Resources for Teaching

WAYS OF
READING

An Anthology for Writers
Third Edition

o—o—o—o—o—o—o—o—o—o—o—o—o—o—o—o—o—o

Resources for Teaching

WAYS OF READING

An Anthology for Writers

Third Edition

o—o—o—o—o—o—o—o—o—o—o—o—o—o—o—o—o—o

Prepared by

David Bartholomae
UNIVERSITY OF PITTSBURGH

Anthony Petrosky
UNIVERSITY OF PITTSBURGH

BEDFORD BOOKS OF ST. MARTIN'S PRESS
Boston

Acknowledgment

Stephen R. Graubard, "Preface to the Issue 'Myth, Symbol, and Culture.' " Reprinted by permission of *Daedalus*, Journal of the American Academy of Arts and Sciences, "Myth, Symbol, and Culture," Winter 1972, Vol. 101, No. 1, Cambridge, Massachusetts.

o—o—o—o—o—o—o—o—o—o—o—o—o—o—

Preface

   Ways of Reading is designed for a course where students are given the opportunity to work on what they read, and to work on it by writing. This manual is a guidebook to such a course. We cannot begin to imagine all the possible ways that the essays might (or should) be taught. The best we can do is to speak from our own experience in such courses. If we seem at times to be dogmatic (to be single-minded in saying what should be done or how it should be done), it is because we are drawing on our own practices as teachers and they are grounded, finally, in our beliefs about what it means to read, write, and teach. We don't mean to imply that we have a corner on effective teaching or that there is no other way to help young adults take charge of what they do with texts.

   In the introduction that follows you will find a brief opening discussion of the textbook and the opportunities it offers a teacher. The first of these resources is a section addressing the questions instructors often ask us about teaching with *Ways of Reading*. Following this is an essay by one of our former colleagues, Bill Hendricks. Bill taught with us for several years. He is a fine teacher, but more than that he has the rare talent of being able to write well about teaching. (There is no more difficult genre than the pedagogical essay.) Bill talks about the shape and conduct of a course in reading and writing, and he looks at some sample student papers. The next part of this manual is composed of an essay-by-essay discussion of the selections and the three sets of questions that follow each selection, "Questions for a Second Reading," "Assignments for Writing," and "Making Connections," and a similar discussion of the Assignment Sequences. We have also included two aditional Assignment Sequences to give you even more options in the classroom. So that you may hear from instructors teaching for the first time from *Ways of Reading,* we have reprinted seven papers written by graduate students in our department, papers that developed from their work in a seminar on the teaching of composition. To give you a sense of how we deal with the kinds of essays this textbook encourages, we have included an essay on responding to student writing. The final part of these resources is a brief, annotated bibliography.

o—o—o—o—o—o—o—o—o—o—o—o—o—o—o

Contents

Contents

VIRGINIA WOOLF

Part III: Working with Assignment Sequences   129

Contents

Contents

Part V: Responding to Student Writing 262

WRITING ABOUT STUDENTS WRITING ABOUT MICHEL FOUCAULT'S
"THE BODY OF THE CONDEMNED," AN ESSAY IN HONOR OF GOOD
INTENTIONS, IMITATION, AND MALLEABILITY 262
— Anthony Petrosky

Resources for Teaching

WAYS OF READING

An Anthology for Writers

Third Edition

Part I. Teaching with *Ways of Reading*

o—o—o—o—o—o—o—o—o—o—o—o—o—o

Introduction

Several years ago we were asked by the dean of our college to put together a course that combined instruction in reading and writing. The goal was to make students proficient users of the varieties of texts they would encounter in undergraduate education. When we began working on this course, we realized that the problems our students had when asked to write or talk about what they read were not "reading problems," at least not as these are strictly defined. Our students knew how to move from one page to the next. They could read sentences. They had obviously been able to carry out many of the versions of reading required for their education — skimming textbooks, cramming for tests, strip-mining books for term papers.

Our students, however, felt powerless in the face of serious writing, in the face of long and complicated texts — the kinds of texts we thought they should find interesting and challenging. We thought (as many teachers have thought) that if we just, finally, gave them something good to read — something rich and meaty — they would change forever their ways of thinking about English. It didn't work, of course. The issue is not only *what* students read, but what they can learn to *do* with what they read. We have learned that the problems our students had lay not in the reading material (it was too hard) or in the students (they were poorly prepared) but in the classroom — in the ways we and they imagined what it meant to work on an essay.

In the preface and introduction to *Ways of Reading*, we provide an extended glimpse into that classroom. The preface is addressed to teachers; it speaks of the design of the book and the assumptions about reading, writing, and teaching that have informed our work. The introduction is addressed to students. It is also, however, a demonstration of how we have learned to talk to our students about reading and writing, about their work and ours. If you haven't read the preface and introduction, we suggest that you begin there before working with this manual. Many instructors assign the introduction as one of the "readings" for the course. Some have asked students to reread the introduction later in the semester — perhaps after reading the essays by Fish or Rich — and to write a response to it, to provide a student's introduction to *Ways of Reading*. This is a way for students to reflect on the work they have been doing and to articulate a sense of the course in terms that can stand alongside, or outside of the terms that dominate the book. It is a way for students to have a conversation with Bartholomae and Petrosky, to imagine us as writers or as characters, to represent the book as having a point of view.

What follows is a brief additional list of tips and afterthoughts — the sorts of things we find ourselves saying to each other over coffee or in the staff room.

Be Patient. We remind ourselves of this more often than anything else. The argument of this text is that students should be given the very types of essays that are often denied them — those that demand time and attention. The purpose of the course, then, is to teach students how to work on those essays and, in particular, how to work on them by writing. There is work for a reader to do. It is important work and part of the process of a liberal arts education. And yet, because the essays cannot be quickly handled, students' first efforts with them are often halting. You cannot expect to walk into class and have a dazzling discussion of Geertz's "Deep Play," or to pick up a set of papers and see commanding readings of that essay. At least not all at once. You have to teach students to do this. As we have taught such courses, the rhythm goes something like this: Students write papers on "Deep Play" that are beginning attempts, footholds on a difficult essay. It is only through further discussion and revision that students will begin to shape these early drafts into more confident and impressive performances. With time, students will learn to take great pleasure in their accomplishments. They will see that they are beginning to be able to enter into conversations, to do things with texts, that they never imagined they could do. If you move too quickly from one work to the next, however, students will experience more frustration than anything else. They will sense what they might have been able to do, without getting a chance to show their best work.

Write First or Write Later? When students are working regularly from essays, much depends on whether they write before or after those essays are discussed in class. The issues are these: If you talk through an essay in class, there is a way in which the students' papers are prewritten. If a teacher takes a strong line and speaks convincingly about how he or she reads Geertz's references to *King Lear*, it is a rare student who will do anything but say back what the teacher has already said. This student has not been in a position to author, or take responsibility for, a reading. The enabling moment for a reader is the moment of silence, when the student sits down before a text — a text that must remain silent — and must begin to write and to see what can be made of that writing. Even if a teacher is skilled at being slippery in front of class, even if a teacher avoids taking a stand and serves primarily to encourage and orchestrate the various comments of the students, there is still a way in which the pressure to write is taken from a writer by discussion. One student may sit down to write about Geertz and find that whatever she says sounds just like what she heard others say in class. Another student may sit down with the intention of doing no more than trying to piece together what went on in class. In many cases, it is best to let students write first. And then, after a discussion of their papers and perhaps a discussion of the selection, let them go back to those papers to work on them again.

This is not cut and dried, however. While all this makes sense, we have often felt that we would have given students a real head start by anticipating problems in students' readings of the essays before they wrote, and so we often hold discussions before they begin. The discussion to have *before* students write is the discussion that will enable students to be better readers of the essays — a discussion preparing students to deal with Foucault's language or to anticipate the temptation to ignore the difficult sections and stick to the familiar in "The Loss of the Creature." We will often speak directly to these special requirements in the discussions of each selection in the first part of the manual.

Be Patient. This is worth repeating. Students will learn to take charge of the work they do as readers and writers when they are given a chance to go back to the work — when they are given opportunities to reread and revise. If they have a chance to go back to a paper on "Deep Play," they can see themselves as readers in what they have written; they will be able to work on the reading by working on the essay. The act of revision we are thinking of, then, is not just a matter of tightening or correcting a paper; it is a matter of going back to the primary text and reworking what one might say about it. Students will not learn the same lesson by jumping ahead to a new assignment. Getting started on an essay on "Deep Play" is not, in itself, preparation for an essay on Percy. Students will learn more if they can spend time working again and again on a single essay than they will if they start a paper on one and then jump forward to something new. If you think of your course as a course in reading and writing, there is no pressure to cover material. There is pressure to read and write, but it makes no difference whether you cover three selections in the textbook or eleven.

On Revision. Revision has been a standard part of the courses we teach — and by that we mean that revision is part of the weekly schedule of work. It is not an afterthought or something students might do on the side. It is part of the assigned work from class to class. Our students, in other words, know that they can expect to work their way toward a final draft. And they can expect to receive help from us through written comments or conferences, and from their colleagues through class discussions of sample mimeographed papers and through group conferences. Since revision is a group process in our classes, we find that we have to make a point of ensuring that revision is not (at least necessarily) a drive toward consensus. When students write first drafts on, for example, "The Loss of the Creature," we will get quite a variety of responses. When we discuss these papers in class, we call attention to the variety of responses — particularly the strongest ones — in order to demonstrate that there are ways of reading "The Loss of the Creature," not just one way, and that these ways of reading are driven by different strategies and serve different ends. We want students, in other words, to see their papers as evidence of choices they made in talking about the text. And we want them to see those choices in the context of choices made by other writers. The purpose of revision, then, is to enable students to take their approach to a text and to make the most of it. We do not want students to revise in order to say what we would say, or what the group has said about "The Loss of the Creature." Our goal as teachers has always been to try to bring forward the paper that seems to be struggling to be written. That's the paper we want the student to work on in revision. These revisions should show again the variety of the first drafts. We do not want students to rework their papers so that they all say the same thing. We want students to work on readings of an essay; we do not insist that they come to a common point of view.

Background Information. There are classes where it is a teacher's job to know all that he or she can about the backgrounds to the texts under discussion. These are not necessarily composition classes, however. We would be paralyzed if we felt we had to be specialists on Kuhn, Geertz, and Rich before we could walk into our classes. It would keep us from teaching what we want to teach. So what do we want to teach? We want to teach students how to make what they can out of essays that don't lend themselves to quick summary. We want to show students, or lead them to show each other, how to work with what they have. We want to teach them how to draw on their own resources. As a consequence, we have avoided Norton *Anthology*–like footnotes (the footnotes you find are in the original texts), and we have avoided headnotes that cast the essays in the context of the history of ideas. Readers read outside of their areas of professional expertise. And they take pleasure and instruction from reading unfamiliar material. We don't want students to get the notion that, because they lack specialized knowledge, they are unable to read essays like "Deep Play." The essay may be difficult, but we don't want students to imagine the difficulty in those terms. If they do, then there is nothing to do but give up. The argument of the textbook, then, is that readers and writers make use of what they have. No reader catches all the allusions or understands all the words or translates all the foreign phrases — yet readers can make texts meaningful by what they do with them when they act as though they had the ability to make a text meaningful. Your students will learn most as they discover how to deal with complex or unfamiliar material. They will be learning about learning.

So What Is This Course about? It is about composing — reading and writing. You are not teaching Limerick or Geertz, history or anthropology. You are teaching reading

3

and writing. You stand for a method, a way of working with texts, and not for a set of canonical interpretations, a series of approved statements used to represent an understanding of those texts. Your authority as a teacher in this course comes from your ability to do things with texts, not from your experience with all the fields of inquiry represented by these essays. The best way to prepare for your teaching is to imagine the varieties of ways these texts might be read. That way you will not be surprised by what your students want to do when they read, and you will be better able to encourage them to work out the potential of their own approaches to the essays. The worst thing to do is to come to class ready to expound or defend a single reading, one that all your students are expected to speak back to you by the end of the day. Then students will sit back and wait to be told what the essays say; they won't feel empowered to forge a reading on their own. You need to be able to monitor and assist your students as they work on these essays. To do that you will have to be able to enter into their ways of reading. You must do more, that is, than tell them whether they are wrong or right.

Who's the Boss? You are, of course. But this means that you are responsible for evaluating the performance of your students. You may ask the class an open question, one reasonable people can disagree on. This is not, however, the same thing as saying that everyone has a right to his or her own opinion. Some opinions are phrased powerfully, some work closely with material from the text, some acknowledge and represent counteropinions, some push against easy commonplaces and clichéd thinking. Whether they are writing or speaking, students are composing ways of talking about these essays, and the job of a teacher is to encourage, monitor, and evaluate those performances. There is nothing worse than a class where discussion is an end in itself — where a lively fifty minutes is its own justification. Whether students are discussing Geertz's essay or an essay of their own, the point of the conversation should be to bring forward a textual problem and to demonstrate how, with care, attention, rigor, and precision, a person might work on it.

Reading against the Grain. We have tried to write a book that leaves plenty of room for a student to move around in, one that is strongly voiced, or as strongly voiced as the conventions of textbook publishing will allow. In the introduction and headnotes, in the questions and assignments, we wanted students to get a sense of two characters speaking. We did not want them to hear the disembodied voice of Truth or Reason. We wanted, in other words, to encourage students to read the text *as* a text, to see it as representing a point of view, to argue with it, to take it as a prompting to respond in a voice of their own. Students can read with or against the text — with it by participating in its form of instruction, against it by seeing its bias or limitations. Students are asked to read not only with but against the grain of the authors represented in *Ways of Reading*. While it is important for students to pay generous attention to what they read — to give in, to think through someone else's words — it is also important that students feel what it is like to step outside a text, in order to ask questions about where it might lead, what it leaves out, and whose interests it serves and why. We wanted students to imagine that they could read in the name of a collective set of interests ("students") that stood outside the range of, for example, Fish's references to students. Fish says, "No one of us wakes up in the morning and (in French fashion) reinvents poetry. . . ." But that is a tricky "us" — if a student violates the conventions of poetry the consequences are very different than they would be for a professor. Students need to feel their power to step outside a text, and they need to learn how and why it is OK to ask difficult questions or resist the forces of tradition, power, and authority.

Using This Book. And we have tried to write a book that leaves plenty of room for a teacher. You'll notice that the teaching materials are placed both after the selections and at the end of the book. There are second-reading questions and writing assignments after each piece and assignment sequences at the end. This is not to insist that a teacher use either one set of materials or the other. All the assignments in the sequences, for example, assume that students will reread the selections, and the second-reading questions are designed to help students imagine where to begin and how to proceed — so that they are not just reading the words one more time. We hope that students will work back and forth between the questions at the end of an essay or a story and the writing assignments in the sequences. Many instructors have found the assignment sequences a powerful way of representing writing as a tool for learning and inquiry, particularly inquiry as it involves the close and critical reading of texts. The assignment sequences are meant to suggest possible courses of instruction, but they are not meant to be limiting. We have used the book for six years at the University of Pittsburgh, teaching different sequences each year. We always revise the sequences at the end of the book by leaving out some readings and adding others, using the "Assignments for Writing" in place of the writing assignments in the sequence. We have also known several instructors who put together semester-long sequences out of a combination of questions in "Assignments for Writing" and "Making Connections."

Reader's Journal. A reader's journal can serve as a useful adjunct to the more formal writing students do. We think of a reader's journal as both a commonplace book and a double-entry notebook. We encourage students, in other words, to copy out and reflect on passages that grab them in what they read. There are powerful lines and phrases in these essays, and this is one way of acknowledging to students that readers grab on to the minute specifics as much as they do the general argument in what they read. The journal can also serve as a way for students to record the process of reading. They can, for example, make two columns in the journal, using one to note puzzles or problems or reactions after a first reading and the other to comment on those entries after a second reading.

And, Finally. Assume that students will need to read each selection at least twice before they do any of the assignments. First readings should give a sense of the selection and its language; subsequent readings should be focused by the questions or directions in the assignment.

Tell students there are no quick-and-easy ways to read these selections. They will need to reread and pay attention to the passages and moments in each selection that allow them to address the questions in the assignments.

Ask students to take notes and mark passages on their second and third readings of the selections.

Use class discussions of the "Questions for a Second Reading" to help students prepare for the writing assignments.

Ask students to come to class prepared to discuss the "Questions for a Second Reading." They should have notes and numerous references to the selection for each question.

Discuss writing with students before they do any of the writing assignments. Use examples of past students' papers to demonstrate such things as notetaking, drafting, revising, and editing.

Duplicate students' papers for class discussions. Use complete papers and parts of papers to demonstrate students' work on such matters as interpretation, critical commentary, text references, paraphrase, and risk taking.

Encourage students to take notes from the texts and to record their thoughts, other students' comments, class discussions, and their responses to your comments on their papers.

Encourage students to reread their drafts, paying attention to what they say and how they use the selection, and to redraft whole drafts or parts of drafts before they hand in their papers.

Accept students' drafts as drafts. Allow them the opportunity to use drafts and revisions to think through the problems posed by the assignments.

Encourage or require revisions for the assignments that warrant them, especially if a student is particularly involved in an assignment.

Respond to students' writing in stages. Respond first to their completion of the task, then to what they have to say and how they use (or don't use) the text, then to editorial matters.

Write comments and raise questions on students' papers. Press them back into the texts and push against their generalizations and quick summaries.

Limit the number of comments you write on students' papers. Pick two or three things to focus on and avoid mixing comments for revision with editorial suggestions.

Teach students to edit their papers. Show them how to use a ruler and a red pencil to read line by line through their final revisions.

Teach students to work in peer editing groups. Ask them to read each other's papers and to explain to each other the errors that they find.

Try to avoid grading individual papers. Ask students to be responsible for keeping all their papers, including all their drafts, in a pocket folder or portfolio, and grade the portfolio of work at mid-semester and at semester's end.

Hold two or three twenty- to thirty-minute conferences with each student during the semester. Go over papers and note what you would like each student to work on during that semester. Keep a record of these conferences for your files, and use your notes to help with grading.

o—o—o—o—o—o—o—o—o—o—o—o—o—o—o

Questions We Are Often Asked

The writing assignments are often long and difficult, even confusing. Why is this? How do you prepare students to read and work with the assignments in *Ways of Reading*?

Let's take the last question first: "How do you prepare students to read and work with the writing assignments?" It's true that the assignments are long. In comparison to what students are used to (test questions, for example, or writing assignments that look like test questions), they take time to read. This is part of the design of the assignments. Even in their format, we want them to challenge or call into question the assumption that the project before students, their writing, is simple or simply a matter of following instructions.

Our goal, rather, is to set a context, to define the outlines or possibilities of a project (we say to our students) within which students can find interesting work to do. Our students say, "Just tell us what you want." And we say, "We want you to do something interesting, something you care about." But, as teachers, we also want to help our students imagine unimaginable projects, work they couldn't do without our help.

From our point of view, the worst way to read the assignments is to find one sentence or one question and to say, "Aha, *here* is what this assignment is *really* about," as though the rest of the words were simply distraction, a smoke screen. This is a version of the standard technology of mastery, similar to reading an essay for its main idea. You find one passage you can control and you let it stand for the whole essay. You find one question you can answer quickly and you let it stand for the whole assignment. We want our assignments to open up a process of questioning for students, not to present a single question or to signal a routine school task.

The other problem we have observed, and again we can link this to the history of American education, is that students are tempted to take the questions in the assignments and answer them one by one, thus using them to structure their essays. One reason there are several questions in each assignment is to suggest that there are several ways in, several ways to begin to think about a response. They are not meant to serve as a checklist for a writer to follow, item by item. A question, for many students, becomes a straitjacket, an order, a command, a test. We want our questions to be an exercise in questioning.

Most of the questions are designed to turn against what we have taken as the flow of the assignment, to open it up and to suggest a new direction. As we just said, we don't want students to think of writing as following a series of orders. In any case, the questions (at their best) don't function that way. They *aren't* a series but a set of interruptions. They are designed to frustrate the very patterns the assignment has set into play.

The writing assignments, then, are meant to suggest a project. This project usually asks students to do two things: to go back to reread the essay, this time with a specific problem in mind; and to write an essay as a way of thinking through an answer to that problem. Our goal is to set some specific limits on students' work — the assignment might direct students to perform a close reading of passages or to apply the terms of one essay to examples of their own choosing or to read one essay as it is framed by another. At the same time we want to provide room for students to move around; we want to make the assignments "readable" in the sense that there is room for interpretation. We want students to be able to find *their* work in *our* assignments. Now, we're realists. Sometimes they do and sometimes they don't. We realize that. If we have done our work well, students will often find ways of making the work their own. In our own classes, we certainly never set ourselves up as assignment police. We expect our students to read the assignments carefully. We expect them to be able to explain how they read the assignments and how their work constitutes a response. But we do not have a specific answer in mind to our questions and we do not have a particular essay in mind as a response to our assignments. When students ask us, "What do you want?" we answer, "What do *you* want to do?" In a class of twenty-two students, our goal is to get as many different kinds of responses as we can. We use the assignments as starting points. They suggest an approach to the readings ("Look at the poems in 'When We Dead Awaken' and think about how they might represent a series.") and they suggest a project ("Write an essay describing what you consider to be the most significant pattern of change in Rich's poems. When you are done, compare your account with Rich's account."). Because as teachers we can begin with what our students imagine to be the most profitable (or possible) directions to take with this (their sense of what the assignment might mean for them as they prepare to write), our discussions about the work they might do have a focus and a motive they would not have if students were left to determine projects on their own. We think that our assignments intervene in productive ways and enable students to want to do things they would never have imagined doing on their own.

Perhaps it might help to look closely at a couple of assignments. Because we have begun using Rich as an example, we have chosen another assignment from "When We Dead Awaken" and, for the sake of comparison, one of the assignments following Virginia Woolf's "A Room of One's Own." The discussion will treat them paragraph by paragraph (or section by section).

2. In the opening of her essay, Woolf says that the "I" of her text "is only a convenient term for somebody who had no real being." And at the beginning of the last chapter (in reference to a new novel by "Mr. A"), she says,

> But after reading a chapter or two a shadow seemed to lie across the page. It was a straight dark bar, a shadow shaped something like the letter "I." One began dodging this way and that to catch a glimpse of the landscape behind it. Whether that was indeed a tree or a woman walking I was not quite sure. Back one was always hailed to the letter "I." One began to be tired of "I." (p. 748)

It's hard to know what to make of this, as an argument about either the position of women or writing. Read back through Woolf's essay, noting sections you could use to investigate the ways an "I" is or is not present in this text, and to investigate the argument that text makes about a writer's (or speaker's) presence. (See the third Question for a Second Reading.)

Write an essay in which you examine the ways Woolf, a writer, is and is not present in this piece of writing. Where and how does she hide? And why? Whom do you find in her place? How might this difficulty over the presence of the writer be said to be a part of Woolf's argument about women and writing? And what might this have to do with you and the writing you are doing, either in this class or in school generally?

The first paragraph was written to prompt a close reading and to resituate a student in relation to the text of "A Room of One's Own." We focus on a passage, making it a key passage. When students reread, they will be reading for the definition of both the authorial I (the writer) and the presentation of the character who speaks in the first person throughout the essay. And, following the passage, we do what we often do. We take something that we suspect students might feel to be straightforward and announce that it is strange, mysterious or problematic ("It is hard to know what to make of this."). In a sense, the writing assignment sets students the task of making something out of the ways in which Woolf, both in what she says and in what she does as a writer, challenges the standard notions governing the status and presence of a "Person" in writing.

The first paragraph, then, defines the project as a directed rereading of "A Room of One's Own." The last paragraph turns specifically to the essays students are to write. The first few questions are there for students who can't quite figure out where to begin ("Think about how and why Woolf might hide. Think about where she is present."). The remaining questions are there to complicate this project: first, by asking students to think about the connections between the argument in "A Room of One's Own" and the argument represented in its style or method; second, by asking students to think about how this essay might be written for them, as writers, how it might have a bearing on the work they are doing in a composition course. In most of our assignments, we try to find a way of saying to students, "Hey, this isn't just academic, it is speaking directly to you about the way you think and write, about how you live your life."

There is a similar pattern in the Rich assignment.

4. Rich says, "We need to know the writing of the past, and know it differently than we have ever known it; not to pass on a tradition but to break its hold over us." That "us" includes you too. Look back over your own writing (perhaps the drafts and revisions you have written for this course), and think back over comments teachers have made, textbooks you've seen; think about what student writers do and what they are told to do, about the secrets students keep and the secrets teachers keep. You can assume, as Rich does, that there are ways of speaking about writing that are part of the culture of schooling and that they are designed to preserve certain ways of writing and thinking and to discourage others.

   One might argue, in other words, that there are traditions here. As you look at the evidence of the "past" in your work, what are its significant features? What might you name this tradition (or these traditions)? How would you illustrate its hold on your work or the work of students generally? What might you have to do to begin to "know it differently," "to break its hold," or to revise? And, finally, why would someone want (or not want) to break its hold?

This assignment defines a different kind of project from the Woolf assignment. The Woolf assignment asked for a close reading of the text. This one asks students to use a text (its terms, its interpretive frame, its motives) to "read" their own experience, including the material record of that experience.

The opening paragraph sets the terms for this project. The "we" of Rich's essay, it says, is also "you." It suggests where students might go to begin to gather material to write about (not just memory but also old textbooks, old papers). And the end of the paragraph returns to frame their work in Rich's terms, terms that would remain hidden or lost or invisible in the text if we did not bring them forward and make them key terms. We want students to think not just about "*my*" school or "*my*" teacher, but about the past, about tradition, about patriarchy (a word we wish we had featured more prominently in the assignment), and about culture.

The final paragraph restates the goal of the project and then tries to question or complicate students' (or any readers') desire to say — "Oh, I get it, what they want is simply this." We want to forestall the desire to see it "simply." We do this by pointing, again, to the larger social, historical and cultural context of the examples students will be writing about, a context we know from experience will be lost without our prompting. We do this by turning, again, to the words of the text. Our goal is to make this essay also a reading of "When We Dead Awaken." We are hoping that students will refer to Rich and use some of her terms in their discussion ("Nothing in this textbook even suggests, as Rich does, that I might not only need to write a topic sentence but 'know it differently,' even 'break its hold' on my writing"). And, finally, we want students to imagine that the essay speaks to them directly as students in a writing course — that in a sense, "When We Dead Awaken" can be read as a lesson in writing.

How many readings do you teach in a semester?

This is an easier question to answer than the first. Usually four. Sometimes three, sometimes five, but never more than that. We could imagine assigning more essays and using them for discussion, in groups or in class, but only if students' writing was limited to three, four, or five essays.

Our semester has fourteen weeks. We spend at least two weeks on every essay and generally leave time for what we call "retrospective" essays. These essays, which we assign at mid-term and at the end of the term are designed to give students time to reflect on the work of the course (and to give us a sense of what students are thinking).

We give students at least two weeks to work on the readings they write about. There is a simple and standard pattern here. Students write a draft in the first week and revise it in the second. The readings are difficult enough to warrant giving students the extra time, particularly the time to reread and revise, tasks we have come to think of as almost identical. We also want students to feel their achievement as readers and writers. If we were moving quickly from one essay to the next each week, we would worry that students would feel only frustration at their failure to understand. Each first draft would give them a sense of what they might be able to do with an essay, but they would never be able to complete that work — or at least take it to its next stage.

What are your courses like? What is the daily routine?

We have taught from *Ways of Reading* every year. In fact, the first edition began with a collection of the materials we had been teaching over the past several years. The first thing to say is that even at the University of Pittsburgh, where a large staff has been teaching this or similar material like it for a long time, there is a surprising range of differences in the shape of the courses and in the daily routine. Teachers need to teach from their strengths. They need to believe in their courses. Most teachers who work with us make regular revisions in the sequences or in individual assignments, both before the semester begins (to create a different emphasis, for example) and once it is under way (to respond to issues that have come up in class).

There are some generalizations to make, however. We regularly reproduce student essays and use them (often in pairs) as the center of class discussion. Instead of having a general discussion of "When We Dead Awaken," for example, we would focus on two specific readings by two different students. Rather than talk about revision generally, we would use those same two papers to discuss how and where and why they might usefully be revised. As we have already stated, revision is a central part of the course. Students revise as part of their weekly schedule of assignments, not on their own or for extra credit; they do one of the writing assignments one week, receive our comments, then revise it the next week. Revision in this case is represented as something other than "fixing" an essay. We ask students to put in the same amount of time as they did on the first draft. Their goal is to rethink the essay they have begun and to take it on its next step.

Perhaps the best way to illustrate one of our classes is to present an example of a course description and a syllabus. The following course description comes from Bartholomae's current course. (You should feel free, by the way, to take any of this and use it in your courses. Good teachers borrow from each other all the time.)

Sample Course Description
David Bartholomae

A COURSE DESCRIPTION

Introduction: The subject of this course is writing. Writing, as I think of it, is an action, an event, a performance, a way of asserting one's presence. It is a way of asserting one's presence but, paradoxically, in a language that makes the writer disappear. (No matter what you write, the writing is not yours; it's part of a larger text, one with many authors, begun long ago. In spite of what you think you are saying, your text will become what others make of it, what they say you said.)

One of my goals in this course is to arrange your work to highlight your relationship (as a writer) to the past and to the words of others (to history and culture). This is the reason for the assigned readings, and this is the role reading will play in this writing course. You will be asked to read a series of assigned texts and to write in response to the pieces you have read. I want to highlight the ways in which your writing takes place in relation to the writing of others. My goal, as your teacher, will be to make that relationship interesting, surprising, and productive. Those meetings between the past and the present, writing and a writer, those places in your essays where you work with someone else's words and ideas to my mind represent the basic scene of instruction; these are the workplaces, the laboratories, the arenas of what is often called a "liberal" education. It is there, on the page, that the key work of a student is done and not in some private, internal mental space. This, I think, is why a writing course is fundamental to undergraduate education.

The Course: I have asked you to think of a writing course as the representative workplace of a liberal arts education. You might also think of our course as a studio course, like a course in painting or sculpture or composition. You will be practicing your art by working on specific projects. I will be looking over your shoulders, monitoring your progress and, at various points in the semester, assessing work you gather together in a portfolio.

In this sense, the course is a course where you practice writing. You can expect to write regularly, at least one draft or essay each week. You will need to develop the habits and the discipline of a writer. You will need a regular schedule, a regular place and time for writing. There is nothing fancy about this. You need to learn to organize your time so that there is time for writing, so that it becomes part of a routine.

You'll need to learn to work quickly but also to keep your attention inside sentences for hours at a time. This requires discipline, a kind of physical training I can best describe as athletic. Writers need to be able to sit in one place and to think inside sentences for long periods of time. As you begin the course, you will need to set your own goals. I would suggest four hours a week in two two-hour sessions. These are writing times, when you are sitting in one place and working closely with words. You should do nothing else during these sessions. You should work in the same place at the same time every week.

I can insist on this kind of care and attention, but I can't teach it. I can, however, teach you ways of working on your writing. I have come to believe that the most important skill I can teach in a writing course is reading — the ability to read closely and critically. In this sense a writing course is like any other course in an English department. There

11

is one difference, however. In a writing course I am interested in how you can apply criticism to production, to the production of your own writing, your texts. In a course on Shakespeare, you may write about Shakespeare, you may in a sense be said to "produce" Shakespeare's plays by interpreting them and writing about what you have read. But there is a fundamental difference in what you produce, in your writing, and how your writing is valued. In a writing class it is your work that is the center of critical attention, not Shakespeare's. The pressing question is what your writing might say about our culture, about language and imagination, not what his might say. Writing, in this course, is a matter of production — which I have defined as requiring the skills or endurance and attention. And, in revision, it requires critical reading, a form of practical criticism, a protocol that will allow you to read your own writing so that you can begin to work on it again.

So there is more than routine practice in this class. You will be writing, but I will also be asking you to revise — to step outside your writing, to see what it might represent (not just what it says), and to make changes. I will teach you how to read your own writing, how to pay close and critical attention to what you have written, and I will teach you how to make this critical attention part of the cycle of production, part of your work as a writer.

I have learned that the essential work of any writing course is revision. There is more to writing, that is, than first thoughts, first drafts, and first pages. A writer learns most by returning to his or her work to see what it does and doesn't do, by taking time with a project and seeing where it might lead. The course will be organized so that you will work a single essay through several drafts; each essay will be a part of a larger project. When I assess your writing I will be looking primarily at the progress from draft to draft.

I have been taken by something Mark Miller said in *Boxed In: The Culture of TV*. Miller is a professor, journalist, and TV critic (and an author in *Ways of Reading*). This is his definition of the "critical faculties" that would represent an active, discriminating mind: "logic and imagination, linguistic precision, historical awareness, and a capacity for long, intense absorption." And, he said, "These — and not the abilities to compute, apply, or memorize — are the true desiderata of any higher education."

I think I would *include* the abilities to compute, apply and memorize on my list of the true desiderata of higher education, but I was taken, as I said, by the terms on his list, which seemed both more appropriate and more precise than most I had seen in statements about the goals of higher education. "Logic and imagination," "linguistic precision," "historical awareness," "a capacity for long, intense absorption." I find these terms to be useful in thinking about our course and its goals. To this list of skills I would add: "practical criticism, the ability to read critically, to distance oneself from a text, including one's own, and to see the argument behind the argument." In fact, as you will see in the syllabus, I have chosen to use these terms to help organize our semester.

Schedule: I have planned for 14 weeks. You will read four essays (see the "Introduction" to *Ways of Reading* for a discussion of how and why assigned readings will be included in a writing class.)

I have divided the semester into three units (see the course schedule). In the first I will focus attention on writing and revision ("long, intense absorption," "logic and imagination," "practical criticism"), in the second on your work with the words and ideas of others ("historical awareness"), in the third on how you fine-tune and finish your work ("linguistic precision").

You should plan to read each assigned essay *twice* before we begin to discuss it in class. The first time through you should read quickly, to get a general sense of what the writer is doing, what the piece is about. Then (and I would recommend the "Questions for a Second Reading" in the textbook), you should read through a second time, this time working more closely and deliberately with the text, particularly with those sections that seem difficult or puzzling or mysterious. You should read with a pen or pencil, marking the text in a way that will help you when you go back to it (particularly when you go back to it as a writer). If you can't bring yourself to write in your book, you should begin to develop a system using note cards or post-it notes.

Each week you will write and/or revise one essay, both as stages in a larger project. Each week you should prepare two copies of everything you have written, one for me and one for another reader. One copy of *everything* you write for this course must be gathered together in your portfolio. Keep the extra copies in a separate, back-up folder. In order to monitor your progress, I will review and grade your portfolios at three points in the term — around the fifth week, the tenth week, and at the end of the term. Your final grade will be based on my final reading of the portfolio. It will be an assessment of your work over the course of the term. I will be particularly interested in the development I see in revision and across the portfolio. I will *not* add together and average the grades from the earlier portfolio reviews.

I will also read individual essays carefully each week and write comments on them. I spend a lot of time on these comments and I will expect you to take time to read what I have written. If you find that I have written much on your paper, you should take this as a sign of love, not of desperation. It means I was interested, engaged.

The best way to read my comments is to start at the beginning of your essay, reread what you have written, and stop to read my comments along the way. This is how I write the marginal comments, while I am rereading what you wrote. They show my reactions/suggestions at a given moment. The final comment is where I will make a summary statement about your essay. Be warned: I tend to be blunt and to the point. If I sound angry, I probably am not. I want to get your attention, I want to be honest, and I see no reason to beat around the bush.

If your work seems thoughtless or quickly done, I will notice. I have taught writing for many years and I know when writers are working hard and when they are fooling around. I will tell you if I think you are fooling around.

I will not put grades on individual essays. I will grade your performance over 14 weeks, but I see no reason to grade each and every piece you write. In many cases, I will be asking you to extend yourself and to do what you cannot do easily or with grace. It would make no sense for me to grade everything you do. (Please see the separate handout on Error and Plagiarism. I will expect you to consistently and successfully proofread all papers, including first drafts.) I will be available to answer questions or to look at an essay immediately before and after class. I know that my handwriting is a problem. I will not be embarrassed if you ask me to decipher what I have written. I will, however, be heartbroken if you simply skip over what is hard to read.

Class participation: I will regularly reproduce your papers (with names removed) and use them for class discussion. Most of our class time will be spent discussing copies of your essays. This is as important to your education as the time you spend alone working on your writing. I expect you to attend all classes. If you are absent, you are not taking the course and I will ask you to drop or give you a failing grade. Similarly, all written work must be completed on schedule. Because you will be writing every week, and because one week's work will lead to the next assignment, you cannot afford to fall behind. I will not accept work that is late. If you are not doing the writing, you are not taking the course and I will ask you to drop or give you a failing grade.

Writing Groups: I will form you into groups of three. Few writers work alone; they rely on friends and colleagues to listen to ideas, to read drafts and to help with copy-editing. You will be responsible for commenting on one group member's essay or draft

13

each week. When you do, you are to sign your name to your comments. (See the handout on "Working as a Reader and Editor.")

Materials: You will need copies of:

A writer's handbook

A dictionary (there are copies of *The American Heritage Dictionary* at the Bookcenter)

Ways of Reading, Bartholomae and Petrosky

Xeroxed handouts

You will need a sturdy folder with pockets to hold your work and everything I hand out in class. This will become your portfolio.

A Word to the Wise: All your work for this course *must be typed.* If you have not yet begun to use a word-processor, now is the time to begin. In a course like this, where you are expected to revise and to revise regularly, you will make your life a lot easier if you can do your revisions on a computer screen. Typing papers over and over again is tiresome and inefficient. If you need help getting started with a computer or a program, see me immediately.

COURSE SCHEDULE	Readings: Pratt, Anzaldúa, Jacobs, Williams (Sequence Two: The Arts of the Contact Zone)

Writing and Revising: "Long, intense absorption," "logic and imagination," "practical criticism"

Sept 3	Introductions
Sept 8, 10	Read Pratt, "Arts of the Contact Zone"
Sept 15, 17	Assignment 1 due: The Literate Arts of the Contact Zone [Pratt]
Sept 22, 24	Revise Assignment 1; Read Anzaldúa, "Entering into the Serpent," "How to Tame a Wild Tongue," "La conciencia de la mestiza"
Sept 29, Oct 1	Assignment 2 due: Borderlands [Pratt, Anzaldúa]; Portfolios due, 9/29

Working with Texts: "Historical awareness"

Oct 6, 8	Revise Assignment 2; Read Jacobs, "Incidents in the Life of a Slave Girl"
Oct 13, 15	mid-term retrospective writing assignment
Oct 20, 22	Assignment 3 due: Autoethnography [Pratt, Jacobs]; read Williams, "Alchemical Notes: Reconstructing Ideals from Deconstructed Rights"
Oct 27, 29	Revise Assignment 3
Nov 3, 5	Assignment 4 due: The Law of Property [Williams]; Portfolios due, 11/3

Fine-Tuning: "Linguistic precision"

Nov 10, 12	Assignment 5 due: On Culture [Pratt, Anzaldúa, Jacobs, Williams]
Nov 17, 19	Revise Assignment 5
Nov 24	Assignment 6 (to be announced)
Dec 1, 3	Revise Assignment 6
Dec 8, 10	Final retrospective essay
Finals week	**Final Portfolios Due** Friday, December 18th, 4:00 P.M.

Aren't these readings too hard? What do you do with students who claim that they can't read them or that the work is boring? What do you do with students who become angry or who give up?

We get this question all the time. Or people say, "Maybe you can teach this stuff at Pitt, but it would never work on our campus."

The course represented by *Ways of Reading* began several years ago, prompted by our sense that students were being cheated. Textbooks and courses were founded on the assumption that students would be bored or frustrated or angry with the intellectual materials that we ourselves found most interesting, fascinating, compelling, or important. And so, ostensibly to protect students, composition courses gave them simple things to work with. ("Don't worry your pretty little heads," the profession said. "Work on simple essays for simple minds.")

We designed our course, as we say in the preface, to teach students *how* to work with difficult materials. We wanted to bring them into the conversation, to give students a way to begin to work the materials that mattered to us, that we valued.

We don't hide the fact that these essays are difficult and frustrating. They were for us when we read them the first time. Our goal is to give students a course to show them how and why they might negotiate the difficulty. This is why rereading is such an important feature of our courses. This is why the writing assignments are designed to help students work with the readings.

Nevertheless, the questions about the difficulty of the texts are valid, and we don't ignore them. Even if you make difficulty one of the acknowledged features of the course, how do you keep students interested? How do you allow them to believe that they can do the work? One way is to show your enthusiasm and pleasure in the work they are doing. It is important, we've said, for teachers to be patient. If students are going to work on these essays, that work will take time. There will be halting steps along the way. Even at the end, a student's account of Rich's "When We Dead Awaken" will most likely not reproduce the level or intensity of the lecture on American feminism that you or a colleague might be able to give. The point of a course like this is to give students a chance to work on the materials and concerns important to the academy. They will not, however, all attain the eloquence or the conclusions of their professors. So patience is more than a matter of waiting. It requires a willingness to value and show enthusiasm for work that is partial, unfinished, the work of novices, work that we have been prepared to call "error."

The book also offers a protocol for dealing with difficulty. It says indirectly (and we say directly in our classes), "Read through quickly as though it all made sense, get the big picture, get a feel for what the piece is about. Then go back to read more closely, taking time to work on passages that seem difficult or mysterious. Assume that these passages are hard for you because they are indeed difficult and would be hard for any reader, not because you are stupid." We offer questions to help direct this rereading. Students should also think of this stage as pencil work, writing in the margins, connecting sections of the text, working out provisional responses and definitions. We've also found that it is important to help students know when and where to use a dictionary.

The other approach we often take is to use class time to model ways of working on difficult passages. We will begin a discussion by asking students to identify passages that they would like us to work on together, as a group. Then we will use the discussion to work out possible readings and to chart, on the blackboard, the strategies that have enabled them. We will also do this in our discussion of students' essays, asking students to notice how a writer has made sense of a difficult section or (often early in the semester) where a writer has carefully avoided dealing with the parts of text that resisted his or her reading.

Your course seems to put so much emphasis on reading. Where is there time for writing instruction? How is your course a writing course?

We have never thought of our course as anything *but* a writing course. As we interpret reading (working on a text, working out a response), it becomes almost synonymous with writing. Reading, too, is a way of working with meaning and language. We also feel that writing students can learn some of the most important lessons only by writing from readings. By doing so students learn that their ideas aren't simply their own. They learn about convention and context. They learn that they don't invent a subject. They learn what it means to work in the context of a history of writing that comes into play when they sit down to write. This is how we make sense of the metaphor of the "conversation of mankind." There are other speakers already speaking. You enter this moment not alone but in the company of others.

But we are avoiding the crux of the question: Where and how do we give the kinds of instruction traditionally associated with the writing course? There are two answers to this question. The first is simple. The work that surrounds the production and revision of students' essays each week, in class, in groups, in conference, and in our comments on their papers represents our most immediate intervention with the students' writing. In this sense our writing courses follow the standard pattern of "workshop" courses. The one major difference is the degree to which revising here also requires rereading. As we have said elsewhere in *Resources*, the one surprising feature of our classes is the small amount of time we spend, as teachers, talking about the readings. Almost all of our discussion of the readings takes place *through* the discussion of student essays, which we reproduce and use to represent specific acts of reading and writing. Most of the questions we address to the assigned texts, in other words, are delivered through questions we ask about writing. Rather than talk generally about introductions, for example, we would talk about the ways a writer has introduced a project or a text or a quotation. Rather than talk about examples in the abstract, we would discuss the use of examples in a student essay — what examples were chosen from the assigned reading; what examples were ignored; what use was made of the examples; what counterexamples there might be; where and how the writer might bring in examples *not* prefigured in the assigned text.

The second "writing lesson" is represented in the readings themselves. Because we have chosen readings that are about writing, they offer lessons to writers, some directly ("When We Dead Awaken: Writing as Re-Vision") and some indirectly ("Our Time"). And the assignments ask students to consider the readings as having immediate import on their work as writers. "Our Time," the assignment says, can help them to write a similarly multivocal text; "When We Dead Awaken" can help students to imagine why writing and a writing course might matter, how it can be about something other than fulfilling college requirements.

The sequences — how do you write them? How do you use them? Why put so much emphasis on the broad sweep of a course?

These are questions we have tried to address in the introductions to the textbooks and to the sequences. The brief section of the textbook just before the sequences begin ("Working with Assignment Sequences," pages 765–768) explains the idea of a sequence to students. You might want to ask your students to read this before they begin their work, perhaps at the same time as you ask them to read the Introduction. Many teachers have found both these introductions to be useful.

Why do we put so much emphasis on the broad sweep of a course? Writers work differently if they are working on single, discrete weekly exercises than if they are working on longer, academic projects. We think of our course as a project course; and we want our students, as writers, to see and pace their work for the long haul. This requirement is not just a matter of endurance, although endurance counts. Students need to learn that *the* subjects that matter aren't quickly exhausted, that the best ideas come when you think there is nothing else to say, that it is important to turn from the security of newfound conclusions to consider alternative points of view. Students also learn to imagine drafts and revisions differently when they are in service of a longer project. In particular, they learn to imagine revision as a way of opening up an issue rather than finishing it, closing it down, and getting it out of the way. We want to teach our students to imagine intellectual life differently than they have imagined it before (with the pieces they read and the pieces they write standing alone, as single exercises), and we want them to imagine reading and writing as they serve in the long term and not just the short.

The best way to work with the sequences is to imagine that they suggest the possibilities for a project students can begin to believe in and imagine as their own. This approach requires flexibility. We have never taught a sequence, whether in the textbook or not, without making changes along the way. We go into a course with a sense of how to put together some interesting readings, readings that speak back and forth to each other in productive ways, readings that we feel we can use to enable students to think about reading and writing. Once we are into that course, however, and get a chance to watch how our students are reading and working with our assignments, we begin to make revisions. Sometimes, when students are not doing what we want, we revise to get better control of the class; sometimes, when students are doing productive work we hadn't imagined them doing, we revise to respond to directions they have taken.

You need to be flexible, to adjust assignments and readings so that they make sense to you and your students as the semester goes along. In this sense, you and your students are readers. The sequences won't automatically make sense. There is no guaranteed payoff if you only follow from step to step. They represent a plan and, in almost every case, a course we have taught. But during the course of the semester or quarter, you will need to feel that you and your students have begun to take the sequence over, so that it begins to make your kind of sense.

As mentioned earlier, we also have found it useful to ask students at mid-term and at the end of the term to write a "retrospective" assignment. This short essay, in which students stop to reflect on the course and its materials, has a double benefit. It allows us to hear our students' versions of the course they are taking. More important, however, it formalizes our concern that students take an active role in making sense out of the course. We don't want the course to just happen to them; we want them to see it as something they can use to frame and enable their work in school.

The question of how we put the sequences together is a bit harder to answer. This process has changed, actually, since we began to work on *Ways of Reading*. Initially, we would get together with our friends and colleagues to design a course we would teach in the upcoming year. Often we would begin with a single book or essay that had knocked us out over the summer. We would start to gather readings to surround this core text, provide interesting ways of going back to it. In most cases, we would look for readings that would profitably counter the piece we began with.

We continue to use these same principles when we design the sequences for *Ways of Reading*. We collect pieces we would like to teach; we then find other pieces suggested by those we have collected. And then we think about teachable combinations. The biggest difference now is that we will have three or four courses going in a semester, Tony teaching one, Dave another, some of our students teaching the third and fourth.

So we gather materials that we think can be profitably read together. A good example is the new sequence, "Arts of the Contact Zone." We loved the Pratt essay, and Pratt's work generally, and found pieces that could be used to put her argument to the test. In a sense we looked for essays that could stand as alternatives to the Guaman Poma example Pratt employs. When we wrote the assignments, we wanted them to represent a stage to various uses of Pratt's texts; we wanted students to work closely with Pratt's text, to apply the metaphor of the "contact zone" to local scenes, and to use her interpretive scheme to look at alternative examples of writing that could be said to be produced by the contact zone.

The general pattern in most of the sequences takes students into one of the readings (asking them to work closely with the text and to produce a "close reading"). Then students are asked to apply and test a set of terms (and, sometimes, an argument) by turning to alternative examples. Finally, students are asked to step back from what they have done to take a position of their own, adding their voice to the conversation among authors, making space in their essays where they speak and speak at length.

We like to think of the sequences as projects and not as arguments. We would be disappointed, for example, if people saw the sequence "The Aims of Education" as an argument we are making about American education. It would be wrong, to our minds, to work through the sequence asking what point it makes or what the correct final position might be. We would hate students to be trying to guess *our* version of the "right" answer to the implied question, "What are the appropriate aims of education?" The sequence is offered not as an argument but as a way of raising questions about education. Now these selections are not neutral or value-free, of course, but we have tried to offer a variety of positions. The questions have their own thrust and direction. But we have written many questions; and we try to turn the issues back to students and to their understanding (in the case of their sequence) of their own participation in the history and culture of schooling. The argument of the textbook is that readers can read both generously and critically and that such reading does not happen naturally but reading requires work, labor. The argument extends to the sequences. To our minds they would be misread if used as a series of fixed steps or seen as representing an argument students are bound to reproduce.

How do you know your class is going well? What are the signs that a class is working?

It sounds corny to say it, but we can feel it when a particular class works well, or when class meetings have gone well. When they do, it almost always means that students feel comfortable, — they talk about the examples of writing before them, and they get involved responding to each other and commenting on each other's remarks. We invariably conduct our classes around two or three examples of students' writing, and we always work from examples that demonstrate students' successes or admirable struggles with particular "moves" in their writing. We tend to focus on what we call "moves" that occur in students' writing; they depend, of course, on the particular assignment and the student work, but generally we look at papers to see how closely students are reading, speculating about, or interpreting sentences and passages from their readings. We also look at how students use others' sentences and language in their writings, and we pay attention to how students create and use such things as summary statements and paraphrases. And, of course, we look for the "moves" that students make when they revise passages in their papers or whole papers. Such examples of typical "moves" in student writing, represent the kinds of student work that we would bring into class for discussion, given, of course, our particular agenda for the class and for the assignment at hand. Our classes generally run for ninety minutes twice a week, and this allows us enough time to work with two or three student papers or excerpts from papers during each meeting. We focus the discussions with our own questions, even though we invite students to respond and ask questions, because we don't want students' comments to be haphazard. We want them to discuss the work in front of them for the reasons that we've brought it into class. We might, for example, bring into class excerpts from two students' papers that show the students interpreting particular passages from a text. We might ask the class then to discuss these excerpts by first restating what each student seems to be saying that the text says. How, in other words, does each student author read his or her passage? We might then, after that initial discussion, ask the class to comment on these readings. At this point, the class would be working well if the students were involved, if they were talking and speculating and commenting and drawing conclusions about the excerpts from the students' papers in front of them. And the discussion would seem truly accomplished if students were speaking substantively about particular sentences in the work before them rather than talking in general, abstract, terms ("I think she makes her point well," "He has a lot of evidence to back up his point") about why a student's paragraph seems good or strong. These discussions are going well, of course, when stutents are involved, participating, but it takes more than enthusiasm for a class to work well. Students have to be doing the detailed work of writers, and that means that they have to be commenting on sentences and chunks of prose in the examples of writing before them, whether those examples be from students' papers or from the essays or stories they are reading and writing about. This is the "local," important work of talking about writing, and when students do it in class discussions, we feel good.

What do you do about sentence errors?

We approach sentence errors in a number of ways. First, we make distinctions between "accidental errors" that students can and do catch and fix when they proofread carefully and "error patterns" that students regularly make and don't notice, or notice, but don't know how to fix. We have a routine for dealing with both kinds of errors that involves individual work with students' papers and whole-class instruction. The key, at least for us, to working on sentence errors has to do with the atmosphere and rhythm of the class. We want to encourage students to experiment with sentences, and we want them to proofread. Both of these tasks can be accomplished without heavy-handed attention, as a part of the regular routine of the class. Five or fifteen minutes here and there throughout the semester seems much more effective than large blocks of time or whole days of instruction given over to sentences and errors.

Before we describe what we do in class, we would like to make a few comments about how we encourage our students to experiment with complex sentences. Generally, we do this in two ways. First, we like to bring interesting sentences to students' attention. Sometimes this exercise is as casual as reading sentences aloud in class and commenting on why they are interesting or compelling, and other times we might put sentences on the chalkboard and study them more closely for the work that's taking place in them. We use examples from the readings and from students' writing for this kind of casual attention drawing. Occasionally, we might conduct a whole class lesson on a particular kind of sentence (e.g., those that use conjunctions to show causal relationships) or sentence construction (e.g., complex, related sentences joined by a semicolon). Here again, we work from examples in the readings and from students' writing. Tony, for instance, regularly asks his students to use embeddings and appositives to qualify and specify subjects and nouns in sentences. He sees this kind of instruction as a way of helping students understand how qualifications that modify nouns and subjects can help wring vagueness and generality out of sentences. When we do this kind of instruction and attention drawing, we feel it's important for students to realize that they'll make errors as they try kinds of sentences they aren't yet familiar with. Such experimentation can give writers another dimension or plane to work on, but they need to feel there's room for it, and this feeling depends a great deal on how we establish the work of the class when it comes to editing and errors.

From the start of the semester, we ask students to buy and use a writer's handbook. They must proofread their papers, including their drafts. We want them to get into the habit of using a handbook and of proofreading as a regular part of writing. Sometimes we ask them to proofread using red pencils so that we can see which errors they catch and which they don't, in other words, those that are accidental and those that might indicate regular error patterns. If students are proofreading, catching what we call accidental errors, but still having problems identifying or correcting recurring errors, then we step in and help. Usually, for students struggling with errors that repeat from one paper to the next, we'll place a check mark in the margin next to the lines where errors occur. We explain to students that when they get their papers back with these check marks, they should find and fix the errors by turning to their handbooks, getting help from friends, and by going to the English Department's Writing Workshop for help. As part of this work, we ask the students who have persistent errors in their sentences individually to keep logs or error journals where they record their errors, explanations of why they made them, and then the corrected sentences. We seldom ask whole classes to do this kind of error journal, but we have. It's important to conduct this kind of error work individually, as a part of the rhythm of the class, and not to make a big deal of it. If students are proofreading and working to correct their errors, we feel that we can show them how to help themselves.

At times, when it seems appropriate, we conduct whole-class lessons, using students' sentences and paragraphs as examples, on the conventions of punctuation and the more common usage errors we see in our students' writing (e.g., noun-verb agreements, noun-pronoun agreements). We don't belabor this kind of instruction, which we do on the chalkboard as graphically as possible, using circles around phrases and clauses and boxes around the punctuation as part of a visual demonstration of how commas, for example, or semicolons or colons work in sentences. Of course, students can always turn to their handbooks for additional help, but we don't assign exercises. When we conduct whole-class instruction like this, we always center it on discussions and demonstrations involving students' work. We work toward establishing an atmosphere in which students get a feel for sentences as plastic and malleable, as language that can be shaped and formed with the help of a few conventions and procedures.

What about the research paper?

Our students regularly write assignments and work on projects that ask them to read various kinds of texts closely, to study texts for particular purposes, and to work across texts. These ways of reading and studying prepare them for the intellectual work of academic research and writing, which historians, scientists, anthropologists, engineers, and market researchers, among others, must be able to do. As part of their work on these assignments and projects, they learn to use quotations and paraphrases; they learn, that is, to use the writings of others in their research. A number of the instructors who use our book ask their students to cite references and document sources in their papers in one of the commonly used styles (that is, MLA, APA) as yet another way of preparing them for academic research.

We don't, however, teach what might be called the traditional research paper in which students compile research on a subject or issue, although many of our assignments ask students to conduct library research (see, for instance, the assignments for Patricia Limerick's selection), observations, and interviews. Assignments, for example, for Mary Louise Pratt's and Susan Willis's selection offer students opportunities to do both observations and interviews as part of their work on individual texts and larger projects involving multiple texts.

How do you teach the stories?

Students can work with stories just as they would work with any other texts. They can imagine, for example, that stories offer arguments, and they can read to write essays on what those arguments might be. As part of this work, students can learn to refer to passages in the story, just as they would refer to passages in an essay, to demonstrate their positions on what a story's arguments might be. Students can treat stories as cases against which they can test arguments and ideas brought forward in essays or in other stories. They can respond to stories as Stanley Fish's students respond to the "poem" on the blackboard in "How to Recognize a Poem When You See One," and they can use their responses as material for studying how and why readers respond variously to the same text. And, of course, students can read stories to write stories just as they might read essays to write in the spirit of those essays.

Basically, our work with the stories proceeds in four ways. First, we ask students to imagine that stories, like for instance, Harold Brodkey's "A Story in an Almost Classical Mode," present arguments and that as readers, they can take a position in relation to the story that allows them to interpret its arguments. With the Brodkey story, we ask them to imagine that Brodkey is creating arguments for how the mind of a boy works, and we have designed assignments that put students in the position of reading the story for what those arguments might be. As they take this position to do this kind of work with the story, they use strategies similar to those they would use to read an essay's arguments. They identify passages in the story that they can work from, they interpret those passages for what they could be saying, and they cite them in some way in their essays. All of this is rigorous academic work, and students can learn to carry it out with stories as well as with essays.

Second, we often ask students to treat stories as cases that can be used to test particular readings or as frames for other readings. When we ask students, for instance, to read the character Marya in Joyce Carol Oates' s story "Theft" as an example of a scholarship girl in light of Richard Rodriguez's discussion of himself as a scholarship boy in his essay "The Achievement of Desire," we are asking them to use Rodriguez's ideas as a frame and the character Marya as a case to test that frame. When we ask students to read Harold Brodkey's "A Story in an Almost Classical Mode" as fiction and then as nonfiction — as autobiography — we are asking them to use the story as a case to test an issue. In this instance, we want them to test questions of genre definitions and to speculate on how their positions as readers change when the genre assumptions change.

Third, we ask students to respond to significant moments in stories and to go on to explain their responses. As part of this work, we usually arrange for students to share each other's responses and to complete assignments that ask them to account for the differences and similarities in what various students noticed as significant. We present this kind of work in terms of the roles texts and readers play in reading. We ask questions, for instance, that give students opportunities to consider how the text works on them and how they work on the text.

We also use stories as occasions for students to write stories. Their reading and writing of stories can give them opportunities to create characters, dialogues, gestures and telling details, and landscapes or places. Story writing can also teach narrative, the making of ideas and statements through characters that seem believable, and students benefit, too, from thinking and writing about why particular stories (theirs and others) are worth telling. They can learn to handle particulars, the details of faces and bodies and voices, for instance, through story writing. Stories are also great places for students to learn conventions such as the use of quotations and paragraphs. And, of course, story writing can entice students to read fiction on their own outside our classes.

o—o—o—o—o—o—o—o—o—o—o—o—o—o—o

ON TEACHING *WAYS OF READING*
by Bill Hendricks
Temple University

Imagine the beginning: the class has met three or four times. The teacher has introduced the course to her students, talked about her expectations, about what will be required of the students, about classroom procedures. The students have read the introduction to *Ways of Reading*, and the teacher has assigned a first reading, say the Walker Percy essay. The students have read "The Loss of the Creature" and used the "Questions for a Second Reading" in their rereading; they've talked about those readings in class. Today the students handed in a paper for one of the "Loss of Creature" writing assignments. The teacher sits down in front of this first stack of student papers and thinks about how the course has gone so far.

She was pleased with the class conversation about the introduction. She had been apprehensive that the students would be puzzled by, maybe even hostile to, an essay on reading that de-emphasizes information-gathering, summarizing, and reading for main ideas in favor of "strong reading," an aggressive and challenging way of reading that few students are likely to have thought much about. But, happily, the students seemed intrigued, and a little flattered, to imagine reading as enabling them to pursue academic projects that they are responsible not only for maintaining and shaping but, in some ways, initiating. "I like the idea of being able to begin with what I notice," one student said, "of not just having to throw in a couple of sentences at the end of a paper about whether I agree or disagree with what I've read." True, some students objected to Bartholomae's and Petrosky's claim that reading is a social interaction, but other students insisted that to deny that claim is really to affirm it. "How can anybody object to this essay's saying that reading is a social interaction," one student said, "without doing exactly what the essay talks about — making a mark on it and talking back to its writers?"

At the next class meeting, when the class discussed readings of "The Loss of the Creature," several students wanted to talk more about the course introduction, saying that the Percy essay reminded them of it. "I'm not sure I know just who a 'consumer' is," said one student, "but he probably isn't a 'strong reader.' The consumers Percy talks about seem pretty passive." The teacher noted this student's use of one text as a frame for understanding another, and she felt generally hopeful about the class's readiness to see acts of reading as involving construction and struggle.

Thinking about these class conversations, the teacher anticipates a satisfying semester, and she begins to read the student papers in front of her with high expectations. Many of these papers, she suspects, will offer rich readings of the problem Walker Percy investigates in "The Loss of the Creature." "The society of today is mechanical," begins the first paper, "and so are the people of this society. They do what they are told, when they are told, and how they are told to do it." The teacher pauses, taken aback by a reading of "The Loss of the Creature" that reduces the dilemmas Percy works with to terms of universal authoritarianism and regimentation — and marveling at how easily this writer has managed to free himself from such pervasive constraints. The teacher begins a second paper, less portentous than the first, which talks about the writer's success in eluding the preformed symbolic complexes that have threatened him: "the solution is to keep an open mind." But the writer seems to think that this formula needs no explanation. The slogan, maddeningly, stands alone. The teacher turns to a third paper, one which begins with what seems like a commitment to look closely at Percy's essay: "In 'The Loss of the Creature,' Walker Percy tries to understand some very important problems," the paper begins. "Such as," it continues, "how to see the Grand Canyon. This is important because if everyone saw the Grand Canyon in the same way the world would become a very boring place to live."

The teacher reads on. A few of the papers seem more promising, better ways to begin the difficult work on reading and writing she has in mind for the semester, but she finds none of the papers very satisfying. She is surprised most by how little most of the readings notice. Few readings notice Percy's distinction between "experts" and "planners"; no one wants to do anything with "dialectic." Many papers make no attempt to bring forth Percy's key terms and examples through direct quotation, relying instead on paraphrases that do not so much translate Percy's language into the writer's as translate it out of existence: "According to Percy, until people actually make an experience their own, or express their own ideas in their own words, the problem of missing the gift will not be solved, and people will be left merely to admire all the pretty packages." Here, quite neatly, the writer avoids the puzzle of what to do with Percy's "preformed symbolic complexes" by implying that "loss of sovereignty" is a dilemma only for the morally lazy: be true to yourself, and the creature is recovered. There are too many papers willing to portray the problems of the social construction of perception as cartoon conflicts: the expert or planner or "society" is plotting to cheat "individuals" of their rightful claims to authentic experience, and we all need to resist these encroachments through keeping an open mind and appreciating how special and unique we and our surroundings are. But few papers want to extend this fervor for resistance to doing a little resisting of Percy. The teacher finds only two or three papers that question Percy's conclusions about what Cárdenas or Terre Haute tourists see in the Grand Canyon; she finds no papers at all that question the liberating potential of apprenticeship to "great men" or majestic educators.

And she wonders: given the promise of the first few classes, how is it that this first batch of papers is so disappointing, so thin? And what is she going to do next?

Reading and Writing

In every course I have ever taught, there has been a moment like this. Always my students' first papers have been not what I hoped for, less than I wanted. Stubbornly, I continue to be a little surprised by such moments ("This semester," I have told myself, "things will be different"). But at least I have gradually developed, I think, ways of understanding the disparity between my expectations for my students and their initial performance — and strategies to narrow the gap by the end of the semester.

Even if *Ways of Reading* is being used for a first course in college reading and writing, students come to the book with considerable experience as readers and writers. But most students will not have been prepared by that experience for a course in which reading and writing are so tightly bound together — in which, for example, students' readings of an essay are validated largely through what they can do with that essay in writing essays of their own, and in which, further, the writing thus produced is ordinarily responded to with a request that the students validate *it* through going back to do more work on reading, and so forth. This back-and-forth movement between reading and writing creates, I think, special challenges and opportunities for both students and teachers of

23

Ways of Reading. In this essay, I am not suggesting that there is a "right" way to teach the book and that I know what it is. I offer just one teacher's reading of the book, of the questions I imagine *Ways of Reading* posing for teachers and students, and the ways my teaching experience suggests to me to work with those questions.

Like the rest of us, students are practiced at getting along. As you together discuss their readings of the Introduction to *Ways of Reading,* your students may well cheerfully assent to Bartholomae's and Petrosky's ideas about new ways of looking at reading — partly because of the excitement of thinking about reading as a powerful tool for intellectual achievement, partly because of the great respect for students evinced by Bartholomae and Petrosky, and partly because *Ways of Reading* is your students' textbook and you're their teacher. The temptation is very strong: "Yes, now I see. Here's how I can be a better reader and writer and get more out of reading and writing." But as they write their first papers, your students will be relying on what they already know how to do, and what they know how to do probably does not include a way of treating reading as a constructive activity extending over time, as a process.

Reading and writing are not inevitable, not "natural." What people learn when they "learn to read" depends on their culture's (or cultures') ways of teaching and valuing reading. Much in your students' education has probably suggested to them that reading is a highly unusual form of interpretation: while one's parents or friends may inspire baffling mixtures of comfort and irritation, a well-written book is perfectly clear; while two workers may have good reasons for their conflicting evaluations of the same job, if two readers disagree, one of them is probably a better reader; while people may make very different judgments, over time, of their children, their neighborhood, their country, the meaning of a text is properly fixed, unalterable; life is a process, reading happens all at once.

For students to pursue the questioning and aggressive reading process suggested by *Ways of Reading* is difficult, moreover, because their education has often seemed to imply that intellectual pursuits, especially in school, are bounded by fairly rigid categories. It is not just reading and writing that have been presented as separate activities. Disciplines and texts and courses of study have also often been seen as self-contained, discrete, each in its predetermined place: tenth-grade biology, eleventh-grade chemistry, twelfth-grade physics; *The Scarlet Letter* "belongs to" American Literature, but not to History of Psychology; students are expected on a final exam in their Systems of Government course to "know the material," but are probably not asked how they could apply what they have learned to improving the governments around them. The student who identifies "how to see the Grand Canyon" as a significant problem presented by Walker Percy's essay, significant because "if everyone saw the Grand Canyon in the same way the world would become a very boring place to live," is probably not in the habit, as a reader, of seeing one thing in terms of something else. A metaphor is something that poets use.

As the students in your course work at being more self-conscious about and critical of their reading and writing, you can expect that they will become increasingly articulate about their reading and writing processes. The student quoted earlier who talked about Percy, the gift and its trappings, wrote midway through the semester:

```
Generally I play one of two roles as a reader.
For an essay based on an assigned reading, I take what
I call the everything-fits-in-a-neat-little-package-and-
you-can-tie-it-all-up-in-a-bow approach; for an essay
based on personal experience, I use what I refer to as
the sounds-like-I-know-what-I'm-talking-about-but-I'm-lying
approach. The names are long but quite easily under-
stood.
```

The systematic everything-fits-in-a-neat-little-pack-age-and-you-can-tie-it-all-up-in-a-bow approach is best applied in essays which analyze the assigned text of any author. My favorite example: "According to Percy, until people actually make an experience their own, or express their own ideas in their own words, the problem of missing the gift will not be solved, and people will be left merely to admire all the pretty packages." In a way, it is somewhat incredible if you stop to consider what I did. In one slightly longer than average sentence, I wrote what it took Walker Percy ten-and-a-half pages to say! I summed up an entire essay, all its examples, problems and complications, in one sentence. How? I omitted anything he said that confused me and pretended that the complications didn't exist. That way I sounded as though I had Percy all figured out lock, stock, and barrel, case closed, the end. Granted, it is good to have a strong idea and to go somewhere with it, but in the process, I killed Percy. Not really; but I do sound as though I learned everything there was that Percy had to offer, used him up, and am finished with him. That is awful because I am probably sacrificing a lot of interesting ideas in my attempt to appear so conclusive. Perhaps if I dared to explore what confused me, I could have generated some new ideas even if they were not all neatly resolved in the end.

But your students' capacity to be reflective about and modify their ways of reading won't emerge quickly. To work at reading by writing takes opportunity and practice, repeated attempts, time.

It isn't that your students initially can't conceive of the interrelatedness of reading and writing, abstractly considered. They can, but different students will arrive differently (and take varying lengths of time) at ways of putting this interrelatedness to work for them. You can expedite this in part through the language in which you conduct your class, referring, for example, to class conversations and student papers as "readings" of the subject or assignment at hand, but the process of learning to see reading and writing as aspects of a single activity probably won't proceed far until students see the advantages, in the contexts of particular acts of reading and writing, of honoring the interconnectedness. For example, the student who writes, "People do what they are told, when they are told, and how they are told to do it" can be questioned about how he has conceived the relation between reading and writing. This student can write, and he can read, but he is trapped by acting as if there were only the slenderest of connections between reading and writing. He has read the Walker Percy essay, noticed that it could be said to have something to do with conformity, mentally scanned the commonplaces he has stored under "Conformity," and written a perfectly lucid sentence that makes nonsense of Percy and his own experience. He could use his sentence to prove that he has read the essay, or to prove that he can write correctly, but he couldn't use it to show why anybody, himself especially, should take his reading seriously. If, now, this student is asked to account for the reading his sentence represents, he will need to write better sentences, but he can't do that unless he simultaneously makes a better reading and goes to work on his and Percy's texts.

On Teaching Ways of Reading

Reading here, writing over there: *Ways of Reading* is designed to help students work against such fragmentation. This is obviously true of the "Making Connections" assignments and the extended assignment sequences, which ask students to write about how two or more essays or stories might illuminate both each other and academic projects that they can be made to further. But it is also true of the "Questions for a Second Reading" and the initial "Writing Assignments," where students are asked, for example, to apply Paulo Freire's term "problem-posing" to their own educational experiences or to describe their reading process in terms of Thomas Kuhn's generalizations about scientific discovery. There are a number of ways that you can reinforce your students' efforts to practice this sort of constructive, amalgamative reading and writing. For example, in introducing a writing assignment on, say, John Berger's *Ways of Seeing*, you might bring forward a student comment from your class discussion of Berger, that wondered whether Emerson's original audience for the "American Scholar" oration might be seen as having been in a position analogous to the audiences for art before mass reproduction. And both in class discussions and in your marking of student papers, you can attend to and encourage comments in the form of "X reminds me of Y" — the sort of comment that may have been dismissed as irrelevant in your students' previous school experience with reading.

Rewriting, Rereading

But while for most readers to notice that one part of their experiences can be connected to another part, that one text recalls another, that "X reminds one of Y," is by no means irrelevant, it is of only rudimentary usefulness.

In order to read or write a text, any reader, any writer, makes many linguistic connections. Students who in high school have read long books and made A's on tests on those books, and who have written correct and coherent papers in a number of courses, have a legitimate claim to a certain expertise as readers and writers. And even if (maybe especially if) students coming to a course in college reading and writing have been very successful in high school, they won't necessarily be discouraged by a comment on their work that says, in effect, "That's wrong." (They have, after all, a lot of experience in setting things "right," and college is supposed to be harder than high school.) But they may well be baffled and angered by a response to their work that says, in effect, "So what?" "How do you account for this reading? What passages or moments in the text might you use to bring it forward? What is it good for? What does noticing that X reminds you of Y allow you to do that you haven't done already? What's the next step?" Suddenly for such students "to reread" must mean something other than reading an essay twice, and "to rewrite" must mean something other than fixing errors or being clearer — but just what these "others" might be will not be immediately apparent. What lies beyond one more academic hurdle successfully negotiated, one more teacher's approval duly registered?

In trying to assist students to sort out for themselves what might be "in it for them" to pursue writing and reading as ongoing, open-ended, and mutually supporting activities, I have found that I need to combine a number of considerations. Any group of student papers addressed to some question or questions about an assigned text will encompass a great variety of readings. Teachers of college reading and writing encounter, every day, the problem of trying to see these readings on their own terms, different as those terms may be from what the teachers themselves might have chosen to do in addressing the assignment. And this problem is likely to be more acute than usual in a course based on *Ways of Reading*, partly because these essays and stories resist easy pigeonholing or categorization (and thus the variety of student readings may be unusually broad) and partly because in almost every writing assignment students are asked to try to see one thing in terms of some other thing or things — a Walker-Percian reading of Clifford Geertz's travels in Bali, a progression in the creative development of Adrienne Rich's poetry seen through the language of Thomas Kuhn and John Berger. Thus, a teacher is faced with a multiplicity of readings of complex cases. Both in commenting on student papers and in class discussions, I struggle (not always successfully) to suspend the strong readings I myself have made of these cases sufficiently to see what my students' readings have attended to. In class discussions, I often find it enormously tempting to propose my own reading of an assignment question or problem my students are working with. But when I have succumbed to the temptation, I have almost always regretted it. ("Well," too many students think — or at least act as if they do — "that settles it. He's paid to know what he's talking about.")

Usually I can resist the lure, but the more interesting pedagogical problem is how to tie the various readings that emerge in a classroom discussion to further acts of reading and writing. One of the most fruitful class discussions I've been involved in recently had to do with how students read the phrase "the end of education" in Richard Rodriguez's "The Achievement of Desire." Some students argued that the "end" of education means a formal stopping point, Rodriguez's way of acknowledging the completion of his academic training. Other students insisted that "end" here means "goal" or "object," that Rodriguez is identifying the aim of education as an ability to reconcile present and past. Still other students proposed that the phrase suggests a renunciation, Rodriguez's recognition that to desire the past would entail his no longer being able to participate in what he had been calling "education." The class discussion had begun in response to one of the "Questions for a Second Reading" that you'll find after the Rodriguez essay in *Ways of Reading*, but it seemed to me, as I listened to students forcefully articulate these completing responses to a troubling moment in "The Achievement of Desire," that here was an occasion to do more than acknowledge the variety and richness of readers' reactions to a powerful text. It seemed to me that the right move now was to draw on the excitement and energy of this discussion by turning the reading question into a writing problem, by sending students back to the essay to see how they might work out, through writing about yet another reading, their interpretations. The resulting set of student papers was one of the strongest I have received lately. Whatever interpretations they were able to articulate in their writing, all students, as they went back to read Rodriguez's essay again, had somehow to take into account — acknowledge, react against, incorporate, consciously ignore — the other voices they had heard in our discussion.

In a course that provides opportunities for students to read and respond to their classmates' writing students will get further experience in seeing not only the anthology pieces but their own papers as subject to multiple interpretations. However, as I have suggested, it is probably naive to think that students will hear a teacher's comments as only one more voice in the dialogue. Teachers are readers, but they are also their students' teachers; they are responding from a privileged position, even if they wish that this were not so. But I think that it is possible for teachers to take advantage of the power relations implicit in institutional writing to become their students' allies in resisting the silence to which it is all too easy for readers and writers to acquiesce. Later in this essay, I show my marking of a sample student paper on Rodriguez, a paper that I thought was — though coherent and sometimes arresting — distressingly silent just when it most needed to speak up. For now, let me offer a few general remarks on how I approach helping students to become more articulate about what their readings have revealed to them.

Often I get papers in which an odd paragraph stands out, something that is hard for me to integrate with the rest of the paper; not what I'd call a "silent" paragraph exactly, but a paragraph that is speaking poorly — perhaps verbose, or seemingly extraneous or misplaced. Some years ago, when I would routinely comment on such a paragraph — with something like "Is this paragraph necessary?" I'd get back revisions with the offending paragraph (that's how students heard my questions) obediently cut. But it seems to me now that though teachers can always shut students up, they ought to be more than a little nervous about deciding to do so. And now I am generally concerned to encourage students to say more, not less. They aren't writing an essay about Percy or Geertz just to prove that they can do it and end there. I try in my comments to help students advance the work on projects which they have begun or might begin, asking them to make connections, in their revisions, with other essays and stories, or with other papers they have written, or between various parts (especially odd paragraphs) of the paper I am commenting on. And I am more likely than I used to be, faced with a puzzling paragraph, to ask questions about it that direct the student back into the essay of which it is a reading.

After one or more revisions of a paper, students may indeed decide that some sentence or paragraph or section of the paper is extraneous, that it doesn't advance the project they are working on. But rather than knowing what they are going to say or how they are going to say it before they begin to write, students will work out what they have to say as they write, and rewrite. In order to write about a text, students have to listen to what an author says and then, in their turn, talk back to the voice they hear. And then a teacher speaks to the voices in the students' papers, commenting both about ways of reading and ways of writing. And though, as I have implied, I think that it is possible for a teacher to say too much too soon about a paper's rhetorical effectiveness, some of my ways of asking students to be more articulate are very much in keeping with traditional rhetorical concerns. On the most basic level, if I read a sentence or paragraph that seems to me so tangled that I can only respond, "I don't understand," I tell the student that I don't understand. I consider this to be providing the student with humble but useful information. And certainly I often request that a writer extend some remark by supplying elaboration or qualification or specific illustration. My problem, always, is to balance my desire, as a reader, for a stronger argument, against my perception, as a teacher, that there are other lines of argument that might also be profitably pursued — or lines of argument that, though hesitantly or confusedly, the writer might in fact *be* pursuing. "The text provides the opportunity for you to see through someone else's language, to imagine your own familiar settings through the images, metaphors, and ideas of others," students of *Ways of Readings* read. Ideally, this model of reading applies not just to students reading assigned texts.

Teachers respond in their comments not only to a particular paper addressed to a particular assignment, but also to what they know about the student's reading and writing development. I have found that my acknowledging a new direction, a new achievement — something that a student has not been able to do before — can have considerable effect in motivating that student to sustain and increase his or her articulateness. This may entail my praising something that, were I to notice it in the writing of a colleague or a professional writer, I would not ordinarily remark on. It isn't plausible that students will in the course of a semester become as expert as professional writers. But expertise is not really the issue. The essays and stories in *Ways of Reading* "leave some work for a reader to do. They require readers willing to accept the challenge and the responsibility, not experts; perhaps the most difficult problem for students is to believe that this is true." For students to improve as strong readers and writers requires that they take some risks; a teacher can honor their risk taking.

Before I turn to a discussion of some representative student papers and my marking of one of them, I want to say that I think teachers commenting on student papers have to develop some way to mediate between all that they *might* say about a paper and what they *do* say about it. Perhaps you have had the experience, as I have, of responding to a student paper with more words than the student wrote: comments snake about everywhere, densely interlining the text, crawling down every margin, turning corners to the back of the page; end comments expand into small essays. I now think that for students, unless they are already unusually good readers, trying to interpret so much commentary may mean that they can't interpret anything; staring at so many words may mean, strangely, that they can't *see* any of them. And, for the teacher, who doesn't have just one student but twenty (or forty or sixty), such mammoth expenditure of time and energy can quickly sink a labor of love into a dispiriting and debilitating trap. I think that the improvements students make in a college reading and writing class will occur gradually, over time — and continue, at the best, long after they have finished with the class. Certain kinds of instrumental writing may be totally successful at once: a grocery list gets the goods, a memo may be recognized by all concerned as having accomplished some purpose.

But I think that most acts of strong reading and writing entail dissatisfactions of compromise. Understanding in reading is never complete; the performed understanding represented by a piece of writing may occasion, for its writer, just as much anxiety over what it has failed to accomplish as satisfaction in what it achieves. Paradoxically, this dissatisfaction probably increases along with skillfulness. The stakes keep going up. Writers' consciousness that some goal has been achieved, their *knowing* that they know, is often accompanied by a sense of further goals fleeing before them. As a teacher, I ask myself what I can reasonably expect my students to achieve in one semester and try to pitch my comments accordingly. And I try not to ask students to achieve everything at once. One thing I do to restrain the urge to speak volumes on a single paper is to keep a record (very brief) for each student of the accomplishments and problems I note on their growing portfolios of papers. This way I have a firmer sense of what each student has done so far as I sit down to read and comment on a fresh batch of student papers. And I'm more likely to be able to assist them in moving from the writing they have done so far to the writing they might do next.

Ways of Reading and Revising: Some Sample Student Papers

Reading begins with predispositions. When students read "The Achievement of Desire," they do so having already read a headnote that says something about Rodriguez's background and educational concerns, and something about the reception of Rodriguez's book *Hunger of Memory*. In addition, they begin to read with certain assumptions (different for different readers) about the purposes of education, about Chicanos and working-class families, about autobiographies. Further, students come to "The Achievement of Desire" with characteristic ways of reading, strategies that have worked for them in the past in making sense of texts in academic settings. Readers never notice everything that might be noticed; what they notice when they come to a text for the first time largely depends, then, on what they are predisposed to notice. Moreover, in rereading, as students try to articulate what they have noticed about a text through writing a text of their own, they can't write about all they have noticed. Even given the focusing instrument of an assignment question or problem, their rereading, their writing, will have to attend to some things that they might say about the question or problem and ignore others. This narrowing of the field of vision need not be seen as merely confining; it can also be seen as empowering. The selective and structuring acts of attention required by writing can transform what students have noticed into texts they must account for, the beginning of a performed understanding.

In commenting on a student's reading of an assigned text with an eye to having the student revise, I am commenting both on the understanding of what the paper represents, asking that it be strengthened and extended, and on the way of reading that the paper brings forward, asking about what it allows the writer to do and about how alternative ways of reading might enable the student to construct further, possibly more satisfying or complete, readings.

Let me illustrate by looking at some student papers written in response to an assignment that asks students to talk about Richard Rodriguez as a reader by examining the ways Rodriguez makes use of Richard Hoggart's *The Uses of Literacy* in writing "The Achievement of Desire." The assignment is closely similar to the first "Assignment for Writing" on Rodriguez in *Ways of Reading*. Here is the first paper.

```
        Rodriguez  used  Hoggart's  "scholarship  boy"  as  a  role
model  to  a  certain  extent.   Rodriguez  modeled  his  educa-
tion  around  what  Hoggart  made  the  "scholarship  boy"  out
to  be.   After  he  read  Hoggart,  Rodriguez  thought  he
might  become  all  the  more  educated  and  know  so  much
more  if  he  followed  the  ideals  of  the  "scholarship  boy."
```

29

In the beginning, Richard's education and learning
became his first priority. He often resorted to hitting
the books because his family life was folded around him.
The isolation which he felt became the obsession for his
hard work and constant classroom participation. The
time spent on schoolwork made the division between his
social and secluded life apparent. The lack of understanding and support he felt that was not coming from
his parents made him draw further away as his family
life fell to pieces. The only way for him to escape
the confinement which he believed was around him was to
view his teachers in astonishment. His admiration
stemmed from their praise of his work and dedication.
His work and efforts were directed toward some mystical
goal, the goal to be like the "scholarship boy."

In conclusion, I understand and admire Rodriguez's
perseverance and dedication to learn. I once wrote in
a speech, "Anything of any worth or value has to be
worked for. Oftentimes it is a struggle, but when you
persevere and you reach your goal, there is a sense of
accomplishment. And I do feel that sense of accomplishment." And so does Rodriguez.

Ways of Reading assumes that the essays and stories it asks students to read are worth the active questioning and recasting they require of their readers; and *Ways of Reading* also assumes that student papers written in response to these texts are worth similar effort. As I read and respond to papers my students have written, I am trying to see what their readings have noticed and trying to suggest ways in which, when they revise, they might do more with what they have attended to. When I begin to read a set of student papers, the question that guides my first reading is usually: "Which of these papers represent readings that grow out of acts of attention?" Or, as the question could also be put, "Which of these papers do some work with a text, and which don't?" That is, I believe that some papers are not worth revising, and this paper on Rodriguez is one of them.

Consider this sentence: "[Rodriguez's] work and efforts were directed toward some mystical goal, the goal to be like the 'scholarship boy.' " I was puzzled by the sentence, initially, because I couldn't understand how this writer is imagining the young Rodriguez to be pursuing a goal he had never heard of. It occurred to me, of course, that the sentence might represent this writer's way of saying that, retrospectively, the mature Richard Rodriguez was renaming his past through Richard Hoggart's language. (And the same thing could be said, hypothetically, about the sentence "Rodriguez modeled his education around what Hoggart made the 'scholarship boy' out to be.") But I had no way of reconciling these conjectures with the sentence "After he read Hoggart, Rodriguez thought he might become all the more educated and know so much more if he followed the ideals of the 'scholarship boy' " followed by a paragraph describing the young Rodriguez trying to become more educated. Bizarrely, the paper suggests that Rodriguez used *The Uses of Literacy* not as a way of retrospectively framing his experience but as a sort of twentieth-century conduct book guiding, *while* it was occurring, his education.

What way of reading does this paper represent? I believe that this writer has read "The Achievement of Desire" at breakneck speed, probably only once, and attended to very little, grasping at just enough to dash off a paper to hand in — never mind the assignment or trying to become engaged by the text. He has a paper, but he hasn't given himself a chance to make sense out of a puzzling text or a challenging problem. He begins with an assignment asking him to discuss Rodriguez as a reader of Hoggart; he scans the text for the first reference to Rodriguez reading Hoggart and finds this: "Then one day, leafing through Richard Hoggart's *The Uses of Literacy*, I found, in his description of the scholarship boy, myself. For the first time I realized that there were other students like me . . ."); and he goes on to grab enough from the essay to prove that, yes, Rodriguez found himself in the "scholarship boy." The student will not be swayed by assignment language that asks him to "look closely at Rodriguez's references to Hoggart's book," to "compare Rodriguez's version of the 'scholarship boy' with Hoggart's," or to examine "the way Rodriguez handles quotations, where he works Hoggart's words into paragraphs of his own"; he has no time to elaborate on his intriguing claims that "[Rodriguez] often resorted to hitting the books because his family life was folding around him" or "the lack of understanding and support he felt that was not coming from his parents made him draw further away as his family life fell to pieces"; and he especially gives himself no opportunity to wonder about what use Richard Rodriguez is making of Richard Hoggart's *The Uses of Literacy*.

In commenting on this paper, I said to the student, in greatly abbreviated form, what I have just said here, and asked him to go back and write a paper on the assignment. I did not ask him to "revise" his first paper because, for one thing, I believed that to do so would trivialize my idea of revision, a re-seeing of some act of attention. Also, I believed that to ask this student for a rewriting of his first paper would be to patronize him. I think that I would have been saying, in effect, "Sorry, you're just not bright enough to read Rodriguez or do this assignment, but maybe you can polish your prose a bit."

"The Achievement of Desire" is especially suitable to a study of the practices of academic reading and writing because of the many ways in which it could be said to suggest that intellectual achievement, as recognized by (contemporary American) academic communities, involves a continuing mediation between invention and imitation, between freedom and constraint. Students engaged in most academic projects are expected to articulate well-considered personal positions within limits not of their own choosing — limits that, unfortunately, probably cannot even be seen *as* limits in the absence of particular acts of reading and writing. That is, teachers cannot resolve their students' reading and writing dilemmas in advance. And students cannot resolve them until they experience them, until they begin, for example, to work at reading an essay through articulating in an essay of their own what their reading has paid attention to. "What strong readers know is that they have to begin regardless of doubts or hesitations."

I think that, in contrast to the first writer, the writer of the following paper has begun a project that she might usefully revise.

> Richard Rodriguez finds himself in Richard Hoggart's The Uses of Literacy. I thought I identified parts of myself in my Psychology texts, but I was not so feverish about finding them. The anxiety in Rodriguez's life makes his reading of Hoggart more dynamic.
>
> His unease can be seen in the way he jumps from thought to thought throughout "The Achievement of Desire." On almost every page, there is an example of Rodriguez questioning himself. The power that is bound to his anxiety is shown by the emphasis that he puts into his confession.
>
> What I am about to say to you has taken me more than twenty years to admit: A primary

<u>reason for my success in the classroom was
that I couldn't forget that schooling was
changing me and separating me from the life I
enjoyed before becoming a student</u>. That simple
realization!

He sets the confession apart to give it more emphasis and throws in the italics and exclamation for good
measure. It is this angst that characterized Rodriguez
before he reads Hoggart.

When the author finally finds Hoggart, it is a re-
lief for him. He gets much satisfaction from being identified. The description of a "scholarship boy" is held
up as a theme to his life. "Then one day . . . I
found, in his description of the scholarship boy, myself." For most of "The Achievement of Desire," there
is a pattern to Rodriguez's use of Hoggart. He gives
an excerpt of Hoggart's description and then tells of
his early experiences. The way Hoggart is employed almost convinces me that Rodriguez based his life on the
writing of Hoggart.

I must point out that the writer is able to distinguish himself from the generality. In my Psychology
courses, I would read about the different personality
traits and think that I was an example of all of them.
Under close inspection, though, I was able to see that
I was more complex than any one category could portray.
Rodriguez shows reservations about committing himself,
too. He adds qualifications to Hoggart's view of the
"scholarship boy." One instance of setting himself
apart comes when he says that Hoggart only "initially"
shows "deep understanding." Throughout the essay, we go
from Hoggart's concept of a "scholarship boy" to the
more specific reality of the author's life. Rodriguez
sees the differences between the two, but he is content
to call himself "a certain kind of scholarship boy."

Why is it so important for him to call himself a
"scholarship boy"? He is not content to trust his own
words to describe himself. The revelation was made by
himself, but he felt a driving need to find "mention of
students like me." This insecurity parallels his problems as a youth. I have to wonder if he has really
come very far from the imitator he was. In an autobiography, we expect to hear an account in a personal,
original, and direct manner. Here we get Rodriguez's
life framed in the work of Hoggart. I do not want to
say that using Hoggart is not effective for our understanding of a powerful part of his life. There are so
many ways of presenting the subject, however, and his

```
choice strikes me as being odd.   He is very willing to
give up his authority to an "expert."
```

```
        He felt that he must find himself in the reading.
A great deal of energy was bound to his feelings of
loss.   He had to pacify his anxiety.   Hoggart gave a
description that was close enough for identification and
Rodriguez jumped at it.   The reason that he gives us
for reading Hoggart is that it gave him a measure of
his change, but I see it as proof that he has changed
very little.
```

When I got this paper, which was submitted for the same assignment in the same class as the paper I looked at earlier, I saw it as a worthwhile opening move in the construction of a strong reading. The tack that this writer takes in this reading, her insistent emphasis on Rodriguez's "anxiety," was not a direction that most of her classmates chose to pursue, nor one that I would have chosen myself, but it seemed to me that this paper, as I interpreted it, did grow out of an act of attention, one that I felt it worth my time and hers to ask her to question and extend.

Our class had already worked with reading and writing assignments based on Walker Percy's essay "The Loss of the Creature," and I noted this writer's allusion to Percy at the end of the fifth paragraph. I also noticed that the allusion was *only* that, not a genuine recasting of experience through new language. It was what we had been calling a "gesture." Certainly, I thought, her re-seeing her paper in conjunction with Percy's treatment of authority might give this writer more to say about Rodriguez-as-anxious-reader. At the same time, I did not want to overemphasize what for this reader might be seen as only tangential, an issue which, if she pursued it strenuously, might serve to turn her paper into my paper.

We had also, in our class, talked about readers' "roles," and it seemed to me that at times this paper (notably in the last sentence of the fourth paragraph) might profitably be questioned on the basis of the limiting roles it was asking me to assume as a reader — particularly since, in the fourth paragraph, the writer herself speaks of having declined to be limited by a certain kind of reading.

One of my strongest reactions to the paper was, as you might imagine, unease at the paucity of demonstration, illustration, and qualification of the claims being made — even though I was quite taken by a number of the claims. Here the task ahead will sound familiar: to deploy my own variants of the writing teacher's old refrain, "Show me." (Our class's term for unexplored assertion was "labeling.") This is how I responded to the paper.

```
    Richard Rodriguez finds himself in Richard Hoggart's
The Uses of Literacy.   I thought I identified parts of
myself in my Psychology texts, but I was not so fever-
ish about finding them.   The anxiety in Rodriguez's
life makes his reading of Hoggart more dynamic.
His unease can be seen in the way he jumps from
thought to thought throughout "The Achievement of De-
sire."  On almost every page, there is an example of
Rodriguez questioning himself.  The power that is bound
to his anxiety is shown by the emphasis that he puts
into his confession.   Significant? Why have you
            chosen not to demonstrate this in your paper?
```

33

[handwritten left margin: o.k., a reader can grant that you recognize his confession. So what do you do with his noticing? Why is the "angst" significant? How do you account for its interpretation? (The "angst" is not self-explanatory.)]

What I am about to say to you has taken me more than twenty years to admit: <u>A primary reason for my success in the classroom was that I couldn't forget that schooling was changing me and separating me from the life I enjoyed before becoming a student.</u> That simple realization!

He sets the (confession) apart to give it more empha-sis and throws in the italics and exclamation for good measure. It is this angst that characterized Rodriguez before he reads Hoggart.

[handwritten: True? Important? Where's your reading?]

When the author finally finds Hoggart, it is a re-lief for him. He gets much satisfaction from being identified. The description of a "scholarship boy" is held up as a theme to his life. "Then one day . . . I found, in his description of the scholarship boy, my-self." For most of "The Achievement of Desire," there is a pattern to Rodriguez's use of Hoggart. He gives an excerpt of Hoggart's description and then tells of his early experiences. The way Hoggart is employed al-most convinces me that Rodriguez based his life on the writing of Hoggart.

[handwritten: This is the one. It is your reading that parallels the "dynamic" reading you say Rodriguez makes of Hoggart. Here your Rodriguez can discriminate; elsewhere he is over-whelmed; what can you make of this split?]

I must point out that the writer is able to dis-tinguish himself from the generality. In my Psychology courses, I would read about the different personality traits and think that I was an example of all of them. Under close inspection, though, I was able to see that I was more complex than any one category could portray. Rodriguez shows reservations about committing himself, too. He adds qualifications to Hoggart's view of the "scholarship boy." One instance of setting himself apart comes when he says that Hoggart only "initially" shows "deep understanding." *[handwritten: And then?]* Throughout the essay, we go from Hoggart's concept of a "scholarship boy" to the more specific reality of the author's life. Rodriguez sees the differences between the two, but he is content to call himself "a certain kind of scholarship boy."

[handwritten: well?] Why is it so important for him to call himself a "scholarship boy"? He is not content to trust his own words to describe himself. The revelation was made by

[handwritten: what role are you asking a reader to play when you imply that the quoted phrase contradicts Rodriguez's ability to see differences?]

Only labels

himself, but he felt a driving need to find "mention of students like me." This insecurity parallels his problems as a youth. I have to wonder if he has really come very far from the imitator he was. In an autobiography, we expect to hear an account in a personal, original, and direct manner. Here we get Rodriguez's life framed in the work of Hoggart. I do not want to say that using Hoggart is not effective for our understanding of a powerful part of his life. There are so many ways of presenting the subject, however, and his choice strikes me as being odd. He is very willing to give up his authority to an "expert."

How is it effective?

Do you have something in mind by the allusion to Percy? Can you make this more of a gesture?

He felt that he must find himself in the reading. A great deal of energy was bound to his feelings of loss. He had to pacify his anxiety. Hoggart gave a description that was close enough for identification and Rodriguez jumped at it. The reason that he gives us for reading Hoggart is that it gave him a measure of his change, but I see it as proof that he has changed very little.

you need to say more

I admire your willingness to see Rodriguez's achievement at an advanced stage of his education, his way of reading Hoggart, as having roots in long-standing feelings and habits. But I don't think your essay yet demonstrates the reading it wants to claim. Your word "category" struck me. What categories besides "anxiety" could you incorporate in your reading of Rodriguez's relation to Hoggart?

And here is the revision that the student handed in the following week.

In Richard Rodriguez's essay "The Achievement of Desire," we get a sort of record of how Rodriguez responded to reading a book by Richard Hoggart called The Uses of Literacy. But what I can't understand is how to separate how Rodriguez reacted to The Uses of Literacy when he first read it in the British Museum from how he is reading it when he's a professional writer writing an essay he wants to publish.

In the British Museum, Rodriguez says, he found in Hoggart's

> description of the scholarship boy, myself.
> For the first time I realized that there were
> other students like me, and so I was able to
> frame the meaning of my academic success, its
> consequent price--the loss.

At various points in "The Achievement of Desire," we see Rodriguez working out how what he read about the scholarship boy helps him understand why he feels so bad about his academic success. "Good schooling requires that any student alter early childhood habits," Rodriguez paraphrases Hoggart, and then Rodriguez remembers how "after dinner, I would rush to a bedroom with papers and books. As often as possible, I resisted parental pleas to 'save lights' by coming to the kitchen to work." Rodriguez wasn't as upset as his parents were about his need to be alone to study. When he first entered school, he remembers, "what bothered me . . . was the isolation reading required." But gradually, as he was tutored by one of the nuns, he began to feel the "possibility of fellowship between a reader and a writer," not "<u>intimate</u>," but "<u>personal</u>." And he also started to want a power he sensed in reading: "Books were going to make me 'educated.'" So that eventually, Rodriguez often <u>enjoyed</u> being alone with his books--but the enjoyment made him feel guilty and anxious: "Nervous. I rarely looked away from my book--or back on my memories." His parents, he knew, were not "educated."

Hoggart helps Rodriguez interpret his past, but as he writes "The Achievement of Desire," Rodriguez is not always grateful for Hoggart's descriptions of the scholarship boy. Rodriguez quotes a passage from <u>The Uses of Literacy</u> in which Hoggart says that the scholarship boy "begins to see life as a ladder, as a permanent examination with some praise and further exhortation at each stage. He becomes an expert imbiber and doler-out." Here, says Rodriguez, Hoggart's "criticism" is "more accurate than fair." When I first read "The Achievement of Desire," I wasn't sure what Rodriguez meant by calling Hoggart's description here "criticism." After he quotes Hoggart's remarks, Rodriguez restates them in a way that makes me think he sees them as a good description--but he's worried about how "fair" they are. In reading the essay again, I noticed Rodriguez's saying that the scholarship boy "realizes more often and more acutely than most other students--than Hoggart himself--that education requires radical self-reformation." How does Rodriguez know how much Hoggart realizes? I haven't read <u>The Uses of Literacy</u>, and maybe if I did I would find out that Hoggart was not himself a scholarship boy, and this might be related to how much Rodriguez says Hoggart "realizes." Or maybe there are parts of <u>The Uses of Literacy</u> that show Hoggart not understanding what Rodriguez sees--but I don't see that Rodriguez quotes them.

I said earlier that I couldn't figure out how to separate Rodriguez's first reading of Hoggart from all

the rereadings of Hoggart he must have done before he
wrote and published "The Achievement of Desire." I
still think, as I wrote in a previous paper, that
Rodriguez "felt that he must find himself" in reading
Hoggart, but I also think now that Rodriguez also became
anxious not to find himself in Hoggart's book. Maybe I
started to feel this way after Sylvia pointed out in
class something that I hadn't noticed before: Hoggart
says that the scholarship boy is unusual, not a typical
working-class student, not even a typically successful
working-class student. Most successful working-class
scholarship students "manage a fairly graceful transition," Rodriguez paraphrases Hoggart. It is only the ex-
ceptional working-class scholarship student--perhaps "intellectually mediocre" (Rodriguez's paraphrase of
Hoggart) and maybe "haunted by the knowledge that one
chooses to become a student" (Rodriguez's interpretation
of Hoggart--I think)--who becomes a "scholarship boy."
I think that Rodriguez found in Hoggart's idea of the
scholarship boy something he thought he could use to
help him understand his own anxieties about his success.
But I also think that Rodriguez must have understood at
some point (when I'm not sure) that Hoggart's description of the scholarship boy didn't completely correspond
to his own situation. (Does Hoggart talk about race as
well as class? Does Rodriguez really believe that he was
himself of only average intelligence?) When Rodriguez
reacts against Hoggart's description, then, you could say
that it is Rodriguez, not Hoggart, who is not being
"fair." But I prefer to say that Rodriguez, as he
writes "The Achievement of Desire," is being what in our
class we've called a "strong reader."

When Rodriguez says

> A primary reason for my success in the class-
> room was that I couldn't forget that schooling
> was changing me and separating me from the
> life I enjoyed before becoming a student.

I read him to mean that his being unable to forget that
his education was making him lose something he valued in
his relationship with his family kept him continually
anxious to be a big success as a student. If he were
only a little successful, he would have "lost" his family without gaining anything in return. I'm not saying
that as a boy Rodriguez was conscious of this (he says
the "realization" took him twenty years), but I do think
this is how he sees it as he writes "The Achievement of
Desire." Partly, Rodriguez wanted to separate himself
from his parents; he wanted to become "educated." What

he found in books became what guided his feelings about
who he was. But I don't think that it's exactly right
to say that Rodriguez wanted, in Walker Percy's words
from "The Loss of the Creature," to "surrender" his
"sovereignty" to "experts," his teachers and the authors
of the books he read. At some point, Rodriguez had to
see that his way of pursuing education only made sense
if he became the expert. In a way, I know that when I
read my psychology texts and find myself there, I am
only playing at psychology. Even when I realize that I
am more complex than any one psychological "category"
can portray, I also know that I don't yet know enough
psychology to feel very sure about just where I do or
don't fit into the language being used. And I could
understand someone's saying that I am still caught up in
believing, in Walker Percy's words, that "the thing is
disposed of by theory."   But I also suspect that if I
want to become a psychologist (and I do), I can't just
ignore psychological theory. I can't just go around the
words and categories of "psychology"; somehow I have to
go through them.   And I think that Rodriguez was doing
something like this when he reread Hoggart.   In the
British Museum, he wanted an "expert," somebody his education had taught him to respect, to give him a handle
on his life.   But he was also anxious, as he wrote
"The Achievement of Desire," to go beyond Hoggart, to
show that his expertise was greater than Hoggart's.   He
needed to show that he was better able to explain his
own life than his teacher was.   I think that if Richard
Hoggart were to read "The Achievement of Desire," he
might feel both complimented and astonished.

When I compared this revision to the original paper, one of the things that struck me was the change in the writer's manner of using quotations. In the original, the material quoted is all drawn from a cluster of three pages in "The Achievement of Desire"; in the revision, the writer has ranged through much of Rodriguez's essay for her citations. In reading the original, I felt a disjunction between phrases like "on almost every page," "for most of 'The Achievement of Desire,'" "throughout the essay," and the nonarticulation of readings those phrases only gesture at. In the revision, it seemed to me, the writer has needed to lean less on summarizing assertions because she has demonstrated her readings through a much closer working relationship with Rodriguez's text.

But I would not want to say that I think the revised paper "supports" its "points" better than the original (though I can certainly imagine a teacher's saying something like that). Ways of reading that emphasize repeated readings and writings, that posit back-and-forth movements between reading and writing, are probably not well served by talking about "support" (supporting "thesis" statements, for example, by "adding detail"). Students can learn fairly quickly how to generate and support theses; but to present that activity as a goal of writing about readings can mean that that's all students will learn. To write a paper is to perform a reading. Strong reading is dependent on attentiveness, on curiosity; if students see their job as primarily to support a thesis, attention declines, curiosity withers.

I do not think that the writer of the original paper has seen her reading as simply supporting a thesis. She's done more than that. A strong reading of "The Achievement of Desire," one that allows itself to be curious, is likely to end up with a proposition different from the one it begins with. And to some extent this is what happens in the original version of the paper. Like the writer of the first Rodriguez paper I looked at, this writer, in her original paper, begins with Rodriguez's claim to have found himself in Hoggart's description of the "scholarship boy." But she hasn't approached Rodriguez's declaration blankly; she hasn't, that is, adopted the role of a reader who is content to take Rodriguez at his word, a reader who has been entrusted with the key to the essay and need now only locate and assemble all those instances in the text that show that the key works. In fact, almost immediately, the writer decides that her reading of "The Achievement of Desire" will tease out not *that* or *how* Rodriguez finds himself in Hoggart, but *why* he chooses to do so. And this project is further modified by the writer's incorporating a comparison between a reading of her own experiences and Rodriguez-as-reader-of-Hoggart, which leads to her becoming (if only temporarily) cautious about and critical of what she is doing: "I must point out that the writer is able to distinguish himself from the generality. . . ." Throughout the essay, we go from Hoggart's concept of a "scholarship boy" to the more specific reality of the author's life.

But, I think, the writer does not sustain her strong reading. Perhaps daunted by the work she senses it would take to follow up on the differences between Hoggart's "concept" and Rodriguez's "specific reality," or perhaps feeling impelled to conclude her reading unwaveringly, she ties up loose ends with her final sentence: "The reason that he gives us for reading Hoggart is that it gave him a measure of his change, but I see it as proof that he has changed very little." I like the sentence. I find it gutsy and intelligent. But I also think that the sentence is a kind of giving up. It indicates, to me, a writer who does not yet have a way of reading that allows her to be more than sometimes curious about what she is saying.

In the revised paper, the writer takes the risk of beginning with a puzzle that she is not going to be able to solve — no more than any reader could. My guess is that the risk is calculated: that though she knows there is no way to separate with certainty Rodriguez's early and late readings of Hoggart, she recognizes that the problem she poses is one that leaves room for multiple strong interpretations. And it's the sort of problem that she can tie to more ways and acts of reading than Rodriguez's reading of Hoggart in the British Museum. While making a strong reading of Rodriguez, she is also beginning readings of the relations between reading and writing, between reading and rereading, between individual and collective participations in language. Interestingly, these connections emerge (and, yes, they are mostly implicit — there are more papers to be articulated here), I think, *because* she has decided to work curiously and attentively with reading and rereading Rodriguez. In strong reading, the commonplace, "You can't see the forest for the trees," makes little sense. For strong readers, the forest is not a given but a field of possibilities, and whatever possibilities are realized require detailed attention to lots of trees.

Talking about Reading and Writing

As they work through the reading and writing assignments of *Ways of Reading*, students will have many opportunities, in a variety of contexts, to attend to the construction of meaning. Occasionally they will be asked to paraphrase or reconstruct a difficult passage. More often, they will be asked to interpret what they have read, with some specific purpose in mind: framing something in their own experience with the key terms and methods of another writer, in order to learn more about both that writer's methods and their own experience; or turning an essay back on itself by testing out its claims or reconsidering its examples; or seeing how they might use one text to interpret another. Frequently, students will be asked for revisions of their papers, revisions in which they can continue projects suggested by the assignments and their responses to the assignments. Always students are asked, implicitly or explicitly, to reread what they have written, to rewrite what they have read.

Much of this work will go on in the classroom. Students' dormitory rooms or library carrels or kitchen tables are not their only arenas for making meaning; the assignments and anthology pieces, the papers students write and the comments a teacher makes on those papers, are not a class's only forums for engaging in the conversations of reading and writing. What happens in the classroom can reinforce or redirect those other exchanges — and serve to make them more fruitful.

I find that class conversation is facilitated when a class begins to develop early its medium of exchange — a language about language that can be shared. Whatever ways students have, individually, for talking about reading and writing, they probably bring with them to a course in college reading and writing a sort of lingua franca from their various high school English courses: "coherence," "organization," etc. Certainly college teachers and their students may choose to draw on these terms to talk about the work of reading and writing, but I have often been surprised at how slippery this seemingly stable language can be. A couple of years ago, for example, when I returned a set of student papers on which I'd commented to some writers that they were "summarizing," two students approached me after class. The first said that he had just reread the assignment carefully and didn't see it asking him anywhere to "summarize," and that that was certainly not what he had done in his paper, though he could have if he'd been asked. The second student thanked me for the comment but wondered if I'd found anything "wrong" with his paper. Both students, that is, revealed to me that my class had not so far provided a context for these readers to do anything with the word "summarizing." In the absence of our class's having worked out a distinction between "summarizing" and, say, "interpreting," these students could only conclude that "summarizing" meant exactly what they knew it meant: a routine performed by students in English classes — ordinarily when asked but sometimes, miraculously, unbidden.

What I like to try to do is have my reading and writing classes construct — gradually, accretively — a language for language that has had to be interpreted, a language for which we have had to make sense. Many terms in my marking of the student paper discussed earlier — "labels," "gesture," readers' "roles," "demonstrate," writing about a text as "reading" it — are terms that that class had been slowly accumulating since the beginning of the semester. Generally these terms first surfaced in class discussions. Sometimes they were first proposed by me, sometimes by students, as linguistic tools for our class to use to make sense of some text before us. Sometimes the terms first appeared in an assignment. Obviously not all classes will fashion the same tools, and one semester's key terms, metaphors, are not likely to be identical to what gets used the next semester. For example, I can imagine that in one class based on *Ways of Reading*, Stanley Fish's term "interpretive community" might become a point of reference for talking not only about "How to Recognize a Poem When You See One" but about acts of reading generally; the terms may become part of a class's common language. In another class, "interpretive community" may not be established as common currency, though readers' "predispositions" may be. A third class might use both these ways of talking about reading performance and other ways (readers' "roles," for example) as well. In redeploying this language to comment on student papers, a teacher models a version of what students are engaged in as they read and respond to the pieces in *Ways of Reading* — seeing their own projects through the frame of language they have had to come to terms with, redefining preexistent language and routines for their own purposes.

I think that there are certain benefits in devoting much of a class's time together to discussions of student papers. Students whose papers are being discussed get multiple responses to what they have written, and possibly insights into how they might revise.

40

The whole class gets a chance to look at other writers struggling with dilemmas similar to those that they themselves have been wrestling with in their own papers.

Classroom discussion of their papers gives students opportunities to explore the possibilities and problems involved in moving from writing to rewriting, from a reading that has noticed something significant to a reading that can better articulate and account for the significance of what has been noticed. The revised paper on Rodriguez I looked at earlier grew not only out of what the writer was able to do with my comments on her first version but also, as it happened, out of a class discussion of the original paper. Students generally liked and were impressed by the paper, but they were puzzled at times by the reading. One student wondered what the writer meant by saying that Rodriguez "jumps from thought to thought" in "The Achievement of Desire." A second student said that, whatever the writer meant, she should have shown how this "jumping" works. Someone else said that she wasn't sure why Rodriguez's jumping from thought to thought, if he does, might be important in the first place, but a fourth student said that obviously it could indicate, as the writer says, Rodriguez's "unease," an "anxiety," just as Rodriguez's "questioning himself" could — provided the writer demonstrated that. "But self-questioning doesn't always mean anxiety," said a fifth student. "I don't think I'm very anxious, and I question myself all the time. Self-questioning could mean that a person doesn't know enough." "Right," said another student, "or that he knows too much." The conversation continued. This sort of discussion provides not so much a chance for writers to hear that they haven't said what they meant (though it may do that), as an occasion for writers to become more curious about just what they *do* mean. The writer of this paper, as she learned from the discussion, couldn't do a rewriting of her paper, not in any important sense, without doing some more reading, getting back into Rodriguez's text and hers.

And class discussions of the papers students write can offer substantiations of the assumption that there are multiple ways, and many good ways, to read. I talked earlier about a class discussion in which students argued about the interpretation of the phrase "the end of education" that concludes Rodriguez's essay. When I read the set of papers that came in for the writing assignment I made, I picked out and duplicated three of them for class discussion. The first writer argued that his interpretation of "the end of education" as the completion of Rodriguez's academic training derived from noticing that "The Achievement of Desire" is constructed as a series of commentaries on important moments in an academic's schooling; that Rodriguez speaks early on of trying to figure out — "in the British Museum (too distracted to finish my dissertation)" — what that schooling amounts to; and that by the last words of the essay, "the end of education," Rodriguez has come to a resolution — though, this writer conceded, he could also see that Rodriguez retained some unfulfilled "desires." The second writer insisted, also quite convincingly, that, according to her reading, "the end of education" must be the accomplishment the essay's title foregrounds — "The Achievement of Desire"; that the significant incidents in Rodriguez's education can be read (she gave readings) as his holding the past at arm's length; and that Rodriguez is able to stop this repression only when he becomes secure enough in his "educated" identity that it can't be undermined by regret for what he has sacrificed; so that, finally, he can turn "unafraid to desire the past." The third reader, in her paper, while saying that she understood the "end" of Rodriguez's education to be in one sense its completion, thought it most important to notice that Rodriguez calls his schooling, early and late, "miseducation," and that, whatever Rodriguez learns in school, he can't understand himself until he gets outside the boundaries of schooling ("too distracted to finish my dissertation"); so that, as this writer reads the essay, "education" is opposed to both "desire" and understanding. I don't do these readings justice with this outline, but I thought that one of the most interesting outcomes of our class discussion of them was several students' remarking that, since they found all three papers persuasive, they judged that not only do different readers read differently, but a single reader might read a text in various ways. Discussions of student papers, texts articulating readings of other texts, parallel the practice of looking at one thing through something else, which most of the course's assignments ask students to perform. For a class to examine student papers with the same attention and care brought to discussions of the anthology selections by themselves augments students' belief in the value of the strong reading they are being asked to pursue.

A teacher's decisions about how to use student papers in class — which papers to use, how much student text can be profitably addressed in a single class period, what questions to use in guiding the discussion, just how a discussion of some particular paper or papers serves broader discussions of reading and writing — all depend on a teacher's experience, agenda for a course in college reading and writing, and way of imagining how *Ways of Reading* fits into that agenda. I'll end here with just a few more notes from my own experience. I have found that student papers duplicated for distribution and class discussion can focus on the acts of reading and writing represented by the papers rather than on uneasy exchanges governed by diffidence about or defense of the emotional investments that the papers also represent. Generally speaking, students adapt to the convention of authorial anonymity quickly and easily. As much as possible, I try to choose papers for discussion that will give the class opportunities to notice, wonder about, and question efforts at performed understanding — rather than papers that I think exhibit little effort, nonperformance. Ideally, I want my students to see a discussion of papers as an occasion not for sniping at lousy work but for talking about how good work might be extended. For example, I can imagine my using the first Rodriguez paper I looked at earlier only in an early-semester class discussion — using it as a way of talking about nonreading, perhaps pairing it with a much stronger paper. But after the first few weeks of a semester, I would think that that paper no longer has a place (and, indeed, did not seek a place) in our class conversations.

If you are teaching *Ways of Reading* along with other teachers at your college, and if some of you have made similar selections from among the scores of assignments available in the book, you might want to share some student papers along with the other things you are sharing about teaching the course, thus giving each of you a bigger pool from which to draw the kinds of papers you want for class discussion.

Part II: Working with the Readings

o—o—o—o—o—o—o—o—o—o—o—o—o—o—o

GLORIA ANZALDÚA

Entering into the Serpent (p. 25), How to Tame a Wild Tongue (p. 39), and La concienza de la mestiza: *Towards a New Consciousness (p. 49)*

Anzaldúa's book, *Borderlands/La frontera*, is a compelling example of postmodern, fragmented writing that can introduce students to the plasticity of writing, to its possibilities beyond the tired, rationally argued essay that they (and everyone else) have been forced to write for all their academic years. These three chapters from Anzaldúa's book capture the spirit, style, and argument of the book and demonstrate that it is possible, feasible, and perhaps desirable to compose in "montage," presenting complex subjects like identity, sexuality, religion in understandable, passionate, and compelling writing while at the same time allowing for the inherent contradictions and paradoxes of such subjects and such writing. We loved teaching Anzaldúa, and for our students this kind of text was both new and challenging (and fun, once they allowed themselves to work with it rather than trying to "get it"). It's a genuine "assemblage" or "montage" a "crazy dance," as Anzaldúa calls it, made up of sections written in a variety of styles (prose poems, endnotes, stories, anecdotes) and languages. Its argument is unconventionally cast. Rather than logically presenting a case for her mixed identity and languages as a *mestiza*, Anzaldúa juxtaposes passionate statements on her heritages, identities, sexualities, religions, and cultures with stories, poems, and anecdotes. The effect is jarring, powerful, but students will need to spend time sorting out the text's mixed style and arguments.

Immediately questions will arise about the Spanish interspersed in the text. Students will want to know if they need to read Spanish to understand Anzaldúa's arguments. It might be difficult for them to understand, at first, that they don't, that the text reveals its use of the Spanish sections as a part of its style and argument, that they'll be able to work through it as they come to see the text as a representation of Anzaldúa's mixed identity. The best advice for students, then, is to read as if the Spanish passages will defy any attempts at a complete understanding but, at the same time, will offer up sentences, phrases, and larger stylistic patterns that they'll be able to make sense of and connect to the rest of her writing.

QUESTIONS FOR A SECOND READING (p. 62)

1. This is an important discussion question to pose for students, especially since this kind of text will be new and challenging (and fun) for most of them. The central question (So how do you read this text if you don't read Spanish?) is a natural one for breaking the ice before any other discussion or writing assignments. It allows students to relate how they read the selection, how they worked with it, and it serves beautifully as an opening to other questions about Anzaldúa's style and arguments.

2. The idea of an author inventing a reader as she writes gives students a way of understanding a text's creation aside from (or alongside) notions of arguments and "points" being put

43

forward. If students begin their work with this text through the first question in this section on how they read the three chapters, then they are ready to consider how Anzaldúa invents a reader or a way of reading and what her expectations or demands might be. A number of sections, like the one quoted in this question, obliquely reveal Anzaldúa's expectations, and students shouldn't have trouble finding and working from them. They should be encouraged, especially, to work from their own experiences reading the chapters. What kinds of readers were they? How would they describe the ways in which they read?

3. This question prompts students to discuss Anzaldúa's arguments but its primary emphasis is on asking students to explain the arguments' connections across the chapters. Anzaldúa's key terms involve issues of identity, sexuality, religious experiences, and consciousness, especially what she refers to as *la facultad*, the ability to see deeper realities in surface phenomena. It's fair to say that there is no specific number of correct terms that students must identify and explain; but some terms and arguments and examples do carry across the chapters, and students would do well to look to these for their discussions of Anzaldúa's arguments and how they're connected across the chapters. It's critical to place the emphasis on *arguments*, as opposed to *argument*, because Anzaldúa makes numerous arguments, some of which contradict others — this is not a unified text, nor a unified, seamless argument.

ASSIGNMENTS FOR WRITING (p. 63)

1. This is a wonderful writing assignment that allows students to experience the creation of a mixed style from their various positions, voices, and backgrounds. Of course, as the assignment points out, students have not been prepared to write this kind of text, but Anzaldúa's example is strong enough to enable them to do so. The key moment in the assignment is the one that asks students to consider the different positions they occupy. What does this mean? Resist the temptation to tell them. Let them come to see that they are students, sons and daughters, friends, authorities, novices, swimmers, skateboarders, lovers, bikers, enemies, ball players, music listeners, concertgoers, inheritors of particular cultures and traits, and so on. Let them realize that these various selves have voices, often contradictory that students can bring forward in writing, as Anzaldúa does, when they set out to explain who they are, how they understand their experiences and, in particular, what their key or significant experiences are and in what form or style they might be presented.

2. Like the first question in Questions for a Second Reading, this writing assignment asks students to tell the story of their reading of these three chapters, but the assignment goes beyond the simple recounting of a reading. It asks students in addition to consider themselves as readers, who feel at home in the text and then lost in it, who occupy a position in relation to the text and, especially, who read or don't read as Anzaldúa expects. Some passages in the text, like the one quoted in the assignment, voice Anzaldúa's expectations about her readers, and they ask to be answered. Students may align themselves with Anzaldúa's expectations or be put off or angered by them; or they might have different responses at different times in their reading. The goal for this assignment is to let students speak back to Anzaldúa's expectations of them as readers and to use their experiences reading these chapters in that essay.

3. This assignment would work well with the first writing assignment, which asks students to write a mixed text like Anzaldúa's. Students might write this assignment first. It's straightforward in its request to students to locate and define Anzaldúa's woman's voice, her sexual voice, and her poet's voice, to work from specific passages to do this locating and defining, and to speculate how these voices differ from each other and from what Anzaldúa imagines a "standard" voice to be. Although the assignment is straightforward, the task is challenging. It opens up the discussion of what constitutes a voice, where voices come from (the self? language?), and how they're defined. It's not unusual for students to see these voices mixing into each other or to begin naming the voices by the emotional reactions they

elicit. The goal of this assignment is to open up the conversation for students to the idea of voice, not to have them find rock-solid examples of one kind of voice or dictionary or literary definitions of voice. The text offers students plenty to work with, and they should puzzle these voices out from it and from their own reactions to the various shifts in style and tone.

4. This assignment is a slightly different version of the first writing assignment. Like that first assignment, it asks students to write in different voices that are a part of them or a part of an argument they want to make. Unlike the first assignment, this one focuses specifically on students creating an argument (rather than expressing their own selves or their understandings of their situations). For this assignment to work well, students will need to write an argument about which they feel passionate, yet one on which they can see themselves taking various positions, given the different roles (students, sons and daughters, friends, skateboarders, lovers, bikers, swimmers, enemies, and so on) they hold in relation to the argument. In other words, students need to make an argument in which they allow their various voices to speak, as Anzaldúa does; they shouldn't expect to have a logical, unified, seamless case.

The second part of this assignment, the two-page assignment on why a student's argument is worth a reader's attention, serves as a way for students to consider the importance of their arguments. It's a way of asking students to think of their readers and their writing in order to present arguments worth a reader's attention, which will teach, challenge, or show readers something rather than simply reiterating commonplace clichés or generalities. In short, the two-page coda is a way of forcing the issue of asking for writing that is worth a reader's time and attention. If this assignment is to work, students will have to invest the time and energy to create arguments that they care about, that they feel confused or uncertain about, as Anzaldúa does (even though she comes across at times as certain), that they can actually explain in terms of being worth a reader's attention. If the explanation turns to clichés or generalizations, then the argument is most likely not worth a reader's attention. The two-page coda can be used, then, as a way to begin the discussion of the arguments that students produce. The first question might be, "Is this argument worth our attention? Why or why not?"

MAKING CONNECTIONS (p. 65)

1. Students will need to have read both the Pratt essay and the Anzaldúa chapters before working on this assignment. It would be worthwhile for students to work with at least one other assignment (either a second reading or writing assignment) for each selection before they turn to this one. The key terms and notions for this assignment reside in Pratt's use of autoethnographic or transcultural texts as writing in which the writer engages in some way the representations others have made of him or her. Anzaldúa continually refers to and critiques various representations of her identity, sexuality, religion, and culture, and students will need to locate those two or three representations that they would like to work from. But the task they face is larger than simply presenting Anzaldúa's text as autoethnographic or transcultural, because they are also being asked to present Pratt's argument for autoethnographic texts and Anzaldúa's text to readers who haven't read either. In other words, they are being asked to re-present both texts and to use Anzaldúa's as a further example for Pratt's discussion of autoethnographic or transcultural texts. Students, of course, will have to produce some sort of summary or paraphrase of both texts in order to complete the assignment, but that summary or paraphrase is only the frame. They must then go on to present Anzaldúa's writing as part and parcel of Pratt's argument. The summary or paraphrase of these texts serves the purpose of orienting readers unfamiliar with either Pratt's essay or Anzaldúa's text, and this assignment offers a good opportunity for students to test their drafts against readers outside their class.

2. The heart of this assignment resides in students identifying the differences in Anzaldúa's and Rich's arguments about writing, identity, politics, and history and then in attributing them

to the positions each writer occupies. Students will need to resist the tendency to attribute differences in the authors' arguments to personal differences, to the fact, that is, that different people hold different opinions, and to examine carefully the positions each author holds as a writer. How, for instance, they might be asked, does Anzaldúa create her identity in writing? How does Rich? How does each locate herself in her culture? What positions do the two hold in relation to their respective histories? What key examples and terms do they put forward? And how do these terms and examples reflect the different positions that they hold as writers? as people working out identities in writing?

JOHN BERGER

Ways of Seeing (p. 66)

As the headnote says, this selection is the first chapter of a book, *Ways of Seeing*, drawn from John Berger's television series with the BBC. The book actually has five authors — or, as the page opposite the title page says, it is "a book made by" John Berger, Sven Blomberg, Chris Fox, Michael Dibb, and Richard Hollis. Both the spine and the title page, however, carry Berger's name only. For convenience, we refer to the essay as his. Possession and ownership, as Berger argues in the essay, are difficult and problematic concepts.

Berger creates books that are hard to classify, and this one is certainly no exception. There are chapters in *Ways of Seeing* that have no words, only pictures. In the chapter we've included, there are pictures that are clearly part of the text (the argument instructs the reader to look at them), but there are other pictures included as well, and they have a less official status. Some could be said to be illustrations of points in the text. Others have to be worked into the chapter.

We were attracted to this piece by the way it allowed us to extend the concept of reading beyond written texts (to the way one "reads" paintings or images, to the way one "reads" one's culture), and for the act of reading it requires. There is a strong argument in the essay, to be sure, particularly in the discussion of the paintings by Frans Hals, and students can reproduce it without great trouble. But there is still much work left for the reader. There are paintings and pictures that go without discussion. There are moments when common words like "history" are wrenched out of common usage. Berger wants to take common terms and make them problematic, just as he wants to take familiar images and give us a new way of seeing them, yet he is not pushy about definitions; terms remain open to discussion. The structure of the essay also presents a challenge to its readers. While students can begin through discussion to work out the argument of various sections in the essay (his reading of the Hals paintings, the example of mystification, his argument about reproduction, the section on the use of museums), there is no single answer to how these various parts should fit together in a single discussion.

This, then, is one way to teach this essay. Students can begin by focusing on individual sections in order to figure out what Berger is saying and what, as a group, they feel it means ("How do you make sense out of the 'yet' in 'Yet, although every image embodies a way of seeing, our perception or appreciation of an image depends also upon our own way of seeing.'" [text pp. 69–70]?) As teachers, we are willing to be a resource at this point: to say what we see in the painting by Magritte or the figures on museum attendance, or to help students see the lines of demarcation that underlie their various points of view on, for instance, what it means to say that the prose on text page 73 is mystification. We are unwilling to tell our students everything we know about Magritte or Benjamin — at least not until very late in the discussion, when this section of the course is over. We don't want the textual problems in an essay to seem like problems of information. The question is not what students can be told about Magritte but what they can make out of that painting, placed as it is in the text. The issue is not how much they know about Walter Benjamin, but that they know that Berger felt the need to bring forward Benjamin's name and one of his books.

The fun of the discussion comes when students find they have gained a foothold on various sections of the essay and you ask, "How does it fit together? How do you put together the section on the *Virgin of the Rocks* with the section on Van Gogh and Hals? What does this have to do with what you've learned to say about history or about the relationship between a person, an image, and ways of seeing?" These are questions that don't have any quick answer. The uncertainty they create can only in a limited sense be resolved by returning to the text. Berger, in other words, loses his capacity as the authority here. Students might test what they have to say by talking about the charts on text page 82 or the painting on text page 89, but they won't find answers. These are answers that they must create, present, and defend both for themselves and for their colleagues, and in discussion as a prelude to work they might do as writers.

Some Added Notes

The man pictured on text page 90 is Walter Benjamin and not, as it appears, John Berger.

The reproductions in Berger's book are of about the same quality as those in the textbook. They too, are in black-and-white. Many of the frames are dark. The physical relationship of image to text is as close to that of the original as we could make it, so the images you see are similar to those a reader confronts in the original text. There is no reason, of course, why a teacher should not seek out slides or better, full-color reproductions, nor should a teacher apologize for black-and-white. The images your students will be studying are those in Berger's book, and since part of Berger's argument concerns the use and reproduction of images, there is reason to pay attention to — rather than try to overcome — problems with his use and reproduction of images.

QUESTIONS FOR A SECOND READING (p. 91)

1. These questions are designed to take one of the key terms of this essay, "history," and to make its possible meanings the central textual problem for students as they read back through the text. For Berger, who is both an art historian and a Marxist, history is something of a technical term, and he uses it to frame his argument. He puts pressure on the term and forces it to mean more than it does when it is used loosely in conversation. The job for students is to see how they might make sense of these sentences — what, for a reader of Berger, might it mean to be "situated" in history, or to be "deprived" of history?

   Students are directed to pay attention to Berger's use of this term. Once they begin to develop a way of accounting for that use, the remaining questions ask them to put *their* sense of this term, "history" to the test by using it in sentences that discuss the Hals paintings. Students are asked to develop a specialized use for a common term and then to use that term to enable a discussion of an example they share with their colleagues in class (and with Berger, their author). They are asked, that is, to produce a Berger-like discussion, or a discussion that demonstrates their way of reading Berger.

2. This question is intended to allow students to imagine a position outside of Berger's, one from which they can critique Berger's argument. On the one hand, Berger argues that mystification hides that which is "really" there. The assumption, at least at a first reading, seems to be that there are some people who can see with that kind of clarity. On the other hand, Berger argues that we see what we have learned to see. Students are asked, then, to work out Berger's position on the relationship between seeing and understanding, between the individual and the culture, and to turn the terms of that discussion back on Berger himself. Could you say

that he sees the truth in the Hals paintings? Is his perception "shaped" or pure? If you find that you can say that Berger too sees what he has learned to see, does that discredit his argument?

ASSIGNMENTS FOR WRITING **(p. 91)**

1. Accepting the implied invitation of the essays, this assignment asks the reader to see what he or she can make of one of the paintings that is given a prominent position in the text. While Berger has something to say about *Woman Pouring Milk*, he does not give it a full discussion. The problem posed is "What can you make of this painting, if you work on it in Berger's spirit?" One way of framing a discussion of these papers or of preparing students for revision is to turn to Berger's own words: "What we make of that painted moment when it is before our eyes depends upon what we expect of art, and that in turns depends today upon how we have already experienced the meaning of paintings through reproductions" (text p. 88). Students might begin by considering what the authors of the papers under consideration expect of art, how they might have experienced the meaning of paintings through reproductions. What, in those papers, might be attributed to the authors' work with Berger? What might be attributed to our general culture? What might be taken as a sign of some individual or idiosyncratic vision?

   In our experience, the key features for students who have worked on this painting have been the identity of the box and pot on the floor behind the woman, the woman's relationship to this room — is it hers, for example? — and the nature of the task she is performing. One question for a teacher here is the degree to which this project could, or should, involve research. It would be a good idea to decide beforehand whether to provide additional information about Vermeer; to provide art historians' readings of the painting; to suggest that students make use of the library; or students work without any secondary sources.

2. We've had a good deal of success with this assignment. Ideally, students should have ready access to a museum. Berger talks about the ways we have come to experience paintings in museums, and a trip to a museum to look at a painting will give students a way of adding to or reflecting on Berger's argument. But he also talks about reproductions, so we felt justified in adding the option of using art books. If you can reasonably expect your students to get to a museum, however, we think the trip will hold some interesting surprises for you. We usually schedule a class meeting at the museum — just to get the students walking around to think about which painting might be "theirs." Warn students against docents and taped tours — for your purposes, prepared readings of paintings will be a real barrier to writing.

   The students who have had the most success with this assignment have been fairly literal in their sense of what it means to have a "conversation" with a painting. Their essays do not read like museum-guide interpretations, rather like more open-ended and speculative pieces, sometimes cast as a narrative with dialogue, sometimes as pure dialogue. The key is to invite students to talk to the painting, to ask questions, and to imagine rich and ambiguous responses. You want to avoid papers in which students begin with an idea of what a picture is about and simply impose that reading on the material. The paintings need to be imagined to talk back, to counter or open up a student's desire to master and control.

   For revision: In some cases we've found we needed to send students back to the painting and the original assignment, usually because they were more concerned to push through a single reading than to have a conversation with their material. In most cases, however, we used the revision as the occasion to send students back to the Berger essay. As they became involved with the museum assignment, students forgot about Berger, so we used the revision to send them back to see what use they could make of his way of talking about paintings or the museum. "How, for example, could you use the example of your essay to explain what Berger might mean when he talks about 'history'?" The idea is to engage students in a conversation with Berger, where they can draw on their expertise to enter his argument.

MAKING CONNECTIONS **(p. 92)**

1. The assignment points to the common starting point in Percy's and Berger's essays: Both work with the assumption that people see what they have learned to see — we don't "naturally" or "truly" receive scenes in nature or pictures in a museum. Both argue that, if this is the case, one ought to think about ways of seeing, worry about one's habitual understanding of the world, and plan strategies or approaches to improve one's vision. With this Percy/Berger sense of the problem, students are asked to put themselves (and the essays) to the test by imagining approaches to a painting in a museum (although there is no reason why a teacher should insist on a museum — it would be possible to use slides or handouts or the images in the text). Students must step back from what they have done and use what they have written in their essays to compare and evaluate the two essays.

   The only real difficulty in this assignment is the number of steps: Grasp the argument of the essays, write a series of approaches, and evaluate what you have done. There is no reason why these steps can't be separate stages as students work on this essay. Each might be written individually and discussed in class or in groups. All three might then be put together into a single essay in a final revision.

2. Before writing this assignment, students will undoubtedly need to do some preliminary work with the Foucault selection and would certainly be helped by preliminary work with the Berger piece. The second-reading questions for class discussions of both the Foucault and the Berger selections will help students orient themselves to these challenging texts.

   Neither Berger nor Foucault directly defines what he means by power. However, Berger is more direct in his attribution of power to the ruling class and invites us to imagine how power relations might change if people were to understand history in art, whereas Foucault presents power as a force of production in culture that, in a sense, has a life of its own. If students approach this assignment as a single project to explain theories of power, rather than to make a critical judgment about either theory, they'll have a clearer sense of purpose as they reread the texts and mark passages that they can use to represent each author's notions of power. Students will find it more challenging to write about Foucault's arguments about power, which he invests not in people or classes of people but rather in culture as a force that those knowledgeable enough about power can use to channel and manipulate people. But it is difficult to say from either Foucault's or Berger's arguments how power works and how you might know it when you see it. Students will be frustrated if they think that they can get either author's arguments about power down pat, and they will need to write this assignment in an atmosphere of experimentation so that they can acknowledge and write about the sections of both texts that they have trouble understanding. It helps our students to know that anyone reading these texts will have a challenging time of trying to come to grips with the discussions of power, and that this difficulty is an opportunity to speculate and venture explanations that are tentative and uncertain.

3. The best way to approach Geertz's essay might be through this one-sentence representation of his method: The cockfights are a story the Balinese tell themselves about themselves. American teenagers walk around shopping malls doing peculiar but characteristic things. College students decorate dorm rooms in peculiar but characteristic ways. To begin to carry out a Geertzian project, we might say that in each case these are stories people are telling themselves about themselves. What are these stories? What are the key features? How might an outsider interpret them? *What* then, are they telling themselves about themselves?

   This is the basic pattern — from it, and by returning to Geertz's essay, a class can begin to account for the special expertise of an anthropologist and the special concerns Geertz shows for the limits and potential of such a method of analysis.

   Students are asked to speak, with Berger's help, about the peculiar but characteristic ways we make use of images from the past (for Berger, of course, this includes the use of those images outside of museum walls). And the assignment asks students to speculate on what stories we are telling ourselves about ourselves.

A note on the final caveat: Berger's argument about the ruling class will quickly consume the speculative ardor of most students. He says it in a nutshell, they will argue, so there is nothing else to say. We've found that it makes sense to insist that students ought to work toward some other account; then, if they and you choose, they can go back to consider Berger's.

HAROLD BRODKEY

A Story in an Almost Classical Mode (p. 95)

This is for many reasons a curious, almost manic story. Our students read it the same semester that they worked with Anzaldúa's essays from *Borderlands/La frontera*, and it was one of those rare stories that leaves almost everyone who reads it with ambivalent yet intensely involved feelings. It was, too, one of the few stories that we have ever taught that made our students want to write stories about themselves in the manner that Brodkey presents in this seemingly autobiographical tale. It's so well written, so cleverly done that all of my students wanted to believe it was "true," yet it's also terribly flawed with its manic male constructions and point of view. We had a lot of fun discussing and writing about how Brodkey and Buddy, the main character, imagine Doris, the only woman in the story, as well as reviewing the methods the story uses to present Buddy as a self-effacing, egotistical junior hero with a Holden Caulfieldish bent.

Brodkey begins by telling us that his protagonists are his mother's voice and the mind he had when he was thirteen. He lets us know almost immediately that "no one in particular trusted my memory" — and then proceeds to tell us the story from what seems to be a flawless, unquestionable memory. He gives the boy in the story his name, Harold Brodkey. Thus students immediately imagine that the story is autobiography rather than fiction and want to treat it as a true case history rather than as an imaginative invention. The story centers on young Harold and the life he lives with his mother, Doris, who is dying of cancer. The boy tries to imagine his mother's pain by imagining himself a woman, and students seem to find this a compelling aspect of the story even though the woman he imagines and the one he lives with dominate the story as unattractive characters who cause others, but especially Harold, pain and frustration. Brodkey allows Harold to be the innocent in the sense that he mostly bears his mother's problems and spends his life in the story trying to cope and become whole in the face of her relentless misery. Still, the story has powerful effects on students, and it's ripe for critical readings of the characters and the author who creates them.

QUESTIONS FOR A SECOND READING (p. 136)

1. Since Brodkey creates Harold in the image of his own name and puts him in a number of emotionally charged situations, it's possible to attribute a range of attitudes toward Buddy: sympathy, skepticism, anger, trust, distrust, and so on. The key for student discussion of these possible attitudes is in the passages they bring forward as significant. Once they identify the passages and discuss the attitudes that they think Brodkey wants them to hold, they should turn their attention to the attitudes that they do hold. The distinction is worth pointing up; students need to learn to imagine first that authorial intentions, like intended attitudes, are textual creations and then that their own responses in juxtaposition to those are possibly separate and different from what the author might be said to have intended.

2. This discussion question has a number of strands, beginning with the question of the thirteen-year-old boy's mind. How, in other words, do we see this mind at work? Working from telling passages, how might you characterize the workings of this thirteen-year-old boy's head? Then there's the question of the adult creating the thirteen-year-old. What's his head like? How similar is he to the boy? Again, students will need to work closely from passages in the story, or they'll create characterizations that are clichéd and over-generalized. Finally, there's the question of how students might read the boy's and the author's stance toward women. How do these two minds understand women? In other words, how does the author characterize the boy understanding women? And how does Harold, the boy, understand Doris?

3. Students will find this assignment unusual for a story. They're not often asked to take a stance toward stories that allow them to see arguments being created by the author; but this is a particularly good story asking them to do so, because of the way Brodkey creates the interactions between Harold and Doris. You might ask students to begin this discussion by imagining that Brodkey, the author, had an argument that he wanted to put forward, and that this argument has to do with the relationship between Harold and Doris, between a boy and a woman. Harold, the character, often gives his version of what's going on in the story, although other guides (for example, the dialogues, Doris's point of view, the assignment of agency — who gets to be the agent?) don't always support Harold's version of what's going on. Students can have fun with this question by taking a particularly critical attitude toward Harold, the character, and imagining that he plays a part in the argument which isn't told yet, that they have to piece together from other aspects of the story.

4. This question asks students to imagine that there are moments in the story that prepare them to answer the question about what use they can make of the story. Students might consider what methods or devices Brodkey uses (such as allowing the story to seem autobiographical) that bear on how it presents itself for others' uses. There are, too, the dialogues and characterizations to consider. What might they be creating in the story that allows it to be used for a particular purpose by readers? Are there lessons that the story could be said to intend? Are there stances or attitudes it provokes that might be useful to readers? How so? From where in the text might one draw this conclusion?

ASSIGNMENTS FOR WRITING (p. 136)

1. This is a great story for students to use to do a critical analysis of gender. Brodkey and his namesake character, Harold, dominate the narrative and the dialogue, and while doing so they attribute a great many things to Doris. Both try to imagine what it is like to be a woman, and that imagining leads to further revelations of how they understand and fail to understand women. It's important that the students work from numerous moments in the text as they compose their analysis of how Brodkey and Buddy understand Doris; and it's equally important that they take into consideration the narrative, the dialogue, and Buddy's attempts to imagine himself as a woman. It should be clear to students that the men carry the weight of the narrative and the dialogue, so it'll be important for them to identify numerous key moments to work from.

2. In this assignment, students are given the opportunity to approach Brodkey's story from two stances, first, as if it were a "true" story and, second, as if it were fiction. Brodkey seems to invite both readings. He calls this a story, implying that it is fiction, and, through the narrator, Harold ("Buddy") Brodkey, he creates the possibility of its being autobiographical. Without a preliminary discussion of what might be called Brodkey's autobiographical method, most, if not all, students will read this as a true account. With this assignment, and the opportunity to notice how their observations differ depending on whether they read it as true or as fiction, students can speak to the differences in reading given these two points of view. If they are encouraged to play with the notions of memory as a creation rather than an instrument of

accurate recall, they will be in a position to enter a conversation on writing, whether it is autobiographical or fictional, as the play of memory and imagination. Such a conversation, which can proceed from this assignment, will help demystify students' notions of ironclad genres and make other ways of discussing writing (understanding it as memory and imagination, for example) available to them.

3. Students are generally unfamiliar with story writing. This assignment gives them the opportunity to write a story that is, like Brodkey's, worth telling, one that tells the tale of a complex slice of their own lives and seems, still, difficult to understand. By writing this kind of story, and so forestalling the tendency to have everything worked out ahead of time, students put themselves in the position of using the story to explore that which is difficult to understand. Students will need to work through multiple revisions of this assignment. At first, they'll tend to create cardboard characters and clichéd dialogue. You can adopt a number of strategies to help them. First, they'll need to understand how stories literally work on the page. They can turn to the Brodkey and Oates stories to study how narration, dialogue, scenes, and characters can be created. You don't have to belabor this, and students can study the stories on their own, but you'll help them if you tell them to turn to the Brodkey and Oates stories to learn how to write and follow the conventions of stories. They can also help themselves by creating dialogues from actual conversations they overhear or observe. Draw students' attention to how people move, gesture, and use facial expressions when they talk, so that they can create character while creating dialogue. As students work through these kinds of strategies in their drafts, they should focus their discussions of each others' works on whether or not they think the stories are worth telling and, specifically, on those moments in the stories that do or do not seem believable. Those moments can then become occasions for emulation, further work, or complete revision.

MAKING CONNECTIONS **(p. 137)**

1. This assignment asks for a straightforward analysis of the Oates and the Brodkey stories comparing their characteristic methods and styles. Students are directed to work closely from passages in the stories that can serve as examples of the methods and styles they choose to write about. These passages should represent for the students the key moments or terms or methods that each story uses. A particularly challenging part of this assignment is the question that asks students to consider what each author's methods allow or prevent him from doing in the story. Because, for instance, Brodkey's story proceeds with Buddy as the narrator, and because we get to see Doris only through his eyes and through very little dialogue (compared to narration), the story can't create Doris with much detail or complexity, at least not with the detail and complexity it affords Buddy. This constraint in turn bears directly on how the men of the story (Buddy and Brodkey, the author) can understand women, particularly Doris. To create their own reading of what methods allow and prevent, students will want to pay attention to the question in the assignment that asks them who tells the story, what characters get the reader's attention, and what the key scenes or terms seem to be.

3. Juxtaposing the Oates and the Brodkey stories offers students the chance of studying two stories strongly marked by gender. Students will need to remember that the Oates story is a woman's story, in which the narrator is a woman, and that the Brodkey story is a man's story, in which the narrator is a man. These narrators create characters. Brodkey's character Buddy in turn creates the story of Buddy and Doris. Oates's character Marya then creates the story of Marya and Imogene. Both stories, too, represent men and women in dialogue. We see Buddy and Doris in conversation, and we see Marya and Imogene as well as Imogene and her parents and Marya and Matthew in conversations. How do the two authors respectively represent the experiences of women and men? Brodkey gives the weight of his story to Buddy; Oates gives Marya center stage. How then do these major creations, these major characters, differ? In other words, how does Oates represent women and how does Brodkey

represent women? What about men? How are they represented by each author? What, too, students can ask themselves, are the traits of each author's characters — from the author's narrative and from the dialogues? Once students begin to work through these questions, they can understand how these stories might be said, through their narratives and dialogues, to be presenting arguments about the differences between men and women and see in what ways these arguments seem right, wrong, biased, incomplete, surprising.

4. This assignment gives students the opportunity to work on the problems of readers reading. It is a great assignment to use with an entire class as a preliminary study of the effects of readers on stories and stories on readers. Students are initially asked to react to the Brodkey story and are then instructed to work from a set of other students' responses as case material for drawing conclusions about how stories work on readers and how readers work on stories. Students can work from the same set of other students' papers, or they can work from different collections of three or four other students' essays. First they are asked to define which moments in the Brodkey story strike them as memorable or important and then they are asked to say what it is about those moments that they found so significant.

Once they complete their initial essays, they are asked to work from a set of others to comment, in another essay, on the differences between their responses and those of other students. Their goal should be to draw conclusions about how stories work on readers and how readers work on stories. But there's a danger here too. It's easy to dismiss differences in readings to individual differences (everyone reads what he or she wants or prefers to see or is inclined to see) without exploring what accounts for those differences and without factoring the text in to the equations. You'll need to be attentive to students tendencies to dismiss differences as only individual differences and help them to explain how individual reactions can be thought of as learned (as part and parcel of such omnipresent yet seemingly invisible things as culture, gender, race, genre expectations, and so on) and how texts can set up readers, their expectations, and their reactions, by the force of such factors as who the narrator is, what characters get the attention, and what the story's methods allow and prevent.

STANLEY FISH

How to Recognize a Poem When You See One (p. 139)

The very qualities that draw crowds to Fish's lectures at professional meetings make him a star in an undergraduate class: His arguments provide a powerful rereading of "common" sense; his writing is witty, anecdotal, sharply focused, and quick to sum things up in a representative example. The stories he tells in "How to Recognize a Poem When You See One" are stories students can read with recognition and pleasure, as though they were getting an inside view of English teaching. The work for a teacher in this essay is to first get students to find pleasure and recognition in those stories, then to press for the connections between them (the story of the poem and the story of Mr. Newlin's gesture, for example) and the theory in Fish's essay. We've found that students are good at phrasing their version of some critics' objections to Fish — he is too quick to assume that an interpretive community is a single, unified thing; he is too quick to assume the passivity of readers or students; he seems to leave no way out of set ways of speaking and thinking. It is harder for them to sympathetically reconstruct and speak for the details of Fish's argument. It is a powerful argument if only for the currency of a term like "interpretive community" in university discourse, and it deserves a careful reading.

One approach to the essay is to begin with the stories, to get students to retell them and bring forward the interesting — and telling — details. Then you can begin to ask what these stories mean, and move back and forth between what the class says they mean in their terms, and what Fish says they mean in his terms. This is one way to highlight Fish's argument as a statement by a professional. He is not just saying what people are accustomed to say — for example, that students are "programmed" by their teachers or that school is just a game you play in order to get ahead. It is important to distinguish between Fish's argument and the commonplaces that will come forward in a discussion of Mr. Newlin or the poem.

QUESTIONS FOR A SECOND READING (p. 152)

1. The questions in this section take two very different approaches to the essay. The first is the easier. It says that, as readers, students should measure Fish's reading of the examples against their own reading of those examples, and that the most immediate authority students have in doing so is the wisdom of experience. You are a student, the question says. Does all this sound right to you? Can you think of a classroom experience that would fit the frame of Fish's argument? As students reread, they are looking for sections that seem easy to confirm and sections that seem false or problematic. This distinction should give them material to use in writing or discussion.

2. This is the harder question, since it asks students, while they reread, to reconstruct the teaching profession's presence in the essay. As we said in the general discussion above, it is important for students to see Fish speaking to a professional audience as well as a general audience. We don't, in our own teaching, wish to lecture students on Hirsch or Graff or Holland or Bleich, nor do we wish to give a quick guide to poststructuralism. We do, however, want students to see that Fish is being more precise in his discriminations than an editorial writer or a popular writer would be. We want students to imagine his expertise by looking to see what he does that belongs to a specialized discourse. If students can begin as confident readers because they, too, have been in classrooms and watched all this going on, they need to read beyond this level of expertise — to see Fish's essay as representing a method of analysis and not just a set of maxims.

ASSIGNMENTS FOR WRITING (p. 153)

1–2. Both assignments ask students to test Fish's argument on an example drawn from their own experience. Both ask students to bring Fish's language to bear on their world, and both raise the issue of the difference between an expert and a common reading — the issue raised in the "Questions for a Second Reading." Once students have located an example — their primary material — their work on the essay will be governed by their sense of Fish's key terms and methods. The assignments, in other words, do not say, "Choose a similar example, and then say what you want about it." They say, "Choose a similar example and give it a Fishian reading." This is an intellectually difficult distinction. Fish is an expert and students are students, and students are seldom given the authority to act on the same level with "real" writers like Stanley Fish. It will seem as though they are being asked to overstep their bounds, to do what they can't be expected to do. And, of course, that is exactly the point. They should be stepping beyond what they can already do, even if it means that their work may be tentative and clumsy. One way of dealing with this difficulty is to make it the focal point for revision. Students can go back to their essays — essays where the primary energy was devoted to finding an example and a way of talking about it — to work on bringing Fish's terms and methods into play in their discussion, and to do so with a greater confidence and authority.

The first assignment invites students to read against the grain of Fish's essay. We've taught this essay several times, and students have always felt a bit uneasy working within the terms of his argument, uneasy at accepting his account of "studenting" and defining themselves and their experience accordingly. For one thing, our students have said, Fish does not talk about the distribution of power in the classroom. This community may be bound together more by the overriding authority of the teacher than by shared interpretive strategies, due not only to the teacher's ability to set grades but also to his or her ability to ask the guiding questions and determine the tone of the discussion. You can feel this authority in Fish's prose—in the way he addresses the reader, in the Mr. Newlin discussion, in the ways he allows his reader to ask certain questions but not others. The assignment asks students to step out of Fish's discourse by imagining their participation in another community, one where he is not a member — by taking a student's point of view. In a sense, the assignment asks them to puncture or call into question the "we" of Fish's essay.

It is important, however, for students to see that they are writing as members of a collective — of a shared — way of thinking and speaking. It is too easy to write in terms of one's individual freedom ("Well, I've never liked that kind of teacher"). The point is not to imagine a world of individuals — where Fish is a pushy teacher and a student can declare his or her right to independence — but to imagine the classroom as a place of competing interests, where both teachers and students are shaped by the social context, by the history of American education, and by habitual ways of thinking and speaking about the classroom, including those present in Fish's essay.

MAKING CONNECTIONS (p. 154)

1. Although Pratt doesn't allude to Fish in "Arts of the Contact Zone," her essay could be seen as one in a line of critical responses to Fish's notion of an "interpretive community." (This line would include some of Fish's own later work, most notably the essay "Change," first published in the *South Atlantic Quarterly* and later collected in *Doing What Comes Naturally*.) The concept of an "interpretive community" was a powerful one and it helped to set specific acts of reading, writing, and thinking in a social/political/historical context; the problems for many were both practical and political: real-life situations didn't seem so orderly or constrained (people felt as if they were members of more than one interpretive community; not everybody in a specific setting, like a classroom, seemed prepared to interpret in the same ways); the idea of community seemed conservative, seemed to erase the possibilities for seeing and valuing difference or change.

We wrote several assignments asking students in one way or another to imagine the limits of Fish's sense of the classroom as a community. Does his story ring true? Why are his students silent, why no words from students in this essay? Can you imagine a response written from a student's point of view, from a point of view situated within the classroom but not part of the "community" Fish takes for granted? This "Connections" assignment extends that critique by asking students to frame a response in Pratt's terms. Pratt resists the temptation to see the community as unified (a desire she calls "utopian") and argues for the importance of learning to see and understand and value difference in a meeting of speakers, writers, and thinkers. Where Fish sees uniformity, Pratt would look for moments of contact, moments that are hidden or repressed in the "official" account of the class and its work.

There are two ways of imagining students' work with this essay. The primary work could be the work of representing "Fish" and "Pratt" (their ideas *and* their words) in an essay. Here the center of attention is summary, paraphrase, and quotation—what happens when you try to represent all of an essay or its argument through example and citation. This is often how we represent the work of a first draft to students. It is not uncommon to find students who will write a dialogue or dramatic scene. These are welcome moments in the classroom but we've found it important to talk about the problems this format will *not* solve. (Usually, for example, Fish and Pratt become cartoon figures and their ideas rather simple, often comic.)

The other way to represent students' work in this essay is through the question that asks, "Where would you be in this discussion?" Since the students' position is often not repre-sented (or represented only slightly) in the first draft, this is often a useful focus for a revision exercise. Students, we've found, need to feel the pressure to represent their positions as fully as Fish and Pratt do. They have to do more than write one-liners, in other words; they need to explain, illustrate, translate and rephrase, take another start, tell a joke, grab attention, and so on.

2. There is a way in which Fish offers a characteristic Percian anecdote. Percy says that perhaps one way to recover the "thing" from the educational package is to make students suddenly aware of the pressure of context — to put a dogfish, as he says, on the student's desk in the English class and a Shakespeare sonnet on the laboratory table in biology. Fish's students, in a sense, found a dogfish on their desks and quickly turned it into a sonnet.

In the second half of Percy's essay (p. 434), Percy talks about the circumstances under which the "thing" in the classroom is restored to students: by ordeal, by apprenticeship to a master, or by virtue of some special strength of character in an individual student. This assignment asks students to write a new section to Percy's essay, and to do so by making Fish's story one more representative anecdote in Percy's discussion. Where would he fit in the story of the poem? What would he say about it? What relation does it bear to the other stories he tells?

An additional exercise might ask students to imagine that Fish has read what Percy has done with his example, and to write out Fish's reply. Another might ask students, when they have finished this imaginary dialogue, to make a statement of their own about "studenting" and about Percy and Fish.

JOHN FISKE

Madonna (p. 156)

"Madonna" is taken from Fiske's new book, *Reading the Popular*, which is part of a two-book set. Its companion, *Understanding Popular Culture*, is designed, Fiske said, to "develop the theoretical and political" arguments about the ways in which popular culture is received and understood. *Reading the Popular* was designed to show the arguments in practice and, as a school book, to develop analytical skills. It moves "from readings to theories" rather than "from theories to readings."

This was part of the attraction of "Madonna" for us. We were looking for a piece that gave a close reading of some area of contemporary American popular culture. (We were looking for a replacement for Simon Frith's essay, "Rock and Sexuality," which seemed to us to be too British and too dated.) Fiske's essay provided not only a strong reading of Madonna but also an extended reflection on its own critical methods, charting the strategies that have enabled critics to read the "texts" of popular culture and theorize their reception.

In this sense, Fiske's project in "Madonna" seemed to parallel that of Jane Tompkins in "Indians." Both provide a look behind the scenes, in a sense, at how academics think about and understand the work they do. "Madonna" provides not just a reading of Madonna but also a commentary on how that reading is produced (with some glance at the problems produced by the production of that reading).

While Fiske is somewhat self-critical in "Madonna," he too easily (for our taste) becomes the hero of his story, the man who can reveal the truth about the lives of young women and set them free. We try to point to this flavor in his account in our questions. When we've taught the essay, we've found students quick to be critical of Fiske. While we encourage a critical reading, we've discovered that, our students' initial instincts are not always to be trusted. We found that students, for reasons that are consistent with Fiske's argument, share in the general notion that close attention to "trivia" (Madonna, TV, exercise programs) is obsessive, stupid, bizarre, a form of "academic" nonsense. And, again for reasons that can be seen as part of Fiske's argument, they find it difficult to construct a first-person narrative where they are anything but individual agents exercising free choice.

As teachers, we have had to work hard to see that students gave "Madonna" a generous reading — that is, paying attention to its account of how Madonna is received and used by her fans and taking seriously Fiske's account of the war between the young and the old, men and women. Later — in a later discussion in class, in a revision of a draft — we try to put an edge to the role Fiske plays as a critic, to highlight Fiske's representation of both the Critic and the Populace (the older man and the younger girls) to give students a lever to step outside his argument. Fiske charts the workings of a patriarchal culture without ever acknowledging the problems or irony in his own position — that of an older man taking possession of and speaking for young women. It is just too easy for him to account for the "real" thoughts and desires of Madonna's fans. And from this perspective, it is not difficult to see Fiske as allied with traditional interests (including the moguls of the music business) in the struggle for power and control.

In our classes we try to work from a generous reading of Fiske to a more critical position. Once our students begin to understand Fiske's account of Madonna and her fans, we want them to think of what Fiske says not as "the truth" about Madonna or youth culture but as an alternative narrative of power and knowledge, as Fiske's (and those critics like Fiske's) representation of Madonna and her fans (What generalizations does he make about young women? Why are these necessary? Whom does he leave out?), or of criticism and its functions. Our students can most quickly and profitably work out this understanding of Fiske when we ask them to think about or write about the Critic (as represented by Fiske) and the role (as represented in this essay) the critic plays or would hope to play in the imaginations of Madonna's fans.

The other problem we have encountered when teaching this essay is its language. Here, in a sense, the comparison with "Indians" breaks down. "Indians" is conceptually tough, but Tompkins is a wonderful writer and the difficulties are productive. Fiske is a less graceful writer, and the difficulties in his prose at times seem as much a product of inattention as anything else. In almost every case, the writers in *Ways of Reading* are writers whose prose we admire greatly. Fiske is an exception. We love his attempts to represent alternative voices, not only the words of Madonna's fans also but the prose of his students, represented by Robyn Blair, whose paper he cites at the end. Students' voices are present in this essay. This is not a text where only the great man gets to speak. In this sense Fiske takes seriously the problems of understanding the minds of young adults, as he takes seriously the challenge of writing a prose that acknowledges the presence and validity of alternative voices. His own prose, however, seems directed at a professional rather than a general audience, and as a result "Madonna" seems written to put students in their place.

QUESTIONS FOR A SECOND READING (p. 173)

1–2. It is important for students to imagine a context for "Madonna." We want them to see it as part of larger attempt to understand and value the materials and experience of popular culture. Fiske is rejecting the cultural studies' early versions of the "populace," as passive "dopes" manipulated by capitalism and its interests. And he is trying to chart out the methods critics use to imagine and represent the experience of popular culture. In this sense he is also arguing against the more general notion that popular culture is trivial and unimportant, not worth serious attention and not a force to be considered when considering the forces at work in contemporary life (or a force simply to be condemned for ruining the minds and values of late adolescents).

The first question asks students to try to infer an argumentative context by thinking about the positions Fiske feels compelled to challenge, bracket, or defend. The second asks students to pay attention to Fiske's account of cultural studies, its concerns and methods. Unfortunately the first few pages of the essay (up until the "Lucy" discussion) are the densest. It is here that Fiske makes quick references to semiotics, signifiers, structuralism, and patriarchal capitalism. It is useful for students to push through this opening section on a first reading, then to spend more time with it the second time through, particularly with the goal of being able to summarize or reproduce Fiske's account of the cultural studies. The question goes on to ask students to test Fiske's account of Madonna's fans against their own experience. It is important to remind your students as they do this that for Fiske and the cultural critics, "common sense" is often seen as unreliable, as part of the problem, as something produced and enforced by the dominant culture to keep consumers from asking difficult questions.

3. The third question is designed to prepare students to read against the grain of Fiske's presentation of the Critic in "Madonna" (see the discussion above). The question turns the tables on Fiske by suggesting that his critique of the packaging of Madonna could be applied to his packaging of John Fiske, the cultural critic. At one level, the questions ask, "What good is this criticism? What is its function? What (or whose) purposes might this essay serve?" At another, the questions turn more specifically on the figure of John Fiske, the critic, the figure in the text, and his position in the complex struggles between men and women, old and young.

ASSIGNMENTS FOR WRITING (p. 173)

1. This assignment gives students two options: an autobiographical essay ("A Fan's Notes") or an essay that provides a reading of the discourse of fans (interviews, letters to the editors, talk on talk shows). The assignment is meant to enable students not only to participate in Fiske's project (trying to represent and understand a fan's use of a star) but also to answer back. When we taught this assignment, our goal was to give students a body of closely discussed material they could use to talk back to Fiske or to test and extend his discussion. ("The women I spoke to spoke differently of Madonna. . . .")

If students pick the autobiographical essay option, be sure that they imagine this genre as fully as possible (since "Madonna" doesn't provide much of a model). Students will need to use the resources of narrative (scene, dialogue, character). The best of these we received worked, actually, through a series of parallel scenes (different stars, different points in time, different accounts of a single concert). It helps to ask students to believe that they are adding material to Fiske's files. (In fact, there is no reason not to send essays to Fiske.) Students might imagine, in other words, accounts that are richer and more detailed than Lucy's or Robyn's.

For revision: in most cases, when our students begin to work on a second draft of this essay, their primary concern is to fill out the account — to make it more detailed, more storylike, to find interesting alternative scenes, voices, or points of view.

If students pick the second option, they will need to be able to anticipate the importance of good fieldwork. These essays will be interesting to the degree that students accept the challenge of finding and collecting their "archive," their materials. If they write about the first item that comes to hand (or the easiest) they will have invested little in the methodological difficulties that are part of this kind of work. They should not be writing from hearsay but from carefully collected materials. We have found it useful to ask students to gather material and write (or talk) about what they are going to select from their files to write about. In this case, we assume that students will collect more than they can use; part of their work will be to discuss how and why they made the selections they did when they prepared to write.

For revision: It will take the first draft for students to organize and present their material. In revision, they can begin to step forward, as Fiske does, to comment on that material, to teach a reader how to read it, to reflect on the project and what it has accomplished, to think about how their position is different from (or a supplement to) Fiske's.

2. This, in many ways, is the easiest assignment in the set. It focuses all the issues in the essay on Fiske's representation of and use of the young women he chooses as his representative fans. As always when teaching essays like this, remind students to work closely with the text, presenting it so that a reader will be able to imagine Fiske and his argument without going back to look at pages, and working closely with the language in order to make a point about the key terms — and missing terms — in Fiske's representation of his fans.

One thing missing from the assignment as it is written is a question that would look at the examples themselves as a limited set — that is, we might have asked, "Whom did Fiske leave out? What principles or desires or fears seem to have guided his selection of examples? What point is made by these choices? Have we caught Fiske by asking these questions, or did he prepare us to ask them?"

3. This assignment follows a standard pattern for us. It asks for a summary, an interested summary. It says, in a sense, "Give a generous account of Fiske to someone not willing to be generous." But it also says, at the end, "OK — now that you have represented Fiske's position as he would want you to represent it, what do you want to add? Do you take his position as your own? Where would you differ? Why?" We tend to feel that summary is a valuable tool; it is strategic, a way of getting a position on the table in order to move on to something else. And, as noted in the discussion above, we believe it is important for students to do the work necessary to provide a generous reading of Fiske's argument. One way of providing more of an edge to the turn at the end of this assignment would be to ask students, after they have spoken from Fiske's position (that of the cultural critic) to speak from the position of the fan or consumer or member of contemporary American youth culture. Students would thus have to speak from a position other than just that of "my experience" or "my taste." The pressure to see one's ideas in the context of an interested position is a useful one, particularly for undergraduates.

For revision: With essays like this, revision for us always begins with rereading, and in doing so, asking the following questions: "What have I missed? What have I left out because it was too hard or too weird?" The goals of revision, in our classes, have been to expand and complicate the representation of Fiske and "Madonna," and to work out in greater detail the position of the student writer.

MAKING CONNECTIONS (p. 174)

1 – 2. We have asked a version of this question of all the cultural critics in *Ways of Reading*. Assignments like these are one way we have found of getting students to think about essays not as a body of information but as the enactment of a method, a way of reading the world. All critics of popular culture work within a system of representation that requires two figures: the "common" reader and the critical reader. This assignment asks students to look at how each of these readers is represented in "Madonna" and in the work of one of the other critics in the anthology.

In a sense, our goal is simple. We want students to be able to do more than reproduce an account of Madonna; we want them to understand both the methods and the interests represented in an account like Fiske's. It is not that he knows the truth about Madonna and her fans; he has a certain kind of story to tell (about resistance and domination). One way for students to begin to see the limits and possibilities of a critical method is to first *see* it as a method and then to see it in relation to others. This is the other goal of the assignment: to place Fiske's account of women and resistance (let's say) next to Susan Willis's. They are different, and although the differences are not obvious, noticing them will help students evaluate and characterize Fiske. Because Fiske writes about young women, the easiest point of comparison will be Willis's essay, although Theweleit also provides an account of fantasy, desire, and the production of the "gendered subject." Miller's essay, because it works with TV ads (which seem less profoundly present in the cultural landscape) and because he is less interested in the questions of gender, will seem the most remote. In its methods and in its concern for the position of the consumer, however, it really is not very distant from Fiske's.

For revision: We have found that the difficulty of representing the positions of the various authors—the difficulty of figuring them out, finding passages to use, presenting the material—is sufficient to dominate students' attention in the first draft. It is in the second that students can best begin to look for differences and try to establish some critical purchase on the essays they have read.

MICHEL FOUCAULT

The Body of the Condemned (p. 176)

For more information on teaching Foucault, see the introduction to Sequence Twelve: Working with Foucault (manual p. 174).

As odd as it may seem, students will like this selection a great deal, and will likely refer to it as one of the most important or impressive selections they have worked with during their college careers. Our students felt this way, and so did the students of every instructor we spoke with who taught this piece. The opening example of the torture of Damiens captures everyone's attention, and Foucault's notions of non-linear progress, "soul" as a creation of supervision and constraints, and the body-power-knowledge relationship was so new and refreshing to students that they kept working at the selection for three weeks without the usual complaints of how tired they were of the same reading. We enjoyed rereading the chapter as much as they did, and we loved watching them discover these new ways of understanding. Foucault is one of those writers to whom we can return over and over again, partly because he's so abstract and wonderfully difficult to understand at times, but mostly because his ideas, particularly his notions of the "soul" as a kind of supervisor, a reflection of social constraints, and his presentations of power and knowledge as cultural forces located in language and production continually challenge our thinking — and our students— in dramatic ways, leading to other, new ways of understanding of the commonplace ideas about such things as power and knowledge. There is something very seductive, too, about Foucault's willingness to write prose that always attempts to be all-inclusive. His essays, and his sentences, are thick, qualified, and, it seems, always moving at the edge of abstraction.

This selection is not easy, although the opening section, which presents Foucault's comparison of eighteenth- and nineteenth-century examples of punishment is seductive and deceptively simple. Foucault's opening examples of punishment will capture students' attention and they'll feel comfortable working with his comparison of them. The last quarter of the chapter, which begins with Foucault's discussion of the four general rules his study obeys and concludes with his abstract presentation of the relationship of power and knowledge to the body, however, will present students with challenging reading.

You'll find that students will want to gloss over this abstract, difficult last quarter of the chapter, but this is where the work of reading Foucault pays off. It's important to take the time to hold class discussions of this selection in relation to the opening examples, whether those discussions proceed from second-reading questions (see p. 201) or students' writing assignments (see p. 202), so that everyone can see that the difficulties of Foucault's abstractions on power and knowledge are challenging to everyone, including instructors. There is no way to "get" this last section of Foucault's argument, but it can be worked on, and speculated on; and students can draw conclusions about power, knowledge, and their relationship to the body and to production that will allow them to think about power not in terms of a possession or "right" of certain powerful people or classes of people but rather as a cultural force, one that people use and manipulate as they use and manipulate (or control) the body, production, and knowledge.

QUESTIONS FOR A SECOND READING (p. 201)

1. It's important for students to deal with the whole of Foucault's argument in this chapter, rather than to stay in the safe territory in the early part of the piece. It's equally important for them to see that he is making an argument here, one that stands in opposition to common ways of imagining such things as power and progress. This discussion assignment gives then a method for marking and, consequently, "seeing" that argument in its stages or steps, as the assignment calls them. We have found it very useful to hold this discussion before students begin writing or along with their first attempts to write this selection. It is imperative that they work closely from passages — phrases, sentences, and paragraphs — in the text to trace the stages or steps of Foucault's argument. Generally speaking, the argument he makes moves from his examples — the torture of Damiens, which stands for the corporal nature of punishment, and the prison timetable, which represents the move to noncorporal punishment with traces of torture — to his conclusion that this shift is not the result of linear progress as we generally think of it but of the changing relations between the power to control and the knowledge that allows for that control. He thinks of the soul as the product of supervision and constraint rather than in traditional Christian terms; and he understands the soul, individual bodies and minds, and power as social or public "constructions," not as individual (or group) creations or possessions. Students will find these arguments and their development in the selection fresh and provocative.

2. "Progress" as a nonlinear occurrence, as a change in social and object relations, is a key term in Foucault's argument; and his notion of it will be quite different from students' common perception of progress as linear evolution through the accumulation of more and better knowledge. It's critically important that students work from passages in the text to follow Foucault's thinking; otherwise they'll want to transform his notion of change, or progress, into the common idea of it that they probably hold.

3. This is a challenging question. It plays into Foucault's notion of progress and change in power and object relations, and his juxtaposition of examples to highlight change that retains traces of the past in the way that the nineteenth-century prison timetable contains traces of corporal punishment and torture while appearing to be essentially a form of noncorporal punishment. Needless to say, students will need to identify the passages and examples Foucault employs; and they will find it easier to draw conclusions about how and why he uses the texts of the past if they juxtapose his examples, study them for what might be said about how the juxtapositions reveal changing social and object relations while still retaining traces of the torture and spectacle, and analyze how the language of the texts he employs presents and enacts those differences. Foucault notices traces of the past's torture in present examples, and his initial comparison of the eighteenth- and nineteenth-century punishments is the place for students to begin to draw conclusions about how and why he uses the texts of the past.

ASSIGNMENTS FOR WRITING (p. 202)

1. Although this assignment presents itself as an opportunity for students to write an essay that summarizes "The Body of the Condemned," it's important that students take the position of presenting Foucault's arguments and key terms to other readers, perhaps to members of their class who are also trying to figure out what Foucault's key arguments, terms, and conclusions are. It's equally important that they understand this as work in progress on a text that will refuse to be mastered or re-presented in a summary. Most likely students will attend to the

first three-quarters of the chapter and shy away from the difficult concluding section, where Foucualt presents an abstract discussion of power and knowledge as social constructions and political technologies, which metamorphose rather than proceed in linear progress. As students work on and discuss their drafts, they'll need to ask themselves what they've left out and what they couldn't explain or understand. Undoubtedly they will need to revisit this challenging last section of the selection. They'll need to raise questions to help themselves with this section and they could benefit from thinking about how Foucault's notions of power as a cultural force, a part of the social fabric of control, beyond anyone's ownership, differ from ones they hold. They might also help themselves by referring to the four rules (p. 195) that Foucault claims his study follows and find places in one test where they "see" those rules at work. This would give them another way to imagine the outline of his project.

2. Working from their own examples to understand and test the terms and directions of Foucault's argument about the production of the soul is a wonderful way for students both to familiarize themselves with Foucault's unusual notion of how a "soul" is produced and to test the notion against their own experiences. Foucault, as the assignment and text argue, thinks of the soul as that which is produced in people through their experiences in situations that train, supervise, punish, and correct. In a way, his notion of the soul is akin to the psychoanalytic notion of a superego, but this isn't important for students to know. It is, however, important for students to work closely with the sections of the text where Foucault discusses the way souls are produced and then to work closely with an example of their own, to read it as Foucault might, as another example of supervision, correction, or punishment producing a soul. To this end, students might reflect on the characteristics of the soul that would be produced in the example they're working with. What, for example, is the nature of the supervision or punishment in the particular situation? To what aspects of one's life, one's behavior, or one's beliefs does it apply? How does the particular supervision or correction or punishment affect the people subjected to it?

3. Like the other second-reading questions, this assignment puts students in the position of producing a summary of Foucault's argument, but for this project students will have to orient themselves and their readers to the chapter through the opening two examples rather than through the structure of the argument and how it literally develops over the pages. Here again, students will need to present examples from the text that touch on the key terms and definitions in Foucault's argument. Essentially, this assignment emphasizes the role of the opening examples and how they continue to play out in the developing arguments about such things as progress, the change in punishment from corporal to noncorporal, the production of a soul, and the relationship of power to knowledge and the body.

MAKING CONNECTIONS (p. 204)

1. Of course, students will need to read both the Berger and the Foucault selections a number of times before taking on this assignment. As for other connections assignments, it would be a good idea to present students with each selection through either a discussion from second-reading questions, a writing assignment, or both. These are difficult selections and preliminary work on both is necessary.

   Essentially, students will need to identify a number of substantial passages that represent how each author thinks about power, where it comes from, how it works, and so on. Berger thinks power comes from privileged positions, from individuals with the wealth and heritage to mystify art and to turn it into a commodity. Basically, he allows members of the ruling classes to hold power as a form of control over others and their perceptions, but he also makes it possible for ordinary people, those without wealth and privilege, to have power when they learn to demystify the art of the past and thereby come to "see" that art is situated, opinionated, not in any way "objective," and always, then, a commentary on the relationship of its subjects and its creators. Foucault, working from examples of how punishment changes (rather than progresses), thinks of power in terms of social relations, as a cultural force that evolves from the control of the body — both the physical body of individuals and the social body, the body politic. For Foucault, people like jailers, priests, and psychiatrists, for example, use and direct power by virtue of their control over others. Unlike Berger, he doesn't locate power in privileged individuals or classes, but individuals can use power as it exists as a "bond," one could say, in social situations and peoples' relations to each other and to each other as "objects." Of the two authors, students will find Foucault's notion of power new and compelling, but they'll have to work to unpack abstract sentences where he describes power in terms of "the 'body politic,' as a set of material elements and techniques that serve as weapons, relays communication routes and supports for the power and knowledge relations that invest human bodies and subjugate them by turning them into objects of knowledge." That's about as definitive as he gets, but you can see, even from this dense sentence, that power is a kind of "bond," and has to do with a "set of material elements and techniques that serve as weapons, relays of communication routes and supports."

2. Both Theweleit and Foucault offer complex, challenging examples and explanations of power. Students will need to work with both of these texts before going on to complete this assignment. Discussions centered on second-reading questions, writing assignments, or both would help students orient themselves to both of these texts so that they can go on and treat them as one project, as a set of examples for their investigations into the body and its relation to power and knowledge.

Theweleit's selection proceeds from multiple examples, most of which are texts that he quotes, while Foucault works primarily from two examples in the opening section of his chapter. These authors write quite differently. Theweleit writes and argues more by association and juxtaposition than by linear arguments, whereas Foucault is more interested in bringing forward an equation (body-power-knowledge) than in a carefully constructed logical argument, although he does proceed to develop his case in steps or stages more systematically than Theweleit does. For different reasons, then, both selections will be unusual and challenging to students.

Students will likely read Theweleit's examples of military trainees in Foucault's terms, and this will provide them with multiple examples of one thing: boys in highly supervised, controlled, and punishment-producing situations. As students work through their drafts and discuss each other's work, you might find it helpful to raise questions about what the military recruits' "soul," in Foucault's sense, would be like. How would it be created? What would the effects be on the young soldiers? Where in Theweleit's examples can they see the physical and psychological traces of souls created from supervised situations? Students will need to spend time coming to grips with Foucault's notion of a soul as that which is produced under the constraints of supervision rather than that Christian soul produced from sin. You might offer them the opportunity to discuss Foucault's notion of a soul and how it would apply to the situations that Theweleit presents as a part of the work on their revisions of this assignment.

Students will also need to work continually on the body-power-knowledge equation that Foucault develops to explain how power works. They should understand that this is difficult material for anyone, including their instructor, and they'll benefit from overlaying the equation on Theweleit's examples. How does the body-power-knowledge equation play out in the examples that Theweleit presents? To what power-knowledge relationships do the recruits belong? How do the recruits gain power? How, then, does the equation develop or change as they find power available to them? What changes, in other words, happen to them — their physical and psychological selves — as they are supervised, trained, and thus made available to power relations? You should anticipate that students will need to write multiple revisions of this assignment, that they'll need to focus on the body-power-knowledge relationship instead of simply trying to discuss power, and that Foucault's "soul" gives them a way into understanding how the recruits in Theweleit's examples are being formed or changed by the body-power-knowledge equation of their particular situations.

PAULO FREIRE

The "Banking" Concept of Education (p. 206)

This essay provokes students. They either feel strongly sympathetic to Freire's condemnation of "banking" education, where students are turned into "containers" to be "filled" by their teachers, or they feel strongly that "banking" education is the very education they need to be competitive and successful.

Assume that your students will need to reread this selection a number of times as it poses challenging conceptual problems, and Freire's terms, like "problem-posing" and "creative transformation," are usually part and parcel of the conceptual problem. The essay has momentum, though, and once students begin to follow his argument — that education that only transmits information, that is conducted through teacher narratives and student silences, stands opposed to "problem-solving" education, which is conducted by teachers and students working together in a dialogue to solve genuine problems — they'll react to it, largely because their personal experiences serve as quick validations of Freire's central concepts.

QUESTIONS FOR A SECOND READING (p. 219)

1. This discussion assignment is designed to allow students to "problem-pose" Freire's concepts by testing them against their own experiences and by imagining them in classes and subjects with which they are familiar. You will want to move slowly, perhaps allowing two or three class sessions to work your way through the assignment's questions. Students will need to be constantly moving between the essay and examples they come up with. When they discuss problem-posing in English, for instance, they'll need to turn to Freire to put his concept in their own language. Then they'll need to imagine an English class where reading, writing, and discussion are used by the teacher and students to "work" a problem that has some significance to them — for example, growth and change in adolescence. When they turn to Freire's examples, as the second half of this assignment asks them to, they'll need to pay particular attention to what he means when he discusses students as spectators and students as re-creators. You can make connections between their examples and his by asking them to include a discussion of students as spectators and students as re-creators in their examples of problem-posing classes in the various subjects.

2. This assignment focuses students on two important concepts that Freire borrows from Marxist thought, and it serves as a good follow-up discussion to the first assignment. Because of its narrow focus, it's not good as an opening assignment, although a discussion of praxis and alienation could certainly be broadened to include Freire's concepts of banking education and problem-posing education.

   Students will need to stay close to the text to discuss these terms, and you'll want to ask them to reread to find those passages and moments that present Freire's use of the terms. Once they've located and noted those, they're ready to put them into their own words and create what I. A. Richards called a "radical paraphrase."

3. There is a way in which Freire's voice and his explanations invite response. Readers often mention their inclination to talk back as they read and reread Freire. Although some of this can be explained by his accessible subjects (education and teachers and students) and his accessible metaphors (banking and working together in problem-posing), he takes a stance that both gives information and invites response by posing education as a problem for readers to work on. Although he frames the question with descriptions, explanations and a few examples, he doesn't offer any final solutions. Instead, he insists through his posture and commitment that readers begin to examine their experiences from this problem-posing

perspective. Still, he does offer information and it is quite strong stuff, raising the question of whether banking and problem-posing are as clear-cut as Freire would have us believe. Students will need to speak from his text, so they'll need to reread to find those moments when Freire can be said to be both depositing information and allowing for a dialogue. You might turn your students' attention to his voice by asking them to characterize the kinds of voices that speak in banking education and the kinds that speak in problem-posing. Ask them to recall those times when they experienced each. Where, you might ask, would Freire's voice put him — in banking or problem-posing? What passages or moments in the text lead them to make this appraisal?

ASSIGNMENTS FOR WRITING (p. 220)

1. This challenging writing assignment offers students the opportunity to see a significant learning experience of their own through Freire's eyes. You might consider turning to this assignment after some extended discussion of the essay, perhaps after spending two or three class sessions working with the questions for the first of the "Questions for a Second Reading." Students will then be familiar with the essay and with framing their own experiences in its terms.

   You might consider asking students to identify a rich and illustrative incident in which they learned something from their own experience, without paying much attention to whether it fits or doesn't fit in Freire's view of education. Once they have identified the incident — and it should be one that they can write quite a bit about — they can begin the work of seeing it through Freire's terms. They'll need to reconstruct the incident with as much detail as they can, and they'll need to pay attention to conversations and what specific people did during or as a result of the incident. If the incident involved school experience, they'll want to write about what they worked with (textbooks, assignments, etc.) and how they worked (what they did, what other students did, what teachers did). Once they've reconstructed the incident, you'll want to turn their attention to a Freirian reading of it. They might consider whether it could be said to be a banking experience or a problem-posing one. What about the experience allows them to talk about it as one or the other? Was it an experience that would allow them to write about an "emersion" of consciousness? or perhaps a submersion?

   For revision: In their first drafts for this essay, students often tell lively stories of an individual's experience in school or provide a tightly organized demonstration that their experiences show that Freire was right. The goal of revision, we feel, should be to open these accounts up, to call them into question.

   Perhaps because they are young adults, and perhaps because they are, by and large, Americans, students translate Freire's account of social, political, and historical forces into a story of individuals — a mean teacher and an innocent student. One way to pose problems for revision, then, would be to send students back to Freire's essay to see how he accounts for "agency" — who is doing what to whom in Freire's account of education. Once students have reread the essay with this in mind, they can go back to their own pieces, making this story of individuals a story of *representative* individuals. Here, teacher and student play predetermined roles in the larger drama of American education and are figures through which the culture works out questions of independence and authority, production and reproduction of knowledge, and the relationship of the citizen to society.

   The first drafts often make quick work of Freire. We asked one of our students how he was able to sum up in three tidy pages everything Freire said. He replied, "It was easy. I left out everything I didn't understand and worked with what I did." This is a familiar strategy, one that is reinforced by teachers who have students read for "gist." Another strategy for revision is to have students go back to the sections of Freire's essay that they *didn't* understand, or couldn't easily control, and to see how they might work those sections into what they have written. This is an opportunity for a dialogue with Freire — not a debate, but a chance to put his words on the page and to say, in effect, "Here is what I think you are saying." This revision will put pressure on students' resources for including quotations and representing and working on text. It makes a big difference, for example, whether a student uses Freire to conclude a point or uses Freire's language as material to work on. These different approaches to Freire provide handy illustrations for a discussion of problem-posing education.

2. This writing assignment would follow nicely from two or three class sessions devoted to a discussion of the first of the "Questions for a Second Reading." You might also consider using the third question as part of prewriting discussions.

Students will have to imagine themselves as teachers determined to adapt Freire's practices to a class working with his essay. They'll have to enact problem-solving through a writing assignment or a set of discussion questions, guidelines, or instructions for this essay. You might consider asking them to examine the questions and assignments in the book to see which, if any, they think fit Freire's notions of problem-solving tasks. They'll need to engage in some discussion of the questions and assignments to say why the tasks do or do not reflect Freire's thinking about problem-solving, and this could help them begin to conceptualize criteria for translating his theory into learning tasks. Once they've participated in these discussions, they'll be ready to write their problem-solving tasks. Then they'll have to complete their own assignments. You might consider a follow-up discussion on what students thought their tasks were asking of them. From there, they could go on to revise their tasks.

MAKING CONNECTIONS (p. 221)

1. Students need to use one of the essays in the book as a starting point for posing a Freirian problem. Then they need to begin working on that problem, responding to it in writing. It's difficult to say ahead of time what essays or stories will trigger students' thinking about a genuine problem that interests and involves them. You might go through the text table of contents and comment on the essays and stories with an eye towards presenting their subjects or issues so students could pinpoint essays to consider. The introductions to each selection will give you a sense of what each one touches on.

Once students have decided on an essay or story to use as a starting point, they'll need to pose a problem or question. It will probably be one that is raised by the selection, but they should understand that the problem can extend far beyond the selection itself. For example, if students were working on Rich's essay "When We Dead Awaken: Writing as Re-Vision," they might raise questions about what a famous poet's account of her position within a patriarchal culture might have to do with their position as students in a writing class or as participants in the general culture. In what ways might they be said to be "drenched in assumptions" they cannot easily understand? What does this have to do with revision or the writing of the past, both familiar concepts, neither appearing to have anything to do with sexual politics nor, in Rich's terms, survival? It is possible to read Rich's essay as though it were not addressed to students, as though it could not make contact with their lives. To pose the essay as a problem means finding, even mechanically at first, such possible connections. "How might I use this phrase in a sentence or paragraph about myself, a sentence, or a paragraph I believed in?"

These become difficult questions, to be sure, but they can lead students to imagine genuine problems. They can bring to consciousness strong, often unspoken experiences. They can make the usual, familiar language suddenly fraught with danger or previously unthought-of implications. They can lead writers to be smarter about themselves and the language they use to represent their world.

When students have posed their problems, you might consider conducting two or three class discussions to examine those problems so students can revise them before they write.

They'll have to present their problems, including brief summaries of the selections they have worked from, and they'll need to explain why, in Freire's terms, their problems are Freirian. Consider using questions about how this writing differs from what they are accustomed to doing. Another assignment might ask them to look back on the essays they wrote in response to their own problems or questions.

2. Students will have to have read Rodriguez's essay and to have spent some time discussing it, perhaps in response to the "Questions for a Second Reading," before they can write this imagined dialogue between Freire and Rodriguez. You might suggest that they begin by imagining questions Freire and Rodriguez might ask each other. They could also reread the Rodriguez selection and note passages or moments that they think Freire would comment on, and they can do the same for the Freire selection by rereading from Rodriguez's point of view. It's important for the dialogue that students avoid turning this into a debate where someone challenges someone. The stance should be conversational — two people from different backgrounds and different sets of beliefs talking with each other about education. They ask questions and comment on things each has said in the essays, and try their best to answer and further explain their comments.

CLIFFORD GEERTZ

Deep Play: Notes on the Balinese Cockfight (p. 223)

"Deep Play" is a brilliant performance and a rare example of the potential for wit and playfulness in academic writing. Geertz speaks in different voices and runs through a range of styles as he demonstrates the methods by which an anthropologist tries to represent and understand his subject.

While it will be hard for students to get a fix on Geertz and what he is doing, it is not a difficult essay to read until the final two sections (beginning with "Feathers, Blood, Crowds, and Money"). Part of the difficulty here is that Geertz suddenly begins talking about literature and literary criticism, and he does so as if he hasn't changed subjects at all. The last two sections are truly difficult — conceptually difficult. We have read them many, many times and, while we have found ways of speaking about what we have read, we wouldn't say for a minute that we are confident that we have "got it" or exhausted those pages. Students need to know that reading presents difficulties that one can only respect or work on, difficulties that one can't resolve. These difficulties are no reason for shame or silence.

The best way to teach the essay might be to lead up to, even dramatize, the turn in the final two sections. We have taught classes where we conscientiously avoided the last two sections until late in the lesson. And our interest in the opening sections, beyond the opening questions that try to chart out the argument — what does Geertz see? what does he say about what he sees? — is directed toward the stylistic differences in the various sections. We are interested in having students consider how a way of writing could be said to represent a method, a way of seeing and understanding. The narrative in "The Raid," the punning and wordplay in "Of Cocks and Men," the careful exposition in "Odds and Even Money," the numbered list in "Playing with Fire" — all represent different ways of approaching or shaping information. All say something about Geertz's skill and method as an observer. All give us a different view of the cockfight. We want our students to sense the various textures in the essay, and to speculate on why Geertz would have made use of them. It is only after we have had such discussions, or after students have written about these problems, that we are willing to invite students to make what they can of the final two sections.

The essay is drawn from a special issue of *Daedalus* (vol. 101, 1972). In the preface, the editor speaks about the origins of the essay and includes a letter from Geertz and Paul de Man inviting scholars to a conference on the "Systematic Study of Meaningful Forms." "Deep Play" accompanied the letter. The full text of the preface follows.

Stephen R. Graubard

Preface to the Issue "Myth, Symbol and Culture"

As many readers of *Daedalus* are aware, almost all issues of the journal depend on a series of closed conferences where authors discuss their draft essays with interested critics. Such conferences generally follow smaller meetings where the issue is planned. On occasion, the deliberations of the planning group persuade the Editors and planners that the time is not propitious for a particular subject to be treated in *Daedalus*, and that there is some advantage in not proceeding. More frequently, the planning committee's decision is to go ahead and to ask for papers from authors who have an obvious interest in the subject.

This issue of *Daedalus* has a history that is worth telling. It began with the suggestion from Clifford Geertz, now at the Institute for Advanced Study at Princeton, and Paul de Man, now of Yale University, that we consider inviting scholars from many disciplines, but principally from anthropology and literature, to discuss the possibility of a *Daedalus* issue on what they called the "Systematic Study of Meaningful Forms." Invitations went out to twelve scholars, both in this country and abroad, for a conference that was to meet in Paris. The planning sessions persuaded all of us that the problems of interdisciplinary discourse are even more substantial than is generally admitted. Disciplines have languages that are specific to themselves; it is not always easy for a scholar in one discipline to appreciate the significance of the intervention of a scholar who comes from a quite different field. More than that, the relations between the particular disciplines are not always apparent, even after days of intensive discussion.

In this instance, the subject itself was so intrinsically difficult that a decision to abandon our original intention, and not go forward with plans for a *Daedalus* issue, would have been entirely understandable. We were dissuaded from that course by three considerations: first, the letter of invitation to participants in the planning meeting seemed to many of us a document of major import; second, though the conference itself had not seen any single theme emerge, individual interventions at the meeting had aroused very substantial interest; finally, one of the conveners, Clifford Geertz, had been moved by the meeting to write more fully on a theme he had treated in one of his lengthy conference interventions.

The Editors were persuaded that there were good reasons for going forward. Clifford Geertz's paper, "Deep Play: Notes on the Balinese Cockfight," together with an invitation to write, went to scholars in widely separated disciplines. They were invited to write on texts or themes that had significance for them. The results of their efforts are apparent in this issue.

We believe that there may be some purpose in reproducing the original letter of invitation that went to members of the planning group. Professors Geertz and de Man wrote as follows:

> We write to tell you about a conference that the American Academy of Arts and Sciences, through its journal *Daedalus*, proposes to hold in Paris on October 29, 30, and 31, 1970. We hope very much that your schedule will permit you to attend this meeting. Its purpose is to plan an issue of *Daedalus* on a theme whose importance is increasingly recognized. The idea for the conference and the *Daedalus* issue arose out of a shared feeling that the question of the relationship between the social sciences and the humanities is often approached in the wrong way.

   General efforts to connect the work of scholars we take to be occupied with "The Humanities" with those we take to be occupied with "The Social Sciences" tend to adopt a "two cultures" sort of formulation. The "relations" between humanistic and social scientific methods, outlooks, concerns, ambitions, and achievements are described in a rather external fashion, as though two wary sovereign powers were drawing up a treaty of mutual coexistence in order to allow a certain level of carefully regulated commerce between them while guaranteeing their mutual autonomy and right to live their separate lives. Thus one gets discussions, whether or not they are actually called such, of "The Implications (Impact, Convergence, Irrelevance . . .) of Structuralism (Evolutionism, Gestalt Psychology, Generative Grammar, Psychoanalysis . . .) for History (Literary Criticism, Musicology, Law, Philosophy . . .)" and so on. (The Sciences being masculine and the Humanities feminine, the causal arrow is only rarely pointed in the other direction.) Some of these discussions have their uses, if only as statements of a larger faith — or, in some cases, lack of it; but they tend not to contribute much, or at least as much as the grandness of their conception would seem to promise, to the specific development of the fields of study thus "related." They are, a few exceptions aside, part only of parascholarship, public declarations for public occasions which, like Auden's "poetry," make nothing happen.

   Yet, in the face of all of this, the conviction continues to grow among leading figures in the Humanities and the Social Sciences that, as the cliché goes, "they have something to offer one another." The problem is how to effect the offering, reasonably unburnt.

   It is our assumption that this will best be done not by general, programmatic considerations of how the humanities, or some corner of them, and the social sciences, or some corner of them, are "related" to one another, or even of what overall presuppositions they share in common, nor again of their supposedly complementary or contradictory roles in the functioning of modern culture. Rather, it will be done, if it is done at all, when some of the more creative people in specific disciplines discover that they are in fact working, from their contrasting methods, on quite similar problems or ranges of problems.

   It is when two (or more) scholars realize that, for all the differences between them, they are attacking highly similar issues, trying to solve closely related puzzles, that communication between them begins to look like a practical policy rather than an academic piety. Specific commonalities of intellectual interest make scholarly interchange possible and useful; and the creation of such interchange demands, and indeed consists in, the discovery and exploitation of such commonalities. It is the coincident perception by historians concerned with the authorship of the Federalist papers and by statisticians concerned with Bayesian interpretations of probability theory that they are confronted with the same kind of problem — how to evaluate "subjective" judgments — which causes them to become genuinely interested in one another. Academic ideologies celebrating the unity of knowledge, decrying the evils of specialization, or dissolving substantive differences into rhetorical agreements do not achieve the same objectives.

   Clearly, such commonalities of concern among otherwise discrete disciplines cannot be formulated without prior inquiry. Looking both at the work of our own fields, literary criticism and cultural anthropology, and at that of fields more or less adjacent to them, it seems to us that one such commonality is what might be called — or, when we actually come to look into it, might not — "the systematic study of meaningful forms."

   There are a lot of elastic and ill-used words crowded into this little formula — only the article and the preposition seem straightforward — but that it points, in its awkward and preliminary way, to a general area in which "humanists" and "social scientists" (even, in a few cases, some we call natural scientists) are simultaneously engaged in study is beyond much doubt. In the social sciences, structuralist anthropology, sociolinguistics, cognitive psychology, and phenomenological sociology, merely to list a few labels, all represent a sharp turn toward a concern with the analysis of meaningful forms, whether they be South American Indian myths, urban speech styles, children's categorical systems, or the taken-for-granted assumptions of everyday life. In the humanities, where the study of meaningful structures has been a traditional concern, recent developments in the philosophy of language and in the analysis of artistic and literary forms all show a markedly heightened awareness of the need for devising ways of coping more effectively with such structures.

What, dimly perceived, these assorted enterprises seem to have in common is a conviction that meaningful forms, whether they be African passage rites, nineteenth-century novels, revolutionary ideologies, grammatical paradigms, scientific theories, English landscape paintings, or the ways in which moral judgments are phrased, have as good a claim to public existence as horses, stones, and trees, and are therefore as susceptible to objective investigation and systematic analysis as these apparently harder realities.

Everything from modern logic, computer technology, and cybernetics at one extreme to phenomenological criticism, psychohistory, and ordinary language philosophy at the other has conspired to undermine the notion that meaning is so radically "in the head," so deeply subjective, that it is incapable of being firmly grasped, much less analysed. It may be supremely difficult to deal with such structures of meaning but they are neither a miracle nor a mirage. Indeed, constructing concepts and methods to deal with them and to produce generalizations about them is the primary intellectual task now facing those humanists and social scientists not content merely to exercise habitual skills. The surge of interest in "myth," "fiction," "archetype," "semantics," "systems of relevance," "language games," and so on is but the symptom that this transformation in viewpoint has in fact taken place, and — from the very multiplicity of the terms — that it has taken place in intellectual contexts much more isolated from one another than the commonality of their concerns would warrant.

Considerations such as these have led us, in collaboration with Professor Stephen Graubard, editor of *Daedalus,* to summon a small group to Paris in late October. Our hope is that some of the commonality of concern that undoubtedly exists may be concretely expressed and that this may have, as one of its effects, a reduction of the mutual isolation that is so frequently noted.

The focus of this conference will not be on a general discussion of the study of meaning, nor on the virtues of interdisciplinary communication, but on specific examples of such study, so cast that their arguments and conclusions, and particularly the conceptual foundations upon which they rest, may be accessible to others working toward similar ends in different ways. The conference will include a variety of scholars from various of the social sciences and humanistic disciplines (and possibly some from the natural sciences as well), actively working, in one way or another, on the systematic analysis of meaningful forms, and especially on the theoretical bases for such analysis. As we do not envisage a generalized discussion of "the meaning of meaning," so also we do not envisage a set of particular empirical studies presented crystalline for admiration, but rather the exemplification and explication of a range of theoretical approaches to our topic on the part of people not ordinarily in one another's company. In such a way, not only should the subject of the conference be advanced, but the usefulness of the work of humanists and social scientists for one another be demonstrated rather than merely debated or proclaimed.

This issue of *Daedalus* is, at best, a first tentative step toward realizing certain of the objectives outlined in this letter. Our gratitude to Professors Clifford Geertz and Paul de Man is very real. They have done much to make this issue possible. We wish also to express our deep appreciation to the Ford Foundation for the grant it has made to the Academy to support interdisciplinary study.

QUESTIONS FOR A SECOND READING (p. 261)

1. The first of these questions directs students to think about Geertz's stated objective as they reread the essay. It is possible to assume that all of the exposition is devoted to a demonstration of what the cockfight says, its commentary upon Balinese life. If that is the case, then one can reread to get a fuller sense of that story, including a fuller sense of the key details and episodes. When Geertz says that the cockfights don't reinforce the patterns of Balinese life but comment on them, he is also arguing with his colleagues. Students don't need to know all the details of that argument (we don't), but they can feel the force of the distinction he is making and his insistence that observed behavior be treated as text.

2. This question directs students to the stylistic differences in the various subsections. We spoke earlier about why these have been important in our teaching. It is important not only to invite students to notice the differences but to give them a way of talking about what the differences represent, particularly in a project of observation, interpretation, and report.

3. This question is an invitation to students to read against the grain of Geertz's essay. Each of the sections in "Deep Play" could be said to reveal its own ideological apparatus. In the first section, for example, both Geertz's wife and the Balinese are turned quickly into cartoon figures to serve a narrative designed to establish Geertz's position as the hero of the story and to provide his authority as an insider, as someone who can know and understand the natives. The political and historical counterpoint to this happy story intrudes in parentheses: "As always, kinesthetically minded and, even when fleeing for their lives (or, as happened eight years later, surrendering them), the world's most poised people, they gleefully mimicked, also over and over . . ." and so on. This could be read as the classic case of the imperial imagination. And the second section opens with a figure familiar to academic writing: The scholar looks over the literature, sees something that has been rarely noticed — the cockfight — and proceeds to show that what appears to be the case is not what is really happening at all. (For extended versions of this critique of Geertz and of ethnography, see the essays by Mary Louise Pratt and Vincent Crapanzano in *Writing Culture: The Poetics and Politics of Ethnography*, edited by James Clifford and George E. Marcus.)

We've taught this essay several times, and the argument we inevitably hear, whether among the staff or in the classroom, is over whether we've "caught" Geertz in making this critique, whether we've found the seams of his text that he is blind to. The counterargument goes something like this: Geertz's text offers its seams to a reader; the reason it is broken into pieces and written in different styles, the reason it is self-conscious and self-consciously playful, is that Geertz is showing the necessary limits and conditions of ethnography. The limits of the discourse are part of the subject of the essay. The parenthetical allusion to a different, historical narrative — shifting from a comic story to a story of political violence — is not a slip but a strategy. Part of the argument of the essay, in other words, is that the work is never pure, that understanding the Balinese means translating their lives into our terms, talking inevitably about Shakespeare, Dickens, or Aristotle.

In teaching the essay, we feel it is important for students to read generously before asking them to try to question the texts in these terms. It is too easy for students to dismiss the essay by saying that it is *just* a story of a white man asserting his dominance over the Third World. That can become a way of not reading. At the same time, it would be irresponsible to finesse

71

these questions altogether. For us this is a matter of timing. While students are working on this essay, there comes a point at which we encourage these questions. If they don't emerge, we raise them ourselves, usually by returning to the opening section, which students say is the easiest and most fun to read. We use it as a way of talking about its familiarity, then about what the familiar story might represent.

4. The hardest of the four questions, this one invites students to imagine a specialized audience and its methods, issues, and concerns. Geertz is not just offering information on cockfights, and he is not just demonstrating, by his own performance, the ways an anthropologist goes about his business; rather, he is making a point to his colleagues in the social sciences. He is arguing that they need to think of themselves also as literary critics. Students can't master this argument — nor can we — but if they begin to sense its outlines, they can use the essay as a way of imagining not only the complex purposes of academic writing but also the different conventions and assumptions of the academic disciplines.

ASSIGNMENTS FOR WRITING (p. 262)

1. In the general discussion and in the second of the "Questions for a Second Reading," we alluded to stylistic differences in the subsections of the essay. Since the assignment is conceptually difficult, it is helpful for students to know that they themselves can organize their papers in terms of seven subsections. The eighth subsection is the one where they stand back and take stock of what they have done in the first seven. This is a difficult assignment and deserves time for revision, particularly if students have the opportunity to see at least some of the first drafts of their colleagues. They will learn much by seeing what others have noticed in Geertz's sentences, and in hearing what others have to say about what they noticed. This assignment will work best, however, if students write their first draft before the subject becomes an issue for general discussion. This is not to say that there should be no prior discussion. Students generally need to learn how to talk about sentences in just these ways. It might be best to have a general discussion of one of the subsections, and then to let students see what they can do with the rest, before returning again to open discussion.

2. This has been a successful assignment for us. It asks students to demonstrate their reading of Geertz's method by putting it to work on characteristic scenes from their own surroundings. Geertz's method can be represented by his phrase "saying something of something" — an event can do this. The cockfights are a story the Balinese tell themselves about themselves. Similarly, American teenagers walk around shopping malls, doing peculiar but characteristic things. College students decorate dorm rooms in peculiar but characteristic ways. To begin to carry out a Geertzian project, we might say then that in each case these are stories they are telling themselves about themselves. Such events say something about something else. The question is what. But what is being said? And about what? What are these stories? What are their key features? How, as a writer, might one interpret them? What are these people telling themselves about themselves? It is important for college students, if they write on college students, to insist on their separateness, to speak of *them*, not *us*. For the exercise, it is important that students act as though they are interpreting someone else's story and not their own.

    The purpose of the assignment is to turn students to their own immediate culture and to invite them to imagine and carry out a Geertzian project. It is important that they act like anthropologists — that they work from recorded observations, not just from memory, which leads students inevitably to the commonplace and clichéd and deprives them of the very details that can make their work rich and interesting.

3. Following from the third of the "Questions for a Second Reading," this writing assignment asks students to write up a reading that runs against the grain of Geertz's essay. For a full discussion of that reading, see the entry for question 3 above. While we present the assignment here as an independent one, we have often used it as a question to guide revisions

of the first assignment. If students begin with this essay, it will be important to discuss it before students write. They will need to hear and imagine an argument against Geertz, at least in part. Students are asked to imagine a position either for or against that contrary reading.

MAKING CONNECTIONS (p. 263)

1. Because he writes about Bali, a distant and exotic place, Geertz is too unquestioningly an expert for most student readers. He is given a kind of intellectual authority ("the man's been there, he's suffered for his wisdom, he knows the real story") that, at least as we read the essay, he neither invites nor deserves. This assignment was designed to put Geertz (as someone who sees, interprets and records) into a more familiar context, one where students will feel some knowledge and authority of their own. The assignment asks for a comparison with Willis, Tompkins, or Fiske. We are usually hesitant to write "comparison and contrast" assignments, since the acts of comparing and contrasting too easily become ends in themselves. Here, we think, the comparison provides the necessary starting point for an interesting project — a reflection on the possibilities and limitations of these authors' methods of interpretation.

   When we have used this assignment, we have been particularly interested in turning students' attention to methods: How does Geertz get his information, how does he, as a writer, work on it? This question becomes easier when Geertz is seen next to (or through) Willis, Tompkins, or Fiske, whose methods are more easily imagined by students (in a sense, they live in the same world of reference). In addition, even though Geertz sets out to write about the act of interpretation, his discussion is difficult and illusive compared to those of Fiske, Willis, and Tompkins.

   A word of warning: our students were quick to argue that Fiske and Willis are dogmatic, that they begin with arguments or positions that predetermine what they will find to say about the material they study. The deck is stacked, in other words. By comparison, they found Geertz to be "open," "receptive," "objective," less of an ideologue. Our goal was to use the assignment — and Geertz — to question the notion of "objectivity" and the scholarly production of scientific truth. We might have begun with the third assignment in "Assignments for Writing" before turning to this comparison. As it was, we needed to make the revision assignment one that questioned the terms of (or the reading in) the first draft. Actually, we often engage in this process in revision assignments. The difficulty is that it produces a second draft that is, at least in conventional terms, no more "finished" than the first.

2. In the opening section of "The Loss of the Creature," Percy talks about the strategies one might use in order to recover the Grand Canyon from the "preformed symbolic complex," from those texts and expectations that make it something else. This assignment asks students to consider Geertz and his account of this experience in Bali, including his professional interpretation of the cockfight, as one of Percy's representative anecdotes. They are to work out a Percian reading of "Deep Play." Percy tells the story of tourists in Paris, in Mexico, and at the Grand Canyon. What might he do with the story of Geertz in Bali? Has Geertz solved the problem that Percy charts in his essay?

   As a variation on this assignment, you might ask students, once they have completed their essays, to write Geertz's response to Percy. What would Geertz have to say to Percy about his account of Geertz's work? The two essays represent a complex and difficult conversation about the relationship between method and understanding. While it would be dizzying for students to consider this debate in the abstract, it can be nicely represented in terms of a dialogue between these two characters. In a further essay students might be invited to bring their own voices into the conversation — to write a paper in which they identify the issues that matter to them in this conversation between Geertz and Percy, and in which they talk about why these issues matter to them.

HARRIET JACOBS

Incidents in the Life of a Slave Girl (p. 264)

While this is not a difficult piece to read, it presents some interesting problems in the classroom. Students read it and feel moved, yet the most appropriate response seems to be silence. What else is there to say? It seems almost disrespectful to begin talking about the text as a text, to turn this into material for an English class. One way to begin is with Jacobs's statement that she does not want a reader's sympathy. Why might she say this? What is wrong with sympathy?

Our approach to "Incidents," in fact, has been through the moments where Jacobs addresses her readers directly. In a sense, she anticipates the problem of silence, of a "liberal" reading, and teaches her reader how to read. We ask students to mark the sections where they feel Jacobs is speaking to them *as* readers, to talk about the readers Jacobs assumes and to identify the ways she wants to prepare them and revise their expectations. We also try to get students to imagine Jacobs's relationship to the conventions of storytelling, to the usual stories about growing up and having children, in order that they might find evidence of the difficulties of this relationship in the prose. This is why we introduce Houston Baker and Jean Fagin Yellin's accounts of the problems of slave narratives in the headnote.

One of the difficulties we've had teaching "Incidents" is that it so quickly becomes a familiar story, translating the experience of slavery into familiar terms, transforming an unwritten — and unwriteable — experience of slavery, love, and human relations into the general public discourse. This tendency to see the other in our own terms, to master that difference, places us in a structural relationship to Jacobs that mirrors her relations with the slave owners. We need to feel the difficulty of that position and we need to honor her attempts, as a writer, to make the problems of the "autobiographical act," in Baker's terms, part of her writing.

QUESTIONS FOR A SECOND READING (p. 305)

1. We added this question as a direct response to a problem we had as a staff (about twenty of us) teaching the Jacobs selection in our introductory course. The question says, "This text makes it impossible to say what we are prepared to say: that slaves were illiterate, uneducated, simple in their speech and thought." We were amazed at how many students said just this about Jacobs — that she was illiterate, uneducated, and so on. We decided there was some pedagogical gain in saying from the outset that "the text" made this probable reading "impossible." (We are happy to offer ourselves as figures in a classroom argument over whether it is possible to read "Incidents" in this way or not.)

   It is not surprising that our students would say or write this. As a culture, we know so little about slavery and its conditions that we turn to stereotypes and pat phrases. It is through this fixed sense of The Slave that our students tried to find a way to characterize the author of "Incidents in the Life of a Slave Girl." As an author, she was invisible to them. Even as a character in a narrative, she was quickly reduced to stereotype.

   We wanted students to acknowledge both the highly literate quality of the text and the position of its author. We found that we also had to make it difficult for students to grab onto the counterposition (that Jacobs wasn't "really" a slave, that her education and reading and her position in the house had made her something else, and that "slavery" was therefore not a useful term in a discussion of this text).

This process was both troubling and productive. At least it was productive when these misreadings could be cast as part of our cultural legacy, evidence of our readiness to misinterpret slave narratives rather than an indication of racism or racial insensitivity.

2–3.   Both of these questions are designed to enable students to begin to read "Incidents" as a text, as an act of writing. As we have said, students will want to read the story as a window of human experience, to feel sympathy for this character, to feel that they now know and understand the real experience of slaves in the South. It is important for students to sense the limits as well as the benefits of this way of reading.

We want students to have a feel for Jacobs as a writer as well as a character, and to see in her writing a commentary on and a representation of her relationship to the dominant culture. We try to make a sharp distinction between the story in the selection and the story in the writing. The story of the writer and her relationship to her audience and her subject is also a story about freedom and slavery. The first question asks students to chart the places where Jacobs, the writer, interrupts the narrative to directly address the reader. If these, too, are part of the story, what is that story? How does Jacobs imagine her white reader? How does she imagine the problems of her relationship to that reader? The second question counters students' attempts to slot the narrative into familiar categories. It asks students to look at the codes governing the construction of the narrative, codes that challenge the readings students are prepared to perform. Students want to read, for example, in terms of a simple arrangement of black and white. Jacobs, on the other hand, works with a much more complex sense of color difference. She represents herself, for example, as different from other slaves, and she makes similar distinctions among the members of the white community. Is she judging individuals or is she working within a value system? How should we understand the distinction she draws between Dr. Flint and Mr. Sands, the father of her children, when both men could be said to treat her in the same way and represent her as the same type? Is this evidence of Jacobs giving her story over to a familiar narrative, one that requires a sympathetic lover? Her account of family lines in the South is offered as a corrective to the assumptions of "women in the North." How does the family in slave culture defy conventional representations?

ASSIGNMENTS FOR WRITING (p. 306)

1.   Following up on the second of the "Questions for a Second Reading," this assignment asks students how the story of slavery is represented in Jacobs's work as a writer, in her relationship to her readers, her subject, and the usual stories of growing up, falling in love, and having a family. Students' success with this assignment will depend on their ability to work closely with the text, to select passages, to work them into their essays, and to take the role of teacher or commentator, showing readers how they might read and understand these passages. It is useful to help students make the distinction between Jacobs the writer and Jacobs the character. Your goal is to enable students to see the narrative not as a fiction, but nonetheless as something *made*. Why, for example, does she offer "incidents"? How are these incidents arranged? Is there a predictable structure? Is it useful to have students look particularly at those passages where Jacobs interrupts the narrative to speak to the reader? What is she doing? To what degree might these be said to be spontaneous outpourings? To what degree might they be said to be strategic? It is tempting for students to assume that Jacobs is an untutored "natural" writer, someone who just wrote. You need to bring forward the drama of Jacobs's interaction with reader, text, and convention.

For revision: Students will devote most of their energies in the first draft to locating, reproducing, and describing what they take to be key sections of the text. In organizing revisions, we like to send students back to "Incidents," this time to notice what they left out, whether deliberately or unconsciously. We want students to return to the text to see how it might serve the project they now have under way, but also to challenge them to revise that project. And we want the revision to be the occasion for students to begin to ask questions of their material. Once they have described what they see, students feel they have exhausted the material. They can, however, begin to ask questions of their own experience as readers — how, for example, do they see themselves in relation to the reader Jacobs assumes? They can ask questions in terms of race and/or gender — how might the writing represent the problems of a minority writer writing to a white audience? "Incidents" seems to be self-consciously addressed to women — how does it distinguish between a male and a female reader? a male and a female reading?

2. This assignment asks for a written response to the third of the "Questions for a Second Reading." It asks students to read the narrative as a document from another culture, to look for the peculiar codes that govern human relations and the participants' understanding of human relations. The difficulty in reading this text, we've argued, is that it invokes familiar narratives; it wants to be read as more of the same, even as it describes a world outside of our familiar representations. Students who choose this assignment will need to pay dogged attention to a single area of slave life as represented in the narrative. They will need to understand that the details that matter most will come forward only after several readings. A student might trace the family connections between blacks and whites to see how these color differences cover a complicated set of relationships. Who were Jacobs's grandmother's parents? Who were Jacobs's? How does she define her relationship to other slaves? To what degree does she speak of them as different from her? What terms mark those differences? Or a student might chart out the relationships between men and women. The point is that students will need to understand that they are *searching* for material, for a hidden code or logic or system. They are not simply describing what they take to be obvious — nor what Jacobs seems to offer as obvious.

    For revision: Students will most likely need to return to the text to complete their projects. They should look for material that doesn't fit quite so quickly or conveniently, either to complete their case or to make it richer. The difficulty lies in reading against Jacobs, in working as though she is not a source of pure understanding (a slave who can tell the truth about whites and about slavery, a position Jacobs defines as her own) but a product of competing ways of seeing, some of them belonging to slave culture and some to the white world. This is the difficult burden of Houston Baker's account of the slave narratives. If we read them to feel that we know the truth of slavery, we are ignoring their cultural context, the ways in which they participate in the very representational system that justifies and organizes slavery.

MAKING CONNECTIONS (p. 308)

1. This assignment asks students to consider how Jacobs might fit as an example in Walker's argument and to imagine why her name is missing from Walker's litany of African-American women. The answers are simple. While the text of "Incidents" was available to scholars at the time Walker was writing "In Search of Our Mothers' Gardens," it was the work of Jean Fagin Yellin and her 1987 edition of *Incidents in the Life of a Slave Girl* that brought Jacobs's text forward as an important and authentic slave narrative. Whether Walker had access to "Incidents" or not, the assignment is designed to give students a way of thinking about the range of names and examples in Walker's essay. (Our point is not to question whether or not Walker had done her homework.) Students will certainly not be familiar with all the artists Walker alludes to; they will be familiar, or can become familiar, with some. Jacobs provides a way of thinking about these names as a specific set, as something other than a comprehensive reference to all African-American women. Some women are more appropriate examples than others.

    The point of this assignment is to enable students to question Walker's representation of the past by asking them to imagine what she might do with "Incidents." Would she find inspiration in Jacobs's narrative — where? and why? In what ways might "Incidents" be said to invite or resist Walker's reading of the past?

2. This assignment is similar to the first of the writing assignments above, with the exception that it asks students to frame their reading in terms of Rich's argument about revision, the past, and the position of women within a patriarchal culture.

3. Mary Louise Pratt's essay, "Arts of the Contact Zone," provides a useful alternative to Houston Baker's account of the slave narrative. For Baker, the "authentic, unwritten self" is necessarily displaced — or appropriated — by the public discourse. In her representation of "autoethnography" and "transculturation," Pratt allows us to figure the author differently, so that we can imagine Jacobs *engaging* with the standard representation of an African-American woman and her experience, and with the standard representation of a woman of virtue, but not giving up or giving in to it; where the point is, in Pratt's terms, to "intervene" with the majority understanding, where the purpose is corrective, and revisionary, and where the writer is allowed a position from which work can be done (where the writer can do more than merely repeat the master narrative).

This assignment asks students to begin with and to use Pratt's terms ("autoethnography" or "transculturation"). It is important for students to see this as something other than a dictionary assignment ("According to Webster, 'ethnography' is . . ."). The point, in other words, is not to come up with the "right" definition but to see how these words, together with the text that accompanies them and the example of Guaman Poma, can provide a way of reading "Incidents." Students need to work back and forth between the two essays, seeing how and where Jacobs might be said to demonstrate her own version of the "literate arts" of the contact zone.

THOMAS KUHN

The Historical Structure of Scientific Discovery (p. 310)

One of our motives in gathering the essays for this book was to give students access to some of the key terms and key figures in the conversations that haunt a college or university campus. We were therefore eager to find something to represent the work of Thomas Kuhn. The individual chapters in *The Structure of Scientific Revolutions* were heavy sledding for beginning undergraduates, however, so we were pleased to find "The Historical Structure of Scientific Discovery," a readable and effective introduction to his argument about the relationship between the community and the individual, between convention and change.

The problem in teaching this essay — whether through discussion or writing — is to enable students to pull Kuhn's theory out of specific cases. Students will tend to read from example to example, like leaping from rock to rock when crossing a swollen stream, and they will not attend to the terms or the precise distinctions in the discussion of observation and conceptualization or anomaly, to take two examples. It's good to begin by asking students to return to the cases under consideration, to piece out who did what, when, and why, and to ask what the point is. As students account for the meaning or significance of the examples, they will bring forward both common wisdom and the more precise terms of Kuhn's analysis. At this point we work very hard to keep the two moving but distinct — to elicit both their account and Kuhn's, and to document both on the blackboard. At some point we can begin to ask the class to describe the difference and to feel the power of a term like "structure," which, while it has meaning in everyday conversation, has a meaning for Kuhn, for whom it becomes almost a tool for analysis. Phrases like "internal history" or "anomaly" or "structure" disappear into the general echo of the essay unless students are given both a method and a reason for paying attention to them.

QUESTIONS FOR A SECOND READING (p. 321)

1. There are two reasons for sending students back to Kuhn's essay with the phrase "new vocabulary" in mind. One is that Kuhn's new vocabulary, because it is not a jargon, looks deceptively like our old vocabulary. He takes words and forces a rigor and precision into their use that is both telling and inspiring. He also demonstrates or enacts the very process he describes in this history of scientific discovery, saying, to put it crudely, that differences and distinctions remain invisible to us until we see them in new terms. The phrase "internal history" gives the reader a new and striking view of discovery. The whole essay, while written in a straightforward manner, has the effect of reordering a familiar landscape.

2. This is the more difficult of the two questions, asking students to imagine the concerns and assumptions of specialists who read this essay. Kuhn is carving out a project for himself that requires him to redefine what it means to write a history. From one point of view, the sentence "Oxygen was discovered" is obvious and self-evident. From another, the sentence is nonsense, meaningless. Students cannot be expected to reconstruct for themselves either the terms of this debate or its complexity (we certainly cannot); they can, however, sense the broad outlines of the debate and feel Kuhn's urgency. This is not just an abstract matter. The question of how knowledge is changed and who gets the credit has real bearing on, and calls into question, much that we take for granted in schoolwork as well as in life.

ASSIGNMENTS FOR WRITING (p. 321)

1. This assignment argues its own case. There is no reason for students to sit silently in front of Kuhn's essay because they lack experience or knowledge in the sciences. If they can't add scientific examples or question the ones Kuhn presents, they can work on his key terms and his method by applying them to their own range of experience. Kuhn's terms can open up an experience one takes for granted in surprising ways. The problem for students writing this essay will be in making full use of Kuhn — that is, in making a study of Kuhnian analysis. Students will use up much of their attention and energy in locating and describing an event, and they will often tell difficult and emotionally loaded stories. As a consequence, the analysis will often be more commonplace ("The scales fell from my eyes," "You just can't tell a book by its cover," "I saw her true nature") than Kuhnian (where the word "anomaly" must somehow become a functional term).

   There may be a natural history to the development of such essays. We would hate to push students away from subjects close and important to them, yet these are the very subjects that will resist specialized analysis. It may be best to allow time for revision with this essay, so that students can go back to Kuhn's essay and the job of understanding their story in his terms.

2. This is a much more difficult assignment. While students may be accustomed to thinking reflectively about moments when they have suddenly seen things in a new light, they are not accustomed to thinking about the process of reading or about themselves as readers. This is obvious to anyone who has tried to teach a "reader-response" course. For many student readers, "The book was read" is as complete and final a statement as "Oxygen was discovered." This may be exactly the reason why the assignment is worth trying, particularly if students work on it *while* they are reading an essay. If they can keep records and consider themselves subjects in a case study, Kuhn will provide a structure and a language for considering the historical structure of reading.

   We have used this assignment to help students account for their reading of Rich's "When We Dead Awaken: Writing as Re-Vision." Students grumble a bit when they begin working on it, but it has always been a pivotal assignment, one that both students and teachers return to later to comment on what they've learned or how their work has changed. It is important for students to take seriously the request to tell a *story* of reading.

MAKING CONNECTIONS (p. 322)

1. Both Kuhn and Rich could be said to be revising the history that assigns an epic role to William Herschel. Both are concerned with the ways "structures" of understanding determine the ways we view (and value) people and events. Both, in their practice, have worked to write in spite of or in opposition to those structures. Students will have to read more than Rich's poem to work on this essay, since the poem is meant to represent a language problem (and her response to it) that is discussed at length in the essay, but the two essays provide rich material for a paper on methods of writing (or rewriting) history. The best papers, however, will work from very specific and limited examples — by looking at language, that is, and not by just talking in the abstract about patriarchy or hero worship.

2. This assignment has a structure that is repeated again and again in our textbook. Students are asked to use the key terms of one text (in this case "The Historical Structure of Scientific Discovery") to read another ("Deep Play"). Geertz's essay is a tough one, one of the toughest in the book, and the assignment will work best for students who have already written about it. Geertz implies (if he doesn't announce) that he is redefining or reimagining the nature of anthropological inquiry. He would not offer himself, that is, as one who is offering "mere additions or increments to the growing stockpile of scientific knowledge." If Geertz is providing a new way of seeing for anthropologists, it is interesting to ask whether his "discovery" follows the lines of Kuhn's argument. Students, of course, cannot be expected to have an insider's knowledge of the history of anthropology or the nature of Geertz's relationship to his sources of anthropology or the nature of Geertz's relationship to his sources or his field. They do, however, have the references in the text, and they have his footnotes — which, with this project in mind, make interesting reading. Students are not going to write a definitive study of Geertz, but there is an interesting project here and the very limits on available information are what make it manageable.

PATRICIA NELSON LIMERICK

Closing the Frontier and Opening Western History (p. 324) and *Empire of Innocence* (p. 338)

We are great fans of *The Legacy of Conquest*, the book from which these two selections were chosen. Limerick is a wonderful writer — funny, eloquent, surprising. The book provides a powerful rereading of the narratives of western expansion that we have come to take for granted, even to take for granted as wrong. Her argument — that the West was not empty, waiting to be filled by settlers from the East, that the usual stories leave out key characters (women, the Spanish and Chinese settlers, native American accounts of contact with Europeans) — has become a familiar one. Limerick adds a mix of passion and balance to its making, she makes deft and striking connections with contemporary American public policy, and she adds a wealth of anecdotes, "mini-histories" of characters and events from the early history of the American West. She works by putting together striking sets of examples and counterexamples, illustrating through her prose part of her argument that a historian must learn how to find, reconcile, and honor multiple points of view.

We chose the introduction, "Closing the Frontier and Opening Western History," and the first chapter, "Empire of Innocence," to represent the book. These were the chapters

79

in which Limerick speaks most directly about the writing of history, which seemed to us to be important for an anthology for writing classes. And we liked the way the two chapters worked as a pair. In the first, she situates the work of the historian in its professional, disciplinary context, talking about how the discipline and its key figures, for example, Frederick Jackson Turner, both enable and constrain the work of individual historians. It is a chapter about how knowledge is produced and preserved in an academic discipline. In the second, she places the work of the historian in a more general intellectual context. Here the problems facing the writer are problems of point of view (maintaining multiple points of view), of one's relation to myth and stereotype (creating moral complexity without losing "mythic power").

We taught these chapters in two different semesters. When students went back to reread them, we found we had to draw attention to the Turner discussion in "Closing the Frontier" and to the concluding paragraph in "Empire of Innocence." As far as the Turner discussion is concerned, Limerick provides enough information about Turner in the chapter for students to know who he is and to understand the role he played in establishing the "meaning" of the West. We found it useful to prompt students back to this section as a way of thinking about how historians work. This was a difficult exercise, since students tend to think that academics just *have* ideas, good ones and true ones, and then write them down. The discussion was a chance for us to ask students to tell the story of Limerick's work (a story of preparation and composition) and to tell stories of our own. This discussion helped students to see the chapters as writing, as the result of a composing process that is historical, social, cultural.

The concluding paragraph in "Empire of Innocence" serves as a nice way back into that chapter because of the ways in which it identifies Limerick's ambitions — or the ways in which it complicates the figure of the historian as critic. Her work is, without question, critical. She wants to unwrite certain versions of the West. But she also imagines herself as a storyteller, occupying the very role she critiques in the name of Turner. The chapter is about innocence and point of view (both have multiple versions); it is also about a storyteller, Limerick (or this is how *we* wanted to frame the rereading of the chapter). We wanted to ask questions about how the chapter was organized, what the author was trying to do and why.

QUESTIONS FOR A SECOND READING (p. 355)

1. This question is designed to frame the chapters as both a critique of practice and a practical guide. Partly in honor of what we take to be Limerick's intentions, and partly because of the kinds of courses we teach, we wanted students to see these chapters as reflections on method. Without this prompting, we found, students read the chapters for "content" — stories from the American West (about Julia Bulette or Narcissa Whitman) or an argument about "innocence" and "empire." As we said above, we like the ways the two chapters parallel each other, one looking at the problems of historical writing as disciplinary, the other looking at the problems of historical writing as more generalized problems of understanding others and the past.

2. This question, in a sense, asks students to notice the references to Louis L'Amour and Ronald Reagan when they read through for the second time. Limerick has a wonderful way of indicating the presence of the past (or conceptions of the past) through jokes, asides, and quick references to current items in the daily papers. She does this in her lectures (she is a brilliant lecturer) and she does it in her writing. There is more to notice, however, than this interesting and telling pair of references. There are other ways in which Limerick's work might be said to speak to the present. We might have asked the question this way: "Historians write about the past for readers who live in the present. Why do they do this? How might you

explain or justify the time we spend reading and studying history? How might you explain or justify it, drawing specifically on the example of these two chapters from *The Legacy of Conquest?*"

ASSIGNMENTS FOR WRITING (p. 355)

1. There are two options in this assignment. The general goal is to have students perform a reading of Limerick by writing a history — showing, in a sense, what they have learned in what they can do, defining the presence of the writer (Limerick) through the possible ways she might influence other writers.

   The first option sends students to the library or local historical society. This assignment was prompted by the teaching of Jean Ferguson Carr, whose courses at Pitt almost always include some kind of archival project and of Pat Bizzell, who has her students at Holy Cross research local accounts of European settlements written by Native Americans. We were frustrated by the degree to which students feel removed from library archives and the degree to which our teaching (and the textbook) seems to enforce that remove. Needless to say, this first option will seem to be the harder of the two, and students will need some prompting or challenge or rewards to choose it. Remember that an assignment like this will take more time than usual; it takes time for students to find the library and spend enough time in the stacks to make the experience profitable, more time than for them to do a quick search for the one book that will get them through the assignment. We've also found that we need to make the process of search and selection an acknowledged part of the work of the course. We ask students to collect folders of material, to present them to others (to the class, to groups), and to discuss in their essays how they selected the material they chose to write about. Selection is of some special importance for this assignment, since Limerick's work points to the importance of finding the otherwise hidden alternative story.

   The second option cuts out the library time, although it will work best if students take the challenge of making this more than a "personal essay." In fact, when we asked students to write this assignment, "personal essay" became a useful negative term, a way of indicating what their work needed to transcend in revision. Here is how we made the distinction between "history," as represented by Limerick, and personal essay. Gathering materials was important; essays became histories when they incorporated materials (photos, diaries, interviews) that would not have been found if a writer had not felt responsible for more than his or her own immediate experience. Structure, too, became important; essays also became histories when they included more than two "stories" and more than a single point of view. In fact, much of the work of revision was represented in just these terms. Students went back to write more stories ("counterstories," in Limerick's style) and to write from points of view not their own (their parents', a neighbor's, a friend's, a teacher's). They added stories and points of view; and they worked to establish paragraphs, like Limerick's, where they stepped forward to speak as historians about the material they had gathered. The key moments in the best essays we received came when students realized that they had to break the "unity" they had been trained to value, when they added the story that didn't seem to fit, or wrote from outside their own point of view.

2. This writing assignment is linked to the second of the "Questions for a Second Reading." That question asks students to imagine how and why Limerick's work might be said to speak to the present. Why, we ask, read history? What can you make of the references to current American public policy? This assignment repeats those questions and tries to imagine a forum where students might use Limerick's work in a public statement of their own. Hence it is framed as a review/essay or a piece for a newspaper op-ed page. You should not feel limited by these formats. There may be outlets for writers or events on your own campus that would be more appropriate or convincing.

MAKING CONNECTIONS (p. 356)

1–2.   Both these assignments point students toward an examination of different ways of writing about, representing, and understanding the past. The goal in each is to have students attend to differences in an area where they believe there are none, where methodological problems are hidden or seem settled.

The first assignment represents differences in disciplinary terms. Tompkins and Pratt, both in literature departments, work with the past and its stories, figures, and records; but each one's work is different from the other's and, more strikingly, different from Limerick's. For one thing, Pratt and Tompkins find the problems of history more fundamentally textual, invoking the status of the text and its various interpretations. There are, however, many other ways of thinking through their differences (in their use of examples, their presence in the text, the ways they write notes and citations, the ways they address their audience). We present Wideman as a novelist whose nonfiction is inflected by his training and preparation. Wideman's reasons for writing about the past and the problems he faces in representing the past (problems of innocence and point of view) are strikingly similar to Limerick's. In fact, as we read the essays, his position is closer to Limerick's than is Pratt's or Tompkins's. (Both Wideman and Limerick, we would be inclined to say, begin with a sense of themselves as writers, not readers. These are differences of training and vocation; they also reflect differences in the ways the "truth" of their work is assessed by their readers.) With the Wideman question, we have pointed particularly at the differences in approach and asked questions about all the writers and what their methods both allow and prevent.

In all of these assignments, the quality of students' writing will reflect the degree to which they work directly with passages from the texts. In revision, we have found that it helps to raise questions about the passages students have selected to write about in the first draft (what do *those* choices reflect? what was left out? why?), and it helps to point to the position the student writers have occupied in their texts in relation to those passages (are they left to speak for themselves? does the writer intervene to teach? translate? summarize? to what end?)

MARK CRISPIN MILLER

Getting Dirty (p. 358)
and
Cosby Knows Best (p. 368)

We selected two of Miller's reviews (with two "Afterwords"). Miller's work, however, is driven by theory and, in the headnote and the assignments, we tried to provide some examples of Miller talking *about* his practice. Most are drawn from the essay that introduces *Boxed In*. We want to make it possible for students to see Miller's work as systematic and informed by a purpose — to educate the viewer, to revise the culture of television. Students' tendency will be to see the account of "The Cosby Show," for example, as show-off, as the scholarly world expressing its disdain for popular culture. There may be some justice in this, but, to make this case, students need to be able to imagine how, in Miller's terms, he is neither showing off nor trashing TV.

When we have taught these two brief essays, we have asked students to use them as a way of charting or understanding a critic's method. We have had to forestall students' desires to use them as the occasion to talk about "The Cosby Show" or their favorite ad. There comes a point at which we encourage students to try out their roles as critics and to write about ads or shows, but we want them to do this in the name of criticism, to imagine what it would be like to read television this way.

1–3. The first two questions are intended to give students a way of going back to the reviews to ask questions about them as critical practice. Miller says he is demonstrating how we might take television seriously, paying attention to both detail and "historical situation." How does one pay attention to detail? What is the "larger context," and how does one read TV? The first question asks students to chart sections of the essay that will enable them to talk about the figure of the critic — his relationship to the public, his audience, and his material. The second asks students to mark sections that show Miller establishing the larger context, a version of the culture of television of which the individual shows could be said to be representative examples. The third asks students to imagine Miller's audience — who reads this criticism and why? It is particularly interesting to use these to get a sense — even if it is Miller's — of the industry.

ASSIGNMENTS FOR WRITING (p. 376)

1. Here, students get to try their hand at Miller's brand of criticism, taking his methods and applying them to new material. Students' success with the assignment will depend on their ability to represent to themselves Miller's method *as a method*, and it will depend on the degree of detail they work with in representing their ad or show. They most likely will not be able to use pictures, but Miller's writing sets a good example here. He teaches his readers how to look at the screen by the example of what he notices and remembers. Students will need to work with close detail, to define a contrary relation to the common-sense reading of their example, and to imagine that their job is to ask questions, including the big one — "Just what is going on here?" As the note says, the hard question is one that even Miller refuses to take head-on. One of his devices as a critic is putting agency into a show — saying, for example, that the Shield ad *offers* women a fantasy of power and control. The story he is trying to tell is not the usual narrative of an artist creating an effect, but of a shaping force that is bigger than an individual artist or writer, one that committees or producers grasp only partially. Students should be aware of the need to talk in unusual terms about the source of television's effects.

For revision: Students, perhaps properly, will at first devote their energy and attention to producing an account of their show or ad — describing it, noticing some features and ignoring others. There are two ways we have approached revisions. We have asked students to step back from their account to imagine what it necessarily misses because of its angle of vision, and we have asked them to use the revision as an occasion to turn their attention to larger, interpretive questions. If the first draft was the occasion to pay "meticulous attention to concrete detail," the second is to see how those details "illuminate the larger context . . . so that the reading of TV contains and necessitates a reading of our own moment and its past."

2. This question is a variation on the first, but it invites students to counter Miller's criticism. Students, we've found, feel uncomfortable with what Miller does; there is something unseemly or improper about looking closely at TV, of refusing to be a "normal" viewer. Students feel that they too know something about TV, even if they miss the sexual politics of the Shield ad. Here is an opportunity for students to define their position in response to Miller's, to speak in the name of the public Miller says is mystified by television's sophisticated rhetoric. In fact, this essay might be cast as a chance for a representative of the viewing public to speak back to Miller, to account in the same detail, and with reference to motive, for the ordinary experience of TV. The difficulty lies in not giving in to self-righteous critic-trashing, and in enabling students to see the "normal" as a practice, a method for reading TV, one that is not naturally there but a product of the culture, learned by watching.

1. Both of these questions follow the same introduction, which contains two passages from Fiske's essay on Madonna. We included those to provide an example of a writer talking about agency, about the *ways* cultural forms might be said to work on an individual's imagination and the ways an individual imagination might be said to work on cultural forms. Fiske wants to imagine the consumer as active, capable of resistance. He is arguing, that is, against the earlier notion of consumers as simply manipulated by special interests (provided with a false consciousness). This account of the dynamics of reception is striking and surprising to students. Fiske's language is sometimes heavy-handed and jargon-laden, but the account he offers of domination and resistance is not difficult or complicated. What *is* hard for students is to imagine themselves and others through the figures offered by Fiske, Miller, Berger, Pratt, Rich, Theweleit and Willis. We have found, for reasons consistent with Fiske's argument, that students share in the general notion that close attention to "trivia" (Madonna, TV, exercise programs) is obsessive, stupid, bizarre, a form of "academic" nonsense. And — again for reasons that can be seen as part of Fiske's argument — they find it difficult to construct a first-person narrative in which they are anything but individual agents exercising free choice.

   The two assignments direct students to imagine themselves and others as products of their culture or as participants in a process of cultural production. The first assignment asks students to account for the key terms and concepts in the criticism of popular culture by looking at the practice of individual critics, choosing from among a list of critics represented in *Ways of Reading*. Students are asked to work from specific passages in the essays they choose. Their success will depend on how closely they work with the texts. It is important, however, to counter students' tendency to lump all of this work together; that is, it is useful to ask students to look for differences rather than similarities. In the search for similarities, it is too easy to settle for quick generalizations. Finally, the assignment casts students in the role of experts — they are asked to write to an audience not familiar with these critics and their work. We added this element in order to put pressure on students to represent the work of each critic through both summary and quotation. To us, both methods are important academic skills. You may prefer to have student jump into the arguments and write to an audience more immediately familiar with the essays under consideration.

2. This assignment asks students to write an autobiographical essay. You might refer to it as a chapter of their autobiography, one that shows their participation in American popular culture. The key here is to get students to tell a good story, to turn to anecdote and example. It helps to make this point in your loudest voice — you are asking neither for a Millerian essay nor for the usual school exercise, but rather for a narrative in which the student is the central character. Of course, the assignment asks for more than *just* a narrative, since it asks students to write a piece that can be read as a response to Miller. This may necessarily be a focus for revision, once students have told their story. It is important, however, for students to imagine that theirs is a story about an individual's relationship to the culture, one that demonstrates what it might mean to say that a person is or is not a product of culture. You want more than a story of "my favorite TV shows"; you are looking for a sense of the relationship between those shows and a life or a person, and this relationship is neither simple nor easy to write.

JOYCE CAROL OATES

Theft (p. 380)

Marya and Imogene are sophomores at a small college in Port Oriskany. Marya lives in Maynard House, a rooming house for girls, and Imogene lives in a sorority house where most of the girls appear to be from wealthy families. Marya, who comes from a poor family, studies relentlessly, puts her schoolwork above everything, and steals. In her words, she's fascinated with that moment when objects pass over from belonging to one person to belonging to another.

Imogene is a drama major who lives dramatically. She likes good clothes, handsome men, and attention. Marya and Imogene meet in a class and awkwardly, for strange reasons, become friends, friends who seem to be continually on the verge of becoming enemies — which they do by the end of the story.

The story reads like a case study of zigzagging friendships and thefts. Students will be taken with its ease. It reads well without being simple or simple-minded and invites close attention.

QUESTIONS FOR A SECOND READING (p. 419)

1. Students are asked to reread by going back over the thefts in the story. People, including Marya, steal things from each other, but there are also thefts, some that Marya imagines, involving such things as knowledge, friendship, and personal rights like the right to privacy, self-expression, or specific goals. Students will need to locate the passages in the story that deal with actual thefts and those that might be said to represent imagined or metaphorical ones. You might point to an instance of the latter, like Marya's sense of reading as stealing, to help students see what you mean by imagined or metaphorical theft, but most of the work will have to come from students' rereading, locating the moments that deal with stealing, and trying to imagine how the world must look to a person like Marya, who thinks about people and things in terms of what's hers and what's theirs. She spends considerable time separating the world into dichotomies — them and her, rich and poor, the haves and the have-nots. You'll want to ask students to make the connections between those passages dealing with her stealing — including her talk about stealing — and those moments in the story when her view of the world seems to come forward.

2. To explain the relationship between Marya and Imogene, students will have to look at what it means or represents to both of them. They'll need to find passages in the text that allow them to talk about the friendship, how it develops, and why it develops. Pulling the rereading together will stand for what the story offers. Students might, in the spirit of paying attention to what the story offers as an explanation of the friendship, look closely at narrative moments that describe the girls and their friendship. What bias or slant might Oates be offering? What are key terms in Oates's narration of their friendship? Then, once they've looked closely at the story and what it offers to explain the friendship, students can turn to what they see as the key or significant terms and moments in the story. Which moments and terms, regardless of what Oates seems to be pushing, strike them as significant? How does their reading compare with Oates's slant? What might account for the differences?

ASSIGNMENTS FOR WRITING (p. 420)

1. To begin this assignment, students need to go back to the story to find the section where Marya is described in terms of that moment of things passing over to her. Why, they should ask themselves, does this interest her? Students will need to locate other key moments in the story where things (or people or states of being — like privacy, or fitting in, or friendship) pass over to belonging to Marya. What, they should ask themselves, might these moments be saying about Marya and stealing? Why does she steal?

You might ask additional questions of students when they revise. If they're working from passages that bring forward moments when things pass over to Marya, ask them to consider what kind of problem this might be, or how much of a problem it is. Marya thinks it's natural to be fascinated with those moments of belonging, including belonging in friendships, but how else might her fascination be read? What in the story points to other ways of reading her attention to those moments? And what passages might help in accounting for why she's so taken with those moments? Is there evidence to say it comes from her poor background, her personality, her obsession with success, her outlook on life?

2. How might Marya's successful academic career be related to her thievery? Students will need to reread the story to find significant passages that deal with her success and others that deal with her stealing. You might point them in the direction of the passage where she portrays reading as "a secret process," and ask them to begin there by finding an equally significant passage that describes what stealing is to her. They might then turn to finding other passages that address academic success and stealing; when they have found three or four passages for each, they can begin a draft of their paper. The problem is too complex to work quickly from one or two examples, so you'll need to keep pressing them to return to the story for other points of comparison. Ask them to also look at those moments when her success and her stealing are threatened. What happens then? What might be the point of comparison here? What do the passages that refer to it allow them to say?

3. This assignment draws students' attention to Oates's methods in "Theft" by asking them to think of the story in a particular way — as "fragmented" or "circling back on itself" rather than as a linear unfolding or progression. Students will have to identify a character or event that they wish to write on, and then they'll need to locate those sections of the story that struck them as significant in their understanding of the character or event. The idea here is to get students to study the story across those significant sections so that they can write about the connections they make in terms of those sections' details, dialogues, narrations. How, in other words, did they work, as readers, to pull those sections together? How did the sections, too, work on them? How, in other words, was their attention drawn from one section to another? What might they call the controlling features of the sections? And how did those features play out across the sections? What significance, too, would they attribute to the order of the sections? How, that is, does the order in which the sections appear bear on the kind of work students do as readers?

MAKING CONNECTIONS (p. 421)

1. The Brodkey and Oates stories are terrific selections for asking students to consider how gender, in this case the female characters, is created. Brodkey gives Buddy, his narrator, a great deal of weight in the story; through Buddy, who is of course created by Brodkey, we come to understand Doris. Students need to study both the narrator and the dialogues in which Doris is created by Brodkey. How is Doris allowed to think and behave? What does the fact that we learn about her through Buddy make possible or impossible for her to do or think or behave? And, too, working from the narrative and the dialogues, how does Oates create Marya or Imogene? What does the story make possible or impossible for them to do or think or be? These are the kinds of questions that students will need to address as they work through their rereadings and notetaking on the stories. Once they have created a method for studying the authors' creations of the characters — Doris and Marya or Imogene — they need to consider how, given what they've learned, it would be possible to conclude that each author is making an argument about women. What would Brodkey's argument be? Oates's? The critical move in the students' essays will be how they draw their conclusions about each author's view of women, based on the materials they have worked with.

2. Is Marya a scholarship girl? How is Rodriguez like her? How can those likenesses be used to explain his relationship to others? to the culture he lives in? Before students begin writing, they'll need to read and reread the Rodriguez selection, paying particular attention to what he has to say about scholarship boys and why he thinks he is one. They'll also need to find those passages where he seems to be talking about himself, his friends, and his family in much the same way Marya does. What likenesses do those passages point to? Students will need to consider what moments in the Oates story make good comparisons with those in the

Rodriguez selection. You might ask them to begin by paying attention to passages where Rodriguez discusses relationships to others, to family and friends. Then they can turn to those moments in the Oates story where Marya does the same.

Once students have done the rereadings, paying attention to and making notes about what makes Rodriguez a scholarship boy and Marya a scholarship girl, and how they deal with relationships, they're ready to write. Students will tend to get lost in the assignment. They might answer the first question about Marya being a scholarship girl and quickly gloss over the business about Marya and Rodriguez responding similarly to relationships. When you're working on revisions, you'll want to be sure they have gone beyond the initial part of the assignment and that they're using it, along with the material they have collected on how both Marya and Rodriguez deal with relationships, to work the main problem — which is to say how Rodriguez and Marya are examples of people with similar responses to growing up, entering the world, and becoming educated.

WALKER PERCY

The Loss of the Creature (p. 422)

In the assignments, we define Percy's method in "The Loss of the Creature" as an enactment of his argument: The world is disposed of by theory; to strive for a more immediate experience of the "thing," one must resist packages and packaging; the job for the writer is to resist the desire to translate examples into generalizations; the job for the reader is to attend to the varied richness of detail, not to search for the hard outline. Percy talks about the value of the indirect approach and shows how it works and how it feels once you climb inside.

Percy does his best to unsettle his readers, to keep them from turning his argument into a fixed, abstract statement. Students, to be sure, will try to sum the essay up — to tame it and make its weirdness manageable — by saying something like "Percy says that we have to work hard to be individuals" or "We must try to live every day to the fullest." When you place these sentences against Percy's own ("The layman will be seduced as long as he regards beings as consumer items to be experienced rather than prizes to be won, and as long as he waives his sovereign rights as a person and accepts his role of consumer as the highest estate to which the layman can aspire," text p. 436), or when you place them against those wonderful, almost parable-like anecdotes (the weary, sophisticated tourist who seeks out the Greyhound package tour with the folks from Terre Haute), you sense the degree to which this writing resists a reader's desire to put it into a box and tie it up with a bow.

The terms of the argument resist summary or translation into common terms. The examples seem almost to deflect, rather than to support or to illustrate, the argument. Sometimes, in fact, the argument seems playfully, or willfully, absurd: Are we really to believe that Cardenas saw the Grand Canyon without any preconceptions? that he didn't see it as an example of God's grandeur or as property for his queen? And what about the bogus precision of assigning a fixed value (P) to the experience of seeing the Grand Canyon? And the examples, as they accumulate, seem to say to readers not that they are getting closer to a final, summary statement but that they are going to somehow have to find the point of all this somewhere in the spaces between the examples. They all approximate something that is ultimately beyond saying.

We find students alternately puzzled, frustrated, and entranced by this essay. Percy doesn't do what a writer is supposed to do. Yet he seems to be upbeat, and on the side of students, in favor of freedom and against dull courses. "What if we wrote like that?"

We have been asked. "Give it a try," We've said. When students talk or write about the essay, we have found it important for them to focus on the examples, particularly on those that seem mysterious, that defy their efforts as readers. When students talk about the tourists at the Grand Canyon, they inevitably turn to the examples of tourists who get off the beaten track ("That's what Percy is saying — we have to take the road less traveled") and ignore the difficult talk about dialectic and the complex soul who sees through the predicaments of others. The former comes to students without effort; the latter is hard to explain (or there is no ready explanation). The complexities become invisible or unimportant to students unless a teacher brings them into the foreground.

When we teach this essay, we are interested in keeping track — for the class — of what students notice and what they fail to notice, of what they take as significant and what they allow to disappear from attention. Then we can ask why they read the essay as they do, and ask how their difficulties with the essay fit into Percy's argument about the problems of seeing the Grand Canyon or a dogfish. Students, we've found, read on the assumption that the examples are equivalent, that they all illustrate the same thing. It is harder to look for differences, or to imagine why Percy has piled example on example ("If they are all the same, then why wouldn't one or two do the trick?"). We insist that they work on a phrase like "dialectical movement," both because it is a powerful phrase — in the academy and in this essay — and because it marks a point at which Percy's essay makes an argument with more precision and rigor than the version students will offer in everyday language ("Be yourself! Don't fall into the same old rut!"). Percy talks about elaborate packages and coverings; students will want to talk about hidden meanings. The problem of translation is a central one in the essay. We want students to go back and *work* on this essay — to do more than just take pleasure in its anecdotes. We want them to see the demands the structure of the essay makes on them as readers; we want to call attention to the difference between the language of the essay and the language students will bring forward to represent and displace it.

The discussion and writing assignments begin with particulars and move outward. There is a point at which we want students to work on the largest structural problem in the essay — the relation between the first and second sections. An appropriate question would ask students, given their reading of the essay and their sense of its method and agenda, what sense it makes to compare the experience of the tourist with that of the student. The essay insists on the comparison — or contrast — without coming forward and making it, without speaking directly of the relationship between parts I and II. Students will have to fill in this silence, and at the risk of making fixed and simple that which is presented as open and complex.

There is a way in which this essay is a trap. It is extraordinarily difficult to write about it without packaging it, and thereby becoming a consumer or a theorist and wearing the Percian badge of shame. Still, it is extraordinarily powerful to feel the problem of knowledge and representation in just this way. If you are concerned about leading students down this shady lane, then perhaps the most appropriate writing assignment is one that asks students to imitate Percy's project rather than write *about* it, hence the seeming indirection of the two "Assignments for Writing" on text pp. 437–38.

If we can lead students to sense that there is a trap in this essay — or that Percy is playing a slippery role, having his theories and denying them at the same time — we will have some successful classes. The difficulty is getting a class to move beyond the certainty that Percy is simply telling them, if elegantly, what they already know.

QUESTIONS FOR A SECOND READING (p. 437)

1. The first of these directs students to what we referred to earlier as Percy's method. It asks students, as they reread, to think about what it is like to read this essay or to think about the

demands it makes upon them. We've found that this distinction is a surprising but often an enabling one for students. When students consider that the essay is, in a sense, teaching them how it wants to be read, they suddenly have a very different sense of what an essay is and what it means to be a reader. They are not, in other words, receiving information the way they might receive it from a textbook. The essay makes different assumptions about the nature of information and the roles of both reader and author.

2. Students are asked to imagine that the essay is not just performance — that Percy has an argument to make, however indirect the presentation, and that the argument has bearing on the life of a student. It is, for that matter, an essay *about* the life of the student. The problem with inviting students to reread the essay with the argument in mind is that it can be an invitation to misread if students are not given advance warning that Percy is trying to undo them as readers. Without a warning, many students will read the essay as though it were no different from a piece in *Reader's Digest*, and see it as saying exactly what they have learned to say to each other: Be yourself, beware of school, count every daisy, don't lose the trees in the forest. With the warning, a rereading with these questions in mind can give students a way of beginning to talk back to Percy. Once students can make Percy's terms work for them, they can begin to imagine what it would take to stand outside that argument and speak back: Why must the "thing" be beyond words? What is the argument against this theory of education? (Rodriguez, in "The Achievement of Desire," offers one counterargument.) What about the people who can't afford trips or Sarah Lawrence — do they have an equivalent loss? What would be the consequences for a person who could step outside his or her culture and see the Grand Canyon? If such a thing is impossible, and if people nonetheless care about seeing natural phenomena, then what else might we struggle for or worry about?

3. This question is intended to make it possible for students to imagine the essay as the demonstration of a method, and to imagine how that method might be said to be problematic. There are written accounts of first encounters with the Grand Canyon dating back at least two centuries. And, of course, there are Native American accounts of the canyon. It would be possible to conduct a scholarly analysis of what actual people have actually said. Percy's essay can be read as a deliberate rejection of the archive, the interview, and the survey. Once students begin thinking about the essay in these terms, it is interesting to ask what is gained and what is lost. It is surprising that an essay about the limits of cultural packaging deals largely in stereotype and caricature — in the quick, representative example (his tourist, his islander, his student, and his "great man"). At the same time, one could argue that the figure of the novelist or artist, while not named directly in the essay, stands behind Percy's essay as the expert who stands outside time and culture. This is a familiar longing, and the essay can be used as a way of examining a general desire to imagine such a position.

ASSIGNMENTS FOR WRITING (p. 437)

1. Here is a writing assignment that frees students from the burden of theorizing about an essay that condemns theorists. It asks them, rather, to do a Percian thing — to carry out a Percian project. The assignment points students in two directions. On one hand, they will have to be good storytellers; whether they should tell Percian anecdotes is another issue. On the other hand, they will have to arrange and comment on their stories using Percy's terms and methods. This is the occasion to work on the use and meaning of a word like "dialectic" (and to work on the use and meaning of the word as Percy uses it and makes it meaningful). It is not the occasion to "forget all that stuff" and turn naively to personal experience. The experience is important, but the way it is shaped and phrased by a writer who is carrying out Percy's project is equally so.

We don't want to underplay the difficulty of this, and it is a difficulty that can be represented in a cycle of drafts and revisions. Students will have access to related stories, and they will care about those stories well before they sense the attention that is required to work on them in Percy's spirit. Such Percian work may make more sense to students when they are working on a later draft, particularly if you direct comments or discussions of sample papers in class toward the relationships between the stories and the shape of the essays or the presence of a voice that speaks in general terms.

A note on the final sentence: It seems rather weak to say "Feel free to imitate Percy's style and method," as there is much teaching to be done if students are to take up the invitation. One issue, however, is whether students will ground their papers in "real" stories from their own experience or representative anecdotes crafted to serve the occasion. The latter is much harder for students to do well, but to realize this is to realize something telling about Percy in this essay. In this apparent guidebook to daily living, he never turns to the detail of his own life, and this allows him a purity and status that students won't have if they bring forward memories of family trips or favorite teachers.

2. This assignment takes the central metaphor of the common and the complex and asks students to use it to imagine that there is more than one way of reading "The Loss of the Creature," that reading can be imagined as a matter of struggle and strategy. Students are asked to imagine a common reading and to write an essay showing what it might look like. Then they are asked to plan and to put into action a strategy to enable another form of reading, one they would be willing to label complex. Finally, they are asked to step back and comment on what they have done.

The all-at-onceness of this assignment is hard for students. This too is an assignment that benefits from stages. If students work on one reading before the other, they are more likely to develop essays on "The Loss of the Creature" that are real essays — in length and seriousness — than if they are preparing miniatures. The same could be said for the final section of the essay. If it is to serve as the occasion for reflection, that reflection can be greatly assisted by time and by group discussion of sections I and II.

MAKING CONNECTIONS (p. 439)

1. We offer this same assignment also in the "Making Connections" questions after Geertz's essay "Deep Play: Notes on the Balinese Cockfight."

In the opening section of "The Loss of the Creature" (text pp. 425–27), Percy talks about the strategies one might use in order to recover the Grand Canyon from the "performed symbolic complex," to see it from a position outside of culture and its expectations. This assignment asks students to consider Geertz and his account of his experience in Bali, including his professional interpretation of the cockfight, as one of Percy's representative anecdotes. Geertz talks at length about his assumptions and methods — about theory — yet he seems content that he has seen something that is there. Is he simply blind to Percy's concerns and gloom?

Percy tells the story of tourists in Paris, in Mexico, and at the Grand Canyon. This assignment asks students to imagine what he might do with the story of Geertz in Bali. Has Geertz solved the problem Percy charts in his essay? Where would he place Geertz's story in the essay? How would he tell it? What would he notice and miss? Or what would he include and leave out? What would he say about it?

The goal is for students to work from within a set interpretive frame, to read one essay in terms of another. The difficulty is that Geertz keeps leaping out of the frame of what he is saying — first the narrative, then the professional account — to comment on what he has done. Students might do best if they ignored the last two sections while working on the paper. They might go back to them when they are done, particularly as a way of considering what Geertz might have to say to Percy, imagining now that Geertz has had a chance to read this Percian account of his work.

2. This assignment is a variation on the first. Here students are asked to add to the repertoire of representative anecdotes, to use their story as a response to the stories featured by Percy and Fish. The key to students' success will be spending time working with the stories in "How To Recognize a Poem" and "The Loss of the Creature." Fish's essay, like Percy's, depends upon anecdotes — the poem, Mr. Newlin, etc. Fish's anecdotes, however, are drawn from recollected experience, not invented for the occasion, as are Percy's. Even if they are invented, they are not invented in quite the same way. Fish is clearly creating a figure in this presentation of this teaching, one that we can hold alongside Percy's great man with the grubby thumb. You will want your students not only to think about the story they will tell but about storytelling, or about themselves as storytellers.

One decision you will face with this assignment is whether you want it to stand as a commentary on Fish and Percy, whether you want your students to name Fish and Percy and to allude to their work in their essays. When we have taught this assignment we have made this an issue for revision, since we do want the students to acknowledge Percy and Fish as sources in their work. Without any reminders, the first draft will most likely be primarily a story. This, we think, is a fine place for students to begin — thinking about their story and about the type of story they want to tell. In revision, we remind them of the other context — the relationship of their story to Percy and Fish. We ask them to make it clear to the reader, when they revise, how their account is a commentary on those prior essays.

MARY LOUISE PRATT

Arts of the Contact Zone (p. 440)

For a long time we felt that Mary Louise Pratt's work — particularly her essay, "Linguistic Utopias," and now her new book, *Imperial Eyes* — had much to offer those interested in writing and the teaching of writing. So much of the work on writing pedagogy was, in her terms "utopian," assuming as its end a common language commonly valued; and while we understood why teachers were prone to utopian beliefs, often expressed in the name of "community," we felt that the current version of the promised land worked against those conceptions of writing and teaching that gave priority to the social, historical, and political contexts of the classroom (and the individual act of writing). We had been greatly helped by Pratt's representation of writing and the classroom, and we had been looking for a piece of hers we could use in our undergraduate courses. We finally settled on "Scratches on the Face of the Country; or, What Mr. Barrow Saw in the Land of the Bushman" (first published in *Critical Inquiry*; there is a version of it in *Imperial Eyes*).

We taught this, we felt, with some considerable success. The essay is a wonderful demonstration of close reading (Pratt is reading excerpts from eighteenth- and nineteenth-century accounts of travel in Africa), which makes it very hard for students to write the conventional paper about exotic others (travel essays, essays about roommates, and so on). "Scratches on the Face of the Country" was on our list for inclusion in the third edition of *Ways of Reading*. However, the essay was also very difficult reading, particularly the first five pages, which are written in the style of 1980's poststructuralism (with puns on "sight" and "cite," for example).

We heard "Arts of the Contact Zone" when it was first delivered at the literacy conference in Pittsburgh and then saw it in *Profession 91*. Partly because it was written as a lecture (and partly, we believe, because Pratt had been working on this project for several years), its argument (about "contact zones" and the clash of cultures as represented in the production and reception of written texts) was similar but much more direct and would certainly put fewer roadblocks in the way of undergraduates. Parts of "Arts of the

Contact Zone" serve in the introduction to *Imperial Eyes*, which we also considered, but that piece removes the references to education and the undergraduate curriculum. It was these references, we felt, that made obvious the connections we wanted to make in our classes between colonial expansion, travel writing, a letter to King Philip III of Spain, and the contemporary American classroom.

The teaching problems the essay presents are fairly straightforward. We don't get to see much of Guaman Poma's text, so the demonstrations of close reading come with the discussion of the illustrations (which are wonderful). We have supplemented this discussion with a xeroxed copy of a page from "Scratches on the Face of the Country," in which Pratt works with the text of an early travelogue. It is important to get students to feel that they can talk about Guaman Poma (and not just Pratt's kids and baseball cards). Students will be thrown a bit by "autoethnography" and "transculturation," which is the point. Turning these into working terms requires going back to the essay (not the dictionary). It was important to some of our students to note that Guaman Poma was himself a member of the elite. We can cast him as the subaltern in his relation to King Philip, but on his home turf who knows what role he played in representing the lower castes of the Inca empire? (Positions, in other words, are situated, not pure.) The passages that provoked the most pointed discussion are those we point to in the assignments. They include those in which Pratt defines her alternative (for many students, counterintuitive) sense of community and culture, as well as those in which she lists the arts of the contact zone. The lists were extremely useful in prompting discussion, helping students to think out instances of the "rhetoric of authenticity," for example, or to imagine "unseemly comparisons" and how they might function for a student writer.

QUESTIONS FOR A SECOND READING (p. 456)

1. It is interesting for students to imagine the intellectual context in which one might turn quickly from children's talk, to the *New Chronicle*, to the undergraduate curriculum. On the one hand, there is a training or sensibility evident here that erases what seem to be obvious barriers of time and place, of personal and professional. On a second reading, we want students to try to imagine Pratt's imagination — her way of thinking about and reading the material around her as she prepares to write. On the other hand, we want students to go back to the argument of the essay and to its key terms (like "community" and "contact") to see how they hold together the pieces Pratt brings forward for discussion.

2. This is, for us, a standard application question. We want to direct students' attention to the material that they can command and use to extend Pratt's project — in this case, the classroom. As a frame for rereading, the question asks students to look for passages and terms they could bring to bear in an examination of their own educations.

3. This question emerged from our experiences in class, specifically concerning the obviously difficult terms. We wanted to acknowledge that the difficulty is strategic — part of the text, not part of students' "poor" preparation — and we wanted to suggest when and where and how a dictionary can be useful. But we also wanted to point to what was for our students the hardest term to get a handle on: "culture." In particular, we wanted to focus attention on the ways in which Pratt, revises the essay's usual use for her readers (making the "unnatural" definition the operative one, arguing against utopian thinking). To this end, we wanted students to think from both positions (a linguistic version of the "face and cup" pictures that appear in psychology textbooks).

ASSIGNMENTS FOR WRITING (p. 457)

1. The first assignment is an "inventory" assignment, asking students to collect documents that could stand, like the *New Chronicle*, as evidence of the literate arts of the contact zone. Pratt's

essay provides a frame to organize the search. Students should imagine that they can break this frame; that is, they can take it as a challenge to find the document that would surprise Pratt, that she would overlook or never think of. Her essay thus provides the terms for a discussion of the material, or representative examples from that material that they collect.

This assignment offers two options. The first sends students to a library (or historical society) to find documents from the past. We tried to suggest the many possible moments of contact in local history (between slaves and owners, workers and management, women and men, minority and majority). This assignment was prompted by Jean Ferguson Carr's teaching at Pitt (her courses almost always include some kind of archival project) and Pat Bizzell's teaching at Holy Cross (where she has students research local accounts of European settlements written by Native Americans). We were frustrated by the degree to which students feel removed from library archives and the degree to which our teaching (and the textbook) seemed to enforce that remove. Needless to say, this option will seem to be the harder of the two and students will need some prompting or challenge or rewards to choose it. One thing to remember is that an assignment like this will take more time than usual, since it takes time to find the library and spend enough time in the stacks to make the experience profitable, more than a quick search for the one book that will get you through the assignment. We've also found that we needed to make the process of search and selection an acknowledged part of the work of the course. We ask students to collect folders of material, to present them to others (to the class, to groups) and, in their essays, to talk about how they chose the material they chose to write about.

The second option sends students out into their local culture to look for the "documents," which can be defined loosely to include music (like rap), transcripts of talk shows, films, documentaries, and so on. Students should feel that they can follow Pratt's lead and turn to their brothers and sisters (or their children) and to educational materials, including papers they are writing or have written recently. You should think carefully about whether or not you would want students to choose papers from your course. It is an interesting possibility, but it will be hard for students to write about you and your class as anything *but* a utopia, paradise on earth. You may be disappointed if you invite students to take your classroom as an example.

With either option, students are asked to present their material as part of a project Pratt has begun. We have found it important to remind students that they need to *present* "Arts of the Contact Zone," even to their fellow students who have read it. You cannot assume, we remind our students, that readers have it freshly in mind or that they will be willing to get the book off the shelf and turn to pages. And we have found it important to help students imagine the role they will play in this text. They will need, in other words, to do more than simply cite from or summarize what they have gathered in their inventories. They will need to step forward as Pratt does to teach, translate, make connection, explain, comment, discuss, think this way and that. Students, at least our students, are often too quick to let the wonderful material they gather speak for itself.

2. Whereas the other assignments in this set ask students to use Pratt's term, "contact zone," in an intellectual project, this assignment asks them to write an "autoethnography" from the contact zone, to show how they understand Pratt's argument through their practice.

It is important, as a starting point, to ask students to imagine how this task might be different from writing an "autobiography." In a sense, autobiographies have historically been read as "autoethnographies." But as these terms define a *writer's* motive, it will be important for many students to imagine from the outset that they occupy a position likely to be ignored or unread or misread. It can be useful to think of the ways writers signal that they are "engaging with representations" others make of them ("many people would say. . . ," "I have been called. . . ," "some might refer to this as. . . ," "from a different point of view. . . "). This is also a good time to return to the lists Pratt offers of the literate arts of the contact zone ("parody," "unseemly comparisons," "bilingualism," "imaginary dialogue," and so on). These lists can serve as a writer's tool kit or, perhaps, as a way of beginning to imagine revision.

3. This assignment is the most straightforward of the three. It asks students to use Pratt's key terms in an essay in which they provide the key examples, in this case examples of "scenes" of education (assignment 1 asked for examples of texts). We have found it useful to ask students to provide parallel accounts of a scene (the utopian and anti-utopian, the pre- and post-Pratt). You could cut this if it seems too arbitrary or distracting. We added it not just as an exercise in thinking from alternative points of view but also as preparation for the final question, which asks students to think about the consequences of this shift — the practical consequences as well as the consequences to one's sense of the order of things. As we usually do, we try to phrase assignments asking students to take a position in such a way as to remind them that their "position" is not autonomous but links them, whether they choose the connections or not, with a more generalized interest, a "group."

MAKING CONNECTIONS (p. 459)

1. One of the pleasures of working with Pratt's essay was that it gave us a new way of reading our Table of Contents. Several pieces could stand as examples of writing from a contact zone (or could be said to illustrate equally the "literate arts of the contact zone"). We chose to point to the slave narrative, "Incidents in the Life of a Slave Girl," and selections from the "mestiza" text, *Borderlands/La frontera*. You could also use the selections by Rich, Rodriguez, Steinem, Walker, Wideman, Williams, and Woolf. This is an application assignment — it asks for a generous reading and extension of Pratt's work. As always, students should feel free to exceed their example — to argue with Pratt, to notice things she wouldn't notice, to add to her list of the literate arts of the contact zone. And, as always, it will help to give students a sense of what they will need to provide for their readers. They will need to present Pratt's essay, that is, establish it as a context; they cannot simply assume that it is there, in full, in their readers' minds. And they will need to present their example, providing an introduction to (let's say) "Incidents" and working closely with the text, including passages in quotation. Since Pratt does not provide examples of the close reading of passages in "Arts of the Contact Zone," it might be useful to provide supplementary examples. As stated earlier, we have worked with pages from "Scratches on the Face of the Country." You might also help students prepare by working on a set passage from Jacobs or Anzaldúa in class.

2. This assignment asks students to read "How to Recognize a Poem When You See One" through the frame of Pratt's argument about the contact zone. You could use other representations of the classroom or of teaching in the anthology as well. Fish provides an interesting counterexample, since (at least as he represents it) his classroom seems utopian, free from "unsolicited oppositional discourse, parody, critique." One of our goals in this assignment is to give Fish a chance to speak, too, since it seemed as though he would get chewed up once we made Pratt the starting point. For this reason we have invited students to imagine the defense of Fish's position, or a dialogue between them. Usually we have asked students to imagine that they, too, have a place to speak from. It may be best to have students work on elaborating their positions once they revise. It will take a first draft to represent Fish and Pratt and to handle the technical difficulties of quotation and paraphrase.

3. This assignment is very similar to the third writing assignment in "Assignments for Writing," which asked students to present a scene from their own education from two points of view: the view that values a unified scene and Pratt's view, the view that honors scenes of contact. Similarly, this assignment asks students to write about a scene from their own experience and to consider it in relation to both Pratt and Oates. As we read Oates's story, we were struck by the way it revises the standard (and "utopian") narrative of college and college life. Oates, it seems to us, is similarly intent on making manifest moments of contact and inequality

(through the metaphors of property and theft) and on challenging the standard ways of valuing and understanding community, including intellectual community.

ADRIENNE RICH

When We Dead Awaken: Writing as Re-Vision (p. 461)

While the opening sections of this essay may sound like shop talk to students, once they get beyond them, students are taken by the force of Rich's argument and a sense that the essay addresses a familiar but controversial topic. Students feel the force of Rich's argument, and they feel empowered to speak their own versions of women's or men's rights, but without careful teaching they will do so without paying attention to detail — that is, to the poems that Rich uses to ground what she has to say. As a consequence, their conversations and essays will consider the social behavior of men and women rather than, as Rich would have it, the problems women have finding a way of speaking inside the language and structures of a patriarchal culture. This is ultimately an essay about reading and writing — students tend to read it as an essay about "life." Students speak and write well when they attend to detail; they speak and write dreadfully when they speak and write about "life" (or at least when they begin with this as their motive).

The best way to teach this essay might be to show students how to pay attention to the details. Use the language and structure of the essay itself as a way of testing and extending Rich's argument. As students pull out sections that address the situation of the woman writer, it becomes interesting to turn what Rich says back on her own essay. Another approach is to spend time working on the poems Rich brings forward as evidence. Even for a professional reader, the bearing of the poems on the argument is not self-evident. We find that we have to stop and read the poems the way we read poems; we can't pass through them as quickly as we can exemplary material in other essays we read. This is one of the things we admire about this essay — Rich's willingness to put her own work in this context, and her patience in including the poems whole, rather than in fragments.

The essay provides the occasion for a teacher to talk with students about poems as they belonged to a moment in a poet's life and allowed her to work on a problem — a language problem, but one not as divorced from real life as students like to imagine. Rather than lecture students on the poems, ask students, after reading one poem out loud, to imagine just where it is in the poem that they find the illustration the essay calls for. Once sections have been identified — and we doubt there will be agreement — ask just what it is that is being illustrated. Let students work on the poems in the spirit of the essay — don't try to remove them and treat them as poems in an anthology. We are interested in hearing from students just how the poems are different, how they chart the progress of a poet. We ask them to move from the changes in the poems to what Rich says about the changes in her work as a writer.

When we think of the poems in context, the most interesting to us is the last, the one on Caroline Herschel that concludes the sequence. The placement puts a certain burden on it, at least within the structure of the essay. Rich says of the poem, "At last the woman in the poem and the woman writing the poem become the same person" (text p. 474). This is a statement whose meaning seems constantly to elude us. We think we know what it means until we get back inside the essay again. It is one of those statements that wonderfully frame a real conversation a teacher can have with students. We're interested in what it means and in what students can say about how the poem serves the argument of the essay. Rich includes it without any direct final commentary. We want to encourage students to take the challenge and do what they can to complete their reading of the essay.

1. We've found that the central problem in this essay is imagining how a feminist argument can be applied to writers and writing. Students are familiar with arguments about housework and the social and sexual relations between men and women, but the argument about language and culture seems difficult and mysterious. One agenda for rereading is to focus on the argument as an argument about writing, one appropriating familiar terms like "revision." Simultaneously students must attend to the essay as a text that can demonstrate or deny the very argument it is making. It is important for students to think of the piece in relation to its genres — autobiography, academic discourse, political oratory. They need not only to hear familiar refrains but also to see where and how Rich resists the familiar even in the very act of mixing genres. And they need to see the consequences of assigning gender to conventions of discourse, to think about conventional phrases and structures as belonging to a patriarchal culture.

2. This variation on the first question directs students' attention not to the text but to its unusual examples, the poems. By studying the poems and the surprising things Rich notices and says about them, students can read them in context — in the context of an argument about women's writing, of a poet's discussion of their place in her own history, of a poet's sense of what makes a poem interesting. It is possible for students to go back through the essay to learn how to better read it, and also to become better readers of poems.

1. Rich says that language can transform by renaming the world, and this anthology is designed to showcase pieces of writing that have just that power. This can be a local phenomenon, however. There are phrases or words that grab a reader and add not just a word to a vocabulary, but a way of seeing or understanding what we would otherwise miss or take for granted. Ordinary terms suddenly have extraordinary power, and a person can use them as tools to reorganize textual material. Rich does it here when she renames writing by calling it "re-naming." This is a powerful term, and the assignment is designed to enable students to feel its power by using it as a tool for analysis. In a sense, the assignment asks students to put Rich to the test — if writing is renaming, take one of her poems and talk about it as an act of renaming. What is transformed into what? and to what end? With this term to organize their analysis, students should be able to do something with, or to, the poem that they could not have done before. The assignment asks them to use this language to speak of a poem, and then to reflect on what they have done.

2. In the course of her essay, Rich says, "I have hesitated to do what I am going to do now, which is to use myself as an illustration" (text p. 467). For illustration she uses her own story, but she also selects and presents four of her poems, each of which represents a moment in her growing understanding of her situation as a woman writing. This assignment asks students to enter into the argument of the essay and to extend it by considering, at greater length than Rich, the history that is represented by the poems. Students are asked to consider what they take to be the key differences in the poems, to construct an account of what those differences represent, and so compare that account with Rich's.

    As the final note says, the best papers will be built around carefully presented, detailed examples from the poems. A general discussion will never reach the level of language present in the poems. In speaking of the last poem, "Planetarium," Rich says, "At last the woman in the poem and the woman writing the poem become the same person" (text p. 474). Students might look at the speakers in the poems to see what they say about the changes they see. Rich's statement that only in the last poem are the speaker and the poet the same is not obviously the case; there is something for students to work on here. Rich has set a problem for her readers, but it is not one she neatly solves.

It is probably best for them to work with the poems in context — to begin with the challenge the essay raises, to see the poems as illustrations of a poet's development or of a writer solving certain language problems. We would not invite students to begin their essays by working out the kinds of readings they may have learned to perform in an introduction-to-poetry course. Students should begin with the poems themselves, and then with the task of imagining a method (a way of talking about those poems) that is in keeping with the spirit of Rich's presentation of them.

3–4.   Both of these assignments were new to the second edition of *Ways of Reading*. Rich speaks powerfully about the need to turn criticism to the material of daily life, yet our original assignments kept students working with her essay solely as a textual problem. There were no assignments asking students to read their experience in Rich's terms. Some of our graduate students argued that we were avoiding the central, and difficult, questions raised by the text. While we hadn't chosen to avoid them, our students were right, and we set out to write additional assignments. We have used both of them over the last two years with considerable success.

Both assignments ask students to write from inside the "we" of Rich's discourse, to imagine that the essay is addressed to them. They take these as key phrases: "Until we can understand the assumptions in which we are drenched we cannot know ourselves" and "We need to know the writing of the past, and know it differently than we have ever known it; not to pass on a tradition but to break its hold over us."

Assignment 3 asks students to follow Rich's lead and to write autobiographically, not in celebration of their individuality but in order to cast themselves as representative of the way a certain group — named perhaps in terms of age, race, class, or gender — is positioned within the dominant culture. It asks them to use the occasion to try out some of Rich's key terms, like "revision" and "patriarchy." The difficulty students will have is in imagining their personal experience as representative of a collective one. You will, in other words, not get papers about the pressure of culture but about key individuals — fathers, mothers, teachers, lovers, grandparents, and coaches. In some ways this is inevitable. Both our students' age and the distinctly American versions of personal experience lead our students to write "frontier" stories, stories with no sense of the social, the political, or the historical. These are the concerns we highlight for revision: In what ways is this story more than your story? Where can we find the cultural context? In what ways are you, as a character, cast in relation to ways of speaking, habits of mind?

Assignment 4 asks students to imagine that the writing of the past is made up of more than a literary tradition, that it includes the practice of all writers, that it is handed down not only through Great Books but also through popular writing and lore, that its evidence can be found in the predictable features of students' own writing. Tradition is not just sonnet form; it is also topic sentence and book report. Students' success with this assignment will depend greatly on their ability and willingness to turn quickly to a close reading of actual examples, as Rich does with her poems. Students will need texts to work with. We have used this as a retrospective assignment, where students reflect over the work they have done over a semester, in our course and others, but we have also used it early in the term for students who have files containing old work. This assignment is an occasion for students to think about their own writing; it is also, however, an occasion for them to think about how writing has been represented to them by their culture and through their education. They hear, often for the first time, much of the emptiness of the usual talk about writing and they have a chance to reflect on whose interests are served in those representations of writing — where ideas are meant to be controlling ideas, where examples must support conclusions, where conclusions take us back to where we began.

We have found that students tend to avoid or overlook the final questions in their first draft. They devote their energy to a study of their own writing and do not step back and reflect on how or why, in their terms or Rich's, one would want to revise the writing of the past, to break its hold. This has been our primary concern when students revise the essay.

MAKING CONNECTIONS (p.479)

1. Both "A Room of One's Own" and "When We Dead Awaken" began as public lectures delivered to university audiences. Both have become classic texts. Both have become major statements in the development of a feminist critique of writing and culture. Our goal here, however, was to have students notice the differences — this, we believe, will lead them to a close analysis of both essays and to a more fine-grained account of the problems of writing and culture. There are many places for students to begin. Rich refers directly to Woolf — students could begin by "reading" her reading of Woolf. Both push against the stylistic limits of the genre — and both avoid the limitations of a "phallocentric" discourse. Students could begin by looking at the differences in the ways each essay revises the conventional genre. Or students could begin at the level of paraphrasable argument — how and why do Woolf's and Rich's accounts of the position and possibilities of women's writing differ?

One of the problems with the assignment is that it is too open-ended. You could forestall such problems by requiring students to work with a set number of passages from each text by rewording the assignment something like this: After rereading both essays, choose two examples from each text, four total, and use them to write an essay in which you discuss "When We Dead Awaken" as a demonstration of Rich's efforts to reread and rewrite the writing of the past.

This assignment is ambitious enough that students will benefit greatly from working through at least one draft under your supervision. They will get a paper started in the first draft that they can't completely imagine or control, and the goal of a revision should be to achieve increased control over the material. We realize that this is a problematic thing to say when students are invited to work against a patriarchal rhetoric, one that values understanding and control.

2. This is a different kind of assignment altogether. Rather than asking students to read one text *through* another, it asks them to compare and contrast. The material to be held together is a selection of two or three essays by feminist writers. The assignment pressures students to look for differences, and it does so in order to allow students a more complex sense of feminism than they would be allowed if they were invited to reduce all three to a single statement. If students look for similarities, they will tend to fold all three essays into a set of overriding issues and reduce the rich and difficult work of the feminist project to its lowest common denominator. It is better, then, for students to look for variation, to make fine distinctions, to see that Rich, Anzaldúa, Williams, and Willis could be making not only different arguments but different kinds of arguments. Finally, the assignment is the occasion for students to account for these differences, to think about the role of history, experience, and ideology in the construction of these positions. With the other "Making Connections" assignment, this one is ambitious enough that students will benefit from working through at least one draft with your help. The first draft may be the occasion for drawing the material together, the second for rethinking what to do with it.

RICHARD RODRIGUEZ

The Achievement of Desire (p. 480)

Part of the power of the Rodriguez essay in an undergraduate class is the way it allows students to frame, even invent, a problem in their own lives as students. Throughout *Hunger*

Hunger of Memory Rodriguez argues that his story is also everyone's story. It takes some work on the part of a teacher to make this connection work, however. Students will read Rodriguez with either sympathy (because he is an oppressed person) or annoyance ("What's he got to complain about — he got good grades, he went to a good school, he was offered a good job). But it is not at all uncommon to hear students claim that their situations are different: "Well you see, I'm not on a scholarship. I'm not a scholarship boy." It takes some teaching, then, to get students to imagine "scholarship boy," or "scholarship girl," as a metaphor representing a complex relationship between a student, his or her past, and school and teachers.

Those who praise Rodriguez's book often praise it in just these terms, by saying that Rodriguez's story is "everyone's" story, that he had identified a universal in human experience. This is a problematic reading of the text, since it erases the ethnic and class distinctions that could be used to explain and describe Rodriguez's position. Those who are not sympathetic to the book say that Rodriguez not only turns his back on his parents and his Hispanic roots, he writes a general justification for this act of turning away. (Note the two reviewers in the headnote.) If Rodriguez's story is everyone's story, then there is no reason to investigate the particular determinates of ethnicity and class in America. Rodriguez's conclusion to "The Achievement of Desire" reflects this thematic displacement of class. He talks about the tradition of pastoral: "The praise of the unlettered by the highly educated is one of the primary themes of 'elitist' literature." But the relationship of high to low, of Hispanic laborers to this graduate of Berkeley, is defined finally not in terms of an elitist culture but in terms of the difference between the "passionate and spontaneous" and the "reflective" life.

We need to find a way of enabling students to read the essay, as Rodriguez says he read Hoggart's *The Uses of Literacy*, to frame their experiences — as a tool, that is, to enable a certain form of analysis and understanding, both in the terms and metaphors it offers and in the example it provides of a process of self-examination. In graduate and under-graduate classes, this essay has inspired some of the best personal essays we have ever read.

Students read the essay to frame experience and as an example of the process of self-examination — we can use this claim to describe two approaches to the essay. We have had students write a kind of "framing" exercise for ten minutes or so at the beginning of a class. We have asked them to go to a phrase or a scene, to write it out and to use it as the starting point for a kind of reverie drawing on their own memories. The same opening move can function in discussion or in more formal writing assignments. The basic assumption is this: Something in this essay will grab you, and often for reasons you can't begin to describe; for us it is the phrase "middle-class pastoral," the story of the "hundred most important books of Western civilization," and the ambiguity of the final phrase "the end of education." One can begin here, in the manner of a preacher working from a text, to draw forward and shape (or "frame" — as in "frame" a house, "frame" a painting, and "I was framed") the recalled (or invented) stuff of one's own experience. This is a way of paying attention to the text — if not to its argument then to its richest moments — and of drawing a connection between it and oneself. It is also a Rodriguez-like thing to do.

We are also interested, as in the case of many of these essays, in having students turn to rich examples, like the story of the boy's reading program, and moving back and forth between their own and Rodriguez's ways of accounting for them. We want students to see Rodriguez's stories as open texts, but we also want them to feel the difference between his characteristic ways of interpreting those stories and their own.

Students as we have said, can read the essay as an example of a process of self-examination. We like to make this a minute, textual issue. One of the most characteristic features of Rodriguez's style, for example, is his use of parentheses. They are a sign of his desire to speak in two voices at once — what he might call a public and private voice — or to say contradictory things and mean both at the same time ("I wanted to be close to my parents, I wanted to push away from my parents"). If you ask about the characteristic features of Rodriguez's sentences, students will turn to the parentheses, or to the sentence fragments and the sentences that trail away to nothing. Once you gather together three or four examples, you can start a conversation about what they represent. Why are they there? What's the effect? What do they tell you about Rodriguez as a writer? about his skill? about the problems he has as a writer? We think the parentheses, in other words, are a method in miniature, a way of using language to shape experience. They provide a tool that Rodriguez uses over and over again. Our students begin relying on parentheses in the papers that follow their reading of Rodriguez.

We will give one more example of a close-up look at Rodriguez's method. Students generally have difficulty working quoted material into their own essays. On the one hand, this is a mechanical problem, and students have to learn about punctuation, ellipses, and the conventions of block quotation. But the concerns a writer faces in using someone else's words are not just mechanical ones. It is interesting to consider Rodriguez's use of Hoggart. He first quotes Hoggart on page 482, but we don't hear about Hoggart until page 483. Then, as you look at the block quotations, you find an interesting variation in the relationships between the words that are quoted and those that surround the quotations. There are occasions where the two become indistinct, as though Hoggart could speak for Rodriguez and Rodriguez for Hoggart. On other occasions, Rodriguez insists on a position beyond the quoted passages — a position from which he can claim his own authorship, that allows him to comment, to disagree, to put Hoggart into perspective. Since the essay is about the relationship between students and teachers, or about the relationship between mimicry, imitation, and identity, the small scene in which Rodriguez struggles to define his relationship to Hoggart's words represents a larger issue, in which Rodriguez struggles with his parents, his teachers, and the public world of middle-class, English-speaking America.

QUESTIONS FOR A SECOND READING (p. 500)

1. This essay is not ostensibly difficult, so students will not feel the need to reread to bring it generally under control. Our purpose for sending students back to the essay is to allow them to complicate matters. The purpose of this question is to have students read as though Rodriguez's story could serve as a means of framing their own experience, as though Rodriguez could stand to them as Hoggart does to Rodriguez. This is an invitation to call Rodriguez's bluff — to say, "Wait a minute" to his desire to place the burden of his sadness on all of us, to offer his story as everyone's story.

2. In the preface to *Hunger of Memory*, Rodriguez speaks about the double nature of his text: It is both essay and autobiography. He refers, in fact, to his refusal to grant his editor's wishes and make it more of a series of personal sketches (his editor has asked for more stories about Grandma). He refused because he felt he had an important argument to make — about education in general and about bilingual education in particular. This question asks students to reread the chapter in order to pay attention to the argument it contains both in the exposition ("His story makes clear that education is a long, unglamorous, even demeaning process — *a nurturing never natural to the person one was before one entered a classroom*") and in the arrangement of anecdotes and argument.

ASSIGNMENTS FOR WRITING (p. 501)

1. These assignments represent, in written exercises, the two concerns raised in the opening discussion. The second asks students to frame their story in Rodriguez's terms and style. This one asks them to turn Rodriguez's argument about education — about the relationship

between students and teachers — back on the essay by considering the relationship between Rodriguez and Hoggart as a case in point. The general question is this: Is Rodriguez still a scholarship boy? Is he still reading "in order to acquire a point of view"? The earlier general discussion explains why we send students to look at the use of quotations. There are other ways of talking about the relationship between these two men, but our concern is to make these problems textual problems — problems that hold lessons for readers and writers.

This can be a more complicated question than it appears, depending on how far you want to push it. Some students will argue that Rodriguez is still a blinkered pony. Some will take his argument on its own terms and argue that he rejects Hoggart in the end for being "more accurate than fair" to the scholarship boy. There is the larger question of Rodriguez's use of Hoggart's book *The Uses of Literacy*, a book about the class system which strives to speak in the general and not to sentimentalize individual stories. It is possible, if you and your students have the time, to send students to Hoggart's book in order to construct a more complicated and comprehensive account of this reading.

2. Here, students are asked to reinvest their own lives by framing their stories in Rodriguez's terms. It becomes a more powerful exercise if students try to do it in Rodriguez's style. As an opening exercise, they might write out a paragraph of his, using the shape of his sentences but filling in the names and details from their own experience. There is no reason, however, why students cannot write a personal essay that is more loosely suggested by Rodriguez's. They might lay a Rodriguez-like commentary over it, or include one with it.

The revision process will differ in each case. If students are concerned first with telling their own stories and then in speaking of them in Rodriguez's terms, then that commentary may be the focus of revision. If the essay is more completely a stylistic revision, then we would reverse the emphasis. The first thing students want to attend to is the form that will enable the writing — sentences and paragraphs and the relationship of anecdote to commentary. Then, in revision, they can best attend to the richness and detail of their own stories. As Scholes says about autobiography, the tension is between beauty and truth. You want to shape a story but also to honor the details of memory and investigation. In the revision we would ask students to try to honor the truth of the stories they are telling.

3. Essentially, this is an assignment that asks students to locate and characterize Rodriguez's methods, his "ways of speaking and caring," his ways, that is, of presenting and valuing what he presents. He's making an argument about being a scholarship boy and, finally, about the differences between the reflective and the "passionate and spontaneous" life. Students need to consider how he presents his arguments, his materials (Hoggart, his recollections, and so on), and how he thinks through them on the page. They need, too, to name and characterize the ways he "speaks" and to figure out what it is he cares about now, in this text, and what he cared about during the various stages of his education. What can he do now, in writing and in his thinking, that he says he couldn't do earlier, in other moments of his evolution into a "speaking and caring" guy?

MAKING CONNECTIONS (p. 502)

1. Freire spent much of his life teaching peasants. There are many reasons why Rodriguez should not be considered a peasant. But Freire also speaks generally about the relationship between students and teachers and the way that that relationship determines the nature and status of knowledge in the classroom. At first glance, Rodriguez seems to offer both a perfect example of oppression (an ape and a mimic) and, in his success, an example of the conservative counterpoint to Freire's plan for a democratized education. If students can work out a Freirian critique of Rodriguez in such black-and-white terms, we are not sure that they are violating the spirit of Freire's project. We are not convinced, however, that Rodriguez can so easily be labeled a conservative and Freire a liberal, or that Rodriguez as a child received

little more than deposits from his teachers. And we would want to push against students' attempts to organize their essays in such set terms.

2. Stanley Fish, in his stories of the poetry class and of Mr. Newlin's raised hand, offers a counterpoint to Rodriguez's early stories about imitation and his desire to be like his teachers. Perhaps counterpoint is too strong a word. Both offer representative anecdotes calling into question the relationship between individual motive and convention in the process of education. It is tempting to simply ask students to consider, at a general level, how Fish and Rodriguez define and value imitation, but the power of both essays lies in the ways the narratives complicate the general argument. For Fish, the complication is represented in a specialized discourse — he locates his examples in current debates over issues in literary criticism and textual interpretation. Rodriguez speaks to a more general audience.

There are two ways to push this assignment. If Fish's student is taken to be a figure for Fish, if the student can speak the terms of Fish's argument, then the job for the writer is to read Rodriguez's story (or one or two characteristic moments) in Fish's terms. The account the student would give Rodriguez, then, would be Fish's account. And, as a next step, the writer would have to imagine Rodriguez's reply. Rodriguez, it is worth reminding the class, was also an English teacher, so he could be expected to hold his own here.

It is also possible to imagine that the student in the assignment is a more naive participant in Fish's class. He had that experience in Fish's classroom, but he could not begin to speak of it in Fish's terms — he was in the class, that is, but he did not read "How to Recognize a Poem When You See One." That will make his account of Rodriguez and Rodriguez's response quite different. In this case, both could be imagined to be trying to figure out how to think about what went on.

GLORIA STEINEM

Ruth's Song (Because She Could Not Sing It) (p. 504)

This moving essay is a good example of powerful political writing based on personal experience. Steinem tells a number of stories about her mother, Ruth, stories that represent Ruth as a child might have seen her, stories about her schooling, her career, her marriage, and her nervous breakdowns. When Steinem puts the stories together to try to understand what might have transformed her mother from an energetic, independent, intelligent person into a dependent, fearful, bewildered one, she puts the responsibility for Ruth's transformation on "the formidable forces arrayed against her," and claims that they are as much to blame as any purely personal or accidental causes.

One of the best aspects of this essay is its openness, its accessibility to readers and its invitations to interpretation. It's not a difficult selection, but it lends itself to deeper digging, because Steinem doesn't wrap it all up. She introduces the "formidable forces" her mother had to face — being a woman in a man's world, having no status, being looked down on by male family members — but leaves implicit many of the explanations as to their effects on her mother.

QUESTIONS FOR A SECOND READING (p. 520)

1. This is a straightforward assignment. Students will need to reread the essay to locate the passages where Steinem tells stories about her mother. She tells two different sets of stories, one near the beginning of the essay and the other toward the later part of it, and each set represents her mother differently. In the early stories, Ruth isn't visible to Steinem; although

Ruth struggles with work, family, and her relationship with Steinem, Steinem doesn't see her mother as a person intimately connected to her. In the later stories, Ruth comes forward as a person constantly pressing against oppressive forces, including her own family.

Once students have found the stories, they should use them to discuss how they present Ruth. Press students to discuss the changes in Steinem's image of her mother from the early stories to the later ones. They'll most likely try to reduce her to a few stereotypes, e.g., the woman who went crazy, the feminist. You'll have to counter these tendencies by pushing students back to the specific stories, and then to their interpretations of what each says about Ruth and Steinem's image of her at the time.

2. Students will need to do two or three rereadings of the section of the essay that deals with the absence of Ruth's husband and ends with the death of her dog. It's elusive, and you'll want to ask them to discuss certain aspects of the section, like Ruth's reactions to her husband's absence and what those readings say about her feelings and her attempts to deal with the state of her life. You might ask students to find those parts of the episode that point to the forces arrayed against Ruth, e.g., loneliness and powerlessness, and ask them to say how she tried to fight them, how she tried to save herself. Finally, they should turn to the episode with the dog and ask themselves what this represents to Steinem. How does Steinem read it, coming as it does at the end of her mother's fight to save herself?

ASSIGNMENTS FOR WRITING (p. 520)

1. This assignment doesn't give students very much help in thinking about the forces Steinem regards as responsible for her mother's transformation. You'll need either to work with some prewriting questions to get students to locate and think about moments in the essay that represent those forces, or to use this assignment in conjunction with or following the two "Questions for a Second Reading." Students will have to spend a considerable amount of time rereading the essay and paying particular attention to those moments in it that represent, for Steinem, the forces arrayed against Steinem's mother. The individual stories that Steinem tells about Ruth are good places for students to begin. They might reread them, noting the kinds of things Ruth was up against. What is she struggling with? Students will find personal and accidental things in answer to this question, but there will be others that don't fit, that seem beyond or bigger than personal, e.g., the male family members' attitudes toward women and, especially, toward women with problems.

When students have located these moments that point to the forces arrayed against Ruth, they're ready to write, but they also need to consider how Ruth changed. What was her transformation? What are the differences in the essay's early portrayal of Ruth and its later portrayal? How do the stories Steinem tells about Ruth point to Ruth's transformation, to the effects of the forces on her? You might also anticipate having to ask these questions of students' papers when they revise, but they are questions that they should hold in mind as they write.

2. This assignment asks students to look at the effects of Ruth's life and Steinem's understanding of it on Steinem. Students will have to work with the stories Steinem tells about her mother, so you might consider using this assignment as a follow-up to the "Questions for a Second Reading." If you don't, you'll want to spend some time in prewriting discussions of the stories Steinem tells and what they say about the forces arrayed against Ruth and Steinem's reaction to those forces.

For students the key to this assignment will be using the stories Steinem tells as ways of looking at Steinem herself. When they reread, they'll need to pay attention to Steinem's reaction to her mother's situations, both as she relates them in the story and as she comments on them as a writer reconstructing the past. As students work with each story, writing notes for their first drafts, you might ask them to make that distinction. What, they could ask

103

themselves, did Steinem think of her mother's situation as it was happening, and what does she think of it — and her initial response to it — now as she's writing about it?

You might anticipate that your questions for revision will follow these same lines. Students will want to pick a general reading of Steinem's reactions, like "She didn't know what was going on then but now she does," and run with it. You should press them back into the stories to say, for example, what she thought then, as the story offers it, and what she thinks now, as she offers it in the essay.

3. This assignment is an invitation to give Steinem a less generous reading, to read against the grain. This is difficult, as Steinem's work is about deeply felt personal experience and its presentation is marked by the trope of the "sincere." It seems somehow a betrayal to ask questions about the conventionality or predictability of the narrative. Yet the seriousness of the material — one's relationship to one's parents — is exactly why one should think about the text as a text, why one should investigate the discourse that governs our understanding of the relationship between children and parents.

MAKING CONNECTIONS (p. 521)

1. Ellie Graziano interests students, and once they have the opportunity to discuss her and Ted, they can turn to this retelling of Ellie's story through Steinem's eyes, especially as she might imagine the people and situations of Ellie's life in terms of forces arrayed against her. As usual, students will want to work from particular moments in the interview, and they'll need to weave a narrative retelling of those moments into their Steinemesque reading of Ellie, so one could imagine this being a lengthy paper with two or three elaborated "stories" from the interview, along with extensive commentary that makes claims for these forces arrayed against or influencing Ellie.

2. Students are asked to work with Steinem's essay and either Walker's or Rodriguez's for this assignment. They're invited to see each writer in the context of his or her re-creation and explanation of the past, to examine his or her treatment of subjects and methods. Once students have read Rodriguez's and Walker's essays, they should decide which one they want to work with. When that's done, they can begin locating the authors' stories, the anecdotes and episodes that serve as occasions for recalling and commenting on the past. Students should pay attention to how the authors treat those stories. Do they, like Steinem, use them to show change and transformation? If they do, what episodes do they use that might be said to be like the specific ones Steinem uses? How are they different?

You'll want to help students decide what they're going to look for as they reread both of the essays, so you might anticipate using prewriting questions like the ones above to suggest directions. Other ways into the essay might come from students looking at how each author portrays the forces affecting his or her subjects. Rodriguez discusses family, his obsession with success; Walker discusses racial oppression and the treatment of black women. How, students might ask themselves, are their authors' subjects, their concerns, and their treatments of them different? What moments in the essays can they use to point to and explain those differences?

You'll also want to draw students' attention to the writing differences in the essays they're working with. They could begin those passages they think best represent the voices of the writers. They might ask themselves who is speaking, and how he or she treats the subject and the reader. What kind of attitude toward the subject, the reader, and himself or herself comes through in those passages? They might also look at the sentences and paragraphs and organization of the selections. How are they different? Finally, you'll want to ask them to consider, perhaps in the last sections of their papers, what might account for these differences. They'll want to say that the differences exist because the writers are different people, but you'll want to push them back to the text and ask them what the text points to as possible explanations of the differences, e.g., do their different concerns, subjects, and voices create differences separate from issues of personality?

As with all assignments like this, the difficulty is in enabling students to realize that criticism is not sniping or name-calling. The way to prepare students for this essay is to have them reread what Steinem has written, to look for the ways in which it conforms to the familiar story — whose broadest outlines can be seen in TV dramas or greeting-card sentiments — and where it seems that she is laboring to revise, or, in Rich's terms, to break the hold of, those forms and sentiments. One question we don't ask in this assignment, but which you may want to add, is how students see their work mirrored in Steinem's — "What does her example have to do with you and your work as a student in a writing class?"

For revision: You will most likely need to turn students' attention toward articulating the concerns that justify their criticism. Students will spend their time and energy outlining and describing the predictable and unpredictable sections in Steinem's text; they will not spend as much time asking "Why does she do this?" or "Why does it matter?"

KLAUS THEWELEIT

Male Bodies and the "White Terror" (p. 523)

Our students were amazed by this selection from Theweleit's two-volume work, *Male Fantasies*, and we had a great three weeks working with the reading. We studied it in a sequence of readings that placed it between Michel Foucault's "The Body of the Condemned" and Susan Willis's "Work(ing) Out," but it can certainly stand on its own or be taught along with a number of other selections. When we used it in the Foucault-Theweleit-Willis sequence, it stood as a way of introducing students to what we took to calling "associative" or "juxtaposed" writing, as opposed to the carefully developed, logically argued essay that pays attention to such things as transitions and explications of quotations. Because it ignores such conventions of the traditional academic essay, it at once offers students an alternative way to write and a way to see suddenly, in sharp contrast, the conventional moves of traditional essays. In addition to its usefulness as a demonstration of a particular kind of writing, the selection offers students a powerful way of understanding how one thing — discipline and training — can be thought of as representing something else — the transformation of sexual desires.

Oddly enough, this was not a difficult selection for our students. Even though it's long, the reading held their attention for three weeks' worth of work in discussion and writing. At least half of our students went out of their way to give the text to friends or family to read as an example of the unusual stuff they were doing in General Writing. And although most students thought that Theweleit's notions of sexuality and drill, reconstructing bodies through discipline, and the creation of totality machines were new, they didn't have trouble understanding his arguments, and they enjoyed his humor and his associative writing. We often heard them leaving class or milling around in the hallway repeating, rapping, and parodying quotations that Theweleit had unearthed. One of their favorites, one that they took to parodying in rap, was "I leave tomorrow for the front, to enjoy the embrace of burning grenades, the crackling kiss of gunfire under the ardent eyes of airplanes." They saw a frightening absurdity in the reality of these words, and they were quick to make connections to heavy metal music lyrics and rap.

Our students approached the selection from three angles. First they read it to restate Theweleit's arguments about discipline and drill representing a transformation of sexual desires into militaristic desires; next they read it from a perspective that asked them to study the relationships between the disciplined and the disciplining powers (i.e., the individuals with authority, the military as a machine, the totality culture designed to produce war) responsible for that disciplining; then they approached it as a frame to test Theweleit's notions of the transformation of sexual desires against their experiences with such things as the preparation of boys for athletics, leadership positions, and schooling that might be read the same way, as transformations of sexual desires into other desires. When we worked with Theweleit's arguments for the transformation of sexual desires into other desires, we studied the metaphors that he presents in the quotations he uses from various texts and his own metaphors for transformations. Students were quick to pick up on the metaphors, and not surprisingly, it made sense to most of them, although some preferred to see the emphasis on sexuality as a metaphor for understanding training and war as too overreaching, arguing against the grain of the selection that masochistic violence, as a sickness of the soul, not the transformation of sexual desires, is the propelling force at work in the training and fighting. The illustrations accompany the selection help bolster Theweleit's arguments (and his associative style of working) and, interestingly enough, the arguments for masochistic violence, so it's important to allow students to attend to those as an essential aspect of their readings of Theweleit's arguments and methods.

QUESTIONS FOR A SECOND READING (p. 579)

1. This question aims to turn students' attention to the means that Theweleit uncovers or presents by which young boys are made or changed into soldiers. It's not a difficult task, the means are pretty visible, but you'll want to be sure that students work both from Theweleit's prose and the elaborate sets of quotations that he works from. When we used this question for a discussion with our students, the class ended up focusing on what was being done to the boys and what the boys did or the role they played. This take is interesting, because, as a number of students argued, there were no innocents (except maybe the recruits who refused to play along and left training in disgrace) in this military preparation. We would use this question again, no matter what writing assignments we decided to work with, as a way of getting students accustomed to a close reading of a text and its sources, and as a way of asking students to reproduce Theweleit's complex account of the training. The question begs a sort of summary, for purposes other than summarizing, without making it seem as if it's possible to wrap up a selection like this in a four- or five-page essay.

2. This is one of our favorite types of assignment for students, because it introduces them to a way of performing a critical reading using the text's terms, its metaphors. Metaphors powerfully reveal texts' predispositions, explanations, and messages. The important move for this discussion which you could easily turn into a writing assignment (as we did), is to press students to read the metaphors for what they reveal and hide. If, for instance, a recruit is a "sack," a thing for filling up, a thing to be carried around, what else might he be that the term "sack" doesn't capture or allow? A sack, as one student said, is a thing; the recruit is then not a person. A sack is a container, so it doesn't have emotions. It's empty to begin with, so it doesn't bring anything to its filling up, its training. Students can carry over this kind of move — working back and forth between what's revealed and what's concealed by the metaphors — into other readings and become quite good at over the course of a semester.

3. Theweleit can stand accused of being his own totality machine, a prose machine bent on one course — making one case, with all its attendant arguments — just as he claims that militaristic training produces one kind of man, one kind of soldier. How does Theweleit work? That's the question this assignment probes. What are his methods? One way into this task is to ask students to look at the kinds of materials he presents. How would they characterize them? Are there any deviations? Is there any room for multiple views on recruits' daily routines, for instance, or on their reactions to the training? When there are deviations within the training that affect recruits, how does Theweleit present or explain

them? We view this task also as an occasion for students to study the way Theweleit writes. How does he use his evidence? What passages can students use to defend or critique Theweleit as a writer with or without an agenda that does or doesn't allow for multiple points of view? The case can probably be made that the text is a monomaniacal piece of writing that sidesteps inconsistencies, contradictions, and paradoxes. To pursue this kind of reading, students would need to locate in the text such inconsistencies, contradictions and paradoxes, as well as oversights or sleights of hand where Theweleit seems to ignore alternative explanations in favor of his agenda.

4. The relation of image to text in this selection is clearly purposeful. Students might be asked to consider if their placement is also purposeful; do they bear on the passages they appear with, or do they have an agenda that plays into the text in other ways? If, for instance, students read the images as a sequence aside from the text, what's their story? Is it linear and unfolding? Or is another way of telling a story at work here? If so, what, might it be? How would they characterize the methods of the images' story (stories) as opposed to the methods of the prose story (stories)? This task also clearly provides the opportunity to push the reading of images into current cultural artifacts, like comic books, and to ask students what are the similarities and differences between this imagistic story's methods and those of, say, comic books.

ASSIGNMENTS FOR WRITING (p. 580)

1. This assignment allows students to conduct their own research on a set of texts, as Theweleit does on the written records of the Freikorps, and to test Theweleit's notion that the preparation of young boys (in this case for life as males in the USA) can be referenced to sexual desire and to the ways in which that desire is absorbed, translated, and distorted by preparation or training into the desires, imaginings, and practices of whatever the training or preparation is for — sports, leadership, computer skills, life on the block, manhood (whatever that might be). There are two key moves for students in this assignment. The first is identifying a body or set of texts that can be read as Theweleit reads his sources, that is, a set of texts that deal with the training or preparation of young boys to be something. The second is reading the preparation or training in terms of sexual desire and its implications according to Theweleit. Students don't have to hold this kind of reading to be true or even useful. The point, rather, is that this is a typical academic move, and the Theweleit expression of it is a particularly visible way of enacting a reading where one element — training or preparation — can be read as another — the translation of sexual desire.

2. The reading of metaphors is a critical tool for students to master. This assignment asks them to look particularly at the machine metaphors, the ones that Theweleit aligns with fascism. Students first need to locate examples of these metaphors in the text, then to consider whether Theweleit uses his examples to present the pleasures as well as the dangers of the "totality machine," and, finally, to consider what Theweleit puts in opposition to the "totality machine" and the fascism it represents. Once students grasp the stages of the task here, they'll find the last task the most difficult, because although Theweleit does allude to "the desiring machine, whose principles — 'the joys of roving unrestrained'" stand as the "antithesis" of the machinery, the references in the text to this opposition are scarce. Students will have to speculate, given all the negative examples, as to what the antithesis of the "totality machine" and fascism might be. Even when they locate the few sentences that bring forward the notion of an antithesis, they'll discover that Theweleit's discussion of this is spare, and they'll have to speculate, again, as to what he might mean by such a thing as "the desiring machine" whose principle is "the joys of roving unrestrained."

3. Here, as with other assignments for this selection, students will benefit from paying attention to Theweleit's metaphors. Once they have located a three- to five-page section of the text as a representative example of Theweleit's methods, they can read his metaphors as an initial

step in their work. What are his metaphors? How do they reveal him as an agent working on textual materials? What metaphors does Theweleit use for him working? For the materials he's working on? For the reasons he's doing it all? Students must also consider how he gathers his materials. How does he think them through? And where might he get his authority? Or, better yet, how does he create himself as an authority? What is it about his work, about what he does, that makes him seem smart? an authority? a guy with the right to do the kind of research and commenting that he does? What characterizes his research and commenting? in-depth analyses? readings from a particular perspective? from multiple perspectives? Students can consider here, too, how Theweleit positions or creates his readers. What work does he allow his readers? How do students think he imagines his readers? What, according to them, does he think they know and believe?

MAKING CONNECTIONS (p. 581)

1. This assignment is an excellent follow-up to the third writing assignment above, in which students study Theweleit's methods of work by focusing on his metaphors. This assignment extends the previous one, but here the task of reading has a different spin — students are asked to study how Theweleit and Wideman present and understand the process involved in the production of men or "the male." Students can make excellent use of the methods they used in the third writing assignment to read the process of producing the male in both the Theweleit and Wideman texts. Here, as always, it's a good idea to ask students to work on each text separately before taking on any or most of the Connections questions. They'll want to discuss and write about each text before bringing them together for this assignment; which you can easily turn this into three or four weeks' worth of discussion and writing (including multiple drafts of the various assignments) by working with the two selections individually and then together for this very smart, sophisticated assignment.

2. Using Theweleit along with Willis gives students a very useful contrastive reading. Willis reads the workout and a TV show for how they present the creation of "woman," and she uses similar production metaphors for understanding how women are turned into objects for consumption. We used this assignment with our students along with work on Foucault and Theweleit, and they had a great time with it. A number of students read Theweleit and Willis through Foucault's notions of body-power-knowledge relations, others used either Theweleit or Willis as the grounding frame to read the other. Willis's consumption metaphors were particularly attractive to students who saw the young recruits in Theweleit's selection as being "eaten up," as they put it, by the war machine, rather than being turned into "totality machines" desiring destruction and sexual release through such things as blackouts, pain, and violence. In other words, students can work back and forth in a number of ways with these two selections, and this assignment can nicely serve as the final piece of work students do after they read Foucault, Theweleit, and Willis or after they work with only Theweleit and Willis individually.

JANE TOMPKINS

"Indians": Textualism, Morality, and the Problem of History (p. 583)

Jane Tompkins's essay, "Indians," is a wonderful opportunity for students to look behind the scenes of academic life. The essay is surprising and engaging, and it offers a powerful corrective to notions of what "research" is all about. It offers an alternative to the story told all too often in the textbooks, where research is a fairly mechanical matter of going to the library, finding books, pulling "facts" or "truths" out of those books, and then fussing over organization and footnotes.

The story Tompkins tells is one of reading and writing, of research as it involves the process of interpretation, as it questions truths that appear to be self-evident. Our students have taken great pleasure in this essay's style and its willingness to show that scholarship engages a person, that it is neither a dispassionate nor an impersonal matter. In a sense, it is the character that emerges in this essay — this "Jane Tompkins" — that students find most memorable. They are either confused or disappointed by the conclusion ("Is that all this was leading to?"), but they love to imagine that they have seen into real lives.

There is a powerful lesson for students in this essay, one whose consequences they can feel in a way they don't when they read Brodkey, for example. The lesson comes in the way Tompkins represents a proper relationship to books. Students may have been told that they need to read their sources critically, but they have a hard time imagining what that means. They believe, most often, that they have to catch the author in an error or a logical fallacy. Tompkins demonstrates that reading critically is a matter of working out a book's point of view and imagining the consequences of it — what it inevitably notices and what it inevitably misses. When students write about this essay in retrospect, they return to this theme again and again — how Tompkins shows them something about books and the library (and their possible relations to books and the library) that they had never understood. They had believed that you went to the library to find the truth and that the truth lay in either the biggest or the most recent book on the shelf.

The essay presents few difficulties for students. They need, as we say in the "Questions for a Second Reading," to work out the conclusion and its importance to its audience, if only as a way of imagining such an audience. We decided it was best to finesse the reference to poststructuralism. In the fourth paragraph Tompkins says, "This essay enacts a particular instance of the challenge poststructuralism poses to the study of history." We felt a lecture on poststructuralism would put students in an impossible relationship to the text, particularly since Tompkins says the essay enacts an instance of this challenge. We decided to go at this inductively. After students had read the essay, we asked what they thought this word might mean, what this challenge might be — who would feel it as a challenge, and why. In many ways the discussion could best begin with the title — by asking why "Indians" was in quotation marks, what morality had to do with library research, and why and how history might be imagined as a problem.

QUESTIONS FOR A SECOND READING (p. 602)

1. In *Lives on the Boundary*, Mike Rose talks about how students are so often excluded from the work we present them because that work presumes a familiarity with a conversation that has been going on for some time. It is hard to jump into an academic controversy. The first of the questions asks students to imagine Tompkins's immediate audience, to piece together the rituals and assumptions that bind the members of this tribe, those who find themselves in what Tompkins refers to as the "academic situation." The questions are designed to prepare students to make sense of the conclusion. It would be misleading, and somewhat dangerous, if students were to see only Tompkins's growing sense of the "situatedness" of her sources, and to conclude, "Oh, I get it. It's all just a matter of personal opinion."

2. The questions here are meant to give students a way of stepping out of the narrative and asking questions of Tompkins's work. We are taken with the way the essay makes connections between lives lived inside and outside the library. Tompkins says that the essay replicates her childhood encounter with Indians. It seems to us important to ask how this also might *not* be true, particularly since all of the "naive" historians are implicated in similar "narcissistic fantasies of freedom and adventure." It is also worth asking questions about the *process* of research as represented here, where misconceptions are peeled away, one after the other, in careful order. Finally, we have found it useful to ask students to imagine alternate readings to the long passages Tompkins cites, particularly those on text pages 592–596.

ASSIGNMENTS FOR WRITING (p. 603)

1. This assignment is similar to several in *Ways of Reading*. It asks students to locate in their own work what Tompkins identifies as the problems of reading and writing. These assignments serve a dual purpose. They are an invitation for students to imagine that they are a real audience, not just naive observers. The assignments ask students to imagine themselves a part of the "we" of this essay. And an assignment like this is, in miniature, a course of instruction; it gives students a model or a scheme they can use to systematically review and assess their own work. It allows students to name what they have learned to do, to identify it as a stage or one method among several and it puts students in a position to push off in a new direction. If students write the first of the two essays, it is imperative that they have a body of work to review and quote. They will need a file of papers, either a high school term paper or work they have done or are doing in college. If they work only from memory, the essay will lose its bite; it is simply too easy to be the hero or the victim in a narrative invented of whole cloth. If students are investigating a textual problem, they will need to work from passages from books they read or from papers they wrote. They do not, of course, need to tell the same story as Tompkins — most likely such a story would be impossible. It is a rare student who has learned to reread one of his or her sources. The essay can be the occasion, however, for students to look at how they used sources, to imagine why, and to imagine how those sources might be reread.

    The second option allows students to imagine that the problem Tompkins alludes to is not literally a textual problem — that it does not necessarily involve one's work with books. It says, in effect, treat your memories — your past conversations, your ways of understanding things, the tropes and figures that dominate (or dominated) your way of thinking and speaking — as text. Imagine that they are situated and that they situate you. Ask questions about point of view, about implication and origin.

2. Students write this essay with considerable pleasure. It allows them to imagine themselves as insiders to the routines and the secrets of academic life. They can imagine that they have more to offer new students than survival knowledge, that they can help introduce them to the systems that govern work in the academy. Students feel empowered by this position and they write with energy and verve. The problem for us has been that students tend to lose sight of Tompkins and what she says about the problems of research. We find that we need to turn students back to the text, but this is perhaps best done after students have written a draft in response to their own desires.

MAKING CONNECTIONS (p. 604)

1. This assignment is similar to the first of the "Assignments for Writing." It asks students to adapt Tompkins's relationship to her sources and to use it as a way of rereading two of the essays in *Ways of Reading*. Students will not be able to develop as detailed a sense of context as Tompkins, but they can imagine that they are trying to tell the story of something by using two sources from the textbook and that their job is to read their sources as Tompkins reads hers — as ways of speaking, as representative points of view. We suggest Woolf and Rich, since there is a historical difference here that students might find suggestive, and because Rich offers her own reading of Woolf. Students might also work with Woolf and Walker, Fish and Freire, Percy and Geertz, or Rodriguez and Oates. It's not hard to put the pieces together and imagine that they define a project, an investigation into a single subject. Students will need to spend some time working with "Indians" to follow Tompkins's example in working with their texts.

2. We worry that this assignment, phrased as it is, is deceptively simple. It asks students to compare Tompkins's and Kuhn's representations of the production and distribution of knowledge, and invites them to do this in the name of the broader distinction, the difference

between the practice of science and the practice of social science. These are powerful and important generalizations, and there is every reason for students to be invited to work with them. They should be sure, however, to work *very* closely from the texts of the two essays. They will be comparing Tompkins's account and Kuhn's account, not whatever comes to mind about history and science. If students work from the text, from Kuhn's and Tompkins's accounts of how an individual works inside of communal ways of thinking, this essay will be a difficult one to write, one that deserves time for revision. If they don't work closely with Kuhn and Tompkins, their essays will be easy to write and, most likely, not worth revising.

3. This essay is similar to #2, although not deceptively simple. We have used several assignments asking students to consider Wideman as an expert, to see his methods of inquiry alongside Kuhn's and Geertz's or, in this case, Tompkins's. In retrospect, we're not completely happy with the last sentence of this assignment — it is important, we think, to name the distinction between Tompkins and Wideman, but the phrase "creative writer" is so overused and misused that it is likely to create more problems for students than it will solve. You might want to warn them that they should be working very closely with Wideman's text, particularly with what he says about writing and with what he *does* as a writer, in order to give quite precise definition to the kind of writer he is and how he differs from Tompkins. Both could be called "creative writers"; both could be said to be something else. Students need to feel the pressure to create a working vocabulary here. They should not assume that this tired phrase carries all of its explanations. Beyond this caveat, the work with this assignment is similar to the work in assignment 2 above. It is important that students work closely with the text, with the problems of writing as they are represented in Wideman and Tompkins's work. If their papers deal only in commonplaces, in generalizations that are true whether one looks at Wideman and Tompkins or not, then they are likely to be a disappointment.

ALICE WALKER

In Search of Our Mothers' Gardens (p. 606)

This essay is especially interesting for the way in which Walker develops her notion of "contrary instincts" or conflicting feelings — those feelings or intuitions that rub against socially appropriate behaviors. She points to her mother as a person who felt bound to maintain the status quo as a black woman in a white world but who, at the same time, felt compelled to express herself as a black woman with her own creative instincts. Walker also points to Phillis Wheatley, a slave in the 1700s, whose loyalties were so divided by contrary instincts that, when she struggled to write, she ended up praising her oppressors. Walker calls her situation "cruelly humorous," and the irony in Wheatley's "singing," as Walker calls it, about freedom and liberty is visible and painful.

QUESTIONS FOR A SECOND READING (p. 615)

1. To work with this problem students have to reread Walker to locate those moments in her essay where she discusses "contrary instincts." Once they've done that, they need to go on to say what contrary instincts are. When they've dealt with the definitions offered by Walker, they need to turn to her discussion of Phillis Wheatley, specifically to those passages where Walker explains why she thinks Wheatley was able to praise her oppressors while writing about such things as freedom and liberty. A key question for students has to do with the answers to the Wheatley question that the essay makes possible. Walker offers her notion of contrary instincts as a possible answer, and, if students address it, they'll need to refer to the passages that allow them to explain how contrary instincts might account for Wheatley's

111

behavior. She offers possibilities of other answers, e.g., that the irony of the situation wasn't visible to Wheatley, that Wheatley felt genuine warmth toward her mistress, who treated her well. Students will have to be pressed to find the moments when Walker alludes to such other explanations, and then they'll need to cast their readings of her into their own language.

2. For this discussion, students will undoubtedly need to do some library research to locate works by and references to the artists, black and white, so that they can look for commonalities (and differences) among the artists to whom Walker alludes in her essay. It's difficult to say what names students will recognize, but it's almost certainly the case that they won't know much about their works or their lives and the circumstances of their creativity. You might consider taking this opportunity to introduce students to the works of these artists by asking them to read both a selection and biographical information about a number of them; alternatively, students could work in groups to conduct this research. When you ask students in discussion what they make of these artists being listed together, you'll want them to consider the subjects of their works, the conditions of their creativity and lives, and the heritages they represent. Students will also need to read the Walker essay closely to study how she uses and refers to these artists. What purpose do they serve for her? What do they represent for her?

3. To do justice to Walker's seriousness and individuality, students will need to locate passages in the essay that address or allude to her feelings about her mother, herself, and the pressures on blacks living in a predominantly white culture. Once they've found the passages they want to use, they'll need to make something of them, to say what they reveal about Alice Walker and her feelings about her mother, herself, and the pressures on blacks. They might also address the question of Walker's voice. What's her attitude, in each specific passage, towards her subject, herself, and her readers? How might you characterize her tone? Is she angry? reconciled? resentful? pleased? Do the passages point to contradictions or ambivalences? Are there places or moments in the essay where she talks about reconciliation, for instance, in an angry or hurt voice?

ASSIGNMENTS FOR WRITING (p. 616)

1. This is a wonderful assignment for drawing students' attention to Walker's essay as a creative project. It's unusual for students to think of essays as creative projects (their schooling in genres almost always defines "creative writing" as stories and poems and then includes essays among all other writing). This assignment gives them the opportunity to study how Walker uses the texts of the past, including Wheatley's and Woolf's, within her own project. Students will need, of course, to define Walker's project and what it allows her to know or learn about herself, the spirit of African-American women, and her own mother. Within the context of defining her project, they need to consider how she reconceived, or rewrote, the texts from their original sources or contexts to serve her project. They'll need to ask themselves, for instance, how the Wheatley work existed, what position it held — or what were its purposes — when Wheatley wrote it. The same kinds of questions will be helpful to students when they study Walker's use of Woolf's term, "contrary instincts"; and it would be useful for students to turn to "A Room of One's Own" to study Woolf's use of the term before drawing conclusions about how Walker uses it and makes it a part of her project. How did Woolf originally use the term? for what purposes? for what audiences? How is Walker's use different from Woolf's? for what purposes? for what audiences? Walker's use of her mother's work is also an important part of her reconceiving of other peoples' projects. You'll want to draw students' attention to this, because they'll likely to see it as so integral to the piece that they may overlook it as a "rewritten" source. Again, students should consider how Walker uses her mother's creativity. What were the purposes of, and audiences for, her mother's work? How does Walker reconceive those purposes and audiences for her own project?

2. Walker's essay includes references to many examples of women who expressed creativity in the face of oppression — Bessie Smith, Roberta Flack, Phillis Wheatley, Zora Neale Hurston, Virginia Woolf, her mother, and, of course, herself. Students won't be familiar with all of these artists, and even if they recognize names, they'll need to do some research to fill in for themselves the nature of their works and lives. Once they've done this research, they'll be in a better position to understand what these references stand for and mean to Walker. They'll then need to consider how Walker uses these references and what they allow her to imagine in her argument. What would she not be able to do if she didn't refer to these other artists, including her mother? How are these references related to the issues she raises? How does she connect or draw together this "evidence" from the past? Walker's use of these artists is an important method, especially given that she reconceives them and their works, and students will need some help understanding this. They'll also need help directing their attention to how Walker understands her audience. To whom does she seem to be writing? What methods of hers might be said to represent her consideration of audience? These issues — Walker's rewriting of the past and her consideration of audience — can usually be presented to students in discussions of their drafts, while subsequent revisions can reflect added considerations. Making these kinds of references and suggestions is a tricky business, though, because you'll want students to invent their own terms and names for what Walker does, and you'll want to be careful to let them imagine how Walker works with artists from the past rather than, say, telling them that she reconceives or rewrites them.

MAKING CONNECTIONS (p. 617)

1. If students haven't already dealt with the issue of contrary instincts in the Walker selection, you might turn to the first of the "Questions for a Second Reading" and use that as a way to get them into it. They'll need to discuss the questions or use them to guide their writing about the Walker essay and the way she portrays her mother's contrary instincts. Since the notion of contrary instincts frames this assignment, you might find it well worth your time to turn first to the "Questions for a Second Reading."

   John Edgar Wideman doesn't name as "contrary instincts" his brother's conflicting feelings about wanting to make it in the white world and yet remain uniquely himself, but it's certainly possible to see them that way. For students this is immediately a problem of reading and rereading the Wideman essay to find those places where Robby might be said to be talking (through his brother) about those conflicting feelings or contrary instincts and also to find those moments when he is acting them out or caught in them. Students will have to ask themselves what his conflicting feelings are about, since they are not the same as Walker's mother's. They'll need to ask themselves how John's understanding and portrayal of Robby's contrary instincts differ from Alice Walker's understanding of her mother's.

   Since John is talking for Robby and telling his story, students might best help themselves by seeing him in a role similar to that assumed by Walker, but they'll need to identify the passages in both essays that they'll use to make the contrast. Once they have the passages and some notes on what Robby's and Walker's mother's contrary instincts might be, they're ready to write.

   Robby's conflicting instincts pit him and his sensitivity to love and good people in the "square world" (like his friend Garth) against success in the street world where the slick guy, the gangster with flashy cars and women and cash, is admired. Students will have to locate those moments in the selection that bring forward those conflicting instincts and they might turn first to a close reading of the epigraph to the Wideman selection. John, in Robby's voice, lays out the gist of contrary instincts. Students could find moments in the essay that elaborate on these instincts and make them visible enough to use in their papers.

2. To see Walker's mother's life in terms of the forces that affect her is another way of reading the essay. Students will need to reread, paying attention to the personal, accidental, and what

113

we might call "larger" forces, the forces beyond her control but not accidental, that affect her life. As they reread, students might note not only the passages that bring these forces forward but also the kind of forces — personal, accidental, or "larger."

Students will need to read the Steinem essay at least twice to find passages that present the forces affecting Ruth. As with the Walker essay, they'll want to note the nature of the forces they bring forward. Then they'll be ready to write, paying particular attention to how these forces are similar and different for the two women. Finally, they need to go on and say what lessons Walker and Steinem have learned from their mothers' examples. Steinem seems to have learned about women and the forces affecting them, while Walker seems to have learned about black women and the forces affecting them. Students could look for moments in the essays that point to overlaps and differences in what the two have learned.

JOHN EDGAR WIDEMAN

Our Time (p. 618)

This excerpt from *Brothers and Keepers* tells such a compelling story with such a powerful voice that students are easily drawn into it. John's younger brother Robby is in prison for his role in a robbery and murder. The excerpt picks up the story near the end, and focuses on Robby's friendship with Garth; his growing up in Homewood, a black neighborhood in Pittsburgh; and his mother and his grandfather, John French. Throughout the selection, John asks himself how this could have happened to Robby, how he could end up in prison and John a Rhodes scholar and a college professor with a national reputation as a writer. The problem of writing about Robby bothers John, especially since the book is an occasion for him to get to know his brother for the first time in his adult life, and because John questions his own motives. Am I, he asks, exploiting Robby or am I telling his story, or is it something else I am up to?

QUESTIONS FOR A SECOND READING (p. 660)

1. "Our Time" is about Robby and Homewood, about a family and a community, but it is also about the act of writing, and in this sense it is primarily John's story. This question brings forward those moments when John interrupts the text to talk about its composition. It asks students to consider why he would call attention to the text as a text. It asks them to consider how John might be said to address these problems he faces as a writer. Students will not have any trouble identifying these sections once they reread with these questions in mind. They will, however, have trouble understanding just what Wideman's problems are, and what they have to do with writing. And they will have trouble finding a position on the question "Why?" If he does not want to tell his story, if he does not want to deflect attention from Robby, then why does he do so? And what does he do to overcome the ways in which writing inevitably makes Robby's story his own? Are the author's intrusions a solution? What about the use of fictional devices? and the sections in Robby's voice? All of these are questions that allow you to bring forward the problems of reading and writing as they are represented in the text.

2. There are major passages in this selection where John speaks in Robby's voice, offering talk that might be said to be Robby's but is, in fact, John speaking to us in the voice of his brother. Students will need to locate those moments and to use sections of them that represent Robby's point of view. How do these passages reveal Robby's view of the world? What do they tell you about how he understands and represents the way the world works?

Once students have discussed these questions, they'll need to turn to passages where John is speaking. Direct them to pay attention to the language, not so much to the subject of the talk. They'll need to look at the differences in Robby's and John's language. What, in the ways they use language, in the ways they use their voices, can you point to as indicating differences in how they understand and represent themselves? the worlds they live in? You might ask students to think about the voices. How does the voice in the passages where Robby talks treat his subjects, his readers, and himself? Who talks like this? For what reasons? To whom? And what about John's voice? What does the voice in his passages tell you?

3. To answer the questions on the differences it would make if John started the story with different episodes, students will need to turn to the way he does start the story — with Garth's death. They'll need to reread, looking for moments in the beginning that frame the rest of the selection. You might ask them to look for passages later that use or rely on the opening to present a point of view. Students will need to discuss the point of view of the given opening. What does the passage on Garth's death do for the rest of the story? How can you demonstrate what it does by showing how other passages rely on that opening for their sense or impact?

Once students have discussed the opening, they can turn to the other sections in the selection — the house in Shadyside and Robby's birth — that might be used to begin. They'll have to imagine those episodes starting the piece, and from there try to say how those passages would change or alter the point of view. What would those moments do to other major moments in the selection if they were used to begin it? Students will want to generalize after imagining other beginnings and you should press them to relate how their readings of specific passages in the selection change when the beginning changes.

ASSIGNMENTS FOR WRITING (p. 661)

1. This is the written response to the first of the "Questions for a Second Reading." If you haven't already, you might want to see what we say about those questions and the reasons for asking students to think about the author's intrusions into the narrative.

We've taught this assignment several times and we've found it important for students to work directly from passages in the text. The first thing they need to do is to reread the selection and choose their material. The assignment asks them to choose three or four passages; this may turn out to be too many. Once they have located their material, students do not have great difficulty describing it. They do, however, have trouble turning the discussion to the issue of writing — either the writing of "In Our Time" or writing as a general subject. In their first draft, students should be encouraged to turn from their material to the question of *why* Wideman interrupts the narrative. We have found that students write well and at length about *what* Wideman says, but, when the space is open for them to comment or explain, they feel they have nothing to say. Students can imagine several routes to this question, several ways of imagining their authority. They can talk as fellow writers, imagining from that perspective why a writer might want to bring forward the problem of writing. They can talk as readers, explaining the effects of these intrusions. Or they can talk as students — that is, through their knowledge of other attempts to represent an understanding of race, family, crime, drug addiction, or the black community.

For revision: Our experience with this assignment suggests that students can best use the time allotted for revision to work on the general issues raised in this paper. What might they say about Wideman's narrative intrusions? More particularly, what might this have to do with the writing they are doing — or might do — as students in the academy? What would the consequences be of producing a text that calls attention to itself as a text, as something produced?

2. This assignment turns to "Our Time" as first-person sociology, pushing to the side the question of the text as text. It asks students to use Wideman's account of Robby's family and

115

neighborhood as a way of framing an answer to Wideman's underlying question: What is Robby's story? The question can be rephrased in a number of ways: Who is Robby? How can you explain the differences between Robby and John? In what ways is a man or woman the product of family and environment? How did Robby end up in jail?

Ideally students will be working closely with the text. The evidence they have is here — not in whatever generalizations they can dredge up about crime or the ghetto. And students will need to do more than retell what they find in the text: They will need to assume a role similar to John's. In fact, one way students might get started on the project is to measure their sense against John's, to set themselves apart as someone who can see what he can't.

MAKING CONNECTIONS (p. 661)

1. The danger with this assignment is that students can mechanically compare and contrast Robby's and Theweleit's soldiers (the roles cast for them, the ways they are produced by a culture with interests they can only partially understand or thwart). The value of the assignment is the degree to which the different representations of Robby and the soldiers reflect upon each other. Wideman's narrative is about an individual, his family and neighborhood. Theweleit's is about nations, war, training, propaganda — it provides a wider context to individual development and response. Taken together, the different concepts of the individual and those contexts that matter to individual development allow both texts to be questioned in ways they might not without the comparison as a tool.

   Beyond this, the assignment asks students to think not just about boys and how they become men but about two authors and how they do their work. That is, behind the comparison is an invitation to reflect on the differences (in form and method, in intent and ambition, in the ways in which the writers conceive of and carry out an intellectual project) between these two unconventional and self-conscious texts. The writers differe in how they choose and discuss examples, in how they conceive of argument and investigation, and in how they represent "truth" or discovery. These differences are not simply matters of surface and filigree; they are fundamental to each writer's method of work.

2. It is quite interesting to read the Jacobs and Wideman texts side-by-side. Both are black authors and both call attention to themselves as writers and to their relationship to their readers and their subjects. Both are trying to explain something that can't be explained, and in both cases what can't be explained is the position of a black man or woman in a white-dominated culture. There are many important differences, however, not the least of which is the difference between the 1860s and the 1970s.

   This assignment asks students to take each of the texts as a case of the problem of writing, either as generally conceived or as it is determined by the position of a minority writer in a dominant culture. It asks students to locate and describe the differences between the two cases. It is too easy, and misleading, to assume that they are both the same — that there is no fundamental difference between the texts.

   It also asks students to name and explain the differences they see. The danger here is the way this assignment becomes an invitation to generalizations students can't handle — generalizations about history or race or writing. But this is also the pleasure of the assignment. It asks students to think not in terms of individual texts and authors but in terms of broad historical and cultural forces as they converge in reading and writing, where students are the readers Jacobs and Wideman had in mind and where they need to imagine a response. This is an ambitious assignment; students will benefit from being given the chance to rework a first draft, particularly if you can help them see the terms of their emerging project in it.

PATRICIA J. WILLIAMS

Alchemical Notes:
Reconstructing Ideals from Deconstructed Rights (p. 663)

We came to Williams's work through her wonderful book, *The Alchemy of Race and Rights*. As the title says, it is a book about race and rights, but it is also about writing and teaching. It would, in fact, make a great book to use in a teaching seminar. We had originally planned to include chapters from that book in *Ways of Reading*, but we could not get permission to reprint them. It is the policy of Harvard University Press, which had recently released the paperback edition, not to grant permission to reprint in the year a paperback edition is issued. We wrote explaining that our book was to be used in introductory courses, that the students in these courses were not great purchasers of university press books, even paperbacks and that, in fact, including a selection in *Ways of Reading* might even increase sales, since many students would no doubt want to read more of Williams and therefore seek out the book for themselves and as presents for others.

But to no avail. Policy is policy. We were terribly disappointed, because we felt that Williams's work was important for an introductory writing class. At this point we began to search the law reviews for other pieces she had written and came upon "Alchemical Notes." The article has all the stylistic richness of the chapters in her book. It mixes genres. It crosses the usual boundaries between personal and professional. It resists summary and easy conclusion. One reason we were eager to teach Williams was that her prose enacts an argument about the ideology of style. Another was the opportunity to look into the world of the law review and to let her work stand (as maverick as it is) as a point of access to legal writing and legal training. Williams is, we think, a powerful writer, a significant presence in American letters, and one who makes an important argument about race and rights.

While we have taught Williams's book (which includes much of "Alchemical Notes") we have never taught this essay in this form. We feel confident, however, that we can predict how it will be received by students. Our students in general were intrigued by Williams's writing and interested in the ways in which her prose was hard to read. But the problems you might imagine having presenting an essay like this in class were not the problems we faced. Students seemed interested in the fragmentary nature of the text, its illusiveness, and its mix of styles. They were perplexed by the technicalities of the legal discussions but felt that there was no reason that they shouldn't be perplexed (after all, they weren't in law school); and they took some pleasure in trying to work out what these might mean, even asking friends or parents who had studied law.

The greatest difficulty we had actually seemed to have little to do with what was *in* the text and everything to do with the difficulties of dealing with racial issues in class. In spite of all the care Williams takes to qualify her position, to show her second thoughts, and to make herself vulnerable, our white students read her as angry and dogmatic and "against" whites. The black students often felt up against the wall, being asked to speak for a person whose position they in some cases didn't completely share (sometimes in obvious ways, since Williams speaks from her position as a legal scholar as well as her position as an African-American woman). Students used the text to act out a familiar story of black and white in America, in spite of all the lengths Williams goes to to make her essay not one more version of the usual story.

It is important, then, to bring the discussion quickly to specific passages or sections of the essay, to speak of Williams as a figure in that text (through her representations of herself) and not as a generalized African-American Woman.

As students began to work from the text, they tended to move toward sections they understood or liked or identified with, sections they couldn't understand or found puzzling. So did we work with her prose — on sections, both what they seemed to say and how they were written. We wanted to force at every point the question of her method, how it might be explained and justified, and why it might or might not be seen as exemplary.

With "Alchemical Notes," we would begin by letting students propose sections for discussion, and then push later to see how the essay might be said to constitute a whole. Williams provides a set of terms to explain the organization of the essay ("meta-story," "mega-story"). These were useful, particularly in leading to the questions, "But why? How does this *work* as a way of writing? as a way of thinking things through? what is pushing away or revising?"

One problem you may confront early on is the degree to which the essay assumes a knowledge of Critical Legal Studies (CLS). We try to provide some background in the headnote. We feel that Williams is writing this essay for a general audience (in her writing, she presents a figure of herself as the lawyer who can speak with, and not just for, those outside the law). She anticipates this difficulty and brackets it as "not a problem," which is why she gives as much background to CLS as she does in the opening pages. This is why Peter Gabel stands as a character in a story as well as an author in a footnote. When we teach an essay like this, we are quick to acknowledge the limits of our own understanding and happy to be figuring out what we can about critical legal studies with our students from what we have in the essay.) In *The Alchemy of Race and Rights*, Williams makes it clear that for every lay reader who has trouble with the references to CLS, there will be a lawyer who has trouble with the references to the "celestial city," her great-great-grandmother, her apartment hunting, or *King Lear*. In fact the footnotes, and not just the mix of legal argument, personal narrative, and allegory, seem designed to draw in (or create) a mixed audience, an audience not bound by traditional channels of university preparation.

Note: A part of the postscript to *The Alchemy of Race and Rights* might be useful for class discussion. Williams says:

> I wish to recognize that terms like "black" and "white" do not begin to capture the rich ethnic and political diversity of my subject. But I do believe that the simple matter of the color of one's skin so profoundly affects the way one is treated, so radically shapes what one is allowed to think and feel about this society, that the decision to generalize from such a division is valid. Furthermore, it is hard to describe succinctly the racial perspective and history that are my concern. "Disenfranchised" will not do, since part of my point is that a purely class-based analysis does not comprehend the whole problem. I don't like the word "minority" (although I use it) because it implies a certain delegitimacy in a majoritarian system; and if one adds up all the shades of yellow, red, and brown swept over by the term, we are in fact not. I prefer "African-American" in my own conversational usage because it effectively evokes the specific cultural dimensions of my identity, but in this book I use most frequently the term "black" in order to accentuate the unshaded monolithism of color itself as a social force. (pp. 256–57)

We offer more than the usual number of assignments for the Williams selection. We wanted not only to provide several alternative routes into the essay, given its difficulty, but also to acknowledge the richness and importance of her work.

QUESTIONS FOR A SECOND READING (p. 695)

1. There are two parts to this question: one asks students to take an inventory of the strange or unusual features of Williams's style (and says, in effect, that the prose *is* strange and

puzzling); the other asks students to think of these features as strategic, as a response to (or enactment of) the "ideology of style." We want to counter students' training, which in most cases prepares them to think of style as ornamentation, to say that Williams's writing is designed to be beautiful or to catch attention, but not to think about how knowledge is produced, transmitted, and preserved. We want students to consider how the story of Williams's great-great-grandmother, for example, is not just moving or interesting but part of an argument over what counts as knowledge in professional and legal discourse.

2. In a review cited in the headnote, Henry Louis Gates refers to Williams's work as a "meditation on example." This question is designed to assist students as they reread in preparation for a summary of Williams's argument ("so what is this essay about"), but it wants to acknowledge that part of her argument is represented by the way examples are gathered, placed one next to the other, and interpreted. She is arguing not only against the conception of "rights" promoted by critical legal studies but also with the way legal scholars prepare, develop, and present their arguments. It is not just that they got it wrong, but that they couldn't have *not* got it wrong.

3. The first time we read the essay, we loved the effect of the footnotes — the way, as we say in the question, they establish a kind of countertext. These are missing from *The Alchemy of Race and Rights* and help to establish "Alchemical Notes" as a reflection on academic sources and academic authority. We love both the effect of reading the two texts together and the unusual assortment of references in the footnotes. In a sense, no formal preparation would put *these* sources in one person's head. They represent an intellect (or training) that stands against the usual disciplinary boundaries. Students will not get all the fun that is here, because they will not be able to identify all the references; but they should be able to see that something unusual is going on here. For purposes of demonstration, we would begin with footnote 90 and work to the end. The wonderful mix of sources establishes an often surprising counterpoint, and after a discussion of the final 15 footnotes, students could go to work on the first 89 (!). We also think that a discussion like this (like a discussion of the way Williams uses quoted material in her essay) will help students see the ways in which the technical details of academic writing, such as footnotes, serve basic strategic functions and can be sources of pleasure and worthy objects of attention.

ASSIGNMENTS FOR WRITING (p. 697)

1. We tend to avoid assignments that directly confront an author's argument and prefer those that question method or context. In this case, however, we felt that it would be wrong to side-step the issues of race as argued by Williams. We wanted to phrase the assignment so that students were writing not only about her argument about rights and the historical impor-tance of "rights" for African-Americans but also about "race," as the term is a useful one for describing the differences between Williams and the lawyers she argues with. She is making a point about the experience of African-Americans, particularly aspects of that experience that are invisible even to sympathetic whites. She is also making a point about the legal profession — black lawyers and white lawyers — and the extent to which racial differences count in the ways in which lawyers are prepared, the ways in which they are perceived as professionals (as in the opening example of the hallways of the courthouse), and in the ways in which they think through legal problems and legal questions. Williams, as a writer, sets out to "redescribe" what they (the white lawyers) take to be a common experience — one with a single, clear meaning — so that they can be reconnected with African-Americans and, beyond that, American history. As teachers, we would insist (perhaps at the point of directing students toward revision) that both representations of race relations become part of their essays.

2. We taught a version of this essay when we taught from *The Alchemy of Race and Rights*. We wanted students to be responsible for a summary (if not, we said, it is too easy for Williams

and what she has written to disappear from their intellectual lives); yet we wanted to acknowledge that her prose is a prose that calls summary into question, that is very much aware of what is lost when the complications and subtleties disappear. So we ask for a summary both as an exercise and as a necessary step in a further investigation of the text. We believe, for example, that Williams offers the essay as a unified whole. In that sense it is a complete statement. It is also clear that she offers the essay as a corrective, not simply as an aesthetic or linguistic experience but as a program for action. Things are to change. We therefore ask students how they might represent their version of the "main idea" of this essay. We might have added, "And what, so far as you are concerned, are you to *do* with this idea?" How does Williams define her ideal reader? We then ask students to step back from their summary to think again about the essay as a whole — about what was lost or deflected or changed by this kind of reading.

3. This question follows from the third question in Questions for a Second Reading above. The footnotes, as we think of them, serve two purposes: they offer material representation for the intellectual context within which the essay is written and read; and they offer material representation of the distinctive and peculiar sensibility of the figure of the author, "Patricia J. Williams." (We phrase it this way and put her name in quotation marks to indicate the degree to which the footnotes might be thought of as a self-conscious performance, part of the creation of the figure of the author. We see Williams, in a characteristic gesture, countering the conventional figure of the writer, covering her bases or gathering her 3" x 5" notecards around her and typing them out in order.

4. We wanted to provide one assignment where students were asked to write in response to or in imitation of Williams's example. We wanted to invite students, in other words, to produce a similarly voiced and structured essay and to see how they might put this form of writing to work. The simplest way to represent the essay as a model form is to say that it blends personal narrative, argumentation, and formal academic style. We wanted to work a bit more closely with what we take to be Williams's project, and so we ask students to imagine themselves in a critical position in relation to "governing" narratives.

Williams is acutely aware of the distance between the stories others use to place her and those that she herself might tell. She is also aware that in both cases the stories have been prepared in advance — by history, by our culture, by a legacy of storytelling that constructs what we take for granted as "real." The point of the story she tells about herself and Gabel is not that they are two individuals with different experiences, but that as white man and black woman they are cast in different roles in the social context when they set out to rent an apartment. The value of the "personal" narrative for Williams is that it provides access to the "governing" narratives that define who a preson is — what it means to be male or female, black or white, rich or poor, young or old, trustworthy or untrustworthy, intelligent or stupid, lawyer or client, and so on. In this sense, her writing enacts, in Gates's terms, a "meditation on example." In "Alchemical Notes" that meditation is enabled by the way she frames and positions her stories — as "mega-stories," "meta-stories," and so on. (See her footnote 7 for the intertextual definition of metalanguage.)

It isn't that important for students to follow the "mini-mega-meta" organization. It is a tool or a frame to allow them to begin to work on a text that violates or calls into question most of the conventions they bring to essay writing. Our goal as teachers is to ensure that students imagine they can carry out (and are allowed to try) that kind of experimentation. Once students have projects under way, particulary at the point of revision, we would want to honor their projects and cut them free from any required conformity to Williams's example. In the version of this assignment that we have taught, students wrote fragments, used different typefaces, tried to mix voices, attempted surprising and unpredictable yokings of examples. These were productive exercises in that they enabled students to begin to see the familiar order of topic sentence, example, conclusion as a convention, a choice about how to think about the world.

1. This is a version of a question we have used quite frequently. It is designed to take the notion of "difficulty" and to bring it forward as an acknowledged, even necessary condition. Students, in other words, are prepared to think that difficulty is shameful, a "problem" rooted in their youth or ignorance or poor preparation. We want to make difficulty a condition of certain kinds of text and a reason to value them. We also want all readers to experience difficulty, not just student readers. This assignment therefore asks students to identify "difficult" sections of text, to discuss that nature of the difficulty, and to think about how it might be seen as strategic, productive, necessary. For students to do well with this assignment, it is important to ensure that they work closely with a limited number of passages. Part of their work is the *presentation* and description of difficulty. They need to define what is difficult, in what way, and why before they can step aside and begin to theorize difficulty.

2. Because so many of our students referred to Williams as an "angry" writer, and because this was surprising to us, we thought it might be useful to make "anger" a term for textual analysis. Rich gives a history and motive to anger. This assignment asks students to bring to bear on Williams's prose Rich's argument for the presence of anger in women's writing. We might have added a request for students to compare Williams's prose with Rich's prose (or, for that matter, with the poems cited as examples). It would be interesting, for example, to compare the final paragraphs of each essay. The writer is figured differently in each; they call up different settings (Rich's prose sounds like the kind of call to arms we traditionally associate with male orators). If both are signs of anger, they represent this response differently.

3. This assignment looks specifically at how problems of difference, in this case racial and ethnic difference, are represented textually in strategies that aim to acknowledge difference between the author's position or point of view and the readers', to insist upon it, enable its recognition and understanding and, perhaps, to bridge it. It is of course not the case that Williams, Jacobs, and Anzaldúa write *only* for a white, majority audience. Each writer, however, addresses that audience at some point in her text and imagines its ways of reading to be a problem a writer must address.

SUSAN WILLIS

"Work(ing) Out" (p. 702)

Our students enjoyed working with Willis's essay, and we took great pleasure in reading her book, *A Primer for Daily Life*, which was by far the best of the readings of contemporary culture we reviewed in preparing the new edition. Our students were predictably surprised and pleased to find Barbie and Jane Fonda in a "serious" academic essay. However, they appreciated the urgency and commitment in the piece. Students believed in Willis as a critic concerned for their well-being; they did not believe in Fiske, for example, in the same way. Students also had a sense — we think justified — that this essay took what they termed the "usual" feminist argument one step further.

That further step is represented by Willis's Marxist analysis of the commodification of women's bodies. This, finally, is the subject of her essay, not the battles between men and women. (The men in our classes found it easier to read themselves into the argument of this essay than they have with other "feminist" essays in the anthology. They, too, can be phrased in the essay's terms as gendered products of late capitalism.) Our students were also interested in the historical context of the argument, using the essay as a way of imagining not only the 1940s but the 1970s.

The essay didn't present any unusual difficulties in class. There were predictable problems with the key terms of analysis: "commodification," "patriarchal power," "gendered subjects." We dealt with these as we usually do, as interesting strategic problems calling for rereading rather than as failures of vocabulary training calling for the dictionary. The most profitable work we saw students undertake was that of trying to figure out (to make use of) the phrase "gendered subjects." It was important for students to make the fundamental recognition, assisted by the discussion of the male body at the end of the subsection titled "The Workout," that a gendered subject was socially and not biologically constructed.

Actually, the key moment for many students in reading the text was the discussion (through Jameson) of the "utopian dimensions" of mass culture. Students, took sides as sides are loosely outlined in American public discourse, where Jane Fonda is a feminist and exercise is an expression of freedom, and they couldn't figure out why anyone would want to question feminism and freedom. It was important for students to see that Willis was *not* another liberal but was in fact critiquing the liberal point of view, which is the farthest to the left that most of our students can imagine. Once they saw that Willis took this position, they could begin to work out its terms, its way of rationalizing itself (Jane Fonda is not a feminist and "freedom" is not freedom but a form of mystification and enslavement).

Once they learned to use Willis's terms when they began to reread, students had little trouble with the stages of the argument, except for the discussions of Cindy Sherman and Jem and the Holograms. The Cindy Sherman discussion was difficult because the text contains no copies of her photographs. (We tried to get permission to include some in the textbook, but without success.) It might help to bring in a reproduction. The discussion of Jem is hard because it stands — at least structurally — in the place of a conclusion. It seems to be offered as a final position; and yet it is difficult for students to think through its relationship to the many discussions along the way. Our way of solving the problem in class was to ask students to turn to the ways in which Willis does offer the discussion of Jem as a conclusion: presenting Jem as a final image (a "horrific" allegory for the position of the contemporary woman); using the discussion as a review of those ways of reading contemporary culture that Willis has labeled "superficial," "liberal," and "profound."

QUESTIONS FOR A SECOND READING (p. 724)

1. This question focuses attention on what we took to be the key terms of the text: "commodified" and "gendered." These terms did, in fact, emerge as the most interestingly problematic for our students (see the discussion above). One the one hand we wanted students to work out ways of using the terms through rereading, by looking at how, where and why Willis uses them. We also wanted them to think about how the argument is revised once these terms enter the discourse; that is, the references to commodification and gender turn this into an argument about modes of production and their control and not simply about men's interests and women's interests.

2. Students tend to read an essay like this example by example. We wanted a question that would direct students, when they reread, to see and chart stages in an argument. The questions here point in two directions. They ask students to prepare for a summary, an answer to the question, "What is that essay about?" The assignment prepares students to manipulate the essay in that way and also to think about Willis's method — how she writes, how she works through and with her materials.

3. Because we found that students had particular trouble with the final discussion, we wanted a question that would send them back to it — to use the concluding example as a way of working back to the bigger questions about gender and capitalism and history that are worked out in the essay. (See the discussion above).

ASSIGNMENTS FOR WRITING **(p. 725)**

1. This assignment, a standard one for us, asks students to extend Willis's argument through a discussion of examples of their own choosing. You can help students prepare by spending class time considering possible choices of material, thinking about where to look, how to choose, and, in particular, what would constitute an interesting and effective (and surprising) pair. (Runners' magazines proved a fertile source for at least one item in the pair. Once a student has one good example, the real work is finding a surprising source for the second.) Using a pair of examples is important to this assignment, for several reasons. Considering the examples together will cause each to be read differently than if either was examined alone. And finding a pair gives students a chance to provide a historical context if the examples come from different moments in time, or a cultural context if they come from a different cultural scene (if they don't both come from TV, for example, or if they don't both come from the students' "personal" experience).

   When students write this essay, we usually define their task as writers in two ways: first they must *present* their material — set a context, bring it forward in a detailed way for a reader to see and think about and understand (Willis is a good model for this); second, they must *comment* on their material — discuss it, reflect on it, think it through, teach a reader what to see and how to think, and provide an intellectual or analytical context (Willis, again, is a good model). Students, characteristically, move too fast in presenting the material. In revision, they can take time to bring forward detail that would otherwise be lost, and they can begin to think about how to make the presentation interesting and fun. Students are also, characteristically, hesitant to come forward in their essays as intellectuals — teaching, reflecting and commenting. It is hard for them to imagine themselves in these roles, or to assume that they are authorized to step forward in just these ways. Again, working on developing this "slot" in the essay can be a useful focus for revision.

   The assignment asks students to see if they can make use of Willis's terms ("commodification," "gendered subjects"). In our classes, the most important measure of students' understanding of one of the readings is the degree to which they can put its terms to work. We have had colleagues who have argued that we prevent students from bringing in other terms, other frames of analysis, or from coining terms of their own. It is not a matter of prohibition, however. We would not prevent students from doing this. In fact, we can think of cases where we have encouraged it. But there are limits to how much you can accomplish in a semester, and we will admit that with limited time we would give priority to Willis's terms.

2. This is a difficult assignment. It assumes a student who has a pretty solid grasp of Willis's project. It might best follow assignment 1 in this set if you are working up your own sequence. The assignment asks students to think about Willis as a critic by bringing forward for discussion both her critical method and the assumptions behind her criticism. As we envision the task, students will work backwards from the places where she names or identifies her position (as in the passage in the epigram) to examples of Willis in practice (as, for example, in the Jem discussion) and then give a name and evaluative description to what she does. We are asking students to step in where Willis becomes silent, right at the point at which she alludes to her methods as "more profound" than the others. We would not give them a name in advance (like "Marxist criticism") or send students to a book describing critical schools.

3. Because Willis provides a list of further readings at the end of her essay (a gesture we admire and one, we feel, that is directed at undergraduate readers), we wanted to honor what she had done by asking students to work from her list or to add items of their own. (If you haven't looked yet, the list includes Toni Morrison's *Beloved*, Donna Haraway's essay, "A Manifesto for Cyborgs," and Frida Kahlo's paintings.) As in the first assignment in "Assignments for Writing" (see the discussion above), we would define the students' work as writers as providing both presentation and commentary. They need to take time in advance to select

and study their sources; then, when they begin to write, they need to present that material to someone unfamiliar with it and teach a reader how to read and understand what they have presented.

4. This is a fairly straightforward exercise in summary. It asks students to go to the very sections of the essay they would most likely ignore in a summary. Our experience shows that students read Willis in terms of their own (in her terms "liberal") version of the feminist critique, leaving out all references to commodities and "the entire circuit of production and consumption under capitalism." As a result, we felt it was useful to define a summary that began with these terms and to define summary as a teaching tool, a way to help another reader *begin* to come to terms with Willis's essay or her brand of critique. While we didn't do so in the assignment, you might find it useful to emphasize "begin," since that would open up a space for a writer to suggest to his or her reader what else might be done if one were going to work on or with "Work(ing) Out."

5. This assignment is designed to give students a chance to read against the grain of Willis's argument. It provides another source of material for study and another method of analysis (a kind of mini- or weekend ethnography) and opens up the field at least to the extent of allowing exercising women to speak for themselves. We wanted to be quick to put those interviews in place as additional text to be worked with, not as "the truth." We want students to work generously with Willis's account, and not just set it aside. At the same time, this assignment is, perhaps, a bit loaded. We found Willis's account of exercise limited because it leaves out the element of pleasure and because it seems to assume that, for the women in the exercise rooms, there is a uniform experience and no evidence of knowing resistance or play.

It is important, then, that students treat their notes as additional text and not as the final truth that puts the question of exercise to rest. In fact, it is useful to let students understand that their essay should open up new questions and suggest possible counterreadings, not put the whole issue to rest. At the end, we have suggested that students might imagine themselves in dialogue with Willis, partly so that Willis's essay shouldn't be silenced, that it can be used to imagine response and counterstatement and partly (as a more purely technical exercise) to push students to work passages from Willis's text back into their essays after they have made their own argument about exercise.

MAKING CONNECTIONS (p. 727)

1. This assignment asks students to read Theweleit's "Male Bodies and the 'White Terror'" and Willis's "Work(ing) Out" as a pair. There are obvious thematic links (one looks at the construction of the male body, one at the female). Since both make an argument that it is difficult for students to think through (about the construction of subjectivity), it is worth spending time having students first work out the parallel arguments in the pieces and, later, look at the differences. (Theweleit and Willis think differently about the individual, about the shaping forces and contexts, about desire.)

In our own teaching, we have tried to point toward differences in method. There are striking and interesting differences in the ways each essay is written, and even in their use of illustrations; and we have found it important to ask students to see these differences as fundamental, as representations of different ways of doing intellectual work, of thinking things through, and not simply as evidence that different people write differently.

One way for students to begin to see the limits and possibilities of a critical method is first to *see* it as a method and then to see it in relation to others. The other goal of this assignment is to place Theweleit's account of the construction of the gendered subject (let's say) next to Susan Willis's. Although the differences between the two are not obvious, identifying them will allow students a way of evaluating and characterizing Willis.

For revision: We have found that the difficulty of representing the positions of the various authors (figuring them out, finding passages to use, presenting the material) is sufficient to dominate students' attention in the first draft. It is in the second that students can best begin to look for differences and try to establish some critical purchase on the essays they have read.

2. This assignment, following a standard pattern for us, asks for an interested summary. It says, in a sense, "Give a generous account of Fiske and Willis to someone not willing to be generous." But it also says, at the end, "OK — now that you have represented their positions as they would want you to represent them, what do you want to add? Do you take their positions as your own? Where would you differ? Why?" We feel that summary is a valuable tool; it is strategic, a way of getting a position on the table in order to move on to something else. We believe it is important for students to do the work necessary for a generous reading of Willis's (and Fiske's) argument.

One way of providing more of an edge to the turn at the end of this assignment would be to ask students, now that they have spoken from Willis's (and Fiske's) position of the cultural critic, to speak from the position of the fan, or "exerciser," or consumer, or member of contemporary American youth culture. Students would then have to speak from a position other than "experience" or "taste." The pressure to see one's ideas in the context of an interested position is a useful one, particularly for undergraduates.

For revision: With essays like this, revision for us always begins with rereading (and rereading asking the questions What have I missed? What have I left out because it was too hard or too weird?). The goals of revision, in our classes, have been to expand and complicate the representation of Fiske and Willis and to work out in greater detail the position of the student writer.

VIRGINIA WOOLF

A Room of One's Own (p. 729)

A Room of One's Own is one of the classic texts of modern feminism. Two other essays in *Ways of Reading* allude to it — Alice Walker and Adrienne Rich give it more than a footnote. Both wrestle with its words and how they might serve as a source for other women writers.

We spent a long time trying to figure out how to excerpt *A Room*. Most anthologies choose Chapter 3, the section where Woolf imagines Shakespeare's sister. Because this is so often cited, we included an excerpt in the headnote. We decided, however, that we would include the opening and closing chapters in our book, since they were most useful for talking about *A Room* as a piece of writing — or, more properly, for talking about the argument enacted in Woolf's text. Students will still have access to the argument *about* the position of a woman writer, but the first and last chapters enable them to develop a way of using terms of gender ("manly" and "womanly") to talk about style, voice, and structure, about how a writer imagines her — or his — relationship to audience and subject, to tradition and convention.

When we have taught these chapters, we have wanted students to feel the ways in which this is a slippery, surprising, carefully wrought, and playful text. More than with any other selection in the book, we spend time reading sections of *A Room* aloud, trying to imagine the ways they might be phrased or how they might be taken. The opening and the conclusion have so many stops and starts, shift voice and ground so often, that they provide fine examples. We want students to feel the richness of this text, and we are not beyond placing it next to an oral reading of a much more plodding, singleminded, and univocal text. For obvious reasons, we have chosen men for our examples — Fish, Kuhn, Freire, Miller — although we have also read from men's writing that seems similarly responsive and multivocal: Percy, Rodriguez, Berger, Geertz.

The danger lies in letting students launch into familiar and well-rehearsed arguments about who does the housework or whether women should work outside the home. There are reasons to argue the justice or implications of a room and £500 a year, but we have found that these arguments do not serve our purposes as well as arguments about writing — about what writing should or might do, about the limits and consequences of a way of writing determined by men or serving men's interests. It is not difficult for students to identify features in writing — types of introductions and conclusions, or the voices of authority — that seem to be "naturally" and inevitably there ("the way you are supposed to write"), and to name them in terms of gender. Once they are named, students have a way of imagining the history and the politics that govern writing, including their own.

Students tend to be nervous over the literary references and allusions, many of which they will not recognize, and some of which we don't recognize. It is enough for them to read the references and allusions as references and allusions. Woolf is not giving a quiz or testing cultural literacy. In fact, she is so quick to make up names that this seems to be part of the point — that the problems of writing she is concerned with do not reside in single authors alone.

QUESTIONS FOR A SECOND READING (p. 758)

1–3.   All of these questions point to chapters as acts of writing. They are designed to help students look or listen for difference, to see or hear this performance against the background of history and convention, a background we want students to imagine is filled with the texts and voices of men. In each case, we ask students to imagine that what they notice enacts an argument, a demonstration of the possibilities for women's writing. The first questions point to voice. The various openings to Chapter 1 and the various endings to the final chapter are filled with shifts and modulations — it is as though, in both cases, faced with the necessity of beginning and ending, Woolf were seeking out which ways of speaking might serve. The second question points to structural features, but also to tropes and figures. One of our students names those moments when the argument is interrupted by the narrative of Mary Beton's travels — the "Here's the soup" device. When talking about literary history, she is interrupted by events around her — a turn in the road, a door, a bowl of soup. Some students, noticing that the first chapter begins with the word "but" began looking for a variety of contrary gestures. In either case you can imagine students beginning to work out an argument about the position of the woman writer or about the features that might characterize a writing that was more womanly than manly. The third question addresses the problem of identity, the "I" of the text. In many ways this is the hardest question for students to get a handle on. Contemporary feminists argue so often about women's self-assertion that it is hard to imagine why a woman might choose to disappear behind other names. Students have the same problem with a similar gesture in Adrienne Rich's "When We Dead Awaken" (p. 461), particularly in the poem "Planetarium." Students should try to chart all the forms of presentation they can find in this essay, particularly if they imagine it as a public lecture where a historical Virginia Woolf is visibly present, speaking these sentences, taking one name and then another.

ASSIGNMENTS FOR WRITING (p. 759)

1–2.   These assignments ask students to write a response to the "Questions for a Second Reading." We've explained why we think it is important to have students writing about the text as a text. One thing to add is that students' efforts will be successful to the degree that they work from passages. These essays, in other words, are exercises in working with textual material. Students should choose from among the passages they have identified, and work with a limited but representative set. As we have taught these assignments, we have wanted students to read closely, to work in detail with Woolf's language. During revision, we have focused on either their choice of passages — the ones that don't fit or seem beyond comprehension are the ones we want them to work with in revision — or on the placement and use of those passages. To what degree are they left to stand alone, as though they could speak for themselves, and to what degree has the writer taken the role of teaching us what we might see and how we might read?

Finally, when students revise, we want them to bring forward what was inevitably overlooked in the first draft — the connection between what Woolf is doing and what they might do as writers, both inside and outside the academy. Some of our colleagues have told students to ignore questions about what Woolf's example or argument have to do with them as students in a writing class, or have left such questions to discussion. In the latter case, teachers reproduce copies of first and second drafts and move the discussion toward the question of what bearing the argument about gender and writing has on each writer's education. Some object to the question, as it has the tendency to make the students' essays come apart at the end. We are interested in the way personal concerns might intrude on the more academic questions raised. If the essays fall apart in the face of such pressure, a teacher could imagine that this is a valuable lesson, appropriate to an assignment on *A Room of One's Own*.

MAKING CONNECTIONS (p. 760)

1. We spoke in the opening section about our desire to have students name texts as "manly" or "womanly," as a way of indicating their relationship to what might be called the dominant — or phallocentric — discourse. This assignment asks students to use Woolf's terms "manly" and "womanly" as devices for noticing and naming features in texts. Students are asked to choose two texts whose difference they might name in terms of gender, regardless of the sex of the writer, and to explain and justify their choices. The key words are "discuss" and "representative." "Discuss" is a problematic term, and you may want to give your students some help imagining the context of such a discussion. Students might imagine a public lecture, following Woolf's lead, or Rich's, for that matter. They might imagine an audience antagonistic to the very enterprise of naming prose in terms of gender. Or they could imagine that this is a discussion they are having with their colleagues in class, beginning with the common ground of class discussions and taking the next step by turning to new examples. The word "representative" pushes students to imagine that they are talking about forces or interests, figures or conventions, that individual writers can only partially understand, command, or control. This essay should not be a celebration of writers' individual styles, but of how they work within and against a tradition of writing that makes individual difference insignificant.

2. This question raises many interesting questions about influence, and about the spaces between texts. Students are reminded that Rich offers her own reading of Woolf — directly, in her comments on Woolf's style; and indirectly, in a public address that could be said to be either a reproduction or a revision of Woolf's. If one reads this way, there are many striking echoes. Students are asked to look at Rich's commentary as interested or situated, as not necessarily the truth, but as a way of reading Woolf that both acknowledges and is blind to its own fears and desires. Students might be asked: Does your reading of Woolf match Rich's? What does she highlight? What does she ignore? Why? Why might Rich be angry with Woolf? How, in her writing, does Rich follow Woolf's example? Where and how is she struggling with Woolf's powerful example? Where and how might she be said to revise it?

Students' success will depend on the degree to which they work directly with passages from the two selections, and on the degree to which those passages provide rich material. In

(text pages 729–761)

first drafts, students will most likely be drawn to examples that quickly and easily fit whatever they want to say. They will ignore contrary or mysterious passages. One way of directing revision is to have students return to the texts to find the passages they have ignored, either willfully or unconsciously, and to begin revising by bringing those passages into their essays.

Part III: Working with the Assignment Sequences

o—o—o—o—o—o—o—o—o—o—o—o—o—o

SEQUENCE ONE

The Aims of Education (p. 769)

In the introduction to this sequence, we say that these essays confront the relationship between the individual, and structured ways of thinking represented by schooling. The goal of the sequence is to give students the feel of what it would be like to step outside of the assumptions that have governed their own sense of school, assumptions that would otherwise be invisible or seem like a "natural" part of an adolescent's landscape. The rhythm of the sequence has students moving in to look at textual problems in the essays — to look at the essays as methods, as ways of seeing and questioning education — and then moving out to apply this new frame of reference to their own familiar surroundings. The final two assignments are, in the broadest sense, revision assignments. The first six assignments lead students to develop a single-minded view of "alternatives" to conventional education. Assignment 7 asks students to rework their position by imagining ways to include an opposing point of view (Fish's) in what they have already written. The last assignment is a "taking stock" assignment. It says, in effect, now that you have been looking at a single problem for some weeks (we would think twelve or thirteen), let's see what you have to say if you stand back from what you have done and make a final statement. Because the final two assignments ask for major revisions — revisions that are radical reworkings of earlier papers — any work students do revising the earlier papers along the way might best be "local" revision: working on the relationship between examples and generalizations; working on papers by going back to the essays to look for ways to extend or counter positions taken in a first draft.

ASSIGNMENT 1

Applying Freire to Your Own Experience as a Student [Freire]

The most powerful and accessible part of Freire's essay for students is the banking metaphor. They will be able to use (or explain) this long before they can speak or write well about "problem-posing education" or about the "structure" of oppression. Structural analysis of social systems is a method they will learn. The banking metaphor gives a way of imagining teachers and students, not as individuals, but as tokens bound into a social structure. The assignment begins, then, with what students will do best. It asks them to take this metaphor and use it to frame (or invent) an episode from their own schooling. In addition, the assignment asks students to try their hand at using some of Freire's more powerful (or puzzling) terms and phrases. We want students to see how they might understand terms like "alienation," "problem-posing," or "dialectical" by putting those terms to use in commenting on their own experience. The final paragraph of the assignment is really a carrot for the best students — those who will get inside Freire's frame of mind, make his argument, and then feel that they have been denied the fun of speaking back or carving a position of their own. So, in Freire's name, it says, "Don't just do this passively. If you are going to carry on his work, you are going to be expected to make your own contribution, even at the expense of challenging this new orthodoxy."

For revision: When our students have written this essay, their first drafts, at their best, tell lively stories of an individual's experience in school or provide a tightly organized demonstration that their experience shows that Freire was "right." The goal of revision, we feel, should be to open these accounts up, to call them into question.

Perhaps because they are young adults, and perhaps because they are (by and large) Americans, students translate Freire's account of social, political, and historical forces into a story of individuals — a mean teacher and an innocent student. One way to challenge this interpretation in its revision, then, would be to send students back to Freire's essay to see how he accounts for "agency" — "who is doing what to whom" in Freire's account of education. Once students have reread the essay with this in mind, they can go back to their own piece, making this story of individuals a story of "representative" individuals, where teacher and student play predetermined roles in the larger drama of American education, where teacher and student are figures through which the culture works through questions about independence and authority, about the production or reproduction of knowledge, about the relationship of the citizen to the society.

It is also the case, however, that the first drafts make quick work of Freire. We asked one of our students how he was able to sum up everything Freire said in three tidy pages. He replied, "It was easy. I left out everything I didn't understand and worked with what I did." This is a familiar strategy, one that is reinforced by teachers who have students read for "gist." Another strategy for revision is to have students go back to the sections of Freire's essay that they didn't understand or couldn't so easily control and to see how they might work those sections into what they have written. This is an opportunity for students to have a dialogue with Freire — not a debate, but a chance to put his words on the page and to say, in effect, "Here is what I think you are saying." This revision will pressure students to be resourceful in including quotations and representing and working on text. It makes a big difference, for example, whether a student uses Freire to conclude a point or whether a student uses Freire's language as material to work on. And, we should add, these different uses of Freire provide handy illustrations for a discussion of "problem-posing" education.

ASSIGNMENT 2

Studying Rich as a Case in Point [Freire, Rich]

This is a more difficult assignment, partly because Rich's essay seems more accessible than Freire's. Students feel that they "know" the feminist argument (often as an argument about housework or job opportunities) even though what they know rests on relatively unexamined assumptions about the roles assigned to men and women; and most likely what they understand will have little to do with culture or writing. Rich's argument about language and culture seems difficult and mysterious. And then, to top it off, her essay turns to *poems* for its examples. Students tend to skip these, since they are not prose, and to assume that the language of the poems doesn't matter.

You will need to prepare students for the strange shifts and turns in this essay, particularly the way the poems function as examples in Rich's argument. Students will often feel that poems belong to a completely different order of discourse — that they require a different set of tools (a knowledge of prosody, a dictionary of symbols) and they don't say what they mean in the ways that "ordinary" language says what it means. We ask our students to read the poems as part of the essays. If the poems are weird or difficult (as the last couple of poems are), they should assume this is the point — that they *are* weird and difficult. Students feel that the problems these poems create belong only to them, because they are students. They need to recognize that the difficulty is one of the features of the poems they need to confront: If "Planetarium" is somehow a sign of Rich's achievement, how do you account for the fact that it is so disjointed, so hard to read?

And students must learn to read Rich's commentary carefully. They can't, that is, just assume that any combination of words on the page can be attributed to "Adrienne Rich." We have found it useful to ask students to distinguish between several speakers: (1) the character or voice in the poem; (2) the Adrienne Rich who wrote the poem; and (3) the Adrienne Rich who wrote the essay commenting on the Adrienne Rich who wrote the poem. Students will not have too much trouble imagining how and why Aunt Jennifer might not be exactly the same person as Rich, but they will have a much harder time charting the different voices in "Snapshots" and "Planetarium." You might begin by asking how they might account for the quotation marks. Who is speaking? Who is trying to draw the line between persons speaking? And why? We have also found it useful to ask students why Rich might have left the last poem, "Planetarium," to stand on its own. It gets a little preliminary commentary, but the end of the poem marks a major transition in the essay.

The "Freire" questions in this assignment stand as a wild card. In a first draft students will most likely write a three-part account of the poems. You will probably want students to return to their discussion of the poems. We found that students fail to distinguish between the person in the poem and the person writing the poem. Students might return to the text to ask "Who is speaking? And to whom?" When assigning a revision, we found we also wanted to give students a way of stepping outside of the poems as they first saw them (and outside the interpretations Rich encourages in her commentary). Freire is particularly helpful here. The second draft, with the Freire questions, can be the occasion for students to ask some questions about what the progression in Rich's poems might (and might not) be said to represent about revision, transformation or criticism, about the possibilities of breaking the hold of the past.

ASSIGNMENT **3**

Tradition and the Writing of the Past [Rich]

This assignment asks students to write from inside the "we" of Rich's discourse, to imagine that the essay is addressed to them. They take these as the key phrases: "Until we can understand the assumptions in which we are drenched we cannot know ourselves" and "We need to know the writing of the past, and know it differently than we have ever known it; not to pass on a tradition but to break its hold over us."

Assignment 3 asks students to imagine that the "writing of the past" is made up of more than a "literary" tradition, that it includes the practice of all writers, that it is handed down not only through Great Books but through popular writing and popular lore, and that its evidence can be found in their own practice, in the predictable features of their own writing, including the writing they have done and are doing for school. Tradition is not just sonnet form; it is also topic sentence and book report. Students' success with this assignment will depend greatly on their ability (and willingness) to turn quickly to a close reading of actual examples (as Rich does with her poems). Students will need texts to work with.

This assignment is the occasion for students to think about their own writing; it is also, however, the occasion for them to think about how writing has been represented to them — by their culture, through their education. They hear, often for the first time, much of the emptiness of the usual talk about writing and they have a chance to reflect on whose interests are served in those representations of writing — where ideas are meant to be controlling ideas, where examples must support conclusions, where conclusions take us back to where we began.

We have found that students tend to avoid (or overlook) the final questions in their first draft — that is, they devote their energy to a study of their own writing and do not step back to reflect on how or why (in their terms or Rich's) one would want to revise the writing of the past, to break its hold. This trend has been our primary concern when working with students in revising their essays.

ASSIGNMENT 4

The Contact Zone [Pratt]

This is a powerful assignment that gives students the opportunity to represent schooling in the 1990s through stories or images from their experiences. Pratt's argument for the classroom as a "contact zone," a place where oppositional discourses rub against each other, clashes with conventional notions of the classroom as a community of like-minded individuals working toward common purposes. As students begin to imagine the classroom as a "contact zone," as they settle into the identification of experiences and images, they'll want to classify them as "community" examples or "contact zone" examples, and you'll want to push them to see the possibilities between the polarities that Pratt establishes, or to imagine other ways of representing their experiences that don't set up polarities.

Once students have read Pratt, it'll be difficult for them not to classify their experiences, but this assignment relies on them to present representative examples of their experiences and images of schooling, those that come to mind almost immediately when they think of school, and they'll first need to present those. When they turn to interpreting their examples in Pratt's terms, they'll have a way to push against her by taking up the question of what they have to gain or lose if they adopt her ways of thinking.

It might be helpful for students to do their initial draft of this assignment with most, if not all, of their attention focused on rendering the representative experiences of schooling that they want to work from. They'll want to create (or re-create) the people involved in the scenes, the dialogue, and the landscape. Most students aren't accustomed to this kind of detailed scene setting; they'll need to render it carefully enough for readers not familiar with their experiences to see the people at work and the kinds of interactions going on, so that when they discuss the scene as representing (or not representing) a "contact zone," readers will be able to discern the oppositions, resistance, and alternatives being played out. The same holds true if they are representing a community.

The second draft or revision could then focus more directly on students weaving their comments into or alongside the scenes. This would be the paper, then, where they read their experiences in Pratt's terms and come to conclusions about what they stand to gain or lose by seeing their schooling in her terms.

ASSIGNMENT 5

The Pedagogical Arts of the Contact Zone [Pratt]

For this assignment students are asked to imagine their writing class, the one that has presented them with this assignment, as a possible "contact zone." To this end, they are invited to take one of the "exercises" that Pratt presents and discuss how it might work in their class. You'll want to be sure that students think about this invitation in terms of turning their classroom into a visible "contact zone," into a place, that is, where differences are visible and taken as occasions for learning. So, for instance, if students decide to fold storytelling into their work, they need to say what kind of storytelling. What will the stories be about? What will they learn from them? How will the stories act to turn the class into a "contact zone"? The same need for definition holds true for whatever "exercise" students decide on. If they would like to critique, then they need to say what they would critique and how critiquing would act to establish a visible "contact zone." For a number of the "exercises" that Pratt suggests (e.g., "experiments in transculturation," "unseemly comparisons"), students will need to imagine what these are and how they would work in a writing classroom. There's room to move here, but they'll need to read Pratt closely to flesh out her more abstract pedagogical arts.

If students decide to imagine comments a teacher would make on one of their papers so that its revision might be one of these "exercises," they have the same problem of definition to deal with. What would the comments ask them, for instance, to tell a story about? How would the revision act to establish a visible "contact zone"? What would they learn from this kind of revision?

ASSIGNMENT 6

Higher Learning [Fish]

This assignment invites students to read against the grain of Fish's essay. We've taught this essay several times, and students have always felt a bit uneasy working within the terms of his argument, uneasy at accepting his account of "studenting" and defining themselves and their experience accordingly. For one thing, our students have said, Fish does not talk about the distribution of power in the classroom. This community may be bound together more by the overriding authority of the teacher than by shared interpretive strategies, due not only to the teacher's ability to set grades but also to his or her ability to ask the guiding questions and determine the tone of the discussion. You can feel this authority in Fish's prose — in the way he addresses the reader, in the Mr. Newlin discussion, in the ways he allows his reader to ask certain questions but not others. The assignment asks students to step out of Fish's discourse by imagining their participation in another community, one where he is not a member — by taking a student's point of view. In a sense, the assignment asks them to puncture or call into question the "we" of Fish's essay.

It is important, however, for students to see that they are writing as members of a collective — of a shared — way of thinking and speaking. It is too easy to write in terms of one's individual freedom ("Well, I've never liked that kind of teacher"). The point is not to imagine a world of individuals — where Fish is a pushy teacher and a student can declare his or her right to independence — but to imagine the classroom as a place of competing interests, where both teachers and students are shaped by the social context, by the history of American education, and by habitual ways of thinking and speaking about the classroom, including those present in Fish's essay.

ASSIGNMENT 7

Confronting an Alternate Point of View
[Freire, Rich, Pratt, Fish]

Rich and Freire have been offered as radical educators — educators who speak for students' abilities to step out of routine, institutional ways of thinking about the world. Fish is offered as an educator who, at least at first glance, seems to be making a counterargument. If students have begun to speak confidently in the first six papers, the purpose of reading Fish is to require that students consider — and at a level they couldn't imagine on their

133·

own — some other point of view. (Again, it would be useful to review the section in the manual on Fish.) This assignment will work best if it is truly a revision, and particularly if it is a revision that does not settle for saying something like "here is another interesting opinion on the subject." Students should be expected, in other words, to make use of Fish — not to bracket him as an oddball or a conservative (the likely response) or to add him as just one more in a list of four, but to begin to imagine how one argument pushes on and qualifies the other. And this will be done best if students not only represent Fish's argument in general terms, but if they turn, in their essays, to a consideration of one of his powerful examples (either the poetry class or Mr. Newlin's hand). If they turn to an example, they can see what Fish's world looks like through Freire's or Pratt's or Rich's eyes. That is often the powerful beginning of a comparison that pushes against easy commonplaces about freedom and restraint, imagination and imitation.

Note: It would be useful to review the section on "How To Recognize a Poem When You See One" in this manual, since the discussions there address similar assignments.

ASSIGNMENT 8

Putting Things Together *[Freire, Rich, Pratt, Fish]*

This assignment is really meant to allow students to feel that the work they have done has brought them somewhere. There is no epiphany at the end of the sequence, no set of words a teacher (or textbook writer) can speak to make it all cohere, but it is possible for students to begin to fashion those words for themselves. That is the purpose of this assignment. It says, in effect, "Listen, you're not a beginner with this anymore. You've developed some expertise on this subject. Let's hear what you have to say." It is important, however, that students feel empowered to draw on their early work. This is not just a matter of saying that it is okay, but of providing the technology to make it possible (like cutting and pasting, for example). Students should begin this task by carefully rereading everything they have written and imagining what the important pieces are and how those pieces might be put together. There should be new writing, of course — students should think of this as a new project — but they shouldn't have to feel that they are starting from scratch.

．．．．．．．．．．

SEQUENCE TWO

The Arts of the Contact Zone *(p. 780)*

The great pleasure of teaching Pratt's essay is watching students put to work the key terms of her interpretive system; "contact zone," "autoethnography," "transculturation." These terms allow students to "reread" or reconceive familiar scenes and subjects; they also provide a rationale (as well as tools) for working against the grain of the usual American valorization of "community." At first her argument seems completely counterintuitive, then it begins to make powerful and surprising sense. At least this was our experience when we taught the essay. It was difficult, in fact, to get students (at the end of their work) to stand a critical distance from Pratt's position — that is, the image of the contact zone provided a perhaps too easy answer to the problem of difference; or it led students to an unexamined reproduction of "liberal" values: sympathy, respect, different strokes for different folks.

This sequence allows students to work at length with Pratt's essay, first with (and on) her terms, later in conjunction with the work of others. You can imagine the sequence working in two directions. It is, in keeping with a standard pattern in *Ways of Reading*, designed as an exercise in application. Students take the general project represented in "Arts of the Contact Zone," work those terms out through close reading and through application to an example from the students' experience, and then apply it to essays in *Ways of Reading* that could be said to represent examples of the literate arts of the contact zone — essays by Gloria Anzaldúa, Harriet Jacobs and Patricia Williams. Our goal in teaching this sequence, however, was also to invite students to begin to imagine that, through their work with Anzaldúa, Jacobs, and Williams, they were in a position to talk back to Pratt — adding examples, perhaps counterexamples, testing the limits of her terms, adding new terms, thinking about Pratt's discussion of Guaman Poma and her discussion of "community," its usefulness and its limits in a more extended project, drawing not only on the resources of *Ways of Reading* but also on students' readings of documents drawn from their local communities.

If you wanted to shorten the sequence, you could drop one of the readings (Anzaldúa, Jacobs, or Williams). There are several selections in *Ways of Reading* that could be substituted for those we have included here: Wideman's "Our Time," Woolf's "A Room of One's Own," Geertz's "Deep Play," Fish's "How to Recognize a Poem," Steinem's "Ruth's Song," Rodriguez's "The Achievement of Desire," Walker's "In Search of Our Mothers' Gardens," Tompkins's "Indians," Fiske's "Madonna" (where the contact might be named as that between old and young). It is surprising how many of the pieces in *Ways of Reading* can be imagined as representative of the arts of the contact zone.

We chose the selections we did for this sequence because we were interested in working with material new to this edition; we also wanted to focus the term "contact" on racial, ethnic, and linguistic difference. If you add other selections (Tompkins, Fish, Geertz, or Fiske, for example), you might want to focus attention on the range of differences (age, class, nation, institutional or intellectual status) that can be highlighted under the term "contact zone."

For a complete commentary on the selections in this sequence, please be sure to read each essay's selection in this manual, particularly the opening discussion. While we will cull materials from the discussions of individual assignments, we won't reproduce the introductions. And, while the sequences provide writing assignments, you should think about the advantages (or disadvantages) of using the Questions for a Second Reading. In every case, students should read the headnotes in the text, which are designed to serve the assignments and sequences.

ASSIGNMENT 1

The Literate Arts of the Contact Zone [Pratt]

The first assignment is structurally a bit complicated. It offers two options, an "inventory" assignment (for which students collect examples of writing from a contact zone) and an "autoethnography" assignment (for which students imagine themselves, as writers, working in a contact zone). What complicates things is that the inventory assignment also offers two options. There are really three writing assignments listed here, grouped into two categories. You may want to make the choice of assignment for your students, depending on the goals of your course. The autoethnography assignment focuses the issues of Pratt's essays within students' own self-representations, within the context of the "personal" essay. The inventory assignment focuses attention on students as readers (and archivists) of other writers' work. Whichever direction students take, we would suggest letting them come back to revise their essays later in the semester, perhaps after assignments 2 and 3 in the sequence. If you plan to work this way, it might be useful to tell students that they will be working on a draft they can come back to later.

135

1. The first of the two options in assignment 1 is an "inventory" assignment, asking students to collect documents that could stand, like the *New Chronicle*, as evidence of the literate arts of the contact zone. Pratt's essay provides a frame to organize the search (a frame students should imagine that they can break — that is, they can take it as a challenge to find the document that would surprise Pratt, that she would overlook or never think of), and it also provides the terms for a discussion of the material they collect (or representative examples from that material).

The assignment suggests two ways of conducting the inventory. The first sends students to a library (or historical society) to find documents from the past. We tried to suggest the many possible moments of contact in local history (between slaves and owners, workers and management, women and men, minority and majority). This assignment was prompted by Jean Ferguson Carr's teaching at Pitt (her courses almost always include some kind of archival project) and Pat Bizzell's teaching at Holy Cross (where she has students research local accounts of European settlements written by Native Americans). We were frustrated by the degree to which students feel removed from library archives and the degree to which our teaching (and the textbook) seemed to enforce that remove. Needless to say, this option will seem to be the harder of the two and students will need some prompting or challenge or rewards to choose it. One thing to remember is that an assignment like this will take more time than usual, since it takes time to find the library and spend enough time in the stacks to make the experience profitable, more than a quick search for the one book that will get you through the assignment. We've also found that we needed to make the process of search and selection an acknowledged part of the work of the course. We ask students to collect folders of material, to present them to others (to the class, to groups) and, in their essays, to talk about how they chose the material they chose to write about.

In the second "inventory" option, students might go out into their local culture to look for "documents" (which can be defined loosely to include music, like rap, transcripts of talk shows, films, documentaries, and so on). Students should feel that they can follow Pratt's lead and turn to their brothers and sisters (or their children) and to educational materials, including papers they are writing or have written recently. You should think about whether or not you would want students to choose papers from your course. It is an interesting possibility, but it will be hard for students to write about you and your class as anything *but* a utopia, paradise on earth. You may be disappointed if you invite students to take your classroom as an example.

Taking either direction, students are asked to present their material as part of a project Pratt has begun. We have found it important to remind students that they need to *present* "Arts of the Contact Zone," even to readers who have read it. You cannot assume, we remind our students, that readers have it freshly in mind or that they will be willing to get the book off the shelf and turn to pages. And we have found it important to help students imagine the role they will play in this text. They will need, in other words, to do more than simply cite from or summarize what they have gathered in their inventories. They will need to step forward (as Pratt does) to teach, translate, make connections, explain, comment, discuss, think this way and that. Students, at least our students, are often too quick to let the wonderful material they gather speak for itself.

2. This assignment asks students to write an "autoethnography." The inventory assignments in this set ask students to use Pratt's term, "contact zone," to read the work of others. This assignment asks students to write from the contact zone, to show how they understand Pratt's argument through their practice.

It is important, as a starting point, to ask students to imagine how this might be different from writing an "autobiography." In a sense, autobiographies have historically been read as "autoethnographies." But as these terms define a *writer's* motive, it will be important for many students to imagine from the outset that they occupy a position likely to be ignored or unread or misread. It can be useful to think of the ways writers signal that they are "engaging with representations" others make of them ("many people would say . . . ," "I have been called . . . ," "some might refer to this as . . . ," "from a different point of view . . ."). This is also a good time to return to the lists Pratt offers of the literate arts of the contact zone ("parody," "unseemly comparisons," "bilingualism," "imaginary dialogue," etc.) These lists can serve as a writer's tool kit — or perhaps, as a way of beginning to imagine revision.

ASSIGNMENT 2

Borderlands [Pratt, Anzaldúa]

One of the pleasures of working with Pratt's essay is that it gave us a new way of reading our Table of Contents. There are several pieces that could stand as examples of writing from a contact zone (or that could be said equally to illustrate the "literate arts of the contact zone"). This assignment turns students' attention to the "mestiza" text, *Borderlands/La frontera*. You could also use the selections by Rich, Rodriguez, Steinem, Walker, Wideman, and Woolf.

This is an application assignment — it asks for a generous reading and extension of Pratt's work. As always, students should feel free to exceed their example — to argue with Pratt, to notice things she wouldn't notice, to add to her list of the literate arts of the contact zone. And as always, it will help to give students a sense of what they will need to provide for their readers. They will need to present Pratt's essay (establish it as a context). They cannot simply assume that it is there, in full, in their readers' minds. And they will need to present their example, providing an introduction to (let's say) "Incidents" and working closely with the text, including passages in quotation. (Since Pratt does not provide examples of the close reading of passages in "Arts of the Contact Zone," it might be useful to provide supplementary examples.) As we stated earlier, we have worked with pages from "Scratches on the Face of the Country." You might also help students prepare by working on a set passage from Anzaldúa in class.

For us, every assignment (or almost every assignment) in a sequence, goes through at least one revision. We would, that is, spend two weeks on most assignments. If students revise this essay, we would suggest two prompts for their work. When they revise, they should begin by rereading Anzaldúa, looking for those parts of the text that have *not* been accounted for in the first draft. Students shouldn't simply be pasting in more examples but looking to see the interesting examples that were left out and asking why, on a first pass, these fell outside their range of vision/understanding/desire. And they should be looking for ways (or places) to speak from their own positions as authors/scholars. Students should, that is, be looking to see how and where they can find a place in their essays to speak from their own learning and concerns. Here is the place where students begin to talk about the limits and benefits, for them, of Pratt's work.

ASSIGNMENT 3

Autoethnography [Pratt, Jacobs]

"Arts of the Contact Zone" provides a useful alternative to Houston Baker's account of the slave narrative. For Baker, the "authentic, unwritten self" is necessarily displaced (or appropriated) by the public discourse. In her representation of "autoethnography" and "transculturation," Pratt allows us to figure the author differently, so that we can imagine Jacobs *engaging* with the standard representation of an African-American woman and her

137

experience (and with the standard representation of a woman of virtue), but not giving up or giving in to it; here the point is, in Pratt's terms, to "intervene" with the majority understanding, where the purpose is corrective or revisionary, and where the writer is allowed a position from which work can be done (and can do more than merely repeat the master narrative).

This assignment asks students to use Pratt's terms ("autoethnography" or "transculturation"). It is important for students to see this as something other than a dictionary assignment ("According to Webster, "ethnography" is . . ."). The point, in other words, is not to come up with the "right" definition but to see how these words (and the text that accompanies them and the example of Guaman Poma) can provide a way of reading "Incidents." Students need to work back and forth between the two essays, seeing how and where Harriet Jacobs might be said to demonstrate her own version of the "literate arts" of the contact zone.

We would spend two weeks on this assignment, asking students to treat their first draft as a draft and directing a revision in the second week. We would follow the same guidelines we outlined above in the discussion of the Anzaldúa essay.

ASSIGNMENT 4

The Law of Property [Pratt, Williams]

Pratt's essay provides an interesting way of connecting Williams's argument in "Alchemical Notes" with her method. When we have taught Williams's work and asked students to think about her method as a response to the "ideology of style," students have tended to speak in fairly general terms about the conventions that govern "reasonable" address, looking for the interests behind that representation of reason, the writer and the reader.

Pratt gave us a way to ask more immediate and pertinent questions about *this* essay and the design or desire represented in its methods of address. Williams, in Pratt's terms, is trying to represent not only her position (as a lawyer) but also the position of African-Americans relative to (almost archetypal) representatives of the majority (white lawyers). This assignment tries to focus a discussion of style through Pratt's representation of the rhetorical situation, where the key problem facing the writer is not simply getting attention and winning assent or understanding but representing the position of the minority in the terms of the majority without simply giving in and letting the majority's terms represent the "truth" or "reality" of the minority experience. (We are very nervous about terms like "majority" and "minority," "black" and "white." Williams's discussion of the problematic nature of these terms has been useful for us in our own class discussions. We include it in full in the entry on Williams in the earlier manual section.)

This essay assumes that students can produce — as writers, not just as readers — a close reading of sections of Williams's essay. It might be useful to work out an example of such a reading on a particular section, which we would suggest then be out of the running for students' essays. When we have worked with a sequence like this one, we have used an essay toward the end of the term to focus attention on the writerly problems of producing a close reading — both the "technical" issues of producing block quotations, using ellipses, and so on, and the more difficult issue of how to write about the possible (and not single or simple) readings of a passage that has been presented through a combination of summary and block quotation. There are problems of presentation in this form of writing that we in the profession have learned to negotiate. It is important to help students see what these problems are, so that they can begin to imagine how they might be solved. Teachers need to do more, that is, than we do in our assignments when we say, "Be sure to work closely with the text."

We would spend two weeks on this assignment, leading students through a draft and a revision following the guidelines outlined above.

On Culture [Pratt, Anzaldúa, Jacobs]

We often end our sequences with "retrospective" assignments. This one asks students to return to Pratt's essay and to the work they have been doing with it in order to represent that work to someone who is an outsider. For the first time, however, the issue has been represented through the more inclusive term, "culture." This assignment is a way for students to connect the work they have been doing with Pratt with larger questions of culture and community, reading and writing. Directing the assignment at an audience new to this material allows students to work from their strengths and to imagine the distance between what they have learned to say and where they began. To this end, it is important for this assignment that students imagine their audience to be a group of peers, people like them who have not been in this course. Without this warning, students tend to represent the "intellectual other" as a child or a simpleton. The stakes have to be high for this paper to work — students need to imagine that they have to address and hold the attention of their sharpest and most intellectually impatient colleagues.

An alternative to this assignment would be one directed not to students but to Pratt. We often end sequences with this other retrospective, in which the goal, we say, is for students to take their turn in a conversation begun by Pratt. Here the pressure on them is to achieve some critical distance from Pratt, to find a way of challenging or supplementing what Pratt says on the basis of what they (the students) have learned over the course of their work with this sequence.

As we suggested earlier, it might be useful to ask students to go back and work again on the first assignment in this sequence in a second or third draft. That way the issues as they have bearing on what students do (how they read and write) and not just on what they know (in summary statement) will be forward in their minds. From this they can begin to write to Pratt, or to students, perhaps students who would be reading the same materials in this course next semester. After a semester, you will have some of these essays on file. We have handed them out at the beginning of the term as a preview, and then brought them forward again at the end, in a discussion framing students' work with this final assignment.

· · · · · · · · · ·

SEQUENCE THREE

Experts and Expertise (p. 787)

We use the metaphor of apprenticeship several times in the textbook. This is the assignment sequence that features this particular use of texts. The assignments invite students to take on the key terms and angle of vision of each essay, to imagine that each author has begun a project and that the students' job, once they have been given the tools and have gotten the hang of what is going on, is to carry it on in the spirit of the master. The last assignment, in the name of Walker Percy, asks students to look back at what they have done and to question just what is at stake or what can be gained by taking on someone else's way of thinking and speaking in just this way. While we want students to have the opportunity of looking critically at this kind of imitation, we want students to feel the power of it. It is, as we say, heady work. Students are given ways of thinking and speaking that they would not invent on their own — at least not so quickly and not in such rapid succession. And they are given a sense of a Theweleit, Rich, Wideman, Geertz, or Kuhn that goes well beyond an encyclopedia-like recitation of the authors' key ideas.

Note: In the case of each assignment, it would be a good idea to go to the sections in the manual on each author and review what we say there as well. There are statements about the essays and about writing assignments that have bearing on the sequence but that we won't repeat here.

ASSIGNMENT 1

Reading Between the Lines [Theweleit]

Theweleit demonstrates a way of working with different kinds of texts (journals, fiction, official pronouncements, graphics) to represent the preparation of young boys for the Freikorps. It's a dazzling and unconventional performance, partly because he ignores traditional argumentative procedures and proceeds primarily through association, but also because of the materials he works with. One thing leads to another in Theweleit's prose, and although he could be said to be presenting evidence — he doesn't shape it into a traditional argument in which relationships and connections are reasoned out and made visible. By juxtaposing arguments and evidence — evidence that is almost always textual, e.g., quotations from journals and works of fiction — he allows his readers the job of imagining the reasoning that leads to his conclusions and statements. Students will be struck by the force of this selection, and although they'll "feel" that it's different from other essays they've read, they won't be able to say why without doing some work on its methods. You might lead into this assignment with one of the second-reading questions (or a writing assignment) for the Theweleit selection that turns students' attention to Theweleit's methods.

Theweleit understands his material as an expression of how the male body and desires can be transformed through training into the desires and practices of war. Students will need to approach their materials from a perspective similarly focusing on the representations of the male body and male desires. Of course, they don't need to demonstrate how these representations are transformed into the desires and practices of war, but they do need to work in the spirit of Theweleit's project and demonstrate that male bodies and desires are being transformed in some way into something other than their sexuality. Students have no difficulty finding materials to read as examples of young boys' preparation for life in the 1990s in the United States, but they do have a difficult time framing their project in terms of the transformation of bodies and sexual desires into something else as part and parcel of training. They will, of course, need to be sure that they are working with materials that present the shaping, or forming, or training of boys—their bodies and their desires.

A revision helps a great deal. Once students have written a paper working with textual materials, quoting passages that represent the preparation of young boys for something—life, sports, computer games, leadership, and so on—they'll need to make another pass at the paper that allows them to pay closer attention to what this preparation might be said to represent. In other words, can they interpret the preparation they selected as a transformation of male bodies and sexual desires into something else? Does this kind of reading work for their materials? Why or why not?

Students will also need to present Theweleit's arguments as a part of their projects, and they should proceed as if they are writing for others in the class, that is, for people who have read Theweleit but need to be reminded about his arguments and oriented to how their new work extends his project. In our experience, the revision is also a good place to attend to this, as students will spend most of their time in their initial draft presenting and reading the materials they have gathered.

A Story of Reading [Kuhn, Theweleit]

We like to include at least one assignment like this in every course we teach — that is, an assignment that asks students to take their experience as readers, turn it into narrative, and reflect upon what they have written. Following Culler (in *On Deconstruction*), we have called these "stories of reading."

The purpose of this assignment is to bring forward what students suspect they must hide — their sense that Theweleit's writing is weird, difficult and, in their terms, "poorly organized." Students will believe that we should read Theweleit (or that any competent reader would read Theweleit) the same way we read Stanley Fish, that the essays should make sense to us in just the same ways. And, of course, this is not true. When students officially acknowledge the difficulty of the essay, and use it as a way of talking about what Theweleit assumes about his readers (rather than their failure as readers), they are in a position to think about reading as an activity, something that they do and that they might do differently.

Before students write this assignment, we will often have a kind of warm-up discussion of a passage drawn from anywhere in the essay. ("Take us to a passage that seemed weird, difficult or impossible," we'll say, and then we'll begin there, and lead students through a close reading of the passage. Our goal is to give them a way of talking about difficulty as a strategy or a feature in the text and not as a sign of their failure.) Most of all, however, we want students to tell a good story.

For revision: Often the narrative is dull and spare and we encourage students to develop character and action in their writing. Some of the most successful papers we have received break the conventions of the "essay" as students imagine them. We deliberately confused genre in writing the assignment (at one point we ask for an essay, at another we say "tell a story") as a way of opening up the formal possibilities for student writers. We have received diaries, stories with dialogue, and extended journal entries. Students also tend to overlook our request that they put Kuhn's terms to the test. You will have to follow your own judgment here. The last time we taught this assignment we were primarily concerned with having students reflect on the ways they read Theweleit, and we needed the revision to continue that reflection. As a consequence, Kuhn tended to fade into the background. He provided a frame or a method to get the assignment going, but we didn't push as hard as we might for students to return to a consideration of Kuhn's terms.

Looking Back [Rich]

Rich speaks powerfully about the need to turn criticism to the material of daily life. This assignment asks students to write from inside the "we" of Rich's discourse, to imagine that the essay is addressed to them. It takes this as its key phrase: "Until we can understand the assumptions in which we are drenched we cannot know ourselves."

Assignment 3 asks students to follow Rich's lead and to write autobiographically, not as a celebration of their individuality but to cast themselves as a representative example of the way a certain group — named perhaps in terms of age, race, class, or gender —

is positioned within the dominant culture. And it asks them to use the occasion to try out some of Rich's key terms, like "revision" and "patriarchy." As with Theweleit, students need to find a way of describing Rich's methods — both the method she calls for and the method enacted in her essay. It is easy to declare Rich a "great writer" or a "famous person." It is harder to imagine what this talk of "re-vision" might be about, and how it might have bearing on the work of a student. The goal of this assignment is to narrow the distance between Rich and the student, to enable the student to imagine that she or he can both understand and try out Rich's project.

The difficulty students will have is in imagining (or representing) their experience as representative of a collective experience. You will not, in other words, get papers about the pressure of culture but about key individuals — fathers, mothers, teachers, lovers, grandparents, and coaches. In some ways this is inevitable. Both our students' age and the distinctly American versions of "personal experience" lead our students to write stories with no sense of the social, the political, or the historical. These, then, are the concerns we highlight for revision: In what ways is this story more than your story? Where can we find the cultural context? In what ways are you, as a character, cast in relation to ways of speaking, habits of mind?

ASSIGNMENT 4

Seeing Your World Through Geertz's Eyes [Geertz]

At the heart of Geertz's method is the process of taking a characteristic cultural event and seeing it as "saying something about something else." The cockfight is a story the Balinese "tell themselves about themselves." This, in miniature, is an invitation to share in the rigorous form of cultural analysis represented by Geertz's work. This assignment asks students to apply his method to a scene from their own familiar culture. Students, we've found, take great pleasure in this assignment. They are given a method, as well as an occasion, for speculating on the meaning of events central to their own lives. It is important, however, for students to work with real observation. If not, they will be inventing television scripts or cartoon versions of their own lives. The value of Geertz's method is that it is a way of opening up an unfamiliar culture. It is difficult for students to assume that their own culture is mysterious or unfamiliar. They must begin with this assumption, however, and they must work to maintain a conceptual distance from the events they closely observe. They should, for example, be careful not to personalize or to refer to themselves, even to the extent of saying "us" when referring to a population of college students.

For revision: Students, we've found, write this essay with considerable skill and enthusiasm. We have used students' first drafts to begin to direct a critical rereading of Geertz. The seams in students' texts are larger and more immediately visible than in Geertz's. By dramatizing the way students "master" the scenes they describe (by objectifying other people, by writing an interpretation that is total and final, by dealing in stereotypes, by telling familiar stories as though they were new), we can prepare them to look for similar gestures (and motives) in Geertz's essay. And by discussing the way Geertz could be said to be working on the problems of writing in this essay (the ways his expertise includes his work as a writer), we can set the terms for students' revisions of their own essays. If, in fact, the problems we highlight are not problems that can be overcome (all writing is interested, every writer is situated), then what are the options for a writer who wants to work on his or her writing? Geertz, it could be argued, solves the problem of making the problem part of the writing. He is not, in other words, just "reporting" what he "discovered" about the Balinese. And so we would like our students to imagine that they need to think of their drafts as writing problems — not just problems of reporting what they saw.

ASSIGNMENT **5**

Wideman as a Case in Point [Wideman]

Wideman, unlike Geertz, announces that he is writing about the problems of writing. This assignment asks students to look particularly at those sections where he interrupts the narrative to call attention to his situation as a writer.

We've taught this assignment several times and we've found it important for students to work directly from passages in the text. The first thing they need to do, then, is to reread the selection and choose their material. (The assignment asks them to choose three or four passages. This may turn out to be too many.) Once they have located their material, students do not have great difficulty describing it. They do, however, have trouble turning the discussion to a critical analysis of writing — either the writing of "In Our Time" or writing as a generalized subject. In their first draft, students should be encouraged to turn from their material to the question of *why* Wideman interrupts the narrative. We have found that students write well and at length about *what* Wideman says, but when the space is open for them to come forward and comment or explain, they feel they have nothing to say. Students can imagine several routes to this question — they can talk as fellow-writers, imagining from that perspective why a writer might want to bring forward the problem of writing. They can talk as readers, explaining the effects of these intrusions as they experienced them. Or they can talk as students — that is, through their knowledge of other attempts to represent an understanding of race, family, crime, drug addiction, or the black community.

For revision: Our experience with this assignment suggests that students can best use the time allowed for revision to work on the general issues raised in this paper. What might they say about Wideman's narrative intrusions? And, more particularly, what might this have to do with the writing they are doing (or might do) as students in the academy? What would the benefits or consequences be of producing a text that calls attention to itself as a text, as something produced? In particular, we want them to consider how Wideman's writing might stand beside Geertz's and Rich's. His authority rests, we think, on somewhat different grounds. And we would like students to consider his language (and theirs) next to the language they find in their textbooks or other "academic" writing assigned in their courses. If, in fact, these writers might be said to be "experts," how might their expertise be valued in the academic community as students have experienced it (or as they imagine it)?

ASSIGNMENT **6**

On Experts and Expertise [Theweleit, Kuhn, Rich, Geertz, Wideman, Percy]

The first five assignments repeat a basic pattern. They ask students to take on the ways of speaking and thinking of other powerful thinkers — to be apprentices. They imagine (with the aid of a text) a "Theweleit," "Kuhn," "Rich," "Geertz," and "Wideman," and then work in his or her spirit. This assignment invites students to reflect back on what they have done, this time in the name of a "Walker Percy" who says that there is nothing more dangerous for a student than to get into the hands of an expert theorist. Students, in a sense, are being invited to fold their own story into the anecdotes about students in the second section of "The Loss of the Creature." This will be a difficult assignment for students who have done no prior work on Percy. It might be useful, in fact, to either allow time for a preliminary assignment or to allow time for this essay to go through several drafts. Percy's argument lends itself so easily to cliché (partly because he refuses to come forward as a theorist and provide a useful analytical language of his own) that students will need to have a complicated sense of how his essay works if they are to do justice to this assignment. (You don't, in other words, want students to be trapped in the corner of talking about nothing more than "the need to be an individual.") It is also important that students focus in on their work in the previous assignments: They will need, that is, to have good stories of their own to tell as well as the encouragement to select and quote from their own texts.

. . . .

SEQUENCE FOUR

History and Ethnography: Reading the Lives of Others (p. 795)

We had a great time teaching this sequence. Students took great pleasure in becoming local or family historians, in turning "anthropological" intent on the scenes and expressions of their immediate culture. One of our goals in designing this sequence was to demonstrate in precise terms the ways in which intellectual work — in this sequence, work that goes under the names "history" and "ethnography" — is the work of reading and writing. We wanted to define the academy in terms of its practice (or practices) so that it could stand as something other than a museum of ideas or a collection of geniuses; we wanted to define intellectual work as reading and writing so that students could see firsthand their connectedness to academic disciplines and how and why they might be able to develop discipline-specific expertise — to become historians or cultural anthropologists (at least of a certain school).

The opening assignments are fairly straightforward. Geertz and Limerick are offered as representatives of their disciplines. Students work with and on their projects — extending them, reading them closely. We added Wideman to the list in order to yank "reading and writing the lives of others" out of the academy and put it into the realm of "ordinary life" or, perhaps more properly, the general (as opposed to academic) culture. And the Pratt assignment provides students with a motive and a set of terms for an attempt to theorize the representation of the "other."

We also, you will notice, built a series of revisions into this sequence. The point of the revision sequence is to allow students to think of the process of revision as something more than the perfecting or "finishing" of an essay. This sequence is designed to make students first of all see that they are involved in a sequential project, in which they will go back to add more to what they have begun. Secondly, while revision is defined here as "addition," this sequence tries to illustrate how addition can be addition with a difference — adding not simply more of the same, but rather material that was hidden or forbidden or lost to the project as it was conceived the first time through. Students look to the "experts" to see how they have represented the problems of reading and writing the lives of others, then they go to their own work to see what they might add to make their texts more "expert" and less "naive."

If you wanted to shorten this sequence, the best way to do it would be to drop the Pratt assignment and perhaps also the third revision of the opening essay. If you wanted to work in book-length readings, we would recommend Geertz's *Works and Lives: The Anthropologist as Author*, Pratt's new book, *Imperial Eyes*, Simon Schama's *Dead Uncertaincies: Unwarranted Speculations*, or Renato Rosaldo's *Culture and Truth*. If you wanted to work in other essays from *Ways of Reading*, we would suggest using one of the stories — "Theft" or "A Story in an Almost Classical Mode" — as a way of raising the issue of the "realistic" narrative; or Fiske's "Madonna" for a look at another version of ethnography, this time dealing with local subjects; or Willis's "Work(ing) Out," for a different version of "reading" the lives of others; or Steinem's "Ruth's Song," which serves as a parallel or supplement to Wideman's attempt to tell a family story/write a family history.

For a complete commentary on the selections in this sequence, please be sure to read each essay's selection in this manual, particularly the opening discussion. While we will cull materials from the discussions of individual assignments, we won't reproduce the introductions. And, while the sequences provide writing assignments, you should think about the advantages (or disadvantages) of using the Questions for a Second Reading. In every case, students should read the headnotes in the textbook, which are designed to serve the assignments and sequences.

ASSIGNMENT 1

Ethnography [Geertz]

This has been a successful assignment for us. It asks students to demonstrate their reading of Geertz's method by putting it to work on characteristic scenes from their own surroundings. Geertz's method can be represented by his phrase "saying something of something." He insists that scenes and events can be said to do this, to speak and tell a story, even to offer a key to the interpretation of a culture. The cockfights, he says, are a story the Balinese tell themselves about themselves. Similarly, our students walk around shopping malls, form groups and subgroups, and express themselves through ritual and routine. These scenes and activities seem to stand beyond commentary — either as just naturally there or as obvious in meaning and intent. One of our students said, "I don't have a 'culture.' I go home, we watch TV, our Mom brings the dinner into the TV room, she clears it away, we watch until the news, then I do my homework and go to bed. What else is there to say?" Learning both the motive and the method to finding that "what else" is one way of representing Geertz's project.

To begin to extend Geertz's work, students must begin with the assumptions that the scenes and events they describe contain stories they are (without knowing it) telling themselves about themselves. Such events say something about something else. The question is what. What is being said? And about what? What are these stories? What are their key features? How, as a reader, might one interpret them? How, as a writer, might one present them and explain/justify/rationalize one's interpretation? It is important for college students, if they write on groups close to them, to insist on their separateness, to speak of *them*, not *us*, to work from the outside. For this exercise, it is important that students act as though they were interpreting someone else's story and not their own.

It is also important to steer students away from the grand, national generalizations Geertz makes. (This is a route to one way of critiquing Geertz — how does he get to speak for *all* Balinese people?) If they begin to write about America, they will have trouble getting beyond the national narrative of America. They will have an easier time writing about local sub-cultures, local scenes and characters and routines.

The purpose of the assignment is to turn students to their own immediate culture and to invite them to imagine and carry out a Geertzian project. It is important, then, that they begin with the motive to act like anthropologists, even if that means little more than writing something *other* than the usual classroom composition. This is partly a matter of style and arrangement; but it is also a matter of preparation. Students should work from recorded observations, not just from memory. Memory will lead inevitably to the commonplace and the clichéd, to the "life story" as it is enshrined in the composition curriculum, and will thus deprive them of the very details that can make their work rich and surprising.

Students should be reminded that they will have a chance to come back to this essay later.

History [Limerick]

There are two options in this assignment. The general goal is to have students perform a reading of Limerick by writing a history — showing, in a sense, what they have learned in what they can do, defining the presence of the writer (Limerick) through the possible ways in which she might influence other writers.

The first option sends students to the library or local historical society. This assignment was prompted by Jean Ferguson Carr's teaching at Pitt (her courses almost always include some kind of archival project) and Pat Bizzell's teaching at Holy Cross (where she has students research local accounts of European settlements written by Native Americans). We were frustrated by the degree to which students feel removed from library archives and the degree to which our teaching (and the textbook) seemed to enforce that remove. Needless to say, this option will seem to be the harder of the two and students will need some prompting or challenge or rewards to choose it. One thing to remember is that an assignment like this will take more time than usual, since it takes time to find the library and spend enough time in the stacks to make the experience profitable, more than a quick search for the one book that will get you through the assignment. We've also found that we needed to make the process of search and selection an acknowledged part of the work of the course. We ask students to collect folders of material, to present them to others (to the class, to groups) and, in their essays, to talk about how they chose the material they chose to write about. Selection is of some special importance for this assignment, since Limerick's work points to the importance of finding the otherwise hidden alternative story.

The second option cuts out the library time, although it will work best if students take the challenge of making this more than a "personal essay." In fact, when we gave students this assignment, "personal essay" became a useful negative term, a way of indicating what their work needed to transcend in revision. Here is how we made the distinction between "history," as represented by Limerick, and "personal essay." Gathering materials was important — that is, essays became "histories" when they incorporated materials (like photos, diaries and interviews) that would not have been found if a writer had not felt responsible for more than his or her own immediate experience. And structure became important. Essays became histories when they included more than two "stories" and more than a single point of view. In fact, much of the work of revision was represented in just these terms. Students went back to write more stories (counterstories, in Limerick's style) and to write from points of view not their own (their parents', a neighbor's, a friend's, a teacher's). Students added stories, added points of view, and worked to establish paragraphs (like those in Limerick) where they stepped forward to speak as an historian about the material they had gathered. The key moments in the best essays we received came when students realized they had to break the "unity" they had been trained to value, when they added the story that didn't seem to fit or wrote from outside their own point of view.

A Writer's Guide [Wideman, Geertz, Limerick]

If you have time, this assignment could actually become two assignments. It asks students first to read Wideman as an alternative to the "historian" and the "ethnographer" as they have been produced by the academy. Wideman comes to a similar project with a background as a fiction writer. For him, the problems are located more generally in the problematics of writing (and, although he is less open about this, in the problematics of the family, *its* master narratives). Students might take time to work out first an account of Wideman as a counterexample to Geertz and Limerick. The advantage of doing this first in writing is that it will allow students the time and motive to choose and work closely with representative passages from "Our Time."

The assignment also asks students to produce a "Writer's Guide." This can be formatted as a guide — that is, as a set of tips or guidelines with illustrative examples. When we taught this assignment we used a handbook as a model.

You could set this up as two separate assignments. You could let the work on "Our Time" take place in a journal, or in material prepared in groups for class discussion. It will be useful to share examples of the "Writer's Guides" or to create a composite "Guide" from the more interesting material you collect. Students should learn to read and to value these guides before they go on to the revision assignments.

ASSIGNMENT 4

Revision [Geertz, Limerick, Wideman]

This assignment asks students to choose one of the opening two essays and to begin a major revision. We have received wonderful work from both the "history" and the "anthropological" essay. (In fact, we have had students win prizes in our campus writing contest with essays from these assignments.) It is important to allow students to finally define "history" and "ethnography" through their practice and their readings of the selections. Students will not write what might strictly speaking be called an "ethnography," for example. But the point of the assignment is not to insist upon disciplinary rigor or to force their work to fit a predetermined mold. Students are imagining, approximating disciplinary work. The ways in which they get it "wrong" will be as potentially interesting and productive as the ways in which they get it "right."

Choosing which essay to work on will be a hard decision for many students. Our standard advice is for them to choose the one they feel drawn to. We impose only one general rule: Never choose the essay that was a disaster or that you (the student) think the teacher didn't like. We want our students to think of revision as a chance to take a good piece of work on to its next step, not to compensate for a bad start.

We also make much of this distinction made in the assignment between fixing or finishing an essay and taking it on to its next step. When students set out to "finish" an essay, their goal is to preserve the text they have begun. We want to encourage students to think of revision as opening up a text, changing it fundamentally, finding a way of bringing in material that challenges or frustrates its unity or certainty, its transitions and conclusions.

When our students have worked with the guidelines suggested by Geertz, Limerick, and Wideman, they have usually written the following: a text with marked sections, a text in a variety of voices or styles, a text that moves from predictable to unpredictable examples, a text with sections representing different points of view, a text with sections in italics, a text in which they stop and talk as writers about the writing.

ASSIGNMENT 5

Reading Others [Pratt]

We think of this assignment as a way of returning students to the practice of "reading and writing the lives of others," but this time with a bit more conscious theorizing — a little more worry about who (really) is doing what to whom. Pratt, in her work, is one of the most powerful and most generous critics of history and ethnography. She advocates the practice, that is, while pointing to the interests it has served in the past and limits that have been imposed on the genres. At the end of this assignment, we want our students to be in a position to theorize on what they have done and to consider as they prepare to revise that the very skills they have developed can also be conceived of as problematic.

This assignment is an "inventory" assignment, asking students to collect documents that could stand, like the *New Chronicle,* as evidence of the literate arts of the contact zone. Pratt's essay provides a frame to organize the search (a frame students should imagine that they can break — that is, they can take it as a challenge to find the document that would surprise Pratt, that she would overlook or never think of), and her essay provides the terms for a discussion of the material they collect (or representative examples from that material).

This assignment offers two options. The first sends students to a library (or historical society) to find documents from the past. We tried to suggest the many possible moments of contact in local history (between slaves and owners, workers and management, women and men, minority and majority). (For more informatin, see our discussion on how this assignment was prompted on manual p. 146.)

The second option sends students out into their local culture to look for the "documents" (this can be defined loosely to include music, like rap, transcripts of talk shows, films, documentaries, whatever). Students should feel that they can follow Pratt's lead and turn to their brothers and sisters (or their children) and to educational materials, including papers they are writing or have written recently. You should think about whether or not you would want students to choose papers from your course. It is an interesting possibility, but it will be hard for students to write about you and your class as anything *but* a utopia, paradise on earth. You may be disappointed if you invite students to take your classroom as an example.

In this assignment, whether students choose to work with historical or contemporary documents, they are asked to present their material as part of a project Pratt has begun. We have found it important to remind students that they need to *present* "Arts of the Contact Zone," even to readers who had read it. You cannot assume, as we noted earlier, that readers have it freshly in mind or that they will be willing to get the book off the shelf and turn to pages. And we have found it important to help students imagine the role they will play in this text. They will need, in other words, to do more than simply cite from or summarize what they have gathered in their inventories. They will need to step forward (as Pratt does) to teach, translate, make connections, explain, comment, discuss, think this way and that. Students, at least our students, are often too quick to let the wonderful material they gather speak for itself.

ASSIGNMENT 6

Revision (again) [Geertz, Limerick, Wideman, Pratt]

This is the "final" revision. We go to great lengths to put the word "final" in quotation marks, so that it doesn't seem to indicate the end of the road or the end of thinking, so that it doesn't seem to call for some kind of ultimate, oracular conclusion, the peace that passes all understanding. We have, however, found it important to distinguish between a draft that is primarily a draft (where a student continues to work on the intellectual project) and one that must also be "finished" (almost in a carpenter's sense, with a finish applied to the surface). We want our students to worry through the problems of proof-reading, format and presentation, and we want to make this process a formal part of the sequence. We do this, in fact, with every course we teach, although we don't always represent this in every assignment sequence in *Ways of Reading.* The second paragraph of the assignment, then, is an attempt to direct students to the task of producing a "finished" essay, even when we know (or hope) that they aren't finished with the issues that have been raised, or even with the projects they have begun to work on.

As we said in the discussion of the previous assignment, we want this revision to be one where students take on the burdens of history and ethnography — understanding how these textual forms have been used in the past, a sense of their participation in that tradition, a sense of the weight of convention (and not just its support). One possible way of formalizing this process is to ask students to write a separate section, modeled on the final two sections of Geertz's essay, in which the writer steps out of the project to reflect back on it, its writing, and its possible good. Students, we've found, need to be reminded of the pressure to write this final section — or else to find some other way of bringing this level of commentary into their text. Without a reminder, they will simply "finesse" this part of the assignment.

• • • • • • • • • •

SEQUENCE FIVE

Gendered Writing (p. 802)

There are three basic goals to this sequence: to have students read and understand the feminist critique of a patriarchal culture, to enable students to see the consequences of this argument for reading and writing as practices, and to invite students to see the implications in their work as readers and writers. Our experience tells us that students (and teachers) take considerable pleasure in the ways this sequence asks students to both critique and to step outside of the essay as a standard genre, the "voice of the Father." The difficulty of the sequence is in turning the feminist argument (which many students think they know all too well) toward texts, where suddenly it becomes a very new and interesting way of describing and valuing ways of using language. We have found that it is important to invite students to define the differences they see in texts in terms of gender without forcing the question of value, so that the class does not seem to insist on a conversion to feminism, so that students don't feel that they must denounce "the Father." As we describe the course to ourselves, we are asking students to try out this form of criticism, to try out a form of writing or reading that might be said to be more "womanly" than "manly," in Woolf's terms. Hence, when we ask students to hear the voice of the Father in familiar materials, it is to see how it might be both attractive and unattractive, productive and counter-productive.

For a more complete discussion of each of the selections, see the commentary on the individual essays and questions earlier in the instructor's manual. We will not reproduce all of it here.

ASSIGNMENT 1

Writing as Re-Vision [Rich]

Rich speaks powerfully about the need to turn criticism to the material of daily life. This assignment asks students to write from inside the "we" of Rich's discourse, to imagine that the essay is addressed to them. It takes this as its key phrase: "Until we can understand the assumptions in which we are drenched we cannot know ourselves."

Assignment 1 asks students to follow Rich's lead and to write autobiographically, not as a celebration of their individuality but to cast themselves as a representative example of the way a certain group — named perhaps in terms of age, race, class or gender — is positioned within the dominant culture. And it asks them to use the occasion to try out some of Rich's key terms, like "revision" and "patriarchy." Sudents need to find a way of describing Rich's method — both the method she calls for and the method enacted in her essay. It is easy to declare Rich a "great writer" or a "famous person." It is harder to imagine what this talk of "re-vision" might be about and how it might have bearing on the work of a student. The goal of this assignment is to narrow the distance between Rich and the student, to enable the student to imagine that she or he can both understand and try out Rich's project.

The difficulty students will have is in imagining (or representing) their experience as representative of a collective experience. You will not, in other words, get papers about the pressure of culture but about key individuals — fathers, mothers, teachers, lovers, grandparents, and coaches. In some ways this is inevitable. Both our students' age and the distinctly American versions of "personal experience" lead our students to write stories with no sense of the social, the political, or the historical. These, then, are the concerns we highlight for revision: In what ways is this story more than your story? Where can we find the cultural context? In what ways are you, as a character, cast in relation to ways of speaking, habits of mind?

ASSIGNMENT 2

A Man's Story [Brodkey]

Brodkey's story plays out through Buddy's intelligence. We hear a good deal about his desires and little about those of his stepmother, Doris. We get to see Buddy react in detail to Doris and her illness, and we come to know Doris primarily through Buddy's creation of her. In this way, Brodkey's story is a boy's story, and the boy is Brodkey's creation. Because Brodkey gives Buddy his name (Harold Brodkey is the boy's name in the story), students immediately want to read the story as autobiography. It helps if students understand that although it is rooted in autobiography, it is a story. If they work with it as fiction, they can consider Brodkey's creation of Buddy as one of the author's methods and one available for study and critique as it might be said to represent the man writing the story.

Our approach to the story has been to ask students to identify passages that they would use to represent the boy's mind and Doris's. They need to stay close to the story, to the passages, or else they'll generalize about boys, as the story seems to represent one, and how they think. When they have the passages to work with, they can characterize the qualities that mark Buddy's thinking and speaking as a boy's. What does he desire? How does he think of Doris? What other possible ways of thinking of and reacting to Doris does Buddy miss or neglect? What do you learn, then, about Buddy's maleness, his characteristic boy's way of thinking and being, by studying how he sees Doris and how he might see her differently?

Students will have a more difficult time locating the man, the author, in the story, mostly because he blurs himself into Buddy; but they can help themselves by thinking in terms of the narrative. Who is telling the story? Buddy, the character, or Harold Brodkey, the author? Where in the story does it seem one or the other? In those places where it seems that a man, not a boy, is telling the story, how would you characterize him? What are his qualities? Is he a stereotypical figure? How or how not? Students can also look to the dialogue, the conversations between Buddy and Doris, for moments when the boy is telling the story, but it's important that they locate these passages in the dialogue and the narrative by themselves with the help of your questions. They need to be able to make the distinctions between the boy and the man telling the story, to find those passages to represent both, and to draw the conclusions about the two minds at work. What are the qualities of these two minds? How do they represent boys and men?

When students work on their revisions of this paper, they can return to what they have written and to Brodkey's story to draw conclusions about what they might call "male codes" — male ways of thinking and behaving — that underlie the story. Once students

150

have worked with the passages to examine the qualities of the two male minds at work in the story, they'll be ready to talk and write about what they represent. They can begin by asking themselves what particular male values are represented by the passages they've chosen to work with. What, in other words, would they say the author and Buddy value? How, then, would they describe or characterize these values and codes, the underlying or invisible rules and regulations, that could be said to govern the thinking of men and boys? And, finally, are the codes recognizable to them? Are they stereotypical? Or are they revised from what they have come to expect of men and boys?

ASSIGNMENT 3

The Voice of the Unwritten Self [Jacobs]

While "Incidents" is not a difficult piece to read, it presents some interesting problems in the classroom. Students read it and feel moved, yet the most appropriate response seems to be silence. What else is there to say? It seems almost disrespectful to begin talking about the text as a text, to turn it into "material" for an English class. One way to begin is with Jacobs's statement that she does not want a reader's sympathy. Why might she say this? What is wrong with sympathy?

Our approach to "Incidents," in fact, has been through the places where Jacobs addresses her readers directly. In a sense, she anticipates the problem of silence (of a "liberal" reading) and teaches her reader how to read. We ask students to mark the sections where they feel Jacobs is speaking to them *as* readers, to talk about the readers Jacobs assumes and the ways she wants to prepare those readers and revise their expectations. We also try to get students to imagine Jacobs's relationship to the conventions of storytelling, to the unusual stories about growing up and having children, and to see how and where they might find evidence of the difficulties of this relationship in the prose. This is also why we introduce in the headnote Houston Baker's and Jean Fagin Yellin's accounts of the problems of slave narratives.

One of the difficulties we've had teaching "Incidents" is that it so quickly becomes a familiar story, translating the experience of slavery into familiar terms, transforming an unwritten (and unwritable) experience into the general public discourse about slavery, love, and human relations. This tendency to see the other in our own terms, to master the difference, places us in a structural relationship to Jacobs that mirrors her relations with the slave owners.

There are further complications here, however. In Jacobs's account, she is at once both a slave and a woman. Owners are white and they are both men and women. Students will need to work out a discussion of the differences and similarities in the positions of women and slaves and women who are slaves. It will be important for students to work closely with passages from the text that they consider examples of the ways in which she works on her material. They will also need to consider how her work on her materials might be said to reveal or characterize her position as a slave who is a woman writing a story that doesn't neatly fit the conventional ways of telling a life story.

ASSIGNMENT 4

Man-Womanly/Woman-Manly: Gender and Writing [Woolf]

When we have taught these chapters, we have wanted students to hear or feel the ways in which this is a slippery, surprising, carefully wrought and playful text. More than with any other selection in the book, we spend time reading sections of *A Room* out loud, trying to imagine the ways they might be phrased or how they might be taken. The opening and the conclusion have so many stops and starts, shift voice and ground so often, that they provide fine examples. We want students to feel the richness of this text, and we are not beyond placing it next to an oral reading of a much more plodding, single-minded and "univocal" text. And, for obvious reasons, we have chosen men for our examples: Fish, Kuhn, Freire, Miller. (Although we have also read from men's writing that seems similarly responsive and multivocal: Percy, Rodriguez, Berger, Geertz.)

The danger here is letting students launch into familiar and well-rehearsed arguments about who does the housework or whether women should work outside the home. There are reasons to argue the justice or implications of a room and £500 a year, but we have found that these arguments do not serve our purposes as well as arguments about writing — about what writing should or might do, about the limits and consequences of a way of writing determined by men or serving men's interests. It is not difficult for students to identify features in writing (types of introductions and conclusions, for example, or the voices of authority) that seem to be "naturally" and inevitably there ("the way you are supposed to write") and to name them in terms of gender. Once they are named, students have a way of imagining the history and the politics that govern writing.

This assignment asks students to write about the text as a text, as a demonstration of a woman's writing. Students' efforts will be successful to the degree that they work from passages. These essays, in other words, are exercises in working with textual material. In every case students should begin by identifying passages to work with; then they should choose from among the material they have identified; they should, that is, work with a limited (but representative) set of passages. As we have taught these assignments, we have wanted students to perform close readings, to work in detail with Woolf's language. When students revise their essays, then, we have tended to focus on either their choice of passages (particularly as they have left out passages that didn't fit or passages that seemed beyond comprehension; these are precisely the passages we want them to work with in revision), or we have focused on the placement and use of those passages (to what degree they are left to stand alone, as though they could speak for themselves, and to what degree the writer has taken the role of teacher, teaching us what we might see and how we might read).

And, finally, when students revise, we have wanted them to bring forward what was inevitably overlooked in the first draft, and that is the connection between what Woolf is doing and what they are doing, or have done, or might do as writers, both inside and outside the academy. Some of our colleagues have chosen to tell students to ignore these questions (about what Woolf's example or argument might have to do with them as students in a writing class); or they have left these questions as discussion questions. In the latter case, teachers would reproduce copies of first and second drafts and then move the discussion toward the question of what bearing the argument about gender and writing might have on this writer's education. Some teachers object to the question as a question in the assignment because it has the tendency to make the students' essays come apart at the end. We are interested in the way personal concerns might intrude on the more "academic" questions raised in the assignment. If the essays begin to fall apart in the face of this pressure, teachers and students may find this a valuable lesson and appropriate to an assignment on *A Room of One's Own*.

ASSIGNMENT 5

Writing as Re-Vision [Rich, Woolf]

After students have had the opportunity to work with passages from Woolf's essay for assignment 4 that they would use to represent the ways in which she works against traditional expectations for essays, they can turn the same kind of critical eye to their own writing. Only this time they are looking for the ways in which their writing could be said to reproduce a patriarchal tradition. As they identify those passages from their own papers that they would call "manly," they need to perform close readings and to work in detail with their own language in order to figure out what elements in it would allow it to be characterized as "manly," as reproducing a patriarchal tradition. Those traditions often appear in the features of certain kinds of introductions and conclusions, in "univocal" and single-minded arguments or lines of reasoning that present themselves as "natural" or self-evident, in prose that takes on the voice of authority, the voice of The Father, and because it neglects to reflect on its methods and motives, appears a seamless statement of the final word.

Students will need to struggle with these distinctions themselves, and although they have been working with close readings throughout this sequence, they'll have a difficult time explaining why particular passages from their papers "feel" manly. And they'll need to address the goodness of those passages they mark as "manly." What would they say is the best of the tradition in their writing? the worst? and, of course, why? Why, that is, would they call one example the best of the tradition and another the worst? What is it about the writing that allows for these kinds of distinctions? What does the writing allow or prevent?

ASSIGNMENT 6

Retrospective [Woolf]

We've phrased this assignment in Woolf's terms. It is a standard assignment in our teaching. Most teachers have a way of sending students back to make sense out of (to construct the order in) a course of instruction. We thought it might be useful to offer an example. When we teach an assignment like this, it usually comes in on the last day, at the top of a folder containing all the student's work for the semester. It gives the student a way of rounding out the course in her or his terms; and it gives us a way of seeing our students' versions of what we think we have been doing.

SEQUENCE SIX

Methods (p. 811)

Although this sequence takes the methods — the characteristic ways of gathering materials, of thinking them through, of presenting a voice — as its immediate focus, it also walks a line between methods and content that is imaginary, that exists only to frame a concern of the assignment so students might be better able to identify the authors' methods and to understand how the methods are interwoven with the content. Every question in the sequence directs students to discuss how methods might be related to the issues, and since every selection has its own identity — even though they all present similar concerns about women and motherhood, — students ought to be able to move around quite a bit in the sequence (identifying and commenting on various methods within and across the essays), even though they will be working on one specific task throughout the sequence: relating methods to issues.

ASSIGNMENT 1

Studying Walker's Methods [Walker]

This is a moving piece of writing, and it offers students some clear-cut methods to work with, including Walker's storytelling (about a number of people from the past and present) and her use of literature and historical figures. Since Walker doesn't name her

153

methods or anchor them in canonical references, students can take this first assignment as an occasion to invent ways of describing and naming how she works — something that other assignments invite them to feel free to do. It's important to the sequence that students do this inventing (rather than, say, instructors presenting them with the language of arguments or compositions), so they can also invent their own descriptions and names for how issues relate to methods, instead of slotting issues into ready-made rhetorical or procedural formulas. If they invent descriptions and names for what appeared to them to be procedural formulas, that's fine, but it's important that instructors don't give the descriptions and names.

ASSIGNMENT 2

Comparing Steinem's Work with Walker's [Steinem, Walker]

Since students will already have worked on the Walker essay, their job here is to compare what they learned about the relationships between her methods and issues to what they see Steinem doing in her essay. Although at times both authors use similar methods such as the storytelling approach, this is a good opportunity for students to examine similar methods in different contexts. Do the methods and issues connect in similar ways for similar effects? If not, how might the students begin to characterize the differences and the influences of contexts?

They should also pay attention to how these essays proceed through differing methods, and speculate on the purposefulness of various moves in the essays and on the authors that are created by the methods they use. How do an author's methods create the author? the issues? the audience? How do an author's concerns create the methods?

ASSIGNMENT 3

Untangling Anzaldúa [Anzaldúa]

This is a difficult essay, but its difficulty leaves it open for study and speculation, for it proceeds, as Anzaldúa says, as a montage, a beaded work, a crazy dance. Students might be stunned by their first encounter with Anzaldúa's chapters, and it would be a good idea to approach these chapters first through a class discussion, perhaps using one of the second-reading questions that give students the opportunity to sort out some of the challenging aspects of her work (e.g., the Spanish text, the poetry and storytelling within the chapters, the references to myths) and to discuss what her arguments seem to be.

Once students have had the opportunity to explore Anzaldúa's writing, they'll find a great deal to work with for this assignment. Her methods cover a lot of ground — she tells stories, cites all sorts of interesting references, offers up poems and myths, retells history, and makes arguments, to name the immediately visible ones. For students to tell the stories of their readings, you'll want them to focus on Anzaldúa's methods when they write about where they felt at home and where they felt lost; but they should understand, too, that methods aren't empty containers, that they need to couple her methods to what she has to say, to see them, that is, as part and parcel of what she is saying. And they'll want to address Anzaldúa's conception of her readers. How, for instance, does she imagine her readers will react to her methods? to the issues she transports through those methods? How do they, as her readers, figure into what she expects of them?

We often suggest to our students that they approach assignments like this one with a double-entry notebook. In the first column of the notebook, they can track their readings and identify the passages that they felt at home and lost with; in the second column they

154

can comment on those passages by writing about how Anzaldúa's methods work on them as integral parts of what she's saying. This kind of double-entry notebook helps students do multiple things with their readings and rereadings — they can identify the passages they want to write about — and they can begin commenting on those passages in a kind of shuffling that allows them to see patterns and make connections among their examples and their discussions of them.

ASSIGNMENT 4

Experimenting with Your Own Writing
[Walker, Steinem, Anzaldúa]

This assignment purposely leaves the door wide open for students to enter into the conversation that has been represented by their readings of the three selections for this sequence. The conversation is broadly sketched out — it has to do with women and their positions in American culture — and students should feel free to define their issues and positions within the broad context of their past work. They should also feel free to experiment with their methods, as the authors they have been working with have done, and to imagine how they might couple their methods to the issues they raise. What can they borrow from Walker, Steinem, and Anzaldúa? What voices — perhaps contradictory or at least different from each other — do they hear in themselves as they work out the issues and positions they would like to take in this paper? How can they give visible expression to those various voices?

More than anything, students should see this assignment as an opportunity to experiment with their writing; in our experience students welcome this opportunity. You will want to schedule enough class time to allow them both to discuss what it was like experimenting with methods and to get feedback for revisions of these papers.

• • • • • • • • •

SEQUENCE SEVEN

"Popular" Culture (p. 816)

This is an alternative version of the sequence, "Reading Culture." The assignments here stick solely to "popular culture," to television, media images, and rock and roll. When we have taught these assignments, students have taken considerable pleasure in seeing how the material of their daily lives — MTV and "The Cosby Show" — can become the "stuff" of academic inquiry. But there is an edge to this. It is fun to write about rock and roll, but students sometimes find the role of the critic — particularly as defined in the academy — to be awkward and uncomfortable. It just doesn't seem right spending all that time and energy on what people do for fun, turning against what "normal" people do when they watch or listen.

The sequence asks students to observe, chart, and apply the methods of three established critics, Mark Miller, Susan Willis, and John Fiske, and through their example to grapple with the concept of culture as a large, organizing force, one they can neither completely imagine nor completely control, one which shapes and organizes the ways they think, speak, and act. There is a power in this form of analysis that students can feel and share, but it comes at the expense of the usual celebrations of freedom and individuality. The usual ways of talking about experience will be displaced by this sequence. You and your students will have to work hard from the opening moments to keep a watchful eye out for vestiges of the "old" ways of speaking; to stop, now and then, when you hear it at work; to bracket it; to put its key terms on the blackboard; and to imagine why it is attractive and how one might understand its limits.

155

With Miller, Fiske, and Willis, we have found it useful to push students to identify at one point with the figure of the critic (extending the writer's critical project) and at another with the figure of the "common" reader/viewer/listener necessary to each writer's critique. In a sense, this is a way of moving between a generous reading and a reading that calls the assumptions of the piece into question. We are interested, as well, in moving students back and forth between the challenge of understanding the essay (reproducing its argument) and understanding the methods by which Miller, Fiske, and Willis choose and produce arguments out of examples drawn from popular culture. Again, this double perspective is a way of representing readings with and against the grain. To read against the grain, as one of our graduate students, Matt Willen, said, is not the same thing as disagreeing or refusing to buy an argument.

For a complete commentary on the selections in this sequence, please be sure to read each essay's selection in this manual, particularly the opening discussion. While we will cull materials from the discussions of individual assignments, we won't reproduce the introductions. And while the sequences provide writing assignments, you should think about the advantages (or disadvantages) of using the Questions for a Second Reading. In every case, students should read the headnotes in the textbook, which are designed to serve the assignments and sequences.

ASSIGNMENT **1**

TV [Miller]

We begin with Miller by asking students to use his practice as representative material for an inquiry into a critic's methods. The first assignment asks students to try their hand at Miller's brand of criticism, taking his methods and applying them to new material. Students' success with this assignment will depend on their ability to represent to themselves Miller's method as a method, and it will depend on the degree to which they work with precise detail in representing their ad or show. They most likely will not be able to use pictures, but Miller's writing sets a good example here. In a sense he teaches his readers how to look at the screen by the example of what he notices and remembers. Students will need to work with close detail; they will need to define a contrary relation to the "common sense" reading of their example; and they will need to imagine that their job is to ask questions, including the big question of "just what is going on here?" As the note says, the hard question is one that even Miller refuses to take head-on. One of his devices as a critic is to put agency into a show — to say, for example, that the Shield ad *offers* women a fantasy of power and control. The story he is trying to tell is not the usual narrative of an artist creating an effect, but of a shaping force that is bigger than an individual artist or writer, one that committees or producers only partially grasp. Students should be aware of the source or origin of television's effects and the ways in which they need to talk about it in unusual terms.

For revision: Students, perhaps properly, will initially devote their energy and attention to producing an account of their show or ad — describing it, noticing some features, and ignoring others. There are two ways we have approached a revision of this essay. We have asked students to step back from their account to imagine what it misses, what it necessarily misses because of its angle of vision. And we have asked students to use the revision as an occasion to turn their attention to larger, interpretive questions. If the first draft was the occasion to pay "meticulous attention to concrete detail," the second is to see how those details might be said to "illuminate the larger context . . . so that the reading of TV contains and necessitates a reading of our own moment and its past."

ASSIGNMENT 2

The Workout [Willis]

This assignment is a version of the first (and one of a standard form in *Ways of Reading*.) It asks students to extend Willis's argument through a discussion of examples of their own choosing. You can help students prepare by spending class time considering possible choices of material, thinking about where to look, thinking about how to choose and, in particular, thinking about what would constitute an interesting and effective (and surprising) pair. (Runners' magazines proved to be a fertile source for at least one item in the pair. Once a student has one good example, the real work is finding a surprising source for the second.) The pair of examples is important to this assignment, and for several reasons. Considering the examples together will cause each to be read differently than if it were examined alone. And the pair will give students a chance to provide a historical context (if the examples comes from different moments in time) or a cultural context (if they come from different cultural scene — if they don't both come from TV, for example, or if they don't both come from the student's "personal" experience).

For revision: When students write this essay, we usually define their work (as writers) in two ways: they must *present* their material — set a context, bring it forward in a detailed way for a reader to see and think about and understand (Willis is a good model for this); and they must comment on their material, discuss it, reflect on it, think it through, teach a reader what to see and how to think, provide an intellectual or analytical context (Willis, again, is a good model). Students, characteristically, will move too fast in presenting the material. In revision, they can take time to bring forward detail that would otherwise be lost, and they can begin to think about how to make the presentation interesting and fun. And students, characteristically, are hesitant to come forward in their essays as intellectuals — teaching, reflecting, and commenting. These roles are hard for students to imagine, and it is hard for students to assume that they are authorized to step forward in just these ways. Again, working on developing this "slot" in the essay can be a useful focus for revision.

The assignment asks students, when they perform this role, to see if they can make use of Willis's terms: "commodification," "gendered subjects," etc. This has always been important for us. In our classes, the most important measure of students' understanding of one of the readings is the degree to which they can put its terms to work. We have had colleagues who have argued that we prevent students from bringing in other terms, other frames of analysis, or from coining terms of their own. This is not a matter of prohibition. We would not prevent students from doing this. In fact, we can think of cases where we have encouraged it. But there are limits to how much you can accomplish in a semester and, in practice, we will admit that with limited time we would tend to give a priority to Willis's terms.

ASSIGNMENT 3

Madonna [Fiske]

This assignment gives students two options: an autobiographical essay ("A Fan's Notes") or an essay that provides a reading of the discourse of fans (interviews, letters to the editors, talk on talk shows). The assignment is meant to enable students to participate in Fiske's project (trying to represent and understand a fan's use of a star) but also to answer back. When we taught this assignment, our goal was to give students a body of closely discussed material that they could use to talk back to Fiske or to test and extend his discussion. ("The women I spoke to spoke differently of Madonna. . . .")

If students take the first option, the autobiographical essay, you want to be sure that they imagine this genre as fully as possible (since "Madonna" doesn't provide much of a model). Students will need to use the resources of narrative (scene, dialogue, character). The best of those we received worked, actually, through a series of parallel scenes (different stars, different points over time, different accounts of a single concert). It helps to ask students to believe that they are adding material to Fiske's files. (In fact, there is no reason not to send essays to Fiske.) Students might imagine, in other words, accounts that are richer and more detailed than Lucy's or Robyn's.

For revision: In most cases, when our students have begun to work on a second draft of this essay, their primary concern is to fill out the account — to make it more detailed, more storylike, to find interesting alternative scenes, voices, or points of view.

If students take the second option, they will need to be able to anticipate the importance of good fieldwork. These essays will be interesting to the degree that students accept the challenge of finding and collecting their "archive" of materials. If they write about the first thing that comes to hand (or the easiest) they will have little invested in the methodological difficulties that are part of this kind of work. They should not be writing from hearsay but from carefully collected materials. We have found it useful to ask students to gather material and write (or talk) about what, from their files, they are going to choose to write about. In this case, we assume that students will collect more than they can use and part of their work will be to discuss how and why they made the selections they did when they prepared to write. It will take the first draft for students to organize and present their material. In revision, they can begin to step forward (as Fiske does) to comment on that material, to teach a reader how to read it, to reflect on the project and what it has accomplished, to think about how their position is different from (or a supplement to) Fiske's.

ASSIGNMENT 4

Criticism [Fiske, Miller, Willis]

We have asked all the cultural critics in *Ways of Reading* a version of this question. Assignments like these are one way we have found of getting students to think about essays not as a body of information but as the enactment of a method, a way of reading the world. All critics of popular culture work within a system of representation that requires two figures: the "common" reader and the critical reader. This assignment asks students to look at how each of these readers is represented in "Madonna" and in the work of Willis and Miller.

Our goal is simple. We want students to be able to do more than reproduce an account of Madonna, *The Cosby Show,* or Barbie. We want students to understand both the methods and the interests represented in accounts like these. It is not that Fiske, for example, knows the truth about Madonna and her fans; he has a certain kind of story to tell (about resistance and domination). One way for students to begin to see the limits and possibilities of a critical method is first to *see* it as a method and then to see it in relation to others. This is the other goal of the assignment: to place Fiske's account of women and resistance (let's say) next to Susan Willis's. The accounts are different, and although the differences are not obvious, noticing them will allow students a way of evaluating and characterizing Fiske. Because Fiske writes about young women, the easiest point of comparison will be Willis's essay, although Miller also provides an account of fantasy, desire, and the production of the "gendered subject" (in both the Cosby essay and, more directly, in the essay on the soap ads).

Students' success with this assignment will depend heavily on how closely they work with passages from the core texts to "build" their essays from a collection of interesting and representative passages. In other words, students need to begin with examples of the authors at work and then to piece out the key differences (as well as the commonalities) in their methods. We emphasize difference because this leads students to a more fine-grained account of criticism; it keeps them from reducing criticism to its lowest common denominator (or the sentence that is easiest to write, the sentence whose goal is only to lump all of these unusual materials together).

For revision: We have found that the difficulty of representing the positions of the various authors (the problem of figuring them out, finding passages to use, presenting the material) is sufficient to dominate students' attention in the first draft. It is in the second that students can best begin to look for differences and try to establish some critical purchase on the essays they have read.

Students were asked to write a kind of "beginners' guide" to cultural criticism. Most likely this will be a guide to Miller, Fiske, and Willis, which is fine. It would be useful, in revision, for students to add their own voices to this collection of experts. They should carve out a space where, in speaking to their audience, they have a role *other* than the role of translating what others have said. After all, the first two essays in this sequence featured the students' criticism. They should have by now developed some sense of what this term "culture" might be said to represent.

ASSIGNMENT 5

Culture [Fiske, Miller, Willis]

This assignment is meant to stand as a revision of the previous essay — students revise, that is, by changing modes. Here we ask students to write an autobiographical essay, to add their story to Miller's, Fiske's, and Willis's files.

Encourage students to see this as an invitation to an autobiographical essay. It will need characters, scenes, even dialogue. At best students will be recalling moments, not talking at a distance about taste ("I'm the sort of guy who likes heavy metal"). The difficulty this assignment will present to students lies in the request that they tell a story informed by their reading of the critics. To do this, they will need to try to identify music or television as a force, a way of thinking, not simply something one watches or listens to. And they will need to define themselves as consumers, as somehow products of their culture. This runs against the grain of American autobiography, where the individual is defined as though he or she were, in Percy's terms, a sovereign individual, as though the "real" person stood outside history and culture. The first draft, then, will most likely be a story of an individual and his or her tastes and experiences. The problems for revision will be to *place* this character as a type and to see this character in the context of a culture. When students revise they should be reminded that this essay stands as a final comment on the work they did in this sequence.

. . . .

SEQUENCE EIGHT

The Problems of Difficulty (p. 822)

Difficult texts, like the ones in this sequence, present students with problems they are not accustomed to. They will see writers at work, thinking on paper (as Wideman does, for instance, when he questions his own writing of his brother's story), working through complex ideas (as Foucault puzzles through the relationships of the body, power, and knowledge), and presenting unusual and challenging positions (as both Woolf and Williams do in their selections) that question the status quo. For most students, even the idea of working with texts like these will be challenging and new. Traditionally, educational enterprises "dummy down" texts for students, and that has been one of the great failures of American education. Rather than teaching students how to work with and how to write difficult texts, the educational community has moved farther and farther toward providing students with easier and easier texts as the solution to students' problems with reading. The underlying assumption of presenting students with easy texts, texts that students can "get" in one reading, is that reading is easy, that problems, then, are indications of a writer's or a reader's failures. This sequence begins with the assumption that difficult texts often present students with challenging, complex thinking, and that for students to develop into complex, critical thinkers, they need to learn the work of reading and writing difficult texts. The metaphor for this sequence is "work." The work students will do here is textual, and the experience of that work is designed to teach them that a great deal of important reading is hard work and not at all easy or instantaneous.

The five assignments in this sequence invite students to consider the nature of four difficult texts and how the problems they pose might be said to belong simultaneously to language, to readers, and to writers. It is assumed that these texts are difficult for all readers, not just for students, and that the difficulty is necessary or strategic, not a mistake or evidence of a writer's (or a reader's) incompetence.

Since the sequence was designed to serve teachers interested in having their students study the problems of difficult texts, it might be helpful to think of using it (or some of the assignments) after students work with these selections either in class discussions (using the second-reading questions or the writing assignments as discussion questions) or in writing assignments or in some combination of both. You could also use the kinds of questions posed by these assignments for other difficult texts that students work with.

ASSIGNMENT 1

I Will Try to Explain [Woolf]

Students can imagine themselves into this assignment in a number of ways. The assignment suggests that they look for places in the Woolf selections where she seems to saying, "I know what I should be doing here, but I won't." They can also imagine themselves as writers with a wealth of information on how essays are supposed to work and what their standard format is supposed to be. For example, students often draw attention to their experiences with essays as three- or five-paragraph themes that present their "points," continue in separate paragraphs to argue for each one, and finally conclude with a restatement of the points. When they look to Woolf as such a model for their essays, they'll find her style works against the grain of these assumptions. Woolf, for instance, tells stories instead of offering evidence. She is self-conscious of herself working against the grain, and she draws attention to this. Whatever tack students take with this essay, they will need to focus on Woolf's writing as an enactment of an argument about writing.

Some will want to discuss what she says, her ideas; but this assignment asks them to study how and what she writes as an enactment of her arguments.

The questions at the end of the assignment are designed to give students ways into thinking about the writing, and you'll see that they draw students' attention to how Woolf imagines her readers and how her writerly moves might be considered examples of someone working on the problems of writing. What are those problems? Woolf points to the clubby expectations of mostly male academics, and, for example, she works against their kinds of academic arguments by telling stories and by using the stories as a way to question their traditions. Students, working in Woolf's spirit, could consider the kinds of academic expectations in which they are asked to participate as writers and students. What, then, would Woolf's example and her arguments have to say about them as student writers?

ASSIGNMENT 2

Foucault's Examples [Foucault]

Students don't usually have trouble with Foucault's opening examples, and this assignment picks up on those examples and how Foucault uses them throughout the selection to create an argument for the relationship of the body, power, and knowledge to one another. Students will need to invent a way to trace the examples through to the last quarter of the selection, the difficult section, where he discusses these relationships; and they will also need to present Foucault's notions of them to their readers. This task will be difficult. His writing is more exploratory, more thinking on paper, than it is summative, and even the most attentive students (and instructors) will find this last section challenging and elusive. But this is an occasion for students to work at the problem (rather than to "get" it or to get it right); and they can find a way into it by studying the two examples and the way in which they represent the body and control over the body. Once they work through the examples, their job then is to find a way to discuss how Foucault creates his body-power-knowledge "equation" (as one of our students once called it) with and from those two examples. They'll need to say as best they can what the relationships are, and they'll need multiple revisions to work their way through this "equation," but they should always be working in terms of the examples. They can think of these examples, as Foucault does, in terms of how they represent the body, control over it, the power to control and the power of the body, and the knowledge that is both necessary for power to be tapped or used and the knowledge that is created when power is used.

ASSIGNMENT 3

A Story of Reading [Wideman]

This assignment asks students to take an unusual stance towards Wideman's selection — to read it as a text that wants to break readers' habits — and it asks them to take an unusual stance toward themselves as readers and writers — to write down and comment on how they read Wideman's text. Students might begin by identifying moments in the text that they want to refer to, moments where they feel Wideman is deliberately working on his readers, defying their expectations and directing their responses. They'll also need to comment on what it was like for them to read those passages, and to this end, they might help themselves with a version of a double-entry notebook, or rather a triple-entry notebook, because the assignment also asks them to comment on what Wideman is doing and why he's doing it. The first column of their notebook might note in some way the passages they've identified where Wideman seems to be deliberately working on his

161

readers. The second column could tell the story of their reading those sections (in the context of their reading the entire selection), and the third column could indicate their thinking about what Wideman is doing, why he seems to be doing it, and how it affected them as readers. Students will need to read the selection at least twice, but they should begin their note taking for the story of how they read it the first time through so that they can record their reactions to those sections where Wideman seems to be working on his readers. Once they've got their notes fleshed out, students will then need to tell the story of their reading, with careful reference to those passages they identified and with careful accounting of their reactions to their first reading of them. They'll need to continually step aside, so to speak, in their writing — as Wideman does — to comment on the habits Wideman assumes in his readers and why he wants to break them. For students, this paper is a story of reading with references to the Wideman text, narratives on their reactions to it, and asides commenting on Wideman's demands on readers. This, then, is an assignment to read a challenging text and to create another challenging text in response to it.

ASSIGNMENT 4

Word Magic [Williams]

It would be smart to give students the opportunity to enter into Williams's essay and this assignment through class discussions of the questions in the assignment. As for the Woolf and Wideman's essays, the assignment asks students to see Williams's writing as an enactment of an argument about reading and writing. If they approach her essay this way, as an argument for and against certain ways of reading and writing, especially legal writing, what might they say she's for and against? Why? What in the essay points to the positions she takes? How does Williams see her work, this essay, as different from the priests' work, their writings, in the celestial city?

Once students have had the opportunity to discuss the essay, they can turn to the assignment and begin to tell the story of their reading it in much the same manner as they approached the Wideman selection. A triple-entry notebook would be helpful here too. The first column could list references to both passages they felt at home with and those where they felt lost or in need of help. The second column could record their reactions to those passages, but in terms of the positions they took as readers, not simply in terms of how easy or difficult the passage was. To think about their positions as readers during the comfortable and difficult times of reading, they'll need to consider such things as why they did or didn't feel in control of the passages. They'll need to consider how their relationship to the text changes as they feel at home and lost. Why do they feel at home? Why do they feel lost? The point of asking students to explain their changing positions is to give them a way to understand those feelings of being at home and being lost in a text. They can't say simple things like, "it was easy because I knew what she was talking about" or, "I couldn't follow her because I didn't know what she was talking about." They have to explain why they did or did not know what she was talking about and why they did or did not feel in control of those passages.

The third column of the notebook could be where they think about their experiences with the text and what they would say Williams is arguing for or against through her writing. In other words, they need to ask, "What do these passages that I've identified tell me about Williams's arguments for reading and writing? How have my reactions as a reader panned out or fit (or not fit) into her assumptions about readers?" As in their papers for the Wideman assignment, students' papers here will be narratives of how they read Williams with references to passages and asides containing their comments on what they think Williams was up to in those passages (as well as how they played into or didn't play into her expectations for them as readers). This is another difficult reading to which students are asked to respond to with a challenging piece of writing that breaks traditional expectations of a reader's response to a text.

ASSIGNMENT 5

A Theory of Difficulty
[Woolf, Foucault, Wideman, Williams]

Students are asked in this assignment to produce a guide that might be useful to other students who will be asked to work with difficult texts and assignments. It's important for students to understand their stance in this piece of writing. Although they are writing a guide that offers advice, they must write from examples of their reading and writing. The examples must come from their past work on this sequence, and they should feel free to cite and explain everything — from class discussions to note taking to revising papers. The danger with retrospective assignments like this one is that students will turn immediately to generic platitudes, that they'll say what they think is expected of them ("Be prepared to work hard," "Don't see difficult texts as your failure or the writer's failure"). To push against these kinds of moves, you'll need to ask students to work from those moments in their past work that highlighted (for them) ways of reading and writing difficult texts, ways that might help other students who haven't done the kinds of work that they have. Here again they might use double-entry notebooks, first to identify the moments in their work they want to discuss, then to explain what that work stands for or taught them about difficult texts. In their papers or in a third column, they can begin those discussions that tie together what they have to say into a theory of difficulty. Whatever they do with their note taking, they'll need it to stand as an example of good practice in reading and writing about difficult texts. And it's from those examples and illustrations that they should derive their theories of difficulty. While a theory is drawn from generalizations, these in turn are drawn from or anchored in illustrations or cases. So if students don't work from the examples they have at hand, their theory will be based on generalizations alone and will be a string of platitudes instead of an argument rooted in example.

. . . .

SEQUENCE NINE

Reading Culture (p. 828)

When we taught this sequence, students took considerable pleasure in feeling that the material of their everyday lives — television, rock and roll, museums — could be the stuff of academic inquiry. But this was a double-edged sword. It was fun to write about rock and roll, but the role of the critic — particularly as criticism is practiced in the academy (and not the newspaper) — seemed awkward and, at times, uncomfortable. It just didn't seem right spending all that time and energy on what people do for fun, turning against what "normal" people do when they watch and listen.

And, as we say in the introduction, the sequence asks students to imagine culture as a large organizing force, one in which they are situated, implicated, one which "shapes," "organizes," and "controls" the ways they think, speak, and act. There is a power in this form of analysis that students can feel and share, but it comes at the expense of the usual celebrations of freedom, free will, and individuality. The usual ways of talking about experience will be displaced by this sequence. You and your students will have to work hard from the opening moments of the course to keep a watchful eye open for vestiges of the "old" ways of speaking; to stop, now and then, when you hear it at work; to bracket it; to put its key terms on the blackboard; and to imagine why it is attractive and how one might understand its limits. The pattern in this sequence is fairly straightforward. Students read the work of several critics, they are asked to reflect on their practice *as* practice, and they are asked to reproduce (or revise) their methods in critical writing of their own.

The sequence is designed to call into question the standard distinctions between high and low culture. Berger "demystifies" (he would say) high art by taking it from the realm of the purely aesthetic and putting it back into the context of human expression (for Berger, a place of struggle). Willis and Fiske take popular cultural icons, images, and artifacts and give them the close and urgent attention usually reserved for high art.

One goal of the sequence, then, is to put students into a position where they can reevaluate, reimagine, and redefine "culture" once some of its fundamental assumptions are removed. In addition, the sequence is defined to focus attention on the dynamics of cultural production and reception. (The readings emphasize reception, although students can infer arguments about production from them. A good place to begin to talk about production would be with Willis, working to Fiske and then Berger.)

The sequence moves back and forth between summary and application. Students are asked to reproduce a form of critique (extending Willis's project, for example) and then to work closely with the assumptions behind a critical project (like Willis's), asking fundamental questions: How does she do it? Why does she do it? What does this have to do with me?

Like most of the "culture" sequences, this one works by having students alternate between identifying with the figure of the critic (with Berger and Willis, extending the writer's critical project) and that of the "common" reader/viewer/listener necessary to each writer's critique (questioning the figure of the "girl" in Willis and Fiske). In a sense, this process of alternating is a way of moving between a generous reading and one that calls the assumptions of the critical project into question. We are interested, as well, in moving students back and forth between the challenge of understanding both the essays' arguments and the methods by which Berger, Fiske, and Willis choose and produce these arguments out of examples drawn from popular culture. Again, this double perspective is a way of representing readings with and against the grain. To read against the grain, as one of our graduate students, Matt Willen, said, is not the same thing as disagreeing or refusing to buy an argument.

This sequence is accompanied by a minisequence, "Reading Culture (II)." This seemed like a good way of indicating the flexibility we hope is obvious in all the sequences. All of them should serve as a base from which a teacher can work, making revisions to the larger sweep of the sequence or to individual assignments as those revisions seem appropriate or necessary. The Berger-Willis-Fiske combination focuses the question on the production of the image of women — at least this is one way of reading that sequence. If you wanted to pull in some representations of men and men's experience, you could turn to assignments in "Reading Culture (II)" dealing with Theweleit or Miller. Theweleit also offers a very different account of production and reception, in which production is more fully tied to political interests and reception to a psychology, rather than a sociology, of desire. As the first sequence stands, it ends with a move to call into question (in the name of "the student" or "youth") some of the assumptions of Fiske's account of the reception of Madonna — and through him, Willis's and Berger's accounts of the "common" consumer. The second sequence proposes an alternative ending, this time using Tompkins's essay on her work as a way of thinking through and charting the changes in students' understanding of both their subjects and the larger project of cultural criticism.

For a complete commentary on the selections in this sequence, please be sure to read each essay's selection in this manual, particularly the opening discussion. While we will cull materials from the discussions of individual assignments, we won't reproduce the introductions. And, while the sequences provide writing assignments, you should think about the advantages (or disadvantages) of using the Questions for a Second Reading. In every case, students should read the headnotes in the textbook, which they are designed to serve the assignments and sequences.

ASSIGNMENT 1

Looking at Pictures [Berger]

The Berger assignment is designed to familiarize the exotic (by asking students to "converse" with high art). Berger argues that criticism should turn to everyday language, to force connections between life and art. His criticism is set against mystification, and while this might be said also of Willis or Fiske, his method *feels* more "honest" and "humane" to students than Willis's or Fiske's. Berger turns against "academic" criticism to represent what he would like us to believe is the human reality of art and the perception of art. This is both compelling and problematic. Berger speaks in a voice students admire. It is difficult, however, to get students to read against that voice, to question the ease with which Berger assumes he knows the reality of history or the ease by which he assumes a kind of universal human experience, one that he understands because he has cut through the crap.

We've had a good deal of success with this assignment. Ideally, students should have ready access to a museum. Berger talks about the ways we have come to experience paintings in museums and a trip to a museum to look at a painting will give students a way of adding to or reflecting on Berger's argument. But he also talks about reproductions, so we felt justified in adding the option for students to go to art books in the library. If you can reasonably expect your students to get to a museum, however, we think the trip will hold some interesting surprises for you. We usually schedule a class meeting at the museum — just to get the students in and walking around to think about which painting might be "theirs." Warn students against docents and taped tours — for your purposes these prepared readings of paintings will be a real barrier to writing.

The students who have had the most success with this assignment have been fairly literal in their sense of what it means to have a "conversation" with a painting. Their essays, that is, have not read as museum-guide-like interpretations but as more open-ended and speculative pieces, sometimes cast as a narrative with dialogue, sometimes as pure dialogue. The key is to invite students to "talk" to the painting, to ask questions, and to imagine rich and ambiguous responses. It is best to have students avoid papers that begin with an idea of what a picture is about and simply impose that reading on the material. The painting needs to be imagined to talk back, to counter or open up a student's desire to master and control.

For revision: In some cases we've found we needed to send students back to the painting and the original assignment, usually because students were more concerned to push through a single reading than to have a conversation with their material. In most cases, however, we used the revision as the occasion to send students back to the Berger essay. As they become involved with the museum assignment, students (in a sense) forgot about Berger, and so we used the revision to send them back, to see what use they can make of his way of talking about paintings or about the museum. (For example, "How could you use the example of your essay to explain what Berger might mean when he talks about 'history'?") The idea here is to engage them in a conversation with Berger, where your students can draw on their expertise to enter his argument.

The Making of a Woman [Willis]

This assignment asks students to extend Willis's argument through a discussion of examples of their own choosing. You can help students prepare by spending class time considering possible choices of material, thinking about where to look, thinking about how to choose and, in particular, thinking about what would constitute an interesting and effective (and surprising) pair. (Runners' magazines proved to be a fertile source for at least one item in the pair. Once a student has one good example, the real work is finding a surprising source for the second.) The pair of examples is important to this assignment, and for several reasons. Considering the examples together will cause each to be read differently than if either were examined alone. And the pair will give students a chance to provide a historical context (if the examples come from different moments in time) or a cultural context (if they come from a different cultural scene — if they don't both come from TV, for example, or if they don't both come from the student's "personal" experience).

For revision: When students write this essay, we usually define their work as writers in two ways: they must *present* their material — set a context, bring it forward in a detailed way for a reader to see and think about and understand (Willis is a good model for this); and they must comment on their material, discuss it, reflect on it, think it through, teach a reader what to see and how to think, provide an intellectual or analytical context (Willis, again, is a good model). Students, characteristically, will move too fast in presenting the material. In revision, they can take time to bring forward detail that would otherwise be lost, and they can begin to think about how to make the presentation interesting and fun. And students, characteristically, are hesitant to come forward in their essays as intellectuals — teaching, reflecting, and commenting. These roles are hard for students to imagine, and it is hard for students to assume that they are authorized to step forward in just these ways. Again, working on developing this "slot" in the essay can be a useful focus for revision.

The assignment asks students, when they perform this role, to see if they can make use of Willis's terms: "commodification," "gendered subjects," and so on. This has always been important for us. In our classes, the most important measure of students' understanding of a reading is the degree to which they can put its terms to work. We have had colleagues who have argued that we prevent students from bringing in other terms, other frames of analysis, or from coining terms of their own. This is not a matter of prohibition. We would not prevent students from doing this. In fact, we can think of cases where we have encouraged it. But there are limits to how much you can accomplish in a semester and, in practice, we will admit that with limited time we would tend to give a priority to Willis's terms.

Willis as Critic [Willis]

Assignment 2 asked students to extend Willis's project. This assignment asks students to read it as an example of a method — a way of producing readings, like the reading of "Jem" — and of a critical program, one we might call Marxist-feminist. It is useful, however, to let students find their own way of naming it on the basis of their reading of the essay, since the labels tend to be reductive and, for students especially, an excuse for not reading very carefully.

The assignment offers two options: an exercise in summary and an exercise in fieldwork. You may have reasons for guiding students in one direction in preference to the other.

We have done both. The summary exercise is in many ways more immediately productive. It forces students (or leads them or gives them a chance) to work out an account of Willis's argument. We have found it important to make sure that students' representations of the essay and its argument step beyond the individual readings of Barbie, Jane Fonda, and Jem to the big picture, the larger project or argument that makes these examples appropriate and "right." In addition, as the assignment says, we want to position summary as a tool, a device. We want students to come to translate the essay into "common terms" (to have it make "common sense") as a way of beginning to think about the import and necessity of its specialized terms (like "commodification" and "gendered subject") and the sense it makes that defies or stands as a corrective to "common" sense.

The "fieldwork" assignment was designed to puncture Willis's seamless generalizations about women and exercise. (What about pleasure? Can we account for exercise *as* opposition? Is all exercise the same? experienced the same way?) It is difficult, however, to make this assignment work. In the first place, it requires students to do more than sit down and write. If the assignment is going to work, students will have to accept the responsibility of going to a gym, observing and interviewing the women who are there. (We would advise you not to invite students to interview men. Men's accounts will be almost impossible for students to read as text. Students who want to work on "men and exercise" should work from images, following the pattern established in "Work(ing) Out.") But the greater difficulty comes with the status of the material students gather. After all the work of conducting interviews (and in the face of the inherent persuasiveness of the interviews), students will have a hard time doing anything but offering what their subjects say as the TRUTH, firsthand testimony that puts this matter to rest.

With these caveats, here is an account of the two options in this assignment:

1. This is a fairly straightforward exercise in summary. It asks students to go to the very sections of the essay they would most likely ignore in a summary. In our experience, students read Willis in terms of their own (in her terms "liberal") version of the feminist critique, leaving out all references to commodities and "the entire circuit of production and consumption under capitalism." As a result, we felt it was useful to define a summary that began with these terms and to define summary as a teaching tool, as a way to help another reader *begin* to get a handle on Willis's essay or her brand of critique. While we didn't do it in the assignment, it might be useful to emphasize "begin," so that a writer could suggest to his or her reader what else might be done if one were going to work on or with "Work(ing) Out."

2. This assignment was written to give students a chance to read against the grain of Willis's argument. It provides another source of material for study and another method of analysis (a kind of mini- or weekend-ethnography). It also opens up the field at least to the extent that exercising women get to speak for themselves. (We wanted to be quick to put those interviews in place as additional text to be worked with, not as "the truth." We want students to work generously with Willis's account, not just set it aside. At the same time, this assignment is, perhaps, a bit loaded. We found Willis's account of exercise limited because it leaves out the element of pleasure and because it seems to assume that, for the women in the exercise rooms, there is a uniform experience and no evidence of knowing resistance or play.)

It is important, then, that students treat their notes as additional text and not as the final truth that puts the question of exercise to rest. In fact, it is useful to let students understand that their essay should open up new questions and suggest possible counterreadings, not put the whole issue to rest. At the end, we suggest that students might see themselves in a dialogue with Willis, partly to suggest that Willis's essay shouldn't be silenced but can be used to imagine response and counterstatement, and partly (as a more purely technical exercise) to push students to work passages from Willis's text back into their essays after they have made their own argument about exercise.

For revision: For either option, we recommend giving two weeks to this assignment. The first week would be devoted to discussion of the essay and the production of a first draft, the second to discussions of the first drafts and work on a second. The problems of revision will differ with each. For option one, it would make sense to represent students' work as having two goals: the production of the summary and the use of the summary to talk about Willis's "uncommon project." In most cases, the first draft will produce the summary, and in revision students can begin to work on: (1) questioning what is lost in a student's particular summary (what sections of the essay, what terms) and asking why; and (2) questioning what is lost generally in summary (and turning to the ways Willis's account defies translation to common sense, to the usual story). In revising option two, students will need to work on presentation (presenting both the text and context of their fieldwork) and on developing their positions *in* that account as teachers or commentators, as the authorial presence who reads and interprets and comments on the material gathered in the field.

ASSIGNMENT 4

The View from the Other Side [Fiske]

The Questions for a Second Reading in the text should be particularly useful for your students as they prepare to write this assignment.

As we said in the introduction to this sequence, the Fiske assignment concludes the series by asking students to read against the figure of the "fan" as offered by Fiske — and, through Fiske, to read against the figure of the viewer/consumer in Willis and Berger. The assignment doesn't insist on these questions as much as it might. We felt it important to give students a chance to work on Fiske after Willis and Berger but without the distraction of having to work parts of the Willis and Berger essays into their text. We may have been overly cautious here. We could imagine asking students to turn somewhere in their essays, perhaps at the end, to a direct reflection on Willis and Berger and their representation of the "consumer" in light of the discussion of Fiske. Students could even write their account of Fiske and perhaps use revision to look back to the other readings in the sequence.

The assignment asks students to test Fiske's account of Madonna's fans against their own experience. It is important, as your students do this, to remind them that for Fiske and the cultural critics, "common sense" is often seen as unreliable, as part of the problem, as something produced and enforced by the dominant culture to keep consumers from asking difficult questions. The assignment also asks students to read against the grain of Fiske's presentation of the "Critic" in Madonna (see the discussion above). It invites students to turn the tables on Fiske by suggesting that his critique of the packaging of Madonna could be applied to his packaging of John Fiske, the cultural critic. At one level, the assignment asks, "What good is this criticism? What is its function? What (or whose) purposes might this essay serve?" At another, the questions turn more specifically on the figure of John Fiske, the critic, the figure in the text, and his position in the complex struggles between men and women, old and young.

For revision: One way of directing a revision of this essay would be to turn it into a retrospective essay. Students (as we said above) could work from their reading of Fiske back to the earlier selections. As we think of the sequence, it would turn, finally, to questions of reception (How does culture "work" on individuals?) and to questions of method (How do these three critics imagine "culture," its effects, and its reception?). In practice, students would be combining summary (representations of the work of others) with original work

— first-person accounts of being a "fan," say, or the findings of critical projects they have authored.

. . . .

SEQUENCE TEN

Reading Culture (II) (p. 835)

For a full introduction to this sequence, see the introduction to "Reading Culture" (manual p. 163).

This sequence can be used on its own or as a supplement to the earlier sequence. The Berger-Willis-Fiske combination focused attention on the production and reception of images of women. The opening assignments in "Reading Culture (II)" bring into play three readings — "Male Bodies and the 'White Terror,' " "Getting Dirty," and "Cosby Knows Best" — that deal with the production and reception of images of men. As in the earlier sequence, the students move from application (writing the Theweleit-like critique) to a study of method (writing about Theweleit's representation of the making of a soldier). Theweleit offers an account of production and reception very different from those given by the other critics in these sequences. For Theweleit, production is more fully tied to political interests (fascism, the period in Germany between the two world wars), and reception is understood through reference to a psychology, rather than a sociology, of desire. The first sequence ends with a move to call into question (in the name of "the student" or "youth") some of the assumptions of Fiske's account of the reception of Madonna — and, through him, Willis and Berger's account of the "common" consumer. The second sequence proposes an alternative ending, this time using Tompkins's essay on her work as a way of thinking through and charting the changes in students' understanding of both their subjects and the larger project of cultural criticism.

For a complete commentary on the selections in this sequence, please be sure to read each essay's selection in this manual, particularly the opening discussion. While we will cull materials from the discussions of individual assignments, we won't reproduce the introductions. And, while the sequences provide writing assignments, you should think about the advantages (or disadvantages) of using the Questions for a Second Reading. In every case, students should read the headnotes in the textbook, which are designed to serve the assignments and sequences.

ASSIGNMENT 1

The Making of a Soldier [Theweleit]

The two Theweleit assignments mirror the Willis assignments in "Reading Culture" (manual p. 166). The first asks students to extend or apply Theweleit's analysis to material of their own choosing that is more local and more recent.

You should not underestimate the need to help students with the process of selection, perhaps taking a class period to look over some material you have gathered in advance (*Boy's Life* and *The Boy Scout Manual* are ideal sources). We've also found that we needed to make the process of search and selection an acknowledged part of the work of the course. We ask students to collect folders of material, to present them to others (to the class, to groups) and, in their essays, to talk about how they selected the material they chose to write about.

Once students have found their material, they need (as writers) to present it to readers as part of a project Theweleit has begun. We have found it important to remind students that they need to introduce and *present* "Male Bodies," even to readers who had read it. You cannot assume, we remind our students, that readers have it freshly in mind or that they will be willing to get the book off the shelf and turn to pages. And we have found it important to help students imagine the role they will play in this text. They will need, in other words, to do more than simply cite from or summarize what they have gathered in their inventories. They will need to step forward (as Theweleit does) to teach, translate, make connection, explain, comment, discuss, think this way and that. Students, at least our students, are often too quick to let the wonderful material they gather speak for itself.

ASSIGNMENT 2

Theweleit as Critic [Theweleit]

This assignment presents Theweleit's essay not for its content so much as an example of method, a way of gathering, reading and presenting the material record of a cultural process — in Theweleit's case, the making of Nazi soldiers. It might help students if you took some class time to work through an example from the text. When we taught the essay, our students spent a good deal of time talking and thinking through the essay's principle of organization. Theweleit works by association, representing in a sense the weight or density of culture. (This is surely part of the effect of all the illustrations, which stand as a kind of unprocessed counterpart to the extended readings of literary examples in the essay.) And, when he turns his attention to examples, he depends upon a fairly rigid account of male desire. He has a system (one students can learn to paraphrase) that then produces the readings he wants, given whatever material he brings before him. These readings are offered in the name of a "humanity" denied by the Fascists, who make certain assumptions about young men and old men. These are some of the "figures" necessary to tell the story Theweleit wants to tell. At the end of this exercise (whose primary goal is a description of method), students might also be asked to describe this "story," its plot and main characters, and the "fiction" in its representation of the world. In practice, one might say, Theweleit becomes the kind of "totality machine" he cites as the center of the Fascist sensibility. Everything comes to be controlled by his desire for meaning, and the meanings he produces become predictable, routine, fixed.

In saying this, we are turning Theweleit's critique against him. There are more generous readings possible; in the headnote, we cite Barbara Ehrenreich's favorable account of Theweleit's style as an example of the "softness" and "permeability" feared by the Fascists. We would encourage students to begin with a generous representation of the ways in which Theweleit works on and with his material. Students can profitably chart the figure of the "critic," the "reader," and the "young man" in Theweleit's work. As is always the case, the quality of students' essays will be related to how closely they work with the text and their ability to produce (as writers and not only as readers) a close reading.

For revision: We tend to divide the revision of an essay like this in terms of "presentation" and "commentary." We would ask students to reread "Male Bodies," thinking about those parts of the texts they have left out, either strategically or without noticing that they were leaving them out. It would be impossible, of course, to include every one of Theweleit's examples in a discussion of the essay. That is not our point. We are interested, rather, in those terms, examples, and ideas that lie outside the range of terms, examples, and ideas reproduced in the summary. And, we have found, students' essays tend to ignore the needs of a reader, one who does not have the text open in front of her and who is unwilling to go back and look up sections. To work at "presentation," then, students need to go back to the text, to see how it has been presented in summary and through quotation; and they need to look out for their readers, to think about how a reader might best become engaged with the material at hand. Finally, we ask students to think about "commentary,"

170

about the places in the text where they speak from their own positions about Theweleit. These "slots" in the text are usually slim and few and far between. Students will spend a good deal of time speaking for Theweleit but not much time speaking for themselves. This, too, is work for revision.

ASSIGNMENT **3**

Watching TV [Miller]

If Theweleit seems exotic and remote, Miller will seem, at least at first, to take students back to familiar territory. When we have taught these two essays, we have asked students to use them as a way of charting or understanding the method of a critic whose work was different from Theweleit's — in fact, although there are many similarities in the work, we have insisted that students look for differences (most notably, for us, the particularly American brand of close reading practiced by Miller).

To do this we have had to forestall students' desires to use the essays as the occasion to talk about "The Cosby Show" or their favorite ad, material they are more comfortable with than wrestling or striptease. There is a point at which we want to encourage students to try out their roles as critics and to write about ads or shows, but we want them to do this in the name of criticism, to imagine what it would be like to "read" television in this way.

This assignment asks students to try their hand at Miller's brand of criticism, taking his methods and applying them to new material. It invites a response, including one that runs counter to Miller's criticism. Students, we've found, feel uncomfortable with what Miller does; there is something unseemly or improper about looking closely at TV, about refusing to be a "normal" viewer. Students feel that they too know something about TV, even if they miss the sexual politics of the Shield ad. This assignment provides the opportunity to students to define their position in response to Miller's, to speak (in a sense) in the name of the public Miller says is mystified by television's sophisticated rhetoric. In fact, this essay might be cast as a chance for a representative of the viewing public to speak back to Miller, to account in the same detail (and with reference to motive) for the "normal" or "ordinary" experience with TV. The difficulty here is to enable students to do this without giving in to self-righteous critic-trashing, and this ability allows students to see the "normal" as a practice, a method for reading TV, one that is not "naturally" there but a product, something we learn by watching and because we are members of the culture.

Students' success with this assignment will depend on their ability to represent to themselves Miller's method as a method, and it will depend on the degree to which they work with precise detail in representing their ad or show. They most likely will not be able to use pictures, but Miller's writing sets a good example here. In a sense, he teaches his readers how to look at the screen by the example of what he notices and remembers. Students will need to work with close detail, they will need to define a contrary relation to the "common-sense" reading of their example, and they will need to imagine that their job is to ask questions, including the big question of "just what is going on here?" As the note says, the hard question is one that even Miller refuses to take head-on. One of his devices as a critic is to put agency into a show — to say, for example, that the Shield ad *offers* women a fantasy of power and control. The story he is trying to tell is not the usual narrative of an artist creating an effect, but of a shaping force that is bigger than an individual artist or writer, one that committees or producers only partially grasp. Students should be aware of the source or origin of television's effects and the ways in which they need to talk about it in unusual terms.

171

(text pages 835–839)

For revision: Students, perhaps properly, will initially devote their energy and attention to producing an account of their show or ad — describing it, noticing some features, and ignoring others. There are two ways we have approached a revision of this essay. We have asked students to step back from their account to imagine what it misses, what it necessarily misses because of its angle of vision. And we have asked students to use the revision as an occasion to turn their attention to larger, interpretive questions. If the first draft was the occasion to pay "meticulous attention to concrete detail," the second is to see how those details might be said to "illuminate the larger context . . . so that the reading of TV contains and necessitates a reading of our own moment and its past."

ASSIGNMENT **4**

On Schooling [Tompkins]

This is the final assignment in the sequence. It can be the occasion for students to stop and take stock of what they have learned, particularly the bearing this on-going critique of culture might have on their work as students, where they are learning to be products of academic culture, and where they are learning to push against the discourse of the everyday, of common sense.

Jane Tompkins's essay, "Indians," is a wonderful opportunity for students to look behind the scenes of academic life. The essay is surprising and engaging, and it offers a powerful corrective to students' notions of what "research" is all about — it offers an alternative to the story told all too often in the textbooks, where research is a fairly mechanical matter of going to the library, finding books, pulling "facts" or "truths" out of those books, and then fussing over organization and footnotes.

The story Tompkins tells is a story of reading and writing, of research as it involves the process of interpretation and as it puts one in a position to question "truths" that appear to be self-evident. Our students have taken great pleasure in this essay — in its style and its willingness to show how scholarship engages a person, how it is neither a dispassionate nor an impersonal matter. In a sense it is the character that emerges in this essay (this "Jane Tompkins") that students find most memorable. They are either confused or disappointed by the conclusion ("Is that all this was leading to?") But they love to imagine that they have seen into our "real" lives.

There is, we believe, a powerful lesson for students in this essay, in the way Tompkins represents a "proper" relationship to books. Students may have been told that they need to read their sources "critically," but they have a hard time imagining what that means. They believe, most often, that they have to "catch" the author in an error or a logical fallacy. Tompkins demonstrates how reading critically is, rather, a matter of working out a book's point of view and imagining the consequences of that point of view — what it inevitably notices and what it inevitably misses. When students wrote about this essay in a retrospective assignment, they returned to this point again and again — how Tompkins had shown them something about books and the library (and their possible relations to books and the library) that they had never understood. They, too, believed that you went to the library to find the truth and that the truth was in either the biggest or the most recent book on the shelf.

This assignment follows the pattern in this sequence. It asks students to locate in their own work what Tompkins identifies as the problems of reading and writing (or the problems of research). It also serves a dual purpose. It is an invitation for students to imagine that they are a real audience (not just naive observers), and it asks students to imagine themselves as part of the "we" of this essay. And an assignment like this is, in miniature, a course of instruction. It gives students a model or a scheme they can use to systematically review and assess their own work. It allows students to name what they have learned to do, to identify it as a stage or one method among several and, as a consequence, it puts students in a position to push off in a new direction.

If students select the first of the two options, it is imperative that they have a body of work to review and quote. They will need to have access to a file of papers, ideally the work in this sequence. If they work only from memory, the essay will lose its bite. It is simply too easy to be the hero or the victim in a narrative invented from whole cloth. If students are, in fact, investigating a textual problem, they will need to have passages to work from — perhaps from books they read or from papers they wrote. They do not, of course, need to tell the *same* story as Tompkins — but they should be encouraged to follow her example and talk about how they have learned to re-read some of their sources.

The second option allows students to imagine that the problem Tompkins alludes to is not literally a textual problem — that it does not necessarily involve one's work with books. It says, in effect, treat your memories, your past conversations, your ways of understanding things, the tropes and figures that dominate (or dominated) your way of thinking and speaking as text; imagine that they are situated and that they situate you; ask questions about point of view, about implication, and about origin.

· · · · · · · · · ·

SEQUENCE ELEVEN

Ways of Seeing (p. 840)

The four assignments in this sequence introduce students to the problems posed by how we look at art and what these problems have to do with "history," as Berger sees it, the making of meaning, and the expectations and strategies that we use to construct both history and meaning. Berger's essay allows us to extend the concept of reading beyond the written texts (to the way one "reads" painting or images, to the way one "reads" one's culture). He seems to purposely want to take common terms like "history" and "meaning" and make them problematic (just as he wants to take familiar images and give us new ways of seeing them); yet he isn't pushy about definitions, and these terms remain open to discussion. For students, this means that they can reproduce his project, beginning with a close examination of his argument and then a Berger-like "reading" of a painting followed by a "reading" of their own essays in his terms and standards. After working with Berger's argument for three assignments (including tests of it), students are then given the opportunity to go back to their first assignments where they reproduced his arguments and resee them, taking into consideration the work they've done in the sequence.

We are attracted to this sequence, as we are to the problems Berger poses, because it offers students the opportunity to work closely and extensively with a single essay that deals with compelling and challenging arguments about the very acts — reading and making meaning — that students are asked to perform.

ASSIGNMENT 1

Berger's Example of a Way of Seeing [Berger]

Berger argues that we fail to see images because our culture has made us blind to them. We can overcome this blindness by means of new strategies or approaches. And it is "history" that is at stake in all this. This assignment offers Berger's essay as a problem for students as though they were clarifying it for other students in class, who have also read it.

173

ASSIGNMENT 2

Applying Berger's Method to a Painting [Berger]

This assignment accepts the implied invitation of the Berger essay and asks the reader to see what he or she can make of a painting in a museum or a book of reproductions. The problem posed to students, then, is "What can you make of this painting, if you work on it in Berger's spirit?" One way of framing a discussion of these papers (or, perhaps, of preparing students for revision) is to turn to Berger's own words: "What we make of that painted moment when it is before our eyes depends upon what we expect of art, and that in turn depends today upon how we have already experienced the meaning of paintings through reproductions." Students might begin their discussions of papers from the class by considering what the authors expect of art, how they might have experienced the meaning of paintings through reproductions, and what, in their colleagues' papers, might be attributed to the author's work with Berger, what might be attributed to our general culture, and what might be taken as a sign of some individual or idiosyncratic vision.

ASSIGNMENT 3

A Way of Seeing Your Way of Seeing [Berger]

This assignment, in a sense, asks students to give a Berger-like reading to their own essays. If you use his terms and standards, what way of seeing is represented in these essays? The very fact that the essay represents a "way of seeing" will be a powerful revelation for students (who think that they described what was there and who will be surprised to see that their accounts reveal an approach or a strategy). This assignment, then, gives students some experience analyzing — and in a rigorous, disciplined way — a moment of vision.

It is important that students write out their responses to this assignment, although it does not lend itself readily to standard essay form. This might be a journal assignment or a series of notes. By writing, however, students will be compelled to attend to their early papers with an attention they would not otherwise show. And a written record will give them a detailed text they can discuss with others.

ASSIGNMENT 4

Reviewing the Way You See [Berger]

This final assignment gives students the opportunity to pull together what they have learned about "reading" pictures, paintings, and images and what all this has to do with "history." It also offers them the opportunity to revise Berger, to resee his claims in the context of their experiences, extending and testing his argument with their own.

. . . .

SEQUENCE TWELVE

Working with Foucault (p. 845)

Both of us taught Foucault in our composition courses last year. We found, as you might guess, that students needed extra time to work through this difficult material. What surprised us, however, was the eagerness they showed in going back again and again to work on Foucault. When, for example, students had the option of a final revision in the course, they almost unanimously chose to go back and work on a Foucault paper, and the paper they chose to work on was the summary of Foucault's argument. For years we had avoided summaries, which represented a version of reading our courses had been designed to supplant or revise, or used them merely as a tool or device, a step on the way to some other work with a text.

We decided to write a sequence that would organize an extended Foucault project. Students would both summarize Foucault's argument and extend the chapter's interpretive project to material closer to home. In addition, we wanted to use Foucault as a way of questioning the act of summary, its motives and uses.

You could think of this sequence, then, as made up of two threads. One asks students to master "The Body of the Condemned" by working through three drafts of a summary account of the chapter and then writing an essay in which they apply Foucault to an early attempt to normalize evaluation in high school composition courses. The other thread is represented by the "codas" to various assignments. The coda is meant to stand as a kind of final reprise or moment of reflection; it is the place where students stand outside of what they written, in some cases in opposition to it, to see "mastery" as evidence of a problem (a problem rooted in a history of mastery, one that connects a writing class to the penal system) and not simply as a sign of achievement.

Foucault makes these connections in *Discipline and Punish*. Among the illustrations in the book are pictures from students' handwriting guides. We found it an extremely useful exercise, in fact, to ask students to think both inside and outside English as a system of disciplining language and language use. This provided a parallel to the Prison as an organizing term. The technology of control in English was readily available in ways that the technology of control in the law was not. It was easy for students to take the role of the professor and to speak for English. In fact, there was some subversive pleasure in this act of ventriloquism. We used, for example, an extremely powerful paper written by one of our students, a first-person essay about divorce filled with the rhythms and syntax of speech.

It was an essay that exemplified the powerful rhetoric of authenticity. We asked students to "correct" this text by punctuating it correctly and turning it into "prose." Then we asked students to think of this from outside English, as an example of power and knowledge at work to regulate the body (the voice) of this writer. These discussions gave students a sense of the basic oppositional move in Foucault; and it gave them a sense of how he ignores traditional historical or disciplinary boundaries (connecting schools and prisons, the seventeenth century and the twentieth, arguing that it only serves the regime of "truth" to imagine that they are different).

These were our goals in teaching Foucault. We did not use the word "poststructuralism"; we did not make any attempts to connect this chapter to the body of Foucault's work or to the large critical project he has helped to serve. That, to our minds, would be the work of a different kind of course. We wanted students to work with the peculiar difficulties of Foucault's text and to put into play what they could imagine to be his critical project. For our students, the key terms were "soul" and "body." We asked them to struggle to come to terms with what he says about power and knowledge, but this was tough going. We did not bring in terms from his earlier or later work. For our classes, Foucault was only the figure represented in "The Body of the Condemned."

This is a single-author sequence. It could be combined with other sequences in *Ways of Reading*: "History and Ethnography," "Working with the Past," "Ways of Seeing," or "Writing History." You could also work in single selections, constructing your own sequence from the Making Connections assignments or the Assignments for Writing. We recommend reading the following authors along with Foucault: Berger, Fish, Freire, Percy, Rich, Williams, and Willis.

For a complete commentary on the selections in this sequence, please be sure to read each essay's selection in this manual, particularly the opening discussion. While we will cull materials from the discussions of individual assignments, we won't reproduce the introductions. And, while the sequences provide writing assignments, you should think about the advantages (or disadvantages) of using the Questions for a Second Reading. In every case, students should read the headnotes in the textbook, which are designed to serve the assignments and sequences.

ASSIGNMENT 1

Reading Foucault [Foucault]

This is the first of the summary assignments. It positions students as "experts," saying to them, "You be the teacher." Built into the position of the expert are certain assumptions about mastery that the "coda" and later revisions will begin to question. We want students, however, to think about how the role of the "master" is written for them historically and politically — through centuries of American schooling, through centuries of concern about the dangers of the book or of uncontrolled reading. We want this desire for mastery to indicate something other than a personal tick or a feature of human psychology. Students will be quick to turn to psychology (or pop psychology) for an account of the "person" and subjectivity. Working on Foucault requires a radical shift in the language you use to talk about the person and motive and agency. Perhaps the classroom is the best place to make the point that the things we do and that we seem to do "naturally" are in fact constructed and preserved by the culture and its institutions. How else to explain, for example, the strange ways we think about and talk about and value acts of reading and writing. For us, it is important to make these "normal" acts *strange*.

As you can tell from the introduction to *Ways of Reading*, one of the ways in which we make this shift in the class is to talk about the regime of the "main idea" as a way of preserving certain roles for students, teachers, and authors. This is a funny business, since we shock our students into seeing the composition class as an arbitrary construction and yet, as teachers, we tend to preserve many of its routines. When we taught Foucault, we spent a good bit of time stepping into and out of our roles as English Teachers. In a sense, this was a way of preparing students to step into and out of their roles as Master Readers.

In this assignment, the coda asks students to reread the chapter to see what they missed. The usual language of the classroom would call these lapses "mistakes" or "oversights" and it would root them in an account of student readers as "novices" or "beginners." The assignment asks students to think of the story of reading as a very different story altogether, where omissions are not mistakes but part of a technology for dealing with difficulty, which we inherit without thinking of it as a technology. And again — we want students to think of this technology for handling difficulty *not* as the psyche's response to uncertainty but as an example of a larger social, cultural, or political process. Whose interests are served by these omissions. Perhaps it is not just a matter of preserving your pride or your sense of authority — what else is preserved by this way of reading?

ASSIGNMENT **2**

The Technology of Mastery (A Revision) [Foucault]

This assignment asks students to go back to their summary to revise it. This makes simple sense to students, since they know that there is good reason to reread the chapter and then go back to work on their presentation of what it says.

Our concern is to begin to question mastery as a goal of revision. We found it very useful to simply announce that it is possible to say, in an essay, that you don't completely understand what Foucault is saying. It is a simple device, this admission, but it opens up a textual space that would otherwise remain closed. It allows students to write their way into their confusion (or the confusion in the text), to think about possible, as opposed to certain, readings, and to reflect on what it is that makes Foucault's chapter hard to understand. We built this offer into the assignment: "You can make understanding tentative, provisional." But you may want to highlight this part of the assignment. Students will read right past it if you don't. They are not prepared to see these words and to act on them — just as they are not prepared to see and act upon certain words in "The Body of the Condemned."

When students write this revision they should think that they are: (1) working at the way in which their essay presents the chapter to a reader who does not have that chapter fixed in her mind, who does not have the book open in front of him; (2) working on the text of "The Body of the Condemned" by rereading, by working new passages into the summary (we assume that the students' essays will become longer), or by focusing attention on the key terms and the mysterious terms in Foucault's text; and (3) working on writing a provisional summary that talks about what it doesn't understand as well as what it does.

The coda in this case focuses on the *figure* of the writer/reader as the writer/reader is figured in the summary. It is a difficult shift for students to see themselves as somehow characters in a story of reading that they have written, or to make strategic use of the difference between the I and the "I" on the page. It is a very useful device in any writing course to allow students this way of reading their prose. A course that includes Foucault provides an extra benefit, since the shift to see a "textual" self helps students to begin to understand the ways in which Foucault imagines the relationship between a person and a discourse or system. It gives students a firsthand sense of what it might mean to think of a person as written into being by a system of representation that the person did not invent and cannot completely control.

ASSIGNMENT **3**

The Soul Project [Foucault]

As our students worked on the argument in "The Body of the Condemned," it was hard for them to bring the terms "body" and "soul" into play. For one thing, "soul" is a loaded term and even though Foucault announces that he is not talking about the soul in traditional Christian terms, those traditional terms tend to govern students' reading of this part of the text.

In the epigraph, we wanted to focus on the phrase "the historical reality of the soul" and to have students find a way of pointing to its "historical reality" from histories closer to home. This assignment follows a pattern of assignments in *Ways of Reading*. It asks students to extend an author's interpretive project to an example, or examples, that students put on the table. It might be useful to work out a possible example and its preliminary reading in class as a pre-writing exercise, although students should use the class example

177

only as a momentary point of reference, if at all, when they write. (You don't want students recording the class discussion when they sit down to work on this paper.)

ASSIGNMENT 4

Writing, Knowledge, and Power [Foucault]

The work in this assignment mirrors the work in assignment 3. This time, however, we have provided the example. It comes from a book by Earl Hudelson, *English Composition: Its Aims, Methods, and Measurement,* published as a yearbook of the National Society for Studies in Education in 1923. (Bartholomae has written about this book in "Writing on the Margins" in *A Sourcebook for Basic Writing Teachers,* Theresa Enos, ed., Random House, 1987.)

The point of the assignment is for students to question the inevitability of the ranking of these essays. It is easy to account for the "rightness" of the order. It seems to be part of the order of things. The question to raise is what that order might be said to represent. Here are some of the ways our students began to read against the hierarchy.

> It represents not "ability" but income and class. Before the distribution of knowledge came the distribution of power.

> The first tells a story of appetite, the last a story of charity, and those meanings of those stories are predetermined.

> The writer of the essay on getting into a locked house is a smart aleck. You could read the essay, in fact, as a parody of the composition course, its forms and values — it is a kind of *Saturday Night Live* version of the "Essay describing a Process." It is clear why he would be rated below the student who submits to the moral, "Do what your mother says."

> The first essay seems true, real, moving; the last seems phony, B.S., posturing — the writer takes too much pleasure describing the "miserable hovel," the "flabby mother" and the "mangy children" for us to believe in his new found humility.

ASSIGNMENT 5

The Two-Step [Foucault]

This final assignment in the sequence asks students to work on their summary again, this time with a double sense of what it means to speak for (and master) a text. This is a summary with a difference, informed by a sense of original sin. Our goal is to focus the argument of discipline and punish on the practice of reading and writing, as they serve the regime of truth.

This sounds grand and glum. In practice, these essays were high-spirited and fun. Students turned to examples culled from assignments 4 and 5 to give extended demonstrations of how they read Foucault's argument. They worked closely with sections of the text, including the hard ones. They talked about the problem of the text as well as its meaning. The essays were long and students were quite proud of them, usually because of the pleasure they took in mastering a difficult text. While most students could get the point of the critique of mastery, they are still products of a culture that rewards the writer of the Grub Hollow paper and finds the "popo bush" writer to be a problem.

178

· · · · · · · · · ·
SEQUENCE THIRTEEN

Working with the Past (p. 853)

As the sequence introduction points out, students are asked to work with texts by Rodriguez (and Hoggart), Oates, Jacobs, and Walker from a perspective that focuses their attention on how authors (and texts) directly or indirectly write under the influences of others. This is an unusual position for students to take. Our students want to see the past as fixed, as certain, and they tend to treat texts the same way. For them, then, the past and past texts exist as recoverable artifacts, moments and ideas that can be accurately and objectively recovered and represented. The idea that the past changes as the lenses used to recover and represent it also change is new to our students; so is the notion that working with texts from the past involves more than simply accurately presenting them.

The beauty of this sequence lies in the way it asks students to reimagine the past and texts from the past as something other than fixed, objective artifacts, to regard them as materials, that is, that are reimagined and revised as different authors work with them for varying purposes. Work with this sequence can give students the opportunity to understand the larger cultural and historical field that bears on authors and their writing, and it can give students ways of imagining "creativity" and "originality" in the contexts of the influences of the past, rather than as the expression of "genius" free from the influences of the past and past writings.

Some of the assignments in this sequence are adapted from writing assignments in the book. You should be sure to read those assignments and the entries on them in this manual.

ASSIGNMENT 1

The Scholarship Boy [Rodriguez]

Rodriguez makes extensive use of Hoggart's work in his presentation of the scholarship boy, and the extended section of Hoggart's discussion of the scholarship boy makes an interesting contrast both to Rodriguez's notion of a scholarship and to his presentation of Hoggart's ideas. Needless to say, students will need to come to an understanding of how both Rodriguez and Hoggart create and use this notion of a scholarship boy. You might consider asking students to do this kind of work from their readings of the individual pieces (Rodriguez's and Hoggart's) before they begin working directly with the sequence assignments. This first assignment is straightforward and if students follow its sequence of directions and questions they'll see that initially they need to understand how Rodriguez uses Hoggart. The important question they need to deal with has to do with what Rodriguez says Hoggart is saying about scholarship boys. The third paragraph of the assignment lays out the questions that can help students read from outside Rodriguez's point of view to establish a sense of how he could be said to be revising Hoggart while using his text and ideas. Our students, for example, have been quick to point out that Hoggart's working-class scholarship boy is British and living in a culture quite different from Rodriguez's or that of most Americans. Our subsequent question back to them then asks how this distinction (being British and working class) makes Hoggart's scholarship boy different not just from the one Rodriguez imagines but also from the boy Rodriguez imagines Hoggart to be.

The fourth paragraph of the assignment turns students' attention to what they might attribute Rodriguez's strategy in using and revising Hoggart. We assume, as is evident from the assignment, that Rodriguez does reimagine and revise Hoggart, so it's a question

179

of where, how, and why he does. The case isn't clear-cut, of course, because Rodriguez doesn't completely rewrite Hoggart, and students should have a good deal of leeway to make their cases for the where, how, and why of Rodriguez's revision of Hoggart's text. The excerpt from Hoggart is lengthy and substantive enough for students to do the kind of comparison readings this assignment calls for; and Hoggart's tone, or stance, along with his notions of the scholarship boy and how he comes into being and acts out his role, is apparent and detailed. More than anything, though, this assignment is designed to introduce students to the notion of authors working under others' influences and to the idea of the malleability of the past. Both Rodriguez and Hoggart serve as good examples of these.

ASSIGNMENT 2

Theft [Rodriguez, Oates]

Students have a great deal to work with in Oates's story, including the difference between its presentation of Marya, a scholarship student, and Rodriguez's presentation of himself as a scholarship student. This is also a great opportunity for students to understand that Rodriguez, like Oates, is telling a story — his story, of course, but nevertheless a story rather than an essay making an argument — and that Oates, although she is certainly telling a story, can also be said to be making an argument for what a scholarship student is and how her life differs from and is similar to that of other students (like Imogene for instance) who are not scholarship students. We've had a good time asking students to work on this assignment with particular attention to the question that offers both stories as arguments: Where and in what ways might Rodriguez and Marya pose arguments that run counter to each other? What arguments are Oates and Rodriguez (the writer of the narrative) making about education and class, knowledge and identity? One interesting point of intersection that often comes up in our discussions and in students' writing concerns the notions of theft. It can be said that both Marya and Rodriguez steal (ideas, knowledge, culture, and so on), and that perhaps both authors are arguing that the education of scholarship students is a kind of theft, which these students must necessarily come to see and deal with. This is, of course, not the only point that students find these narratives do or do not have in common, but it serves as a good example of the ways in which these two stories can offer students rich examples to work with as they craft and revise their essays influenced by Rodriguez, Hoggart, and Oates.

As a follow-up assignment to this one, you might consider asking students to resee their essays as examples of their revisions and their work with authors from the past. How, for instance, might they say they rewrote Hoggart, Rodriguez, and Oates when they compared them? What did they present from these authors, and how did they present it (and use it) differently from them? What might the students say they ignored or overlooked or were blind to as they did this work for assignment 2?

ASSIGNMENT 3

Telling a Story of Education [Rodriguez, Oates]

Students are quick to point out that they're not scholarship students, even if they're on scholarships, as are Rodriguez or Marya, and you might need to help them get past this literal take on presenting themselves in light of these two narratives. The point of the assignment is to have students tell their own stories of schooling, in light of what they see as their similarities to, and differences from, the scholarship students presented by Rodriguez, Hoggart, and Oates.

180

Writing stories is difficult for students who don't have experience, and this assignment asks for their attention to scene, dialogue, and detail; students will thus need to identify moments of dialogue that can stand for key points or conversations (like Rodriguez's talks with his mother, for example, or Marya's internal monologues) in their educational experience. They'll want to put these conversations on paper, together with the descriptions of scenes that represent their college experience, and they'll need to do so following the conventions of story. They can learn these conventions — using quotations, indenting, weaving descriptions of people's gestures and the place into the dialogue, and so on — from the stories in the book, especially the Oates story, as well as from studying how Rodriguez weaves such things as remembered conversations (or summaries of them) into his narrative.

Students can have fun with this assignment if it's presented in the spirit of experimentation and they imitate the writing (Oates, Rodriguez, Hoggart) before them. They'll need to understand that it's not likely they'll get it right and produce a story that looks like Rodriguez's or Oates's, but they can get very close if they write multiple drafts and you give them the opportunity to take their stories through multiple revisions with comments from each other and from you.

ASSIGNMENT 4

A Life Story [Jacobs]

Jacobs's methods in her narrative are fairly transparent, at least for readers with some experience in the kinds of close readings that would allow them, for example, to identify shifts within the text in the kinds of writing she's doing. She is certainly telling a story, complete with remembered dialogue and conversations, but she also, at times, creates a polemic, a passionate plea for the reader's understanding of the life of slaves, one not likely to be received with sympathy by all of her possible readers of the time. There are moments, too, when it seems as though her writing might be called epistolary, others when it is poetic. She uses sources, she quotes people and texts, and she imagines readers as certain kinds of people.

Students will need to reread Jacobs at least twice to identify those shifts in the text that signal the materials she's presenting and the methods of writing she's using. When students do this work, they will need to the take the perspective that they're reading a writer who is working with the past — both as remembered and imagined materials and as a writer influenced by conventions and traditions of writing. How, too, they'll need to ask themselves, does she imagine her readers? What can they find in the text that gives them clues or signals about the kinds of readers Jacobs imagines? How would they characterize these readers? Why might Jacobs be imagining these kinds of readers? What influences are at work on her as she creates readers in her imagination?

ASSIGNMENT 5

Working with the Past [Walker]

Once students have been working with the notion of a writer creating from written materials from the past, they should be able to move into this assignment without much trouble. It's straightforward, without any unexpected turns, and students will find plenty of examples of texts within Walker's to work with. Our students have turned almost immediately to Walker's use of Wheatley's poetry, which she pretty clearly imagines in ways other than Wheatley might have intended; but even within these examples, there's plenty of room for students to move as they imagine how Walker uses her poetry and the story of Wheatley's life for her project. When we used this assignment in Pittsburgh, the most interesting part was the question that asks students to consider how Walker's essay, with all of its uses of texts and stories from the past, might be read as a part of the tradition of creativity that she charts in her own essay. In other words, how does Walker's project chart the creativity of an African-American woman in the face of oppressions? How, too, does her use of the texts and stories of the past allow her to revise that past, to imagine it as a part of her project now?

You should note that the excerpt from "A Room of One's Own" in the text does not include Woolf's discussion of "contrary instincts"; students will need to do library research to find that discussion in Woolf's book and address the question of how Walker revises Woolf's use of the phrase. It's certainly clear that Woolf wasn't addressing an African-American audience and that she was concerned with the contrary instincts of women trying to write, trying to create intellectual lives; but students will need more than these conclusions to flesh out the differences in Woolf's use of the term and Walker's.

ASSIGNMENT 6

Legacies [Walker, Jacobs]

Actually, this assignment is a revision of assignments 4 and 5, and students should feel free to use what they wrote for those (this is, of course, another example of working with texts from the past), but the purpose of this assignment is considerably different from these other two, and they'll need to reread Jacobs and Walker before proceeding. Essentially, this one asks students first to consider Jacobs as another example for Walker's project and then to imagine how Jacobs's example alters or changes the project. Of course, it can alter it in any number of ways — for example, by changing the focus to Jacobs's desires, or by enriching and broadening Walker's arguments through another strong example — and students should feel free, in their own "creative projects," to speculate on how Jacobs's text might serve or alter Walker's argument.

· · · · · · · · · ·

SEQUENCE FOURTEEN

Working with the Past (II) (p. 868)

As the introduction to this sequence notes, you could use these three assignments to add to those of sequence thirteen or to replace some. The Woolf assignment here (1) could, for example, easily replace the Rodriguez-Hoggart assignment (1), the Woolf-Walker assignment here (2) could replace the Rodriguez-Oates assignment in sequence thirteen (2); and the final assignment here (3) could replace the third assignment in sequence thirteen or be used as the final assignment in that sequence. Or this sequence could be used on its own as a mini-sequence. We are sure that there are other ways to use these assignments along with those from sequence thirteen, and you should feel free to invent your own sequence from these assignments and those in sequence thirteen or to write your own assignments using other texts that revise texts from the past to reinvent this sequence.

ASSIGNMENT **1**

Reading the Past [Woolf]

For students, the key move in working with this assignment is their identification of four moments in Woolf's essay at which they can say that she is saying, or seems to be saying, "I'm not going to be doing what you expect in an essay; instead I'll do this." They will need to identify, in other words, four moments at which Woolf reimagines the essay or lecture and offers other ways of enacting her thinking. Students will need to consider, as the assignment asks, what Woolf is doing — how they can characterize her methods and how those methods might be said to have something to do with the figure of the woman she imagines in place of the traditionally male audience for lectures and essays. Students will also need to consider Woolf's work in this essay as an example of an author working with the writing of the past. How, in other words, would they characterize Woolf's work with the writing of the past — the lecture and the essay? And how would they explain the changes or revisions she makes to that writing? As the assignment asks, what does she preserve? What does she revise?

ASSIGNMENT **2**

Rewriting "A Room of One's Own" [Walker]

Walker's project involves revising texts from the past to construct her argument for African-American women's creativity in the face of oppressive conditions. Woolf serves as one of her examples. She appropriates, and revises, Woolf's term, "contrary instincts," to apply to her own examples, and students should understand their job in this essay as the explanation of how and why Walker uses Woolf. First they'll need to locate the moments in Walker's essay where she refers to Woolf. Then they'll need to comment on how Walker uses Woolf and how her use of Woolf connects with her argument about women's creativity in the face of oppressive living and working conditions. There are other questions to engage students' attention for this assignment, and students should have no trouble speculating on how Walker treats Woolf and why she might have chosen her as an example, especially if they have worked with Woolf's essay from the first assignment.

ASSIGNMENT **3**

On Reading the Past [Woolf, Walker]

This is a powerful assignment, and it's a lot of work for students, so you should expect that they will need to take it through multiple revisions. First, they need to tell some stories about their own education that illustrate how, in their education, they worked with the past. The stories need to stand as powerful examples for the students, as times they felt that something important or useful or exciting happened to them in relation to work they were doing with the past.

The examples could come from any subject area but should concern how they, the students, were dealing with or were being taught to deal with or approach the past, or work from the past. Possibilities include studying art or history, or writing in these subjects, or their past experiences in any form. The field is wide open here for them to locate those moments.

Students will also need to weave their examples in with Woolf's and Walker's, when appropriate of course, but this will be a difficult yet powerful move for them to try their hands at. Woolf discusses the failure of the British essay and lecture to represent the thinking of women and to offer women a space for writing and reading; Walker discusses the failure of American culture to make room for and to honor the creative work of African-American women from the past. What might students' education have prepared or failed to prepare them to do? Both Walker and Woolf offer extremely compelling examples of how the past can be revised and readers prepared to understand their projects. Students, by their examples in this project, can imagine themselves in turn preparing their readers to understand their own education in ways not readily apparent.

. . . .

SEQUENCE FIFTEEN

Writing History (p. 872)

This short sequence could be thought of as an introduction to the academy or, more specifically, to "history" as a disciplinary activity, a way of writing about the past valued and preserved in colleges and universities. Limerick's chapters and Tompkins's essay are presented as opportunities for students to peer behind the veil and get the "true" story of intellectual labor. Limerick's two chapters tell the story of professional writing and professional preparation. Tompkins's chapter tells a more general story of intellectual life, of the ways in which knowledge is made, preserved, and transformed.

The first two assignments put students in the position of the "expert," representing (or translating) Limerick's and Tompkins's work for someone who has not read the selections. We specify the audience for two reasons. We want students (as writers) to think about presentation. The problems they will face, then, are characteristic problems in academic writing — working closely with texts, representing the ideas and positions of others, presenting textual material to those who will not have the text before them, engaging readers with ideas, establishing a position in relation to the work of the others. The other reason for specifying the audience is to put students in the position of speaking as though they were academy insiders. We want students to feel their authority in just this way (as an act of will and appropriation); we want them to imagine learning as just this kind of work with the writing of others. It is important, though, that as students imagine their audience, they imagine it as composed of their sharpest and most intellectually demanding peers. Little is gained if students write to children or to simpletons. The stakes need to be high for students to feel the pressure to become engaged with these essays beyond the superficial level.

If the opening assignments ask students to play the role of the expert, the final assignment situates them as novices, outsiders, trying their hands at writing a history. We have had great success with this assignment. We do not want to argue that students can become "historians" in three or four weeks. Neither are we concerned to design a specific formula for the production of "history." We are interested, rather, in pushing students to imagine that history is, if nothing else, something other than what they would normally write, something other than what they have been prepared to do. And this is how we have worked with that assignment — by letting students formulate their own working definitions of history from their reading of Limerick and Tompkins and through their own work as writers. We don't know what a "history" is, we say, but we know what it is *not*; it's not just a personal essay or a description or a narrative or something written about the past. Something else is involved. This approach puts students in the position of imagining history as a problem rather than a given, as something achieved beyond the ordinary uses of language. That, we found, was a productive motive for students' work, to work from the given to the unknown rather than to any formula or set definition.

This short sequence can be used as it is or it might be profitably added to other sequences: "Working with the Past," "Writing and Real Life," "Methods," "History and

184

Ethnography," to name a few. And it is possible to imagine other readings that might be dealt into this sequence: Wideman's "Our Time," Jacobs's "Incidents," Berger's "Ways of Seeing," Foucault's "The Body of the Condemned," Geertz's "Deep Play," Kuhn's "Historical Structure of Scientific Discovery," Theweleit's "Male Bodies." All of these selections can be read both as "histories" and as reflections on the problems of writing about the past. It is this mix of practice and theory that we are pointing to in this sequence.

For a complete commentary on the selections in this sequence, please be sure to read each essay's selection in this manual, particularly the opening discussion. While we will cull materials from the discussions of individual assignments, we won't reproduce the introductions. And, while the sequences provide writing assignments, you should think about the advantages (or disadvantages) of using the Questions for a Second Reading. In every case, students should read the headnotes in the textbook, which are designed to serve the assignments and sequences.

ASSIGNMENTS 1

The Legacy of Conquest [Limerick]

This assignment is fairly straightforward. It is important, we found, to ask students to pay attention to the different representations of the problems facing a historian in the first and second chapters. In the first, the problem has to do with the discipline and its major figures and key terms, such as "frontier." In the second, the problems are represented more generally as problems of myth and point of view.

Students will need to be able to produce (not only as readers but also as writers) a close reading of Limerick's text. There are several fairly important matters of technique students need to learn to carry this off. For one thing they need to learn how to set up and introduce a text for discussion. They need to learn the mechanics of block quotation and the mysteries of paraphrase. Perhaps most important, they need to learn to feel the pressure to fill the space after the block quotation or lengthy presentation of text. They need to step forward as a reader (one who writes sentences) or a teacher or a commentator. We find it important to reproduce student papers and to point to the space (usually unfilled) that students need to learn to fill.

It is worth directing attention to the final question in the assignment which opens out the context of the assignment. The issue is more than simply, "What does Limerick say about the writing of history?" The writer is asked to talk about why any of this might be important to a student at the early stages of a college or university career. The quick answer is that most students will be required to take a history course. The more interesting answer looks to Limerick's essay for what it says more generally about reading and writing and intellectual life.

ASSIGNMENT 2

Indians [Tompkins]

This assignment mirrors the first assignment in the sequence; much of what we said above therefore applies to this assignment as well. The Tompkins essay is harder to read than the Limerick chapters. It might be worth spending some class time preparing for a second reading (see the Questions for a Second Reading), since Tompkins works against students' commonsense understanding of "fact" and "objectivity." We found, in fact, that the most useful way to work with a rereading of the essay was to begin by asking what seem to be simple questions: What is the story Tompkins tells about her own scholarly project? What are the key moments? What happens at each one? How are they resolved? What is the final chapter?

We've said this before, but it is worth repeating. With both of these assignments, students should imagine that they are writing for their peers, perhaps for students who will be taking the same course and reading the same readings next semester or next quarter. After you have a course under your belt, you will have some of these essays on file and you can use them for class discussion. It is important for students to believe that their job is to give the most subtle and sophisticated possible reading of Tompkins rather than the reading that makes it all clear and simple. In most cases, students are prepared to think that summary (the work of representing someone else's ideas) is *ideally* reductive. You will need to counter this assumption for the assignments to work well.

You may very well find that aiming high becomes the work of revision, where students take the "simple" version of Limerick or Tompkins as a pushing-off point ("what most readers would say," "what most people believe"). If students read their drafts to bracket the obvious and the commonsensical, this will help to clear space for them to begin to write about the subtle and difficult, to take as their goal the revision of "what most people believe" into a knowledge that requires intellectual labor and special understanding.

ASSIGNMENT 3

Writing History [Limerick, Tompkins]

There are two options in this assignment. The general goal is to have students perform a reading of Limerick and Tompkins by writing a history — showing, in a sense, what they have learned about defining the presence of the writer (Limerick) through the possible ways she might influence other writers.

The first option sends students to the library or local historical society. This assignment was prompted by Jean Ferguson Carr's teaching at Pitt (her courses almost always include some kind of archival project) and Pat Bizzell's teaching at Holy Cross (where she has students research local accounts of European settlements written by Native Americans). We were frustrated by the degree to which students feel removed from library archives and the degree to which our teaching (and the textbook) seemed to enforce that remove. Needless to say, this option will seem to be the harder of the two and students will need some prompting or challenge or rewards to choose it. One thing to remember is that an assignment like this will take more time than usual, since it takes time to find the library and spend enough time in the stacks to make the experience profitable, more than a quick search for the one book that will get you through the assignment. We've also found that we needed to make the process of search and selection an acknowledged part of the work of the course. We ask students to collect folders of material, to present them to others (to the class, to groups) and, in their essays, to talk about how they chose the material they chose to write about. Selection is of some special importance for this assignment, since Limerick's work points to the importance of finding the otherwise hidden alternative story. For Tompkins, each new source marks a turning point in her conception of her project. Tompkins's narrative of discovery and revision takes place over a greater period of time than is available to students in a writing course. It is unlikely that students will work through sources following the pattern set by Tompkins. It is reasonable to expect, however, that once students have found a way of reading the material, they can (after Tompkins) also begin to call it into question, suggesting how and where and why they might responsibly begin to doubt themselves.

The second option cuts out the library time, although it will work best if students take the challenge of making this more than a "personal essay." In fact, when we have asked

186

students to write this assignment, "personal essay" became a useful negative term, a way of indicating what their work needed to transcend in revision. Here is how we made the distinction between "history," as represented by Tompkins or Limerick, and the personal essay. Gathering materials was important — that is, essays became "histories" when they incorporated materials (like photos, diaries and interviews) that would not have been found if a writer had not felt responsible for more than his or her own immediate experience. And structure became important. Essays became histories when they were included more than two "stories" and more than a single point of view. In fact, much of the work of revision was represented in just these terms. Students went back to write more stories ("counterstories," in Limerick's style) and to write from points of view not their own (their parents', a neighbor's, a friend's, a teacher's). Students added stories, added points of view, and worked to establish paragraphs (like those in Limerick) where they stepped forward to speak as an historian about the material they had gathered. The key moments in the best essays we received came when students realized that they had to break the "unity" they had been trained to value, when they added the story that didn't seem to fit or wrote from outside their own point of view.

· · · · · · · · · ·

SEQUENCE SIXTEEN

Writing and "Real" Life (p. 875)

The borderlines between what we conventionally call "fiction" and "fact" aren't anywhere near as clear and solid as they appear at first glance. Wideman, discussing his position as a writer telling his brother Robby's story, puts it this way. "Temporarily at least . . . I had to root my fiction-writing self out of our exchanges. I had to teach myself to listen. Start fresh, clear the pipes, resist too facile an identification, tame the urge to take off with Robby's story and make it my own." For our purposes in this sequence, we are interested in posing the boundaries between fiction and fact as a problem for students to work on, not a problem for them to solve, but one that they can work on through writing and studying fiction and nonfiction.

The sequence poses the problem in terms of short stories that could be called "realistic" and of Wideman's work of nonfiction that questions how it represents the "real." Students are asked to read these works from two stances, one that considers the works "real" and the other that considers them "fiction." Besides studying the selections for what it is about them that allows these two stances, students are asked to consider the power or influence of the stances themselves, as Wideman does, at least in part, when he tries to root his fiction-writing self out of his exchanges with Robby and out of his writing about Robby.

Students are also asked to write a story of their own that "plays" with the borderlines by weaving together fact and fiction, and after they work with that assignment, they are given an opportunity in the final assignment to step back and study their own story, its writing, and the general question of the relationship between writing and the real world.

Students can have a lot of fun with this sequence, but there are dangers. One of them concerns how unquestioningly people view facts as easily verifiable and objective; even though the assignments ask students to think about "fact" and its relationship to writing, at least some students will want to argue for the "real" being objective writing and fiction being simply made up. Both of the stories, and Wideman's selection, can confuse those perspectives, but students will need to be willing to engage the questions, to play with the idea that the borderlines pose knotty problems that can't be dismissed by assertions of the "real" as objective and verifiable. You'll help yourself and your students if you offer this sequence in the spirit of "play," as an opportunity for students to work with the plasticity of writing, to suspend their larger philosophical notions of fact and fiction so that they can engage the questions in the assignments and allow themselves to read the selections as "real" and as "fiction." It'll be important, too, to help the class keep its discussions and writings close to the texts and away from abstract declarations about the "real," "fact," and "fiction" — except, of course, when those kinds of statements can be tested against the texts they're working with.

ASSIGNMENT 1

Imagining Landscapes [Oates]

The key moves for students in this assignment have to do with how they use the text of the story to identify and speak to the questions of where Oates gets it right, if they measure the story of Marya and Imogene against their own experiences in college, where she stretches the boundaries (what, that is, violates the "real," for them, and how does it violate it?), and why they think, in reference to the story as a piece of writing, she gets it right, when she does. We like to keep our students working closely with the text for assignments like this one because there's always the danger of students turning their writing and discussions into facile generalizations about how believable the story is or how real Marya seems or how typical the relationships are. These kinds of readings are certainly fair game for this assignment, but students need to work from moments in the text that seem to them, for instance, believable or not believable, and they need to explain fully why the writing does or does not seem believable. They'll want to turn their attention to the characters as possible real-life figures, and that's OK to a point; but they also need to focus on the writing. What is it about the writing that makes a particular episode or description or event seem real or not real? If students think that Oates fails to see or understand something, they need to go on and say what it is about the writing that signals or presents the failure.

The one-page coda is designed to give students the opportunity to take what might be called "the fiction stance" towards the story, but there's a twist to it. Students are asked to speculate what Oates, as a fiction writer, is doing in the story. Is she making an argument? trying to influence her readers in some way? fantasizing? idealizing? offering an alternative to "real life"? Of course, if students take that position, they will need to say what argument they think Oates is trying to make. They'll need to say what the influence or the fantasy or the idealizing or the alternative to "real life" might be. And they'll need to do this with some reference to the text, although one page doesn't give them much room to move in. It's a good opportunity, however, for them to carefully consider their use of the text. Do they need block quotations? How can they identify pertinent passages without quoting?

ASSIGNMENT 2

Using Stories [Brodkey]

To a person our students read this story as true, as autobiography, until we raised specific questions about it as fiction or nonfiction. This assignment takes advantage of the story's methods, which allow it to be read this way, and uses the last line of the story to frame the issue of what readers notice when they take these two stances — fiction and nonfiction — toward the story. At the end of the story, Brodkey says, "make what use of this you like." This assignment asks students to consider how their reading of that line changes (or doesn't) when they change their stance towards the story. Students will help themselves address the questions of this assignment if they actually read the story twice, once thinking of it as nonfiction (you might ask them to read it to write to the final line of the story before giving them the actual assignment that frames their work in terms of fiction and nonfiction) and again thinking of it as fiction. The statement of Brodkey's that comes at the end of the story is difficult to answer in the abstract, and students will need to stay close to the story to find those passages or moments that allow them to make some use of the story. If there's a lesson here (as some of our students said), then what is it? And where is it in the story? What passages allow it to be seen as a lesson? The same kind of move holds true for the story as fiction. If this is a familiar tale, and if students see it too as offering a lesson or a moral, then what is it? And where is it? What passages allow it to be seen in that way?

There's material here, in the students' writing and in this assignment, for a good discussion, perhaps as a part of their work on a revision for their papers, on the changes in their responses to the "make what use of this you like" line when they change stances. Once we worked with the story for a few assignments, we had a mix of responses. Some students argued that the stance didn't matter, the lesson of the story remained the same. Others, predictably, argued that the stance meant everything, that the tale of an innocent child and wicked stepmother was unbelievable and revealed the self-centeredness of the child and the author. The range of possible readings is fairly large, and we don't attempt to present them here, except to say that once the students begin to take stances towards the story, they'll have plenty to talk about in discussions and to consider for their revisions.

ASSIGNMENT 3

Studying Fact and Fiction [Wideman]

Students are asked to take Wideman as a writer and "Our Time" as a case study of the relationships between writing, fiction, and fact. As with the other assignments in this sequence, students will need to work closely from Wideman's text, and the assignment asks them to choose three or four passages from "Our Time" that they can use to address the problems he faces writing on the borderline between fiction and fact. Students will find it helpful, as the assignment proposes, if they identify both passages that seem to best represent the "real" in Wideman's work and those that seem contrived or fictional. The key questions they will need to address once they have chosen the passages to work from involve why they see particular passages as either "real" or contrived and fictional. These are questions of writing, at least as the assignment presents them, and students will need to direct their attention to the passages as writing, as representations of thoughts and episodes, and as methods and devices. So if students are willing to say, for example, that a particular passage strikes them as contrived, as Wideman allowing his fiction-writing self to take over, they will also need to address what it is about the writing that signals or presents this. Is it what he says? an idea or description that seems fictional? What makes it seem that way? a device or method that, perhaps, draws too much attention to the writer rather than to the subject or the reader? a voice, a shift in the subject or in the writer, that seems out of character with either the subject or the writer? There are numerous possibilities for what students might attend to in the selection, including long passages where Robby speaks in quotations, and passages where Wideman speaks for his brother and for himself.

189

ASSIGNMENT **4**

Writing Your Own Story [Oates, Brodkey, Wideman]

Students are asked to write a story that combines fact and fiction, real scenes and scenes made up for this assignment. If your students are like ours, they will have had little, if any, experience writing stories, and they'll need to turn to the Brodkey and Oates stories to learn how to write narrative, dialogue, and details. They'll need to study these stories to see how the conventions of story work, how, for example, dialogue is punctuated, or how dialogue and details, like facial gestures, are woven together and situated in a narrative. There's a great deal for students to come to grips with for this assignment, and it's our experience that this kind of writing needs to go through multiple drafts. Other than the conventions of story writing, of course, students will need to do the assignment. They'll need to tell a story "worth telling and worth reading, not simply an exercise," and students will wonder what this means. You might anticipate their questions by asking them in class discussion why the Brodkey and Oates stories are worth telling and reading. What makes them more than exercises?

There are questions at the end of this assignment on the role of memory, the line between a character and a person, how reality and fiction might be said to serve each other, and how stories are created. These questions can play an important role in class discussions of the stories when you duplicate a few and bring them to class for discussions. They also have a place in the next assignment in the sequence, which asks students to use their experience writing a story that treads the borders between fiction and fact.

ASSIGNMENT **5**

Writing and Real Life [Oates, Brodkey, Wideman]

This assignment offers students the opportunity to comment on their stories in light of the work they have been doing on the borders between fiction and nonfiction, between the "real" and the contrived. It might be helpful for students to see this essay as an afterword or introduction to their stories, one in which they discuss their stories and the writing of them in terms, perhaps, of the questions posed toward the end of the last assignment. Can you, as a writer interested in presenting the "real," realistic characters and episodes, rely on memory? What are the alternatives? Where did you get the details and dialogues for your story? How did you get into someone else's head to create that sense of them, of what they know and think, in your writing? And, of course, how would you say that fiction serves the "real"? How, too, does the "real" serve fiction?

Students might also be encouraged to refer to the work they have done with the Oates and Brodkey stories and the Wideman essay. Wideman might help them find a way, or a voice, to address these issues in their own writing; the sections where he writes about writing his brother's story might also give students a way into this kind of self-reflective, critical commentary.

o—o—o—o—o—o—o—o—o—o—o—o—o—o—o

Additional Assignment Sequences

Here are two additional assignment sequences. You are welcome to duplicate these materials for your students.

A Way of Composing

Paulo Freire
John Berger
Adrienne Rich

This sequence is designed to offer a lesson in writing. The assignments will stage your work (or the process you will follow in composing a single essay) in a pattern common to most writers: drafting, revising, and editing. You will begin by identifying a topic and writing a first draft; this draft will be revised several times and prepared as final copy.

This is not the usual writing lesson, however, since you will be asked to imagine that your teachers are Paulo Freire, John Berger, and Adrienne Rich and that their essays are addressed immediately to you as a writer, as though these writers were sitting by your desk and commenting on your writing. In place of the conventional vocabulary of the writing class, you will be working from passages drawn from their essays. You may find that the terms these teachers use in a conversation about writing are unusual—they are not what you would find in most composition textbooks for example—but the language is powerful and surprising. This assignment sequence demonstrates how these writers could be imagined to be talking to you while you are writing and it argues that you can make use of a theoretical discussion of language—you can do this, that is, if you learn to look through the eyes of a writer eager to understand his or her work.

Your work in these assignments, then, will be framed by the words of Freire, Berger, and Rich. Their essays are not offered as models, however. They are offered as places where a writer can find a vocabulary to describe the experience of writing. Writers need models, to be sure. And writers need tips or techniques. But above all writers need a way of thinking about writing, a way of reading their own work from a critical perspective, a way of seeing and understanding the problems and potential in the use of written language. The primary goal of this assignment sequence is to show how this is possible.

Posing a Problem for Writing [Freire]

Students, as they are increasingly posed with problems relating to themselves in the world and with the world, will feel increasingly challenged and obliged to respond to that challenge. Because they apprehend the challenge as inter-related to other problems within a total context, not as a theoretical question, the resulting comprehension tends to be increasingly critical and thus constantly less alienated. Their response to the challenge evokes new challenges, followed by new understandings; and gradually the students come to regard themselves as committed. (p. 215)

– Paulo Freire
The "Banking" Concept of Education

One of the arguments of Freire's essay, "The 'Banking' Concept of Education," is that students must be given work that they can think of as theirs; they should not be "docile" listeners but "critical co-investigators" of their own situations "in the world and with the world." The work they do must matter, not only because it draws on their experience but also because that work makes it possible for students to better understand (and therefore change) their lives.

This is heavy talk, but it has practical implications. The work of a writer, for example, to be real work must begin with real situations that need to be "problematized." "Authentic reflection considers neither abstract man nor the world without men, but men in their relations with the world." The work of a writer, then, begins with stories and anecdotes, with examples drawn from the world you live in or from reading that could somehow be said to be yours. It does not begin with abstractions, with theses to be proven or ideas to be organized on a page. It begins with memories or observations that become, through writing, verbal representations of your situation in the world; and, as a writer, you can return to these representations to study them, to consider them first this way and then that, to see what form of understanding they represent and how that way of seeing things might be transformed. As Freire says, "In problem-posing education, men develop their power to perceive critically *the way they exist* in the world *with which* and *in which* they find themselves; they come to see the world not as a static reality, but as a reality in process, in transformation."

For this assignment, locate a moment from your own recent experience (an event or a chain of events) that seems rich or puzzling, that you feel you do not quite understand but that you would like to understand better (or that you would like to understand differently). Write the first draft of an essay in which you both describe what happened and provide a way of seeing or understanding what happened. You will need to tell a story with much careful detail, since those details will provide the material for you to work on when you begin interpreting or commenting on your story. It is possible to write a paper like this without stopping to think about what you are doing. You could write a routine essay, but that is not the point of this assignment. The purpose of this draft is to pose a problem for yourself, to represent your experience in such a way that there is work for you to do on it as a writer.

You should think of your essay as a preliminary draft, not a finished paper. You will have the opportunity to go back and work on it again later. You don't need to feel that you have to say everything that can be said, nor do you need to feel that you have to prepare a "finished" essay. You need to write a draft that will give you a place to begin.

When you have finished, go back and reread Freire's essay as a piece directed to you as a writer. Mark those sections that seem to offer something for you to act on when you revise your essay.

ASSIGNMENT 2

Giving Advice to a Fellow Student [Berger]

Yet when an image is presented as a work of art, the way people look at it is affected by a whole series of learnt assumptions about art. Assumptions concerning:

> Beauty
> Truth
> Genius
> Civilization
> Form
> Status
> Taste, etc. (p. 70)

> – John Berger
> *Ways of Seeing*

Berger suggests that problems of seeing can also be imagined as problems of writing. He calls this problem "mystification." "Mystification is the process of explaining away what might otherwise be evident." Here is one of his examples of the kind of writing he calls mystification:

> Hals's unwavering commitment to his personal vision, which enriches our consciousness of our fellow men and heightens our awe for the ever-increasing power of the mighty impulses that enabled him to give us a close view of life's vital forces.

This way of talking might sound familiar to you. You may hear some of your teachers in it, or echoes of books you have read. Teachers also, however, will hear some of their students in that passage. Listen, for example, to a passage from a student paper:

> Walker Percy writes of man's age-old problem. How does one know the truth? How does one find beauty and wisdom combined? Percy's message is simple. We must avoid the distractions of the modern world and learn to see the beauty and wisdom around us. We must turn our eyes again to the glory of the mountains and the wisdom of Shakespeare. It is easy to be satisfied with packaged tours and *Cliff's Notes*. It is more comfortable to take the American Express guided tour than to rent a Land Rover and explore the untrodden trails of the jungle. We have all felt the desire to turn on the TV and watch "Dallas" rather than curl up with a good book. I've done it myself. But to do so is to turn our backs on the infinite richness life has to offer.

What is going on here? What is the problem? What is the problem with the writing— or with the stance or the thinking that is represented by this writing? (The student is writing in response to Walker Percy's essay "The Loss of the Creature," one of the essays in the text. You can understand the passage, and what is going on in the passage, even if you have not read Percy's essay. Similarly, you could understand the passage about Franz Hals without ever having seen the paintings to which it refers. In fact, what it says could probably be applied to any of a hundred paintings in your local museum. Perhaps this is one of the problems with mystification.)

For this assignment, write a letter to the student who wrote that paragraph. You might include a copy of the passage, with your marginal comments, in that letter. The point of your letter is to give advice—to help that student understand what the problem is and to imagine what to do next. You can assume that he or she (you choose whether it is a man or a woman) has read both "The 'Banking' Concept of Education" and "Ways of Seeing." To prepare yourself for this letter, reread "Ways of Seeing" and mark those passages that seem to you to be interesting or relevant in light of whatever problems you see in the passage above.

ASSIGNMENT 3

Writing a Second Draft [Freire, Berger]

Problem-posing education, as a humanist and liberating praxis, posits as fundamental that men subjected to domination must fight for their emancipation. To that end, it enables teachers and students to become Subjects of the educational process by overcoming authoritarianism and an alienating intellectualism; it also enables men to overcome their false perception of reality. The world—no longer something to be described with deceptive words—becomes the object of that transforming action by men which results in their humanization. (p.218)

– Paulo Friere
The "Banking" Concept Of Education

There is a difference between writing and revising, and the difference is more than a difference of time and place. The work is different. In the first case you are working on a subject—finding something to say and getting words down on paper (often finding something to say *by* getting words down on paper). In the second, you are working on a text, on something that has been written, on your subject as it is represented by the words on the page.

Revision allows you the opportunity to work more deliberately than you possibly can when you are struggling to put something on the page for the first time. It gives you the time and the occasion to reflect, question, and reconsider what you have written. The time to do this is not always available when you are caught up in the confusing rush of composing an initial draft. In fact, it is not always appropriate to challenge or question what you write while you are writing, since this can block thoughts that are eager for expression and divert attention from the task at hand.

The job for the writer in revising a paper, then, is to imagine how the text might be altered—and altered, presumably, for the better. This is seldom a simple, routine, or mechanical process. You are not just copying-over-more-neatly or searching for spelling mistakes.

If you take Freire and Berger as guides, revision can be thought of as a struggle against domination. One of the difficulties of writing is that what you want to say is sometimes consumed or displaced by a language that mystifies the subject or alienates the writer. The problem with authoritarianism or alienating intellectualism or deceptive words is that it is not a simple matter to break free from them. It takes work. The ways of speaking and thinking that are immediately available to a writer (what Berger calls "learnt assumptions") can be seen as obstacles as well as aids. If a first draft is driven by habit and assisted by conventional ways of thinking and writing, a second can enable a writer to push against habit and convention.

For this assignment, read back through the draft you wrote for assignment 1, underlining words or phrases that seem to you to be evidence of the power of language to dominate,

194

mystify, deceive, or alienate. And then, when you are done, prepare a second draft that struggles against such acts, that transforms the first into an essay that honors your subject or that seems more humane in the way it speaks to its readers.

Writing as Re-Vision [Rich]

For a poem to coalesce, for a character or an action to take shape, there has to be an imaginative transformation of reality which is no way passive. And a certain freedom of the mind is needed—freedom to press on, to enter the currents of your thought like a glider pilot, knowing that your motion can be sustained, that the buoyancy of your attention will not be suddenly snatched away. Moreover, if the imagination is to transcend and transform experience it has to question, to challenge, to conceive of alternatives, perhaps to the very life you are living at that moment. You have to be free to play around with the notion that day might be night, love might be hate; nothing can be too sacred for the imagination to turn into its opposite or to call experimentally by another name. For writing is renaming. (p. 471)
                    – Adrienne Rich
        When We Dead Awaken: Writing as Re-Vision

This is powerful language, and it is interesting to imagine how a writer might put such terms to work. For this assignment, go back to the draft you wrote for assignment 3 and look for a section where the writing is strong and authoritative, where you seemed, as a writer, to be most in control of what you were doing. If, in that section, you gave shape and definition (perhaps even a name) to your experience, see what you can do to "transcend and transform" what you have written. Play around with the notion that day might be night, love might be hate; nothing should be "too sacred for [your] imagination to turn into its opposite or to call experimentally by another name."

Rewrite that section of your essay, but without discarding what you had previously written. The section you work on, in other words, should grow in size as it incorporates this "playful" experimentation with another point of view. Grant yourself the "freedom to press on," even if the currents of your thought run in alternate directions—or turn back on themselves.

Preparing a Final Draft [Freire, Berger, Rich]

Their response to the challenge evokes new challenges, followed by new understandings; and gradually the students come to regard themselves as committed. (p. 264)
                    – Paulo Freire
        The "Banking" Concept of Education

A piece of writing is never really finished, but there comes a point in time when a writer has to send it to an editor (or give it to a teacher) and turn to work on something else. This is the last opportunity you will have to work on the essay you began in assignment 1. To this point, you have been working under the guidance of expert writers: Freire, Berger, and Rich. For the final revision, you are on your own. You have their advice and (particularly in Rich's case) their example before you. You have your drafts, with the comments you've received from your instructor (or perhaps your colleagues in class). You should complete the work, now, as best you can, honoring your commitment to the project you have begun and following it to the fullest conclusion.

Note: When you have finished working on your essay and you are ready to hand it in, you should set aside time to proofread it. This is the work of correcting mistakes, usually mistakes in spelling, punctuation, or grammar. This is the last thing a writer does, and it is not the same thing as revision. You will need to read through carefully and, while you are reading, make corrections on the manuscript you will turn in.

The hard work is locating the errors, not correcting them. Proofreading requires a slowed-down form of reading, where you pay attention to the marks on the page rather than to the sound of a voice or the train of ideas, and this form of reading is strange and unnatural. Many writers have learned, in fact, to artificially disrupt the normal rhythms of reading by reading their manuscripts backward, beginning with the last page and moving to the first; by reading with a ruler to block out the following lines; or by making a photocopy, grabbing a friend, and taking turns reading out loud.

Reading Walker Percy

Walker Percy
Richard Rodriguez
Clifford Geertz

This sequence is designed to provide you with a way of reading Walker Percy's essay, "The Loss of the Creature." This is not a simple essay, and it deserves more than a single reading. There are six assignments in this sequence, all of which offer a way of rereading (or revising your reading of) Percy's essay; and, in doing so, they provide one example of what it means to be an expert or a critical reader.

"The Loss of the Creature" argues that people have trouble seeing and understanding the things around them. Percy makes his point by looking at two exemplary groups: students and tourists. The opening three assignments provide a way for you to work on "The Loss of the Creature" as a single essay, as something that stands alone. You will restate its argument, tell a "Percian" story of your own, and test the essay's implications. Then Richard Rodriguez and Clifford Geertz provide alternate ways of talking about the problems of "seeing." And, in addition, they provide examples you can use to extend Percy's argument further. The last assignment is the occasion for you to step forward as an expert, a person who has something to add to the conversation Percy began and who determines whose text it is that will speak with authority.

ASSIGNMENT 1

Who's Lost What in "The Loss of the Creature"? [Percy]

Our complex friend stands behind the fellow tourists at the Bright Angel Lodge and sees the canyon through them and their predicament, their picture taking and busy disregard. In a sense, he exploits his fellow tourists; he stands on their shoulders to see the canyon.

Such a man is far more advanced in the dialectic than the sightseer who is trying to get off the beaten track — getting up at dawn and approaching the canyon through the mesquite. This stratagem is, in fact, for our complex man the weariest, most beaten track of all. (p. 425)

– Walker Percy
The Loss of the Creature

Percy's essay is not difficult to read, and yet there is a way in which it is a difficult essay. He tells several stories — some of them quite good stories — but it is often hard to know just what he is getting at, just what point it is he is trying to make. If he's making an argument, it's not the sort of argument that is easy to summarize. And if the stories (or anecdotes) are meant to serve as examples, they are not the sort of examples that quickly add up to a single, general conclusion or that serve to clarify a point or support an obvious thesis. In fact, at the very moment at which you expect Percy to come forward and talk like an expert (to pull things together, sum things up, or say what he means), he offers yet another story, as though another example, rather than any general statement, would get you closer to what he is saying.

There are, at the same time, terms and phrases to suggest that this is an essay with a point to make. Percy talks, for example, about "the loss of sovereignty," "symbolic packages," "sovereign individuals," "consumers of experience," "a universe disposed by theory," "dialectic," and it seems safe to say that these terms and phrases are meant to name or comment on key scenes, situations, or characters in the examples. You could go to the dictionary to see what these words might mean, but the problem for a reader of this essay is to see what the words might mean for Percy as he is writing the essay, telling those stories, and looking for terms he can use to make the stories say more than what they appear to say (about a trip to the Grand Canyon, or a trip to Mexico, of a Falkland Islander, or a student at Sarah Lawrence College). This is an essay, in other words, that seems to break some of the rules of essay writing and to make unusual (and interesting) demands on a reader. There's more for a reader to do here than follow a discussion from its introduction to its conclusion.

As you begin working on Percy's essay (that is, as you begin rereading), you might start with the stories. They fall roughly into two groups (stories about students and those about tourists), raising the question of how students and tourists might be said to face similar problems or confront similar situations.

Choose two stories that seem to you to be particularly interesting or puzzling. Go back to the text and review them, looking particularly for the small details that seem to be worth thinking about. (If you work with the section on the tourists at the Grand Canyon, be sure to acknowledge that this section tells the story of several different tourists—not everyone comes on a bus from Terre Haute; not everyone follows the same route.) Then, in an essay, use the stories as examples for your own discussion of Percy's essay and what it might be said to be about.

Note: You should look closely at the differences between the two examples you choose. The differences may be more telling than the similarities. If you look only at the similarities, then you are tacitly assuming that they are both examples of the same thing. If one example would suffice, presumably Percy would have stopped at one. It is useful to assume that he added more examples because one wouldn't do, because he wanted to add another angle of vision, to qualify, refine, extend, or challenge the apparent meaning of the previous examples.

ASSIGNMENT 2

Telling a "Percian" Story of Your Own [Percy]

The situation of the tourist at the Grand Canyon and the biology student are special cases of a predicament in which everyone finds himself in a modern technical society—a society, that is, in which there is a division between expert and layman, planner and consumer, in which experts and planners take special measures to teach and edify the consumer. (p. 435)

– Walker Percy
The Loss of the Creature

For this assignment you should tell a story of your own, one that is suggested by the stories Percy tells—perhaps a story about a time you went looking for something or at something, or about a time when you did or did not find a dogfish in your Shakespeare class. You should imagine that you are carrying out a project that Walker Percy has begun, a project that has you looking back at your own experience through the lens of "The Loss of the Creature." You might also experiment with some of his key terms or phrases (like "dialectic" or "consumer of experience" but you should choose the ones that seem the most interesting or puzzling—the ones you would want to work with, that is). These will help to establish a perspective from which you can look at and comment on the story you have to tell.

ASSIGNMENT 3

Complex and Common Readings of "The Loss of the Creature" [Percy]

I do not refer only to the special relation of layman to theorist. I refer to the general situation in which sovereignty is surrendered to a class of privileged knowers, whether these be theorists or artists. A reader may surrender sovereignty over that which has been written about, just as a consumer may surrender sovereignty over a thing which has been theorized about. The consumer is content to receive an experience just as it has been presented to him by theorists and planners. The reader may also be content to judge life by whether it has or has not been formulated by those who know and write about life. (p. 430)

This dialectic of sightseeing cannot be taken into account by planners, for the object of the dialectic is nothing other than the subversion of the efforts of the planners. (p. 426)

– Walker Percy
The Loss of the Creature

Percy charts several routes to the Grand Canyon: you can take the packaged tour, you can get off the beaten track, you can wait for a disaster, you can follow the "dialectical movement which brings one back to the beaten track but at a level above it." This last path (or "stratagem"), he says, is for the complex traveler. "Our complex friend stands behind the fellow tourists at the Bright Angel Lodge and sees the canyon through them and their predicament, their picture taking and busy disregard. In a sense, he exploits his fellow tourists; he stands on their shoulders to see the canyon."

When Percy talks about students studying Shakespeare or biology, he says that "there is nothing the educator can do" to provide for the student's need to recover the specimen from its educational package. "Everything the educator does only succeeds in becoming, for the student, part of the educational package."

Percy, in his essay, is working on a problem, a problem that is hard to name and hard to define, but it is a problem that can be located in the experience of the student and the experience of the tourist and overcome, perhaps, only by means of certain strategies. This problem can also be imagined as a problem facing a reader: "A reader may surrender sovereignty over that which has been written about, just as a consumer may surrender sovereignty over a thing which has been theorized about."

The complex traveler sees the Grand Canyon through the example of the common tourists with "their predicament, their picture taking and busy disregard." He "stands on their shoulders" to see the canyon. What happens if you apply these terms—*complex* and *common* — to reading? What strategies might a complex reader use to recover his or her sovereignty over that which has been written (or that which has been written about)?

For this assignment, write an essay that demonstrates a common and a complex reading of "The Loss of the Creature." Your essay should have three sections (you could number them, if you choose).

The first two sections should each represent a different way of reading the essay. One should be an example of the work of a common reader, a reader who treats the text the way the common tourists treat the Grand Canyon. The other should be an example of the work of a complex reader, a reader with a different set of strategies or a reader who has found a different route to the essay. You should feel free to draw on either or both of your previous essays for this assignment, revising them as you see fit to make them represent either of these ways of reading. Or, if need be, you may start all over again.

The third section of your paper should look back and comment on the previous two sections. In particular, you might address these questions: What does the complex reader see or do? And why might a person prefer one reading over another? What is to be gained or lost?

ASSIGNMENT **4**

Rodriguez as One of
Percy's Examples [Percy, Rodriguez]

> Those who would take seriously the boy's success—and his failure—would be forced to realize how great is the change any academic undergoes, how far one must move from one's past. It is easiest to ignore such considerations. So little is said about the scholarship boy in pages and pages of educational literature. Nothing is said of the silence that comes to separate the boy from his parents. Instead, one hears proposals for increasing the self-esteem of students and encouraging early intellectual independence. Paragraphs glitter with a constellation of terms like *creativity* and *originality*. (Ignored altogether is the function of imitation in a student's life.) (p. 497)
>
> – Richard Rodriguez
> *The Achievement of Desire*

"The Achievement of Desire" is the second chapter in Rodriguez's autobiography, *Hunger of Memory: The Education of Richard Rodriguez*. The story Rodriguez tells is, in part, a story of loss and separation, of the necessary sacrifices required of all those who take their own education seriously. To use the language of Percy's essay, Rodriguez loses any authentic or sovereign contact he once had with the world around him. He has become a kind of "weary traveler," deprived of the immediate, easy access he once had to his parents, his past, or even his own thoughts and emotions. And whatever he has lost, it can only be regained now—if it can be regained at all—by a complex strategy.

If Percy were to take Rodriguez's story—or a section of it—as an example, where would he place it and what would he have to say about it?

If Percy were to add Rodriguez (perhaps the Rodriguez who read Hoggart's *The Uses of Literacy* or the Rodriguez who read through the list of the "hundred most important books of Western Civilization") to the example of the biology student or the Falkland

Islander, where would he put Rodriguez and what would he say to place Rodriguez in the context of his argument?

For this assignment, write two short essays. In the first essay read Rodriguez's story through the frame of Percy's essay. From this point of view, what would Percy notice and what would he say about what he notices?

Rodriguez, however, also has an argument to make about education and loss. For the second essay, consider the following questions: What does Rodriguez offer as the significant moments in his experience? What does he have to say about them? And what might he have to say to Percy? Is Percy one who, in Rodriguez's terms, can take seriously the scholarship boy's success and failure?

Your job, then is to set Percy and Rodriguez against each other, to write about Rodriguez from Percy's point of view, but then in a separate short essay to consider as well what Rodriguez might have to say about Percy's reading of "The Achievement of Desire."

ASSIGNMENT 5

The Anthropologist as a Person with a Way of Seeing [Geertz]

> For the anthropologist, whose concern is with formulating sociological principles, not with promoting or appreciating cockfights, the question is, what does one learn about such principles from examining culture as an assemblage of texts? (pp. 250–51)
>
> – Clifford Geertz
> *Deep Play: Notes on the Balinese Cockfight*

You've gone from tourists to students and now, at the end of this set of readings, you have another travel story before you. This essay, "Deep Play: Notes on the Balinese Cockfight," was written by an anthropologist. Anthropologists, properly speaking, are not really tourists. There is a scholarly purpose to their travel, and, presumably, they have learned or developed the complex strategies necessary to get beyond the preformed "symbolic complex" that would keep them from seeing the place or the people they have traveled to study. They are experts, in other words, not just any "layman seer of sights." One question to ask of "Deep Play" is whether Geertz has solved the problem of seeing that Percy outlines.

Anthropologists are people who observe (or in Geertz's terms "read") the behavior of other people. But their work is governed by methods, by ways of seeing that are complex and sophisticated. They can do something that the ordinary tourist to Bali (or Mexico or the Grand Canyon) cannot. They have different ways of situating themselves as observers, and they have a different way of thinking (or writing) about what they have seen. What is it, then, that anthropologists do, and how do they do what they do?

If this essay were your only evidence, how might you describe the work of an anthropologist? Write an essay in which you look at "Deep Play" section by section, describing on the basis of each what it is that an anthropologist must be able to do. In each case, you have the chance to watch Geertz at work. (Your essay, then, might well have seven sections that correspond to Geertz's.) When you have worked through them all, write a final section that discusses how these various skills or arts fit together to define the expertise of someone like Geertz.

ASSIGNMENT **6**

Taking Your Turn in the Conversation
[Percy, Rodriguez, Geertz]

I refer to the general situation in which sovereignty is surrendered to a class of privileged knowers, whether these be theorists or artists. A reader may surrender sovereignty over that which has been written about, just as a consumer may surrender sovereignty over a thing which has been theorized about. The consumer is content to receive an experience just as it has been presented to him by theorists and planners. The reader may also be content to judge life by whether it has or has not been formulated by those who know and write about life. (p. 430)

— Walker Percy
The Loss of the Creature

It could be argued that all of the work you have done in these assignments has been preparing you to test the assumptions of Percy's essay, "The Loss of the Creature." You've read several accounts of the problems facing tourists and students, people who look at and try to understand what is before them. You have observed acts of seeing, reading, and writing that can extend the range of examples provided by Percy. And you have, of course, your own work before you as an example of a student working under the guidance of a variety of experts. You are in a position, in other words, to speak in response to Percy with considerable authority. This last assignment is the occasion for you to do so.

For this assignment, you might imagine that you are writing an article for the journal that first printed "The Loss of the Creature." You can assume, that is, that your readers are expert readers. They have read Percy's essay. They know what the common reading would be and they know that they want something else. This is not an occasion for summary, but for an essay that can enable those readers to take a next step in their thinking. You may challenge Percy's essay, defend and extend what it has to say, or provide an angle you feel others will not have seen. You should feel free to draw as much as you can on the writing you have already done, working sections of those papers into your final essay. Percy has said what he has to say. It is time for you to speak, now, in turn.

Part IV: Graduate Students
on *Ways of Reading*

The seven papers that follow were written by graduate students in our department as a part of their work in a seminar on the teaching of composition. We include them here because we thought it would be helpful for you to hear from people who had taught for a year, and in some cases for the first time, from *Ways of Reading*. We hope that the discussions of their teaching and their experiences with selected readings and sequences will be helpful to you as you teach from our book. We would also like their essays to stand for the kind of work people can do in graduate seminars that make use of *Ways of Reading* for the study of the teaching of composition and literature.

GENEROUS READING:
CREATING A GENERAL WRITING LANGUAGE
by Melissa Bender

Students often come to the General Writing (GW) classroom with certain expectations that are not met. In the classes I have taught some of these expectations surfaced at the very beginning of each semester when I asked my students to read and respond to the introduction to *Ways of Reading*. Many of them found the introduction to be empowering and affirming. They were anxious and excited at the proposed reading and writing ideas. And they could identify with the "old" way of teaching reading and writing that is outlined in the introduction with such phrases as "finding information," or "identifying main ideas." This is what they had expected GW to be like. And yes, they had done that before, and they were tired of doing it. Finally, they seemed to be saying, someone was asking for their opinion. However, in spite of all of its "ready to wear" terms, the introduction does not supply students or teachers with the vocabulary that is necessary for speaking about reading/writing in such a new and unusual way. Terms, if they are to work at all in the GW classroom, must be collectively defined and understood. And, until new terms for talking about reading/writing are defined, the only way to speak about these acts is through the "old" language, the language of expectations.

I didn't realize this immediately, however. I was as mystified by the introduction as my students were. I liked what it had to say about reading and writing but I hadn't considered exactly what it meant, or how I should use it. In my classroom I threw around terms like "framing" and "making a mark" and "reading against the grain," and in return my students stared at me.

At nearly the same time that I was struggling with this issue we discussed a paper written in response to Ralph Waldo Emerson's "American Scholar," which was included in the second edition of *Ways of Reading*. A student, David, wrote: "If I, as the reader, am to make use of these points, I will not take Emerson's word as *law*. . . ." He continued to use the word *law* throughout his paper. "Emerson stresses that books are not *laws*. Anything that is written should not be taken as *law*, but should be left to the reader to make his own interpretation." Perhaps because it was an easy metaphor, or because it reaffirmed their own previously established ideas of reading, or because of the abundance of what I call "courtroom terms" in their vocabularies, my students borrowed the word *law* from David's paper and turned it into a way of defining a reading. In spite of the fact that David seemed to be saying something quite the opposite, the class began to talk about essays as if a reader could "prove" what the author meant. Without necessarily realizing that this definition of reading was being formed right in front of me, and perhaps because I, too, was taken in by the ease of the language, I went along with the class.

Before I knew it, we were talking about how student writers might look for "evidence" in quotations, in order to "support" their "argument." After a few days of this I left the class thinking, "What happened to *ways* of reading, and forging a reading? What happened to student readers who 'can take responsibility for determining the meaning of a text' "? (*Ways of Reading*, p. 7) The language that we were using to discuss reading/writing was working against seeing these acts in a new way. And this language seemed to represent that "old" and "usual" way of talking about reading/writing that Bartholomae and Petrosky imply in the introduction when they write, "This is an *unusual* way of talking about reading, we know." (p. 1) I was amazed at how easy it was for both me and my students to shy away from the challenge of this "new" and "unusual" way of writing and slip back into the "old."

In an effort to revise some of this "court talk," I directed my class back to the introduction of the book, and perhaps this is the moment when our own work as definers began. By collectively rereading parts of the introduction and making lists comparing "court words" and *Ways of Reading* words, we were able to see that, instead of aiding our entry into a new way of reading and thinking about reading, our "court talk" allowed us to do what we were most familiar with. It was time for us, as the introduction states, to begin the work of "imagining other ways of reading." In place of our "court words" we chose and defined terms, some from the introduction and some from students' papers or class comments that seemed to facilitate a way of thinking about reading that was different from reading for facts or main ideas. And, we created a term that now seems to me to symbolize the actual act of thinking about reading in new ways. Instead of the "old" reading position, which one student decided positions the writer as someone who is in a superior position to the reader, we fashioned what became known in my classroom as a *generous reading position*. The word *generous* first came from the "Reading with and against the Grain" section of the introduction:

> A reader takes charge of a text; a reader gives generous attention to someone else's (a writer's) key terms and methods, commits his time to her examples, tries to think in her language, imagines that this strange work is important, compelling, at least for the moment. (p. 11)

However, as we molded it into our own term, it came to mean something more than just giving generous time to a writer's words, which to many of my students didn't seem that different from the old hierarchical configuration of writer as teacher, reader as student. The meaning of *generous reading* came from combining ideas — generous attention, strong reading, close reading, and reading against the grain. A *generous reading* is one that balances that "difficult mix of authority and humility." (Bartholomae and Petrosky, p. 11) It allows a reader both to give attention to the writer's language, ideas, and terms and to "take responsibility for determining the meaning of the text" (*Ways of Reading*, p. 7).

Although we did not eliminate the terms *reading with the grain* or *reading against the grain* from our GW vocabularies, I found that using the term *generous reading* was in fact, more generous to both the reader and the writer. Implied in the idea of reading with the grain or reading against the grain is a choice. A student must choose whether she is going to be generous to the writer, and therefore read/write with the grain, or she chooses not to be generous to the writer so that she can read/write against the grain. While reading with or against the grain implies that the reader is really or rhetorically either agreeing with the writer or disagreeing with the writer, a *generous reading* allows the reader to do both in the same reading. It gives students a way of thinking about such difficult texts as Michel Foucault's "The Body of the Condemned" without getting caught up in whether or not they agree with the writer, and therefore allows them the time to create an enriched and complicated reading.

The term *generous reading* offers students a way of thinking about how they might negotiate the difficulties of balancing privilege between the reader and the writer. A reader can both give time to the writer's ideas and, in the same reading and/or paper, give time to her own ideas — which may or may not conflict with the published writer's. Therefore, from a *generous reading position*, reading with and against the grain are not necessarily separate acts.

In addition to becoming a tool for my students, *generous reading* fits well into my own evolving pedagogy. It offers me a format for thinking about the ways in which I, as teacher, negotiate terms and languages in my classroom. This became clear to me while reflecting on the class's discussion of the use of the word "Saint" in Alice Walker's essay "In Search of Our Mothers' Gardens."

Many of my students interpreted Walker's use of the word "Saint" as a positive renaming of black women. They assumed this in their writing in spite of the fact that Walker states, ". . . they became 'Saints.' Instead of being perceived as whole persons, their bodies became shrines . . ." and "[They] were not Saints, but Artists" (*Ways of Reading*, p. 608). Many of my students seemed to be falling comfortably into a preconceived definition of the word *saint*, one that did not necessarily agree with Walker's definition and I felt as though I should work with them on this reading. I did so, first, because it did not seem to show a close reading of the text, and second, because I thought that it would be a good opportunity for us to again discuss the way meanings of words are constructed.

I asked them to make two lists. One list contained words they would use to describe the word *saint*. The second list was composed of words that Walker uses to describe "Saint" in her essay. When I put these up on the board it was easy for my students to see that their list, which included terms such as "holy," "chosen by God," "exalted," "looked up to," "martyr," was much different from Walker's list, which included such terms as "sexual object," "crazy," "lunatic," "wild," "loony," "suicide," "pitiable." When I had time to think about this class I saw myself as the negotiator of definitions. I moved (figuratively and literally since the lists were on the board) between the two definitions. In fact, I was demonstrating a *generous reading* for my students by moving back and forth between the writer's terms and the reader's terms. However, in this case, I seemed to direct the class toward working more in the realm of the writer's words, assuming that Walker's definitions were more accurate in conjunction with her work than were those of my students.

In retrospect, I believed that I was working with, as Kenneth Burke says, the "impurities and identifications lurking" around the word *saint*. However, the more I thought about it, the more I could not decide which list represented the "impurities." On one hand, my students' list of defining words (their communal definition of *saint*) had prevented them from seeing that Walker might be negating this term. On the other hand, Walker's definition of "Saint" is both dependent on another assumed definition (something close to my students' definition of that term, I suppose) as well as some negative "identifications" with that term. That is, she had to assume that her readers had some idea of what a saint is before she could write of the inappropriateness of that name. Moreover, Walker's readers needed to have some presupposed definition of the word *saint* before they could understand her work with that word.

In my mental revision of the class I would spend more time working in space where the two definitions overlapped. This, it seems, would be a more *generous reading* — a way of privileging both Walker's words as well as my students' — but also significantly more difficult work. It would require a strategy for linking the two lists so that it is apparent why one is dependent on the other.

One of the questions I might use in the classroom to begin this more *generous reading* would be, "Why is it necessary for us, as readers, to understand *your* definition of *saint* before we can make sense out of Walker's?" If students had a difficult time answering this question I would direct them to the place in the text where Walker's definition appears:

> In the selfless abstractions their bodies became to the men who used them, they became more than "sexual objects," more even than mere women: they became "Saints." Instead of being perceived as whole persons, their bodies became shrines: what was thought to be their minds became temples suitable for worship. These crazy Saints stared out at the world, wildly, like lunatics — or quietly, like suicides; and the "God" that was in their gaze was as mute as a great stone. (p. 608)

While constructing her definition of "Saint," Walker draws on her reader's preconceived notion of that word. She does this by using words that have religious or "saintly" connotations in describing these women, and then she turns these words into indicators of oppression and suffering. Walker's "Saint" is pivotal only because of the existence of my students' definition.

The religious self-sacrifice suggested by "selfless abstraction," becomes the means by which these women's bodies are used as sexual objects. These numbed and abused bodies are described as "shrines." Their crazy, lunatic minds are "temples suitable for worship." They have a "God" in their gaze, but he is as unresponsive as the men who oppress them. They are "more even than mere women," they are wild, suicidal saints. *The selflessness, the shrine, the temple, the worship, the God, the elevated position* are all easily related to the list my students compiled. Likewise, they are all words that Walker uses to describe the "Saints" that black women become when their unjustifiable oppression is made acceptable in the name of spirituality. My students' saint and Walker's "Saint" are not the same, but they are both necessary to this particular reading of Walker's text.

A *generous reading*, then, is both a description of the ways in which I negotiate language in the classroom and in my thinking about my teaching as well as an example of one of the terms my students and I have created together as part of our common GW language. Where the students are concerned, however, it will only work if they clearly understand what it means. And, as with almost everything I have noticed about teaching GW, it takes more than one class period, more than one mention, more than one session of defining, for a term to become part of the language of the classroom. Again and again, as issues of the relation between reader and writer surfaced in our textbook and in student papers, I returned to the term *generous reading position*. I asked: "How is this student writer taking a *generous reading position* in relation to the text? What prevents her from doing so? What is her position? How could that position become more *generous*?" After a few weeks of asking these kinds of questions, in class and in my comments on papers, students started to use the term on their own.

I have also found that working with my students on creating a metaphor for a term helps to facilitate their use of it. Our metaphor for *generous reading* came out of the assigned reading of the Joyce Carol Oates story, "Theft":

> It seemed to [Marya] at such times that she was capable of slipping out of her own consciousness and into that of the writer's . . . into the very rhythm of another's prose. Bodiless, weightless, utterly absorbed, she traversed the landscape of another's mind and found it like her own yet totally unlike—surprising and jarring her, enticing her, leading her on. (p. 384)

The landscape, which the class decided on as mountains, became our metaphor for reading. And we agreed that the reading Oates is describing here was similar to our idea of *generous reading*. The character, Marya, allows herself to be both "enticed" and "absorbed." However, she does not minimize herself as a reader. Students pointed to such words as "jarring" and "totally unlike" as indications that Marya privileges her own mind as well as the writer's. Marya is able to find a way of entering a text — stepping into the "rhythms of another's prose," giving "generous attention to a writer's language" — without blindly accepting and admiring a text.

A position of blind admiration of a writer and text, one student said, would position a reader at the foot of the mountain, looking up in reverence at the peak. A position at the top of the mountain symbolized not giving any attention to the writer's "key terms" and ideas. The middle of the mountain, where the foot and the peak are both in sight, was the place where my students found that a *generous reading* might be possible.

Middle of the mountain then became a working metaphor for *generous reading*. In their mid-term retrospectives more students than ever began to use the term *generous reading position*. I think this is because our "mountain landscape" made more visible to them what this term means in relation to reading/writing. I also had a few students who used the mountain as a term for describing their own position as readers within their individual papers.

This is not to say that our work, even with this one term of our "GW language," was entirely successful. Some students were resistant to the idea of leaving the "old" language behind for the "new." I have found that these students were most often the ones who had, in the past, successfully learned to position themselves in English or writing classes where the "old" language was part of the structure of the class. That is, they had performed well in classes where they were at the bottom of the hierarchy, where their main responsibility was to reiterate what the writer's "main idea" was or what the teacher had to say. Naturally, these students wanted to hang on to the "old" language, the language that fulfilled their expectations, because they already knew that they could "do" reading that way. They were not so sure about this "new" stuff. The very idea of a *generous reading* — one where they had to share the responsibility for creating meaning with the writer — caused them to question all that they had assumed about reading and writing.

Some of these students, in an attempt to please me, used the term *generous reading* and the mountain metaphor as buzz words in their papers without showing that they used this language to think about reading. One student, Trish, wrote in her mid-term retrospective, "If I had to categorize myself as a reader, I would say I am somewhere in the middle of the mountain," and gave me no further indication as to why she thought that she was in that position. I believe that Trish used this classroom metaphor in the hope that she was fulfilling some requirement of mine. This hope is grounded in a truism of the "old" language. *The teacher seems to like this word. She uses it all the time so it must mean something. If I use it in my paper I'll be writing the right way.* In Trish's paper the way of reading became the teacher's way, and the "new" language, in spite of itself, reinforced the "old" language of assumptions about students, classrooms, and teachers.

Another student, Eric, who seemed quite angry with me, wrote, "If Ms. Bender would just tell me what she means by a generous reading I would do it." Eric's resistance to the "newness" of the GW language was extreme. The very fact that he addressed me as Ms. Bender (I always make it clear to my students that they may call me by my first name) showed me that, as a student, he was more comfortable in a traditional ("old") classroom where the teacher and writer are the bearers of knowledge and the students the receptacles. Eric perceived me as the keeper of the definition in spite of the fact that *generous reading* was a term that the class had defined together. Just as Eric did not want to take responsibility for determining the meaning of the texts he read, he did not want to take responsibility for defining *generous reading*.

These moments of resistance to the "new" language are not, however, complete failures. They are signs of crises for students who are on the threshold of beginning to question their own assumptions about reading and writing. Trish and Eric were not quite there, but they were well on their way. I responded to both of them by directing them back to themselves. To Trish I wrote, "Why? What reading practices of yours allowed you to categorize yourself as middle of the mountain? How does this show in your writing?" To Eric I wrote, "How would you define *generous reading* based on the things you have read this term, and the discussions we've had in class?" These questions allowed me to respond to my students without giving them an actual answer, which would have fulfilled their expectations in the "old" language instead of helping them work toward building a "new" one.

The work of building a language in the GW classroom is a slow and tedious, but necessary process. Without giving any attention to language we use in the classroom we (teachers and students of GW) risk true communication with each other. If we rely on our "old" ways of talking about reading/writing, like the "courtroom talk" that slipped into my class, it is unlikely that we will ever be able to think about reading/writing in a "new" way. Even the myriad of available terms that can be lifted from the introduction to *Ways of Reading* will not form a vocabulary for talking about reading/writing, unless teachers and students of General Writing work together to give those terms meanings.

o—o—o—o—o—o—o—o—o—o—o—o—o—o

RESISTING THE (GENDERED) SPACE OF THE ESSAY: TEACHING "A ROOM OF ONE'S OWN"

by John Champagne

Once again I'm faced with the same situation presented in a new fashion. The situation is that of equal rights for women. The English department may say that we are discussing gender, but what is gender today — it's equal rights.

– Chuck Hatalsky

Several times this past year I have had occasion to tell the story of my first attempts at teaching a freshman reading and writing assignment sequence that took gender as its subject. I invariably divide my semester into two halves: the first, in which I felt as if I were failing miserably, and the second, in which I achieved some amount of success. While this narrative is undoubtedly a fiction, it allows me to make sense of my experience teaching the course, to isolate what I feel were some of the pedagogical problems I encountered, and to offer to myself some suggestions as to how I might avoid such problems in the future.

The epigraph to this essay was written by one of my students during what I have come to name the "failure" half of the semester. Chuck, who was particularly resistant to what he understood the focus of the course to be, helped me to recognize that I was enacting in my teaching one of the worst-case scenarios of a composition course examining questions of gender. For, while I had hoped that I was teaching a course in which my students and I would explore how gender influences our reading and writing, Chuck's comments made me realize that I was in fact engaging my class in a series of debates on such issues as "equal rights for women" — debates that I of course won.

While I would dispute neither the power nor propriety of bringing issues of equality into the composition classroom, Chuck helped me to identify what was disturbing me about my teaching that semester. For the class had begun to feel strangely "unteachable." My students were coming to associate the discussion of gender issues with the accepting of a correct political position —my position — and one that they learned very quickly to mouth on cue. Class work consisted of identifying the pernicious effects of sexism. Issues of reading and writing fell by the wayside. Worst of all was my realization that while students seemed to recognize some of the negative effects of a sex-gendering system, they could not imagine challenging its *inevitability*. This was made clear to me when, during a class discussion, rather than questioning a way of knowing the world that insisted on someone inevitably being the oppressor and someone else inevitably being the oppressed, my students merely acknowledged that yes, men oppress women, "but why shouldn't they? Someone has to be 'on top,' why shouldn't it be the physically stronger?" As Chuck explained in one of his essays,

> I think that if all of us would take the male
> point of view for a moment this might make a
> little more sense. Since the beginning of our
> country or even time as we "humans" know it, the
> male has been the dominant figure in our society
> in most cases. Then all of a sudden women want
> to be equal in every manner. That thought alone
> sent shivers down the spines of the men in this
> country. Their position on top could be gone, and
> if you have ever been on top you know how it
> feels. You don't want to come down and close it
> so you try to find a way to keep it.

How had a course that had hoped to explore the ways we read and write as men and women managed to deteriorate into a discussion of who ought to be "on top"?

Not surprisingly, it was the readings in the course that helped me to make the transition from the "failure" to the "success" half of my teaching that semester. Specifically, it was the choice of one essay in particular, Virginia Woolf's "A Room of One's Own," that enabled me to shift the focus of my class away from political debates and toward questions of reading and writing.

When I first read Woolf's essay, I feared that its admittedly guarded feminist polemic might lead class discussion into yet another round of debates on "equal rights." But eventually I was able to see how I might use "A Room of One's Own" to build on the work the class had already accomplished. I decided to concentrate not on the specifics of Woolf's polemic, but on the argument enacted by her in the essay's very writing. What did the style of Woolf's essay, its rhetorical turns and formal devices, have to do with the overriding question the class was just beginning to explore: the relationship between gender and reading and writing?

In her essay "Killing Priests, Nuns, Women, Children," Jean Franco argues that cultural spaces are gendered not by the actual biological sex of those who construct and inhabit them, but by the (gendered) values that such spaces accrue.[1] Thus, in different historical moments, real women may have entered — and perhaps even flourished in — spaces gendered as masculine. The particular results of these "transgressions" of gender need to be specified in order to understand the shifting and contested history of a space's gendering. Extending Franco's analysis to the space we call an essay, a space that "constructs" us in the sense of compelling us to write (and read) according to certain culturally defined, gendered conventions, we might ask how a historical figure such as Virginia Woolf managed to find a place for herself as an essayist.

"A Room of One's Own" provides us with a compelling account of a woman in 1928–1929 attempting to inhabit and transform the space of the essay, a space that has historically been gendered as masculine.[2] However, this account lies not in the essay's polemic, but in Woolf's own efforts to resist, in the writing of "A Room of One's Own," what she perceives to be the (masculine) conventions of essay writing. Through this act of resistance, Woolf transforms the essay into a "space" of her own, a room where she can accomplish her work as a woman writer.

Rereading the essay, I was struck by the number of times Woolf outlines what she understands to be her "proper" task as an essay writer, only to go ahead and ignore that task. In her efforts to "defy convention," she seems to be exploring whatever avenues of resistance may have been open to a woman writing in the late 1920s. If there is such a thing as gendered writing, as certain feminists have suggested,[3] Woolf's attempts at defying convention might be gendered as feminine — since she appears not simply to inhabit the (masculine) space of the essay, but to transform that space, bringing alternative values to it. What "alternative," "feminine" values might Woolf, in the writing of "A Room of One's Own," be attaching to that masculine space of the essay? According to Susan Deysher,

> [In "A Room," Woolf] creates for herself a space where she can "offer you an opinion upon one minor point--a woman must have money and a room of her own if she is to write fiction." Therefore, she sets herself up not as an authority on "Women and Fiction," but rather as an authority on her own opinion, as she is the only one who could explain it. This is very different from the way male writing assumes authority.

One of the most commonly explored themes in feminist writing of the past twenty years is that of authority. Throughout its history, feminism has attempted to pose alternatives to a patriarchal, phallocentric conception of authority. In "A Room of One's Own," Woolf confronts, on a number of occasions, the issue of the writer's authority. Throughout her essay, she insists on "shirking her duty" as a writer, refusing to hand her audience "a nugget of pure truth to wrap up between the pages of (their) notebooks." "Lies will flow from my lips," she tells us, "but there may perhaps be some truth mixed up with them; it is for you to seek out this truth and to decide whether any part of it is worth keeping."

It might be argued that the position of authority Woolf occupies in her essay both challenges the gendering of the essay as masculine and is profoundly feminist. Woolf questions her own status as knower *while continuing to speak.* She calls into suspicion rigid distinctions between the true and the false, and suggests to her audience that they may be the ones ultimately authorized to determine the value of her work to their own lives. Her insistence on speaking through a multitude of identities — Mary Beton, Mary Seton, Mary Carmichael, her "own person," — threatens to erode the boundaries between "author" and "character," the knower and the known, the subject who "speaks" the essay, and that which the essay takes as its object. It might be argued that all of these moves work to challenge the essay's masculine gendering. Stated in Lacanian feminist terms, Woolf's attempts both to claim and call into question her own authority as a writer serve to confuse the strict epistemological boundaries of a phallocentric culture, which separates those who "possess" (truth, power, value, the authority to speak) from those who "lack."[4] Woolf presumes neither to speak from a place of mastery over language nor to occupy the silent, unauthorized place reserved by phallocentrism for the feminine. Instead, she attempts, in her writing of "A Room of One's Own," to occupy some alternative place between these poles, and thus transforms the (masculine) space of the essay.

In their own writing about Woolf's essay, students in my course sometimes made gestures similar to those made by Woolf in "A Room of One's Own." Forced to inhabit (as both readers and writers) the space of the essay, a space that they felt they were not completely authorized to enter, students moved both to claim and reject authority simultaneously. Compelled by the work of the course to speak as "experts," and yet fearing that this expertise was somehow unearned, they moved uneasily between asserting their interpretation of Woolf's essay and apologizing for their lack of understanding. At first glance, there would seem to be a tremendous difference between Woolf's deliberate attempts simultaneously to confirm and to call into question her own authority as a writer and students' less conscientious moves in similar directions. And yet both Woolf and my students faced cultural and historical circumstances that positioned them in very similar ways vis-à-vis the problem of the writer's authority. For both Woolf and my students were gendered by their culture as "feminine."

What I am arguing is that the space of "student" is, regardless of the biological sex of those who inhabit it, a space our culture genders as feminine. Our cultural understanding of "student" is "the castrated other" that desires the phallus/knowledge that the patriarch/ teacher is authorized to give. The physical set-up of the traditional classroom, the pro- hibition against speaking without being recognized by the teacher, the subordinate place student writing occupies in most classes — all attest to this gendering of "student" as feminine (and "teacher" as masculine). As "feminine" students attempt to transgress the boundaries of the "masculine" space of the essay, they face the same options faced by Woolf in the writing of "A Room of One's Own": to speak as a (culturally constructed) man (and thus to inhabit the space of the essay without attempting to resist and transform its gendering); to refuse to speak altogether (and thus occupy the place of "lack"); or to resist the gendering of the space, and attempt to forge a place in it for a "bi-sexual" voice of one's own.[5]

In response to "A Room of One's Own," I asked my students to write an essay in which they located places in her essay where Woolf appeared to be "defying convention," and to hypothesize why Woolf may have been defying convention in these particular ways. Here is a section of Jennifer Gottschalk's response to this assignment:

> One thing I noticed that Woolf does, is to pick out small details. These minute details make the essay more interesting to me. <u>I know that I am not a critic of any sort</u>, [emphasis, mine] but I like how Woolf does that. She added details about the riverbank, the food at lunch and dinner, and also about the stray cat. These details are important because they are characteristic of a woman's writing. Men are not seen as writing this way, and usually ignore tiny details. The way Woolf uses details is a very definite feminine style.
>
> This reminds me a lot of my own writing, not for class, but on a more personal level. Most people would ignore objects of a passing glance, as the male writing style has taught us. I guess I admire her because her writing is similar to my own. <u>I know that I should not think of it in that order</u>, [emphasis, mine] because it was her idea in the first place, she had done it before I did. In a way I am very protective of my own writing.

Although I am somewhat uncomfortable with her nonhistoricized description of "masculine" and "feminine" writing (fearing, for both of us, accusations of "essentialism"), what seems most significant to me here are Jennifer's attempts to simultaneously claim and not claim authority over both her reading of Woolf and her own writing. She has enough confidence in her reading to draw attention to what she perceives to be ways in which Woolf defies the conventions of essay writing, and to name Woolf's defiance "feminine." Yet she is quick to point out that she is "not a critic of any sort." Although she recognizes a certain similarity between Woolf's writing and her own (an "unautho- rized," nonpublic writing that she feels compelled to protect from the "masculine" voice of academic criticism), she scolds herself for daring to compare herself with Woolf, and assumes a posture of humility before her.

212

Two additional aspects of these paragraphs are worth noting. First, Jennifer's insistence that men *"are not seen"* as writing this way" implies that gender is a cultural construction — that while a real man may in fact write "like a woman," we have no means culturally of recognizing this writing as feminine.[6] Secondly, her recognition that certain kinds of writing are "not for class" implies not only that the university requires one to learn some other, nonprivate kind of writing, but that this writing may be gendered in opposition to one's own "feminine," "personal" writing.

In his response to "A Room of One's Own," Jim Lakeley notices what he perceives to be a certain failure of nerve on Woolf's part. He is disappointed and confused by the move in her essay away from the richly descriptive fictive passages with which it begins, toward the more sober and directed polemic found in the essay's conclusion.

> In the beginning of the essay she doesn't ex-
> press her feelings in direct dialogue, instead she
> creates a space for the reader to enter so that
> readers can reflect upon the "story" and perhaps
> draw their own conclusions. In the end, she flat-
> out tells the audience what is on her mind. I no
> longer have the pleasure of traveling through her
> space and almost becoming a part of the essay.
> Instead, I am lectured to about the history of
> women, and of "the very low opinion in which
> (women) were held by Mr. Oscar Browning . . . Na-
> poleon and Mussolini." There is nothing outwardly
> wrong with using this style of writing, but in the
> context it is very confusing. Perhaps she has not
> enough confidence that her audience has been recep-
> tive to her use of imagery and fiction. <u>Honestly,
> I do not know why</u> [emphasis, mine] she might go
> back on her earlier promise. <u>All I can do is
> guess</u> [emphasis, mine] that maybe she felt that her
> use of fiction was not strong enough, and she had
> to speak plainly and directly to make sure her
> point was made.

Like Jennifer, Jim notices a significant aspect of Woolf's essay, her decision to end the essay in her own person so as to anticipate two criticisms. He even offers some interesting suggestions to account for Woolf's shift in tone. But also like Jennifer, Jim litters his essay with hesitancies such as "perhaps," "maybe," "honestly, I do not know," "all I can do is guess," the effect of which is to undermine his authority as a writer. Like Jennifer, he appears to be both claiming and not claiming a place for himself within the essay. As a student (thus occupying a feminine space) Jim finds in the (feminine) beginning of Woolf's essay a place where he feels comfortable, capable of making an interpretation. But when the tone of the essay shifts to what he perceives to be a more "masculine" polemic, he feels excluded from the essay, and unauthorized to speak back to it. Interestingly, he is careful to note that there is "nothing outwardly wrong" with this "masculine" writing; he merely finds it confusing in the context of Woolf's essay, and a hindrance to his pleasure.

What is particularly interesting about this passage is the way that, in the midst of all his hesitancies, Jim has some perceptive ideas. Perhaps Woolf did experience a failure of nerve near the conclusion of her essay. Fearing the consequences of too resistant a stance, perhaps Woolf, in an effort to be taken seriously, chose "to speak plainly and directly," like a (culturally constructed) man. Perhaps in the moments of the essay's conclusion, she chose to inhabit the masculine space of the essay without resisting it. All of these ideas are suggested by Jim. One might quarrel with his easy attribution of Woolf's alleged failure of nerve to her, personally, rather than to the historical and cultural pressures brought to bear on her as a woman writer. One might also take issue with his rather monolithic reading of the essay's conclusion, a reading that ignores the fact that Woolf ends her essay with another fictional narrative. But here I want to draw particular attention to the way Jim struggles with the space of the essay, attempting both to occupy and resist a space in which he feels both authorized and unauthorized to speak. Like Jennifer, he neither fully abdicates, nor fully inhabits, the spaces of "reader" and "writer."

How are we as teachers to respond to this double movement in student essays, this gesture both toward and away from the claiming of a certain authority over one's reading and writing? Do we wipe out the traces of students' reluctance, insist that they delete their "I am not a critic of any sort," their "honestly, I do not know why"? Admittedly, my first response as a teacher would be to suggest that they take a stand, forge a reading, omit from their essays the symptoms of their unknowing. But in the act of doing so, I would be removing from their essays all trace of their (feminine) resistance to that masculine space. I would be forcing them to speak as men, to inhabit the space of the essay without transforming it. I would, in effect, be erasing the feminine from their writing. And yet, isn't it my job as a teacher to teach my students how to write with confidence, to write with authority and expertise, as if they are in command of their material? Isn't this the kind of writing the university respects and demands?

I am suggesting that, as teachers of writing, we have a conception of "good" writing. And that conception may well be gendered as masculine. When we force our students to inhabit their essays as if they can assume unquestioned authority over their reading and writing, we are, in effect, acculturating our students into a "masculine" phallocentric position, erasing their attempts to "feminize" the space of the essay. We are reproducing the epistemological distinctions on which patriarchal phallocentrism is based.

Rather than compel students to remove all (feminine) resistance to the essay, all traces of this movement both toward and away from authority, I would suggest that we move them toward their resistance, to make it, in effect, the subject of their writing. We might encourage our students to follow Woolf's example and attempt to defy the conventions of essay writing. We might ask them to explore in greater detail just what it is they are resisting in the essay and why they feel compelled to resist. What might they be able to write through this act of resistance that they felt unauthorized to write before? We might also suggest that they examine what parts of the essay they do *not* wish to resist — those "masculine" aspects which they feel are of value. In Jennifer's case, we might encourage her to explore in her work the boundaries between a "personal" and "public" writing, to attempt to discover how much heterogeneity the space of the essay can bear. To Jim we might suggest that he imagine why Woolf may have chosen to speak in both "masculine" and "feminine" voices. What did this shift from ("feminine") fiction to ("masculine") polemic allow her to say that she might not have been able to say otherwise?

While we are suggesting to our students that they examine their "feminine" resistance to the essay, we obviously need to reconsider our own masculine gendering as teachers. We need to call into question our own status as the site of knowledge and resist the cultural and institutional pressures to position ourselves as (patriarchal) authorities.

Following the Woolf assignment, my class and I were able to move in some of these directions. Our task became to imagine what might constitute a "feminine" practice of essay writing today. I asked my students to reconsider their own writing in terms of issues of gender, to name places in their work as "masculine" and "feminine."

Here is Todd Simmon's reconsideration of his first essay written that semester, in which he wrote a response to Adrienne Rich's "When We Dead Awaken."

> At times during the semester I have written in
> this style that I can now call masculine. My un-
> derstanding of writing through your gender has of-
> ten been difficult. It was in my first paper on
> Adrienne Rich that I can now see what I couldn't
> see before. What was I doing when writing this
> essay? Basically, what I've been doing all my
> life. I guess you could say I was thinking, "Ok,
> here's my assignment, now I've got to try to con-
> vince my teacher that what I'm saying makes sense."
> I was very confused with what I was doing in the
> first place but despite that fact I still felt
> like I had to assume authority and write like I
> knew perfectly well what was going on. My second
> paragraph starts out, "Rich speaks of 'anger' about
> herself and of women. Anger from male dominance
> over the female and a female society that has ac-
> cepted this dominance and. . . ." That is what
> my whole paper is about. Rich does this, Rich
> does that, she means this and wants to say that.
> I did not even say that that is what I believe
> but what was also indeed the correct assumptions
> about Adrienne Rich and her essay. I only started
> to use the ever-so-controversial pronoun, "I," in
> the last paragraph. Why even use it then? I
> don't know, I probably never even thought about it
> at the time and the fact that I can recognize it
> now signifies a substantial change in the things
> that I notice when reading essays now.

There are several things that strike me as significant in this paragraph. First of all, there is the seriousness with which Todd considers his own work. He has the ability and confidence to name his previous writing as masculine, and to argue for this gendering with a specific reference to one of his own texts. Todd recognizes that his writing has changed over the course of the semester, and is capable of articulating how it has changed. He acknowledges the limitations of his previous conception of reading, a conception that required him to presume to know "the correct assumptions about Rich and her essay." He questions his previous understanding of his own authority as a writer, one of the effects of which was a belief that he had constantly to "cover over" his inadequacy in order to have the right to speak.[7] As Todd puts it, despite the fact that he was confused, he felt compelled to write as if he "knew perfectly well what was going on." There is now a place in Todd's writing for knowing and unknowing, a space for that "ever-so-controversial pronoun, 'I,'" as well as for a more formal, less private voice. In his essay, Todd resists and inhabits those ways of reading and writing he "can now call masculine," so that a space might be opened up in his work for both the masculine and the feminine. As he explains, "After doing the Woolf assignment I was prepared to begin using my understanding of what feminine writing might be in my own writing."

If, as Hélène Cixous has argued, writing is the very possibility of change,[8] perhaps students' efforts at both resisting and inhabiting the (masculine) space of the essay are gestures toward a radical epistemology to come, an epistemology incorporating the bisexual. Students' willingness to acknowledge both the masculine and feminine in their own writing may in fact represent a profound act of cultural resistance. Perhaps they already sense what Cixous has argued: "In one another we will never be lacking."[9]

NOTES

1. Jean Franco, "Killing Priests, Nuns, Women, Children," *On Signs*, ed. Marshall Blonsky (Johns Hopkins University Press, 1985). This piece appeared in the second edition of *Ways of Reading*.

2. My assumption that the essay has been historically gendered as masculine is drawn from a number of feminist texts on writing as gendered. See, for example, Hélène Cixous, "The Laugh of the Medusa," *Critical Theory since 1965*, ed. Hazard Adams and Leroy Searle (Tallahassee: Florida State University Press, 1986), pp. 309–20; Jane Gallop, *Reading Lacan* (Ithaca: Cornell University Press, 1985); Luce Irigaray, "The Power of Discourse and the Subordination of the Feminine," *The Sex Which Is Not One* (Ithaca: Cornell University Press, 1985), pp. 68–85.

3. See note 2.

4. For an excellent explanation of the Lacanian terms utilized in this essay, and a more detailed account of patriarchy as an epistemology, see Gallop, ibid.

5. I borrow the term "bisexual" from Cixous, to indicate writing which contains traces of both genders. As Cixous insists, in a patriarchal, phallocentric culture, the masculine can never be fully eclipsed; a "little bit of phallus" must remain in all writing (because the feminine can be defined only in a relation of opposition to the masculine, and never in and of itself). Thus, it is probably more accurate to speak of "masculine" and "bisexual" writing, rather than "masculine" and "feminine." See Cixous, ibid.

6. Cixous insists on something very similar when she claims Genet, Joyce, and Kleist as male writers who write the feminine. See Cixous, ibid.

7. Here, I am paraphrasing Jane Gallop, who insists that one of the effects of phallocentrism is that "one must constantly cover over one's inevitable inadequacy in order to have the right to speak." (Gallop, p. 20) Thus, Todd's reconception of this authority as a writer might be considered feminist.

8. Cixous, p. 311.

9. Cixous, p. 320.

o—o—o—o—o—o—o—o—o—o—o—o—o—o

WHAT THEY DON'T KNOW THEY KNOW: STUDENT WRITERS AND ADRIENNE RICH

by Christine Conklin

There is a line in Adrienne Rich's essay, "When We Dead Awaken: Writing as Re-Vision," that has haunted me since I first read it as an undergraduate. Rich writes, "But poems are like dreams: in them you put what you don't know you know." At eighteen, I was an English major and wanted to be a poet, and those lines were a direct and personal message. Ten years later, having worked with Rich's essay in my introductory composition classroom, where most of my students are neither poets nor English majors, I have come to see that those lines also work as a metaphor for reading; I substitute "readings" for the word "poems." For me and for my students, reading can be a way of coming to know more, not just about a particular subject but about the process of reading itself. And we can work out together the crucial, unarticulated connections between reading, writing, and revision.

My students are in general unaware of what "strong reading" involves and of how it is connected to "strong writing." I hope, in using Rich's essay as I do, to enact and examine reading with them in the classroom. By starting with Rich's poems and moving outward to her text, students can experience what it means to know more about poems and texts than they knew they knew — and therefore also to know more about reading and writing.

In her essay, Rich also "models" for students the way in which closely reading herself empowers and frees her. In doing so Rich presents and complicates several important issues for student readers and writers. She writes,

> Re-vision — the act of looking back, of seeing with fresh eyes, of entering an old text from a new critical direction — is for women more than a chapter in cultural history: it is an act of survival. Until we can understand the assumptions we are drenched in we cannot know ourselves.

Rich has worked best for me in the middle of the term, providing a very real crisis and turning point in a term-long discussion of reading and writing. Students who have struggled already with one or two complex essays have begun to imagine the difficulties of strong reading though they probably won't yet know what it means to perform it.

Rich's is the only essay that I discuss in class before students write on it. I require that students read and mark the essay or make some notes on it before coming to class; in some cases I've also had them write a two-page "position paper" in which they must identify specifically a "difficulty" in their reading of Rich and then suggest a solution to it. (This often surfaces and diffuses tensions about Rich's politics.) The class discussion that follows this initial reading focuses very specifically on two poems in the essay and then moves outward to connect text and poetry, general and specific, past and present. With this plan I hope to model reading, enact strategies, and make concrete some connections between reading and writing, reading *as* writing.

I didn't invent this plan alone nor do I want to present it as a simple formula. It grows out of Ann Berthoff's "double-entry notebook" method and is one way to get started that other teachers and I have used successfully. I can detail this plan here on the page, but I cannot say anything more than how and, perhaps, why it has worked for me and my students.

I ask students to draw a vertical line down the center of a piece of notebook paper. I tell them that I'm going to read the poem "Aunt Jennifer's Tigers" aloud while they read and mark whatever strikes them in the poem, and that I will give them five minutes to write notes on the right side of their paper when I have finished reading aloud. These notes won't be collected, although, I tell them, the notes may be useful when they sit down to write their papers. These notes can be anything that comes to mind after the reading: questions, images or words that strike them for some unknown reason, problems, thoughts, or phrases. Here, I think, is the beginning of a reading, an act of attention or "noticing," divorced for the moment from any purpose except paying attention.

After we've read and they've made their notes, I ask students to describe the structure of the poem. They will notice that it looks square or even "box-like" on the page, that lines rhyme and are equal in length. They may say that it is "traditional" poetry. From there I might ask them to notice what is "inside" the square or box — or who? And, "What words in the poem connect to being in a box?" I've asked. And what images are not "trapped"? Students can then take the discussion in a number of directions — to talk about what Aunt Jennifer's activity is, how she created the scene she creates, what its implications and limitations are. Basically, students take over doing what the New Critics would call "close reading" but their reading goes beyond achieving some single correct meaning, because there can and will be multiple interpretations. I require evidence from the poem for each reading but I don't make any sort of judgment. As students begin to see the possibilities and demands of this kind of reading and supplying of evidence they become engaged with this poem and with their various readings of it. One important move for students to make next is outward: from the poem to what Rich says in the text immediately surrounding the poem and throughout the essay. I ask specifically what passages in Rich's text they can connect to the readings we have made of her poem.

Often students go to the text immediately surrounding "Aunt Jennifer's Tigers," to Rich's description of her "deliberate detachment" and to her "asbestos gloves" metaphor. We discuss these, and I ask them to locate another passage in the essay that seems to connect to whatever we have said. Because they have read the essay ahead of time, they will have underlined passages that struck them in reading, and often they will cite the lines about poems and dreams. They can suggest that Rich's project in "revision" is to look at her own writing to see what she didn't know she knew as she wrote. They may see Rich as a kind of model reader who uses "old" texts to learn something new both about her history and her present. A text can somehow be both a solid record and a malleable one, changed by a new reading/reader.

The passage on revision as an "act of looking back with fresh eyes" is useful here, and if they don't take me there, I take them. I push students to look at the whole paragraph and at Rich's ideas of "how our language has trapped as well as liberated us" and what it might mean to say that her job is "not to pass on a tradition but to break its hold over us." Whatever passages students offer can be worked with, toward the idea of making connections between the poem and the text, and between different sections of the text.

What I hope is happening here, right before students' eyes and because of their own work in discussion, is a modeling of the reading process that involves noticing, thinking, analyzing, selecting, rejecting, connecting, moving constantly back and forth, from text to thought to text. Students can begin to see that it is possible to range through the whole essay; that there are ways into this difficult essay, and there are as many ways to move within it as there are readers.

After this discussion, I tell students that I'll read "Aunt Jennifer's Tigers" aloud again and that then again they will have time to write, this time on the left side of their pages. This shows, I hope, that rereading is necessary and often surprising; it is another way to look again, to revise from a differently informed position. Students can respond in their notes to questions they wrote earlier, to points in discussion, or they can notice new images, words and connections. When they've made these new notes I ask them to look at both sides of their notes and write a paragraph about what they see as having moved or changed — or more generally what they see as having moved or changed in the hour we've spent in this class. Again, I'm hoping to model that reflexiveness, that necessary "vision and re-vision" that reading and writing require. In pointing toward the assignment (and I've used several different Rich assignments from *Ways of Reading*), I hope that students will see that their writing will grow out of these readings and subsequent ones; they will be forced to re-read and then to write again.

I do the same exercise with Rich's poem "Planetarium"; students divide a fresh notebook page, I read aloud, they make notes, and again I begin by asking about structure: "How does this poem look on the page?" They will notice that there is more "space" than there is in "Aunt Jennifer's Tigers," or that it is "more open" or "free verse." They will notice that punctuation is missing, but white space links or separates the fragments and italics and quotations. They may say this poem is about space or about a woman who isn't weighted but "levitates." They can then connect some of the passages in the text, perhaps in terms of "breaking traditions" or questioning assumptions. They can begin to say that here is some specific evidence, in two "records" of Rich, of what it looks like to revise and to rename and to transform one's writing and/or one's self.

This plan has been, for me, a powerful way to enact reading and finding a way to engage with a complex text. The papers that students write after this exercise, however, are not always (or even often) dazzling. Many students simply transfer the class discussion onto paper, or string quotations ("evidence") together; but those moves, too, can provide a way of talking about what *more* is involved in reading and writing a paper that matters. Students in the class who have tried to do more than repeat the discussion will call into question a paper that settles for that tactic. It's a way to talk about notetaking and collaboration and quotation as a starting point, rather than as a satisfactory "answer."

Students have more often taken significant steps in revising these Rich papers. Rich almost forces some movement or decision from writers, I think because she presents a direct way to observe and define the power and complexity of reading and revision. One term, I received revisions from two writers, Kelly and Monica. The two were friends and seemed, by their comments in class and their written work, to have deliberately allied themselves against the idea that a paper ought to be more than clear, logical, coherent, and correct.

Kelly and Monica were responding to assignment 2 in the "Aims of Education" sequence, which asks students to "use" one of Rich's early poems to "test and extend"

Paulo Freire's argument in "The 'Banking Concept' of Education." Students are asked to consider "structures of oppression" and "transformation" and "what Rich learned to do."

Kelly's original paper, which I used in class (anonymously, as always), opens with mention of Rich's oppression and argues that her re-vision is a "transcendence" of "the male style of writing." She also quotes from Freire in this first paragraph, to show that she's "doing" the assignment. I asked students to notice, as I read the rest of the paper aloud and they marked it, how well this writer had read Rich, and how well she had used Rich. Since I ask students to put the page number in parentheses after any quotation, students noticed that Kelly quoted a lot, and that she followed almost exactly the order of Rich's essay. She also inserted some quotations from Freire. In between, she does work at interpreting "Aunt Jennifer's Tigers"; some but not all of her ideas come out of our class discussion.

Kelly gets trapped in her own strategy, however, when she gets to the end of her paper. In effect, allowing Rich to dictate her paper's order means that Kelly can't really move to her own discoveries in writing or concluding. She has to make up a generalized and happy ending in which she assumes the language of the assignment and of class discussion without the burden of evidence.

> Rich can now write in her own style; she doesn't have to write for her father, male writers or teachers. Women can now "name" by themselves without looking at men's examples. Rich "renames" and also "revises" herself by breaking out of her old self. In conclusion, Freire's argument about the way people can bring about change is thus extended through the use of Rich's examples.

Initially, this ending looks pretty good to students, because it seems to answer the assignment and even manages to bring Freire back in. When I asked students to push at it, though, it began to seem unearned. Mainly, each sentence contains an idea or assertion (smart ones, even) that hasn't been introduced or developed elsewhere. These ideas seem general, huge and too "easy" when simply stated and abandoned. Students will say they *want* to believe the writer's ideas because she has shown evidence in her preceding pages that she has read Rich closely. She has done the work to get where she does but she gets trapped into rushing to a general close. She has followed Rich so closely that when Rich stops writing so does Kelly. Rather than using her work with Rich to tease out the threads of her own reading, the writer shuts down her paper with an "in conclusion" flag. As some students said, this sentence tells, rather than shows, that the writer has "done her job." This last sentence seemed particularly easy. A writer who had read and documented as much as Kelly had could do more; perhaps she could make the work pay off in a revision structured by her own reading of Rich — one that she begins to get to in the end — rather than by Rich's order. If the writer could learn to work or control Rich, to listen to what struck her and could be connected by her, then the writer could compose her own essay, not merely echo Rich's.

Monica's original paper shares some of the "problems" of Kelly's in that quotations are strung together in predictable order, but Monica has used more of Freire, intercutting Rich and Freire in a kind of A-B-A-B pattern. Students said that this seemed promising, if in revision the writer worked more to connect the two. As in the poetry/text reading exercise, we had been working all term toward a definition of reading that included "connecting." That is, a reader notices something in an essay and elsewhere she notices something else. When the reader puts two words, sentences, passages, or ideas next to each other on a page and tries to work out for herself in writing *why* she seems compelled to notice them, she is beginning not only to construct a reading ("These two things interest me") but also to consider the process and its product — further reading, writing, rereading, connections, leading to more connections ("These two things together interest me because . . . "). In between the "things" is where the reader does the work of reading, interpreting, connecting, making meaning.

Monica had put passages from Freire and Rich together, but students saw that a *reading* was entirely missing. There wasn't, in this draft, a place where meaning or connections were made. There were opportunities, because the writer had noticed and placed passages next to one another, but at the moment these were "like strangers on a bus" — sharing the same vehicle but not interacting in any way. The writer was going to have to rethink and rewrite pretty aggressively in order to produce an essay in which connections were made. The class said that both writers seemed to "have their work cut out for them" in revision, but at least they had a place to start, with readings to work from.

Before students turned in their revisions, I asked each of them to write a note telling me what they would like me to notice about their revisions. I used both Kelly's and Monica's revisions in the next class, but before students read either revision, I also handed out copies of the notes Kelly and Monica had written to me.

I started with Monica's note, before students saw her revision, and asked what they would expect her revision to look like based on her note. Monica had written,

> This revision is not much different from the original, in fact it is quite similar. The more I read the original the better I thought it was. I didn't think it was that bad. It had some errors and a few problems, which I tried to clean up. I also added a few sentences and changed a few things to try to make the paper more understandable. I changed it mostly where there were comments written. This paper is trying to show Rich's life as a writer; and how she changed in her writing. There's no hidden meaning. I'm <u>just</u> trying to show Rich's transformation in writing from an oppressive style to a free thinking style of writing. I think it's pretty straightforward. I don't know, though. You be the judge!

Students could see that if, as the writer said, her revision wasn't going to be "very different" then it probably wasn't going to represent much rethinking or reworking or rereading of Rich. Moreover, the writer sees me, the teacher, saying her paper is "bad," rather than saying that it can be worked on to extend meanings or make connections. She sees the teacher's comments as condemnation rather than dialogue, and she reacts by saying she has "cleaned up" a few "errors" but otherwise doesn't see that there's anything so terribly wrong. She's changing a few things "mostly where there were comments," to please the teacher and to be "good."

Yet, the writer isn't as submissive as she says she is. She insists, perhaps as a way of warding off further prodding from me, that her mission and her ideas are simple: "I'm *just* trying to show Rich's transformation . . . it's pretty straightforward." In our ongoing definition of "strong reading," complexity was often an issue. With the classroom reading of Rich we saw together that readings can be multiple, and can change; and within readings connections can be contradictory but not necessarily exclusive. A willingness to consider and to complicate ideas can certainly lead to chaos but sometimes also to richer understanding.

I asked the class, "What is this writer resisting?" and they said, "Hidden meanings." I wrote "I hid the _____" on the board and asked students to finish the sentence. We listed their answers: money, keys, books, socks, tapes. Then I asked what these things had in common and students said, eventually, that they are all concrete items that you could put somewhere safe and then find them again exactly as they were. Someone else who knew where you hid them could also find them as you would. I asked, "So, if this writer is talking about meanings being hidden, what are her assumptions about meaning in a text?" This was a way to look back at discussions on making meaning in reading as opposed to finding "it" as a unit, ready-made. The assumptions behind "hidden meanings" are that there is one "correct" little gem of insight that an author has buried, that a clever student could unearth, so the teacher could say "right."

I asked how the phrase "hidden meaning" positions the writer and how it might be a different positioning from that of a writer who thinks that meaning is not already "there" but is made by the reader as well as the writer. I asked the class, "How does this positioning relate to this writer's assumptions about revision?" They said revision seemed to be a "fix-it" notion, a mechanical or formulaic view that related to a mechanical view of the text as having discrete components of meaning, waiting to be "correctly" excavated. I asked, "How are her assumptions about revision related to her assumptions about what a teacher is?" The writer is a victim, a defendant against a "judge" and, as such, I asked, "How might such assumptions trap her?"

This allowed us to move back into Rich, thinking again about that passage on poems and dreams and the one on revision. In reading her note now, would the writer see things she didn't know she knew? Could there be advantages to that "fix-it" strategy? Could there be disadvantages?

From Monica, I had received exactly the same paper she had turned in the preceding week, with new sentences tacked onto the end of every other paragraph. In copying her paper for class, I bracketed these additions, so that her strategy would be obvious immediately. We didn't spend long on her paper. Once the class saw that their expectations of a "nonrevision" were confirmed, and that her assumptions probably had prevented her from doing the work of the assignment, it wasn't worth spending much more time on.

My intention in this discussion was not to reduce or berate Monica but to ask her — and her classmates who may share some or all of her views — to look at the trap her own language and assumptions create and to imagine ways out of that trap — as Rich does. The ways out have to do with risk and ambiguity and struggle, rather than clarity, coherence, and correctness.

I also handed out Kelly's note and asked students to imagine how the revision would look and how the writer had read Rich and herself. Kelly had written:

```
     I'd like you to look at the use of quotes in
my essay and the way I connected my ideas through
the quotes.  I tried to put more of Freire in the
essay, so I'd like you to look and see if there's
more of a connection between Rich and Freire.   I
also described more of what I meant by the "space"
in Rich's poem "Planetarium."  Also, I didn't fol-
low Rich's essay from beginning to end, but tried
to start with "Planetarium" and work back to "Aunt
```

Jennifer's Tigers." I still have things from our class discussion about the poems, but I felt this information was important in explaining Rich's transformation and transcendence.

Students picked up on the cheerleading tone in Kelly's note; it sounds as though she is trying to sell the paper as a "true revision." Although students said they would see for themselves in reading her revision whether this was true, they saw in the note that it might be, if she really did what she said she had. Students also saw that, like Monica, Kelly was reacting to the teacher: The teacher's comments had probably said (as did the class discussion) not to string quotations together, not to follow Rich's order too closely, not to rely too heavily on class notes. But, the class said, to be practical, this is what all students have to do — react to the teacher. Sometimes it's entrapping, like Monica's defensive resistance. Refusing to look for "hidden" meaning precluded all attempts to read strongly; Monica saw herself as having to choose between false polarities — "hidden" or "straightforward." At this point, someone said that maybe there is a difference between reacting and responding. This writer might have responded to the teacher's suggestions because they made sense to her, not because she had to. Maybe this writer could have a conversation with the teacher and learn something about how to revise. I asked for evidence.

Students said that, in this note, the writer directs the teacher to "look at," and "to see if. . . . " This writer, unlike Monica, isn't asking to be "judged"; she is asking for continued dialogue about her revision. As such, I asked, "How are this student's assumptions about revision also tied to her assumptions about teachers and students?" She seems, in her tone, in her directions, and even in her defense of certain inclusions, to position herself to speak, to listen, and to respond.

I asked, "How does this relate to a willingness to consider complexity?" Monica's portrait of teacher/student is black and white, whereas Kelly seems to be able to imagine a grey area (they have, after all, read Freire) where students are teachers and teachers students, where dialogue, exchange, and response occur. Kelly can imagine and begin to compose a different relationship of student and teacher and therefore of student, teacher, text, and revision. The writer of this note, students said, could see revision as an opportunity for dialogue rather than as a punishment; this opened up possibilities to see, hear, and know more about and *through* her own text by revising it. She had hope of coming to know, in revision, more than she knew she knew.

From Kelly, I had received a paper that looked and sounded different. While she still opens with her idea of "transcendence" she also tries to connect that, in the first paragraph, to what it might mean to "rename" and "revise." She seems to begin where she had had to end in her draft; thus she is able to use her initial work as a reader to find a place to start. The ideas of transcendence, renaming, and revising allow her to work with Rich, to connect and examine what she has noticed in the essay. Rather than generalizing and concluding, she sets herself up to move from the general to the specific, with a reading of "Planetarium" and back toward "Aunt Jennifer's Tigers." In rethinking her own structure and rereading Rich, the easy "happy ending" disappears. Kelly attempts to show rather than tell her own connections in her revision. She moves from her reading of the poems to an attempt to define "renaming" as a form of transcendence that she connects to Rich's imagery of Caroline Herschel. This paper is getting somewhere in a way that Monica's cannot.

In her revision, Kelly has worked Freire and Rich hard enough to be able to use them as a filter through which she reads herself. At the end of her paper, Kelly writes,

```
        Rich  finds  new  meaning  for  her  life  by  examin-
   ing  her  old  work  and  ways  of  thinking  and  thus
   Rich  creates  a  new  work,  her  essay,  in  which  she
   shows  a  Freire-like  transformation.   She  defines
   through  her  own  self-examination,  a  method  for  any-
   one  to  find  their  own  meaning,  independent  of  mean-
   ings  that  others  expect  them  to  follow.

        Rich  enters  old  texts  and  old  ways  of  thinking
   and  by  questioning  these  she  has  a  dialogue  with
   herself  and  her  work.  Through  "acts  of  cognition"--
   questioning,  challenging,  thinking  of  alternatives--
   she  renames  her  experience  in  her  own  terms.

        Rich's  revision  of  herself  from  not  knowing
   her  own  oppression  to  at  least  trying  to  know  says
   to  me  that  I  might  do  the  same  thing.   Like  Rich,
   I  might  find  meanings  by  looking  back  and  redefin-
   ing  myself  and  my  experience  in  new  terms.
```

In some ways, Kelly's move echoes Rich's authorial one and grows out of the class discussion and assignment on "structure." Kelly sees herself attempting the work that Rich defines, "enter[ing] an old text from a new critical direction." Kelly works from within what she knows to revise it into a new way of thinking and defining herself as a student/ writer. While Rich works at reforming poetry and patriarchy, some of my students, through Rich, work at renaming reading as experience and process.

o—o—o—o—o—o—o—o—o—o—o—o—o—o—o

BETWEEN CHALLENGING AND A HARD PLACE
by Angie Farkas

> When my General Writing teacher passed around
> the essays we, as a class, would be reading, I
> must admit my heart fell to my knees. After flip-
> ping through the pages of these essays and seeing
> what the essays were like (difficult and compli-
> cated) my heart dropped even further and came to
> rest in my feet. I knew we, as a class, would be
> responding to some sort of readings, but I had no
> idea that they would be at this degree of diffi-
> culty.

In case you're wondering, the author of the epigraph survived. Her name, like mine, is Angela, and she's at home now (Cambridge Springs, PA) resting (I hope) and enjoying her summer break. Angela told me as she handed in her portfolio that she was "looking forward to life again in a small town" — as opposed, I guess, to General Writing (death) in a big city. Angela helps me to begin this essay because I also want to talk about complexity.

It's taken me a while to start writing, to convince myself that I'm a person who should be sharing stories of her experience with teaching the new essays because, to be honest, I feel pretty ambivalent toward them. I'm critical of the specialized language I see in many of the essays, language I believe can be inaccessible without some knowledge of literary theory.

The two essays that my students and I worked with this semester (those by Patricia Williams and John Fiske) rely on terms and theories that I had never heard of until I started graduate school: subject positions, hegemony, signifiers and signified — words you can't find in the *American Heritage Dictionary*. Or, if they are in the dictionary, they usually are not defined in the sense that we use them when we talk about language. A college dictionary's definition of patriarchy as "a system of social organization in which descent and succession are traced through the male line" did not help Angela understand why Fiske sees certain words ("tarty," "seductive") as patriarchal. To understand Fiske's argument, she also needs to know what that system of social organization has to do with language, meaning, and the distribution of value. (To Angela's credit, she admits later in her essay that she can see how Fiske may have come up with that reading, considering "men have virtually dictated thus far in time what has been seen as 'tarty' and 'seductive.'")

Reading my students' work again, away from the crush of last semester, I have the time to look more closely at how they did and didn't manage the complexity of the essays, to consider more carefully the way my students use language in responding to challenging readings. I have chosen to focus exclusively on my students' work with John Fiske's essay on Madonna.

I decided to include Fiske's essay "Madonna" on my syllabus despite my reservations about the highly theoretical nature of Fiske's argument. I assumed that most students know something about Madonna and that familiarity would give them a place to begin to respond to Fiske's reading of her. The essay was particularly attractive to me because Fiske talks about issues of gender as he explores the relationship between Madonna and her female fans. (Unfortunately, that perspective on Madonna also provides many opportunities for students to generalize about women and teenage girls: "Most women still need a lot of encouragement when asserting their rights and needs around men.")

I told myself, when I selected Fiske, that he offers so many examples and makes the same argument so many times — although in different terms — that students could read around some of the more specialized language and still make sense of the essay. (It was my own familiarity with the theories that inform Fiske's analysis that allowed me to comfort myself with that thought.) What I noticed right away, at least in my students' initial response to Fiske, was a tendency for them to target the areas of an essay that are most dense, the areas with the most specialized language — perhaps because students are drawn by the professional sound of the language and the authority it suggests.

To help students with their first reading of Fiske, I asked them to mark a passage from the essay that seemed especially significant to them and to explain why in no more than a page. (Part of the exercise was locating and defining significance: how do you define the significant parts of an essay without an assignment question to make that decision for you?) I was surprised by my student's choices, many of which sounded like the one below:

> All this would suggest that she is teaching her young female fans to see themselves as men would see them, that is, she is hailing them as feminine subjects within patriarchy, and as such is an agent of patriarchal hegemony." (Fiske, pp. 159–60)

While I could see how a reader could be attracted to the first part of the passage, which presents itself as a summary of everything that goes before it (hence its significance), I wondered what students would possibly do with the last part, the part about agency, patriarchy, and hegemony.

Here is how one student, Matthew, approached the passage and the assignment:

> I have found this particular passage that seems to almost stand off the page with its sig-nificance. The opinions of the entire article seem to come to a head within this little passage. The writer feels that Madonna encourages young adoles-cent females to worship men and to submit to male desires. I find this is extremely false.

While Matthew's attempt to sell us on the significance of his passage (without really telling us what makes it significant) is somewhat funny, I don't want to underestimate the seriousness of his effort to answer the assignment. He continues at length about why he disagrees, based on his own observations of female fan behavior at Madonna concerts: "At the concert, I saw many beautiful females, but they were much more interested in watching her instead of scoping out men to submit to."

Matthew's discomfort with the language — a discomfort that perhaps keeps him from actually "seeing" the passage — is not only apparent by the manner in which he talks around the quotation but also in the awkward wording of his interpretation, the redundancy of "young adolescent females," for example. I think he gets tangled up when he attempts to sound equally complex: "I find this is extremely false" instead of "I don't agree," "extremely false" instead of just "false."

Matthew's was one of several responses that I considered to be representative of my students' attempts to make sense of Fiske's complicated language. I typed up a number of these passages and responses — including Matthew's — and used them in class not only to discuss strategies for locating and defining significance but also to discuss whether or not the responses represented "strong readings."

By this time in the semester my students were familiar, if not completely comfortable, with the language Bartholomae and Petrosky use to talk about reading in their introduction to *Ways of Reading* (such as "strong reading"). I treated the introduction as another essay in my class, giving it as much attention as Fiske and Williams. I asked students to write two papers in response to their reading of the introduction, one of which asked them to use some of the introduction's terms to construct a profile of themselves as readers. If I were to do it over again, I would have my students use the introduction to talk about themselves as readers, to locate patterns in their reading and writing, in the middle of the semester rather than at the beginning. That type of mid-term revision might allow them to see for themselves some of the ways in which they respond as readers and writers to complicated language.

The passage Matthew selected as significant proved to be a popular one among my students. Jamie incorporated it into a paper she wrote following the journal assignment on significance and was similarly troubled by it. After quoting Fiske (Madonna is teaching her young female fans to see themselves as feminine subjects within patriarchy), Jamie responds with one line: "Fiske dwells in his work on this simple fact."

What's noteworthy about her response is how it reduces the complexity of Fiske's assertion to a "simple fact." (Jamie, like Matt, is trying to sell us on something, trying to convince us that the passage is so simple it doesn't need further explanation.) It's significant to me that both Jamie and Matt characterize Fiske's assertion as diminutive in some way, as if they need to shrink it before they can consider what it says. Matt seems to be impressed that such a large idea could be contained within such a "little" passage.

And the passage is little if you see only the first half of it. That particular passage serves as a good example of Fiske's rhetoric, of the way he moves in and out of theory (in this case, with a semicolon). The second part of the statement generalizes about the first by putting things in broader, more theoretical terms; it lets us know the significance of the first half — why it is important to make the observation that Madonna is teaching her fans to see themselves as men would see them. As an agent of patriarchal hegemony, Madonna would align herself with the dominant social order, reproducing and perpetuating through her dress, gestures, music, and other texts a structure of power that subordinates women to men. (This is not what Fiske is actually arguing at this point; he is merely reproducing previous criticism of Madonna.) If my students can't read this part of the quotation, it is very likely that they are not going to see the significance of Fiske's argument. The other problem with working only one side of Fiske's assertion (Madonna is teaching women to see themselves as men see them) is that it doesn't leave much room for a writer to do anything but agree or disagree; in both Jamie's and Matt's case it turns the larger project of defining significance into a true-or-false question. While I didn't expect my students to be familiar or even to become familiar with concepts of hegemony in one semester, I did fret a little over what gets lost when students don't take those terms into account.

Some of what gets lost in Jamie's and Matt's readings is the irony of Fiske's assertion. Neither realizes that Fiske distances himself from previous criticism of Madonna in the passage that they work with (perhaps because being an agent of patriarchal hegemony sounds like something someone could go to jail for). Fiske's argument would have been stronger, Jamie says, had he "not chosen to explore Madonna's actions as agents leading to patrilocal hegemony [sic], but that could be because I am a female."

When it comes time to talk back to the author, if only to paraphrase, Jamie, like Matt, experiences problems composing. She has trouble with the word "patriarchy," and on two different occasions transcribes it onto her paper from the text of Fiske's essay as "patrilocal." Some of the slippage may be explained by her need to change an unfamiliar noun into an adjective — somewhere along the way from patriarchy to patriarchal she comes up with "patrilocal." But I think it is more than just a mistyping because it happens twice, and the second time doesn't require a grammatical shift. On that occasion she uses "patrilocal" right after she's quoted the phrase "patriarchal hegemony," leaving me to question how much the term's nearness to "hegemony" had to do with her misappropriation.

Knowing that Jamie is a conscientious student, serious and hardworking, made her error more striking. Knowing how Jamie works, knowing that Jamie works, prevents me from passing it off as carelessness. Certainly that is part of the story, for both Jamie and Matthew, but I would argue that it's only a part.

I haven't been in graduate school too long to have forgotten how alienating theory can be to the uninitiated. One of my first graduate-level assignments asked me to consider Foucault's "What Is an Author" in relation to issues of student authority in the composition classroom. This was my first encounter with the type of theoretical discourse that I would be asked to read and respond to throughout graduate school. Although I read the essay over and over, up until the night before my paper was due, I could not find a way into it — a paragraph, a particular point, anything that I could begin to respond to. I did, however, memorize most of the language. I was a tragic figure, crying over my keyboard late into the night, weighing my inadequacies.

The written comments I received on the paper tell the rest of the story.

> This has such a desultory, fragmentary feel to it — like you're groping for a place to stand. Then on pages 4–6 something begins to emerge that seems to hold your attention. Is that the essay you want to write here? If so, by all means, render it a worthy project.

I remember feeling offended by the final sentence, which seemed to suggest I hadn't already tried to render the paper a worthy project. That, in fact, all I had to do was try harder.

I hear similar things when I read the introduction to *Ways of Reading*: "Read as though it [makes] sense and perhaps it will" (p. 10). Here, the authors are quoting I. A. Richards as a way of developing their metaphor of a strong reader, a reader who "takes charge of a text," who constructs readings that are at once authoritative in the face of complexity and generous to the authors they speak back to.

The metaphor of a strong reader, and especially the advice from I. A. Richards, becomes more complicated for me, though, in the face of theory, whose terms and phrases I think go beyond challenging for students because of their professionalization. I doubted whether pretending or trying harder was going to get Matthew or Jamie any closer to an understanding of agency, patriarchal hegemony, or subject positions (just as trying harder for me at that point in my education was not going to get me any closer to an understanding of that particular Foucault essay).

Like Jamie and Matt, I would channel a complicated passage into a single line: "The author gives rise to a variety of egos and to a series of subjective positions that individuals of any class may come to occupy." In response, I noted that "Foucault seems to be clearing space here for the reader," and then I hurried off in another direction. Because Foucault was actually addressing the author function directly at that point, I was sure that the key to the whole essay depended upon my interpretation of that passage. (This is where things seemed to come to a head for me.)

Only after three years of being surrounded by that talk, that way of thinking, have I come to feel more comfortable with theory. Only now do I feel I'm in a position to begin to respond to that assignment. From this perspective, I realize that there are more accessible moments in the essay I was working with, and more realistic goals I can set for myself as a reader.

I use my experience with Foucault not only to explain my hesitancy about asking my students to read and respond to such specialized language but also to show how I am reading my students' writing: not as signs of carelessness but as indications of the way students may use language when they are "groping for a place to stand." Reminding myself of my own beginnings helps me remain sensitive to my students' beginnings. I don't want to forget how disabling theoretical discourse can be, especially for those who may feel powerless in academic situations in the first place.

I was particularly taken last semester by Jason's beginnings. His strategy for locating significance was one of the best, I thought, since he targeted a point in Fiske's essay where the author seemed to be saying something directly to him (rather than a section that might encourage him to generalize about the plight of teenage girls). Jason chose to work with the following passage:

> If [Madonna's] fans are not "cultural dopes," but actively choose to watch, listen to, and imitate her rather than anyone else, there must be some gaps or spaces in her image that escape ideological control and allow her audiences to make meanings that connect with *their* social experience. For many of her audiences, this social experience is one of powerlessness and subordination, and if Madonna as a site of meaning is not to naturalize this, she must offer opportunities for resisting it. Her image becomes, then, not a model meaning for young girls in patriarchy, but a site of semiotic struggle between the forces of patriarchal control and feminine resistance, of capitalism and the subordinate, of the adult and the young." (p. 160)

Jason sees "hope" in this representation of Madonna. While admitting his distaste for her — he "gets sick of reading about all her obsessed fans and the idiots that worship her" — Jason notes that "something applies to all of us when Fiske says, 'Her image becomes, then, not a model meaning for young girls in patriarchy, but a site of semiotic struggle between the forces of patriarchal control and feminine resistance, of capitalism and the subordinate, of the adult and the young.'" He then interprets that line:

```
     I feel that this sentence spells out
Madonna's true effect on society and how her suc-
cess means that there is hope for all underdogs.
This is an excellent example of how everyone should
have a "never quit" attitude, because that is the
only way to find out what one's capable of.
```

Jason, by the way, is much more optimistic than I am. Since Jason had positioned himself as an underdog in his previous writing, I thought that here was a student who had found a place to stand in Fiske's essay. In an earlier paper Jason told a story about how he was passed up for a promotion at K-mart and questioned how that experience may have been related to his family's economic background. Another paper (for a writing assignment in response to the *Ways of Reading* introduction) expressed his feelings of inferiority as a reader and writer. In this paper, Jason says that he read the introduction over and over again out of fear that I might call on him and embarrass him in front of the other students. "I wanted to understand it as well as some of the kids in class," he says in his paper, and expresses his fear of being "left behind." The way Jason represented himself in his early writing, led me to believe that he connected with what Fiske says in the passage above about struggle and powerlessness.

But because of the length and complexity of the passage Jason chose as significant, he has a hard time articulating the connection he wants to make. He relies heavily on the language that is perhaps most accessible and most attractive to him as a football player: never-quit attitudes, and other formulas for a winning season. Jason's attempt to work closely with Fiske's words — pulling a line from the quotation into his commentary without really responding directly to it — only made more obvious to me his inability to appropriate its terms. Even though Fiske's sentence is at the center of Jason's reading, its language remains completely isolated from his.

I often volunteer (or at least have in mind) a knitting metaphor when I talk to my students about working with other writers' words. I encourage them to move into the quotation, to make important terms their own (weave them into their own writing) as they comment on or explain the significance of the passage they've chosen to respond to. I share with them my own pleasure in making other people's words work for me when I write. The metaphor helps me explain to students the importance of accounting for all the language in a certain passage, not just those words or phrases that appear immediately useful. I imagine a seamless finish.

I mention this now because I see Jason starting to do that with the line that most appeals to him from Fiske's quotation — if only by carrying it out of the longer passage and into his commentary. But he needs to work through the line, not just around it. (I also mention my knitting metaphor because I like how it looks next to "push" and "shove.")

I used Jason's passage in class as a good example of one way to begin a reading of an essay and to make that reading meaningful. I also made sure Jason realized the work that still needed to be done.

Encouraged by my response, Jason carried his "significant" passage over into his first and then his last paper on Fiske. This is what he was finally able to do with it:

> Fiske creates a situation in which [Madonna's] fans are not "cultural dopes" but intelligent people. By creating this scenario, he enables himself to discuss her effect on society as a whole. He says, "Her image becomes, then, not a model meaning for young girls in patriarchy, but a site of semiotic struggle between the forces of subordinate, of the adult and the young." [sic] I feel that this sentence spells out Madonna's true impact and how her success means that there is hope for everybody.

I see Jason trying to work more closely with the passage in this revision. He summarizes Fiske's argument and incorporates one of Fiske's phrases ("cultural dopes") into his commentary. He is also careful to point out that it is Fiske's reading of Madonna he's responding to, rather than Madonna herself. (He's still not ready to give Madonna credit for anything.) Fiske "creates a situation" he says, that enables Jason to see Madonna's fans as intelligent people (rather than as "idiots," which is the way Jason characterized them in his first draft). But he doesn't come any closer to the line that was most striking to him, the line about Madonna as a "site of semiotic struggle." In fact he mistypes it, and he doesn't seem to notice that he's lost a phrase transferring the sentence from his original to his revision. Not surprisingly, his interpretation is still vague. He doesn't tell us what Madonna's "true impact" is, and how he reads "hope" into that line. In his revision, he ignored the marginal comments that asked him to explain what words or phrases helped him develop that reading.

While I'm sure that Jason's work with the Fiske essay was productive for him — if only in giving him some idea of the work that reading, and then presenting a reading, involves — I was disappointed that he was unable to connect with the passage in a way that would help him better articulate his own sense of struggle, his own experiences of power and of powerlessness, rather than talking about Madonna's effect on "society as a whole."

It's probably obvious by now that I feel pretty ambivalent toward theory (and not just the way theory is used in the essays I taught). I think I have a reputation for not liking it. But it's not so much that I dislike it as that I'm uncomfortable with the inaccessibility of some of the language; I'm too aware of the exclusions that are made when someone speaks, writes, or otherwise moves within that discourse. I'm overly conscious of the audiences that can't participate in that discussion. More troubling to me, though, is hearing theory spoken in a tone that conceals its status as a highly academic discourse, a tone that suggests it's common knowledge. To put it another way, it's the "that is," in the passage Matthew and Jamie both quote from "Madonna":

> All this would suggest that she is teaching her young female fans to see themselves as men would see them, that is, she is hailing them as feminine subjects within patriarchy, and as such is an agent of patriarchal hegemony. (pp. 159–160)

As an authorial gesture the "that is" is really curious. Such a move usually indicates that a writer is about to restate an idea in a way that makes everything clearer, but here Fiske restates things in a way that makes them more obscure. And it's done so matter-of-factly. It's almost as though Fiske, at that moment, is speaking to two audiences that he separates with a semicolon. Which brings me back to Angela, who, among other things, was angry at having been shut out of Fiske's discussion of teenage girls and their relationship to Madonna — a discussion that just may have had something, everything, to do with her. In the quotation below, Angela is responding to Fiske's reading of the language a teenager named Lucy uses to describe Madonna. Lucy calls Madonna "tarty and seductive." Her use of these terms indicates to Fiske that she is only able to find "patriarchal words to describe Madonna's sexuality." (Fiske, 161) Angela resents the language that Fiske uses when he reads Lucy's language:

```
         I personally do not even think I have ever
even heard of the word "patriarchy" before reading
this essay; consequently I would not have identi-
fied the things Fiske picked out from what the fan
said about Madonna.  Fiske goes on to say that the
girl "struggles against the patriarchy inscribed in
them {tarty and seductive}," as well as struggling
"against the patriarchy inscribed in her own sub-
jectivity."  (p. 161)  To me the only thing strug-
gling here is the girl because she cannot find the
appropriate words in her mind to describe how she
```

```
feels about Madonna.        I know that I sometimes
struggle and would probably sound similar to the
way this girl sounds because it is as if my mind
goes blank and I seem to talk in circles.   Who
would know that the fan is struggling because she
is "trying to come to terms with the contradictions
between a positive feminine view of . . . sexual-
ity and an alien patriarchal one that appears to
be the only one offered" by everyone and everything
in society as Fiske believes?
```

By the time Angela gets to the end of that paragraph in her paper, her well-ordered argument unravels and becomes all frayed at the end. While she doesn't exactly move through Fiske's language at the beginning, she moves well *with* it, using what she needs and discarding the rest. At her highest point of exasperation she loses even that authority, that thread.

In a way, Angela, a teenager herself, seems outraged that Fiske would be so presumptuous as to assume he can speak for teenage girls — that he can take the words right out of their mouths like that and make them mean something else altogether. Angela offers her own interpretation, separate, she says, from Fiske's, one that doesn't rely on his terms:

```
Madonna does not seem to need men or love and
is not pushed around in a relationship, because she
stands up for herself.   Girls like the sense of
power Madonna exerts in her relationships and would
like to take on this characteristic of Madonna.
(This interpretation can also be found in Fiske's
essay, but I did not get my ideas from his inter-
pretation.)
```

By offering "her own" interpretation Angela can return Lucy's language to her and help Lucy say what she was trying to say in the first place.

The way Angela positions herself alongside Lucy reminds me of Jamie's response to Fiske's reading of Madonna "as an agent of patriarchal hegemony." Jamie doesn't think Fiske should have spoken about Madonna in that way, but "that could be because I am a female," she says. Both Jamie and Angela align themselves with the women who are being talked about, as if they feel the need to protect them from Fiske's intellectual scrutiny, or to rescue them from his language. (I think both also seem to assume that because the language at those particular moments sounds critical or serious, Fiske is being critical, in the negative sense of the term.)

Angela's anger could also be understood as the anger many students express when they are asked to look critically at texts they usually watch, listen to, or read "just for fun" (that is, when their world is threatened or intruded upon by the authorities). If this is true, Angela wasn't the only student who took issue with Fiske's work. Matthew, who was growing more and more frustrated by the class's reading of his passage on significance (they decided that his was a misreading) finally vented his anger: "Why does Fiske have to pick Madonna apart like that?" he asked. He was referring specifically to the place in the essay where Fiske analyzes the introduction to one of Madonna's videos, and in doing so breaks it up into twenty-one shots. ("Twenty-one pieces!" Matthew said.) I thought Matthew's question would be a good question for the whole class to consider, so I turned it into a writing assignment: three pages on what point Fiske is trying to make by "picking Madonna apart" like that. Throughout this essay, the work that I have referred to written by Jamie, Angela, and Jason was done in response to that assignment. I mention this now because I question whether Angela and Jamie interpreted "picking apart" to mean "picking on" Madonna.

While that may account for some of Angela's and Jamie's defensiveness, I still want to claim a difference between the resistance that they voice and the resistance that Matthew voices, a difference I think can be accounted for in terms of gender. Matthew seems to be more upset with the method Fiskes uses in his reading of Madonna ("Why is he being such a nit-pick?") than with the language he uses as he reads her ("Why is he saying those things about her?").

To help my class read Fiske's language I spent part of a session sharing my under-standing of some of the terms that were giving students the most trouble: "hegemony," "patriarchy," "ideology," "semiotics," "signifier," and "signified." I wanted them to realize that these weren't terms they were just expected to know, but terms that represented a certain level of professionalism in literary studies. I let them know that my own under-standing of those terms was tentative, one that I was still working out. This wasn't something I had planned for, but something I thought I should do after seeing the type of trouble my students were having with the Fiske essay.

That discussion stands out for me because I had never before tested out what I knew of those terms in a classroom. The language in graduate seminars seemed so far removed from my own, and moved so quickly, that at times I didn't know how to posit an opinion, a reading, or even formulate a question were I actually to ask one. Somewhere in between college and graduate school, language — all speech acts — became "discourse," and I was left to silently figure the difference. Considering my students' work now, I am convinced that I benefited more from talking through some of that language than my students did.

I think the best thing that came out of discussing those terms for my students that day is the authority I see in Angela's reading of Fiske. She doesn't submit to Fiske's language, to his expertise, but chooses instead to understand "patriarchy" as part of a discourse she isn't familiar with at this moment in her education: "I personally do not even think I have ever even heard of the word 'patriarchy' before reading this essay; consequently I would not have identified the things Fiske picked out from what the fan said about Madonna."

Fiske's reading is not necessarily better, it's just other, or different.

I value also the fact that Angela attends to the complexity of Fiske's language rather than dismissing it or overlooking it, and that she acknowledges the importance of what he is saying:

> Actually, rethinking this [how "tarty" and "se-ductive" come to be patriarchal] I see that Fiske may have gotten this interpretation from the fact that men have virtually dictated thus far in time what has been seen as "tarty" and "seductive."

But at the same time, she places equal weight on her own interpretation, which indicates to me that she knows that what she says and how she says it is are just as important.

RELATIVISM: A WALL WITH MANY WINDOWS
by Ellen Smith

A little past mid-term of a semester last year, in a cross-listed Women's Studies general writing course using *Ways of Reading* as its main textbook, Mary, a student who was usually cool and confident with her assignments, came to my office hours shaking a photocopy of Susan Willis's "Work(ing) Out" and announced that she was "climbing the walls." Willis had so problematized the idea of women and fitness that Mary, an ardent exerciser and feminist, was angry at the critical infinity the essay had opened up. "You could just go on forever reading into popular culture," Mary noted. And she was right. She showed me a draft of her essay in response to Willis's article. The first page was devoted to venting her frustration at the way Willis's analysis glided from one paradigm to the next without closing in and making a prescriptive statement on the feminist stance toward the fitness craze of the 1980s.

I was confused, too, and started climbing the walls with her. It was, after all, my fourth try at teaching this course; and by then I'd pretty much adopted the Jean Kerr variation on the famous Kipling quote: "If you can keep your head when all about you are losing theirs [and blaming it on you], it's just possible you haven't grasped the situation." Mary took her frustrated draft back to her apartment, picked up where the frustration tapered, and in a day or two turned in an essay in which she furnished the conclusion the Willis text nobly refused to furnish. In a loud textual voice, Mary yelled back and forth with Willis and finally decided that exercise wasn't the enemy of women, but that the way exercise was marketed was a partriarchal mediation that women needed to separate from the common-sense good of physical fitness and strength.

I was very happy to see this essay. Mary had waded through the relativism that the critical reading/writing class must encounter if it is to be truly "critical." Her work made me begin to see that critical work follows a kind of ebb and flow, a passage from the sturdy banks of certainty to the Sargasso of relativism and inevitably back to some ground on which to stand, though the ground will never seem as erosion-free as it once did — not as long as there is dialogue.

Through revisions from one semester to the next, I always carry over in my course descriptions a few key concepts that I value in the teaching of composition. One of them is that of "dialogue." This concept is developed in the the introduction to *Ways of Reading* and has been helpful to me in articulating with my students the link between reading and writing. It has become a part of my classroom's critical lexicon and readerly etiquette. I emphasize dialogue because I feel that we all come to writing with strong adversarial models in place (courtroom TV, debate rhetoric). In dialogue, one needn't swing to a markedly pro or con position in relation to a text or set of ideas. The aim is not to vindicate or dismiss a text wholesale; rather, it is to engage it so that both text and reader come away modified by the exchange.

With my students, I set a scenario of a stimulating conversation among friends. It's unthinkable that constant agreement or disagreement would make such conversations worth returning to. I discuss the importance of tension and the give and take that make us return to some conversational milieus and not to others. But anyone who has ever stayed up into the wee hours engaged in an energetic dialogue knows that they never really conclude, at least not decisively. Someone points to the clock or rubs her eyes; maybe someone else offers a provisional conclusion or mentions areas of discussion that still need to be covered in a future meeting; or another throws up her hands in despair the way Mary did. The point is that in closing, we assume that someday we'll return to the discussion. The closing signals a potential beginning.

I hope that this analogy relieves student writers of the burden of having the definitive final word in response to a text. In my critical comments, I often activate the analogy to point out places where the assigned text is being shut out of the discussion and where the student is sitting back and letting it do all the talking just to fill a nervous pause. In large group readings of a student text, a key question is: "What kind of conversation does this student essay represent?"

In a reading sequence that opened with Adrienne Rich's "When We Dead Awaken: Writing as Re-Vision," two analogous reading practices emerged in the first student assignments of the semester. Assignments related to Rich's essay asked students to read certain concepts introduced by Rich through the examples of her poetry that she includes in the essay. Any text will yield these types of practices in the beginning of a freshman writing course, although the Rich piece, whose combination of poetry and expository prose the *Ways of Reading* assignments avoids separating, accentuates the causes for the two types of responses (with some overlap):

(1) The way to be in dialogue with an expository essay is to locate or invent a thesis, to abstract the thesis into issues around the text, and then to proceed to either oppose or augment this thesis.

(2) The way to be in dialogue with poetry, since it is "subjective" and only the author knows its "true meaning," is to defer as much as possible to the author's cues on how to read it; if the author's directives are absent or incomplete, one can go "out on a limb," but only if one states the disclaimer that one reader's interpretation is as good as another's.

With both types of response there are problems in terms of dialogue. I have found it useful to try to use one of each type of response in the initial group readings of student texts. I therefore try to bring in a paper ostensibly dealing with the issue of women's rights and involving very little textual work, along with a paper that refers (or de-fers) to the text with very little intervention on the part of the writer's opinions or experience. Since the notion of "dialogue" is my classroom mantra, what we read for in a large group are relationships between the writer/reader and the text.

An issue-oriented, polemical student essay entitled "Defense of a Republican Redneck" presented itself as almost a caricatural version of the first type of response. It seized not so much on the Rich text but rather on the political values the student inferred from it. It was as if they had asked Rich to "step outside" the text and duke it out over the issues. One student blamed his fighting posture on Rich's "tone":

> My point is that I can understand different
> ideologies, but by no means can I ever approach
> the subject with a cool and open mind when my own
> values have been violated in an aggressive style,
> much as Ms. Rich has done. . . . Ms. Rich man-
> ages in one essay to offend all that is holy to a

conservative, young, white heterosexual, old-school
male.

I opened classroom discussion with this question: "With what parts of the Rich essay
is this writer in dialogue?" The first student to speak looked sheepishly at me, asking
if I wanted his honest opinion. His honest opinion was that he "wished he had written
it." Like the student writer under discussion, this student held that the "aggressive" tone
of Rich's text deserved a response in kind. If you ever teach the Rich essay, be sure to
take time to develop a collective working definition of "tone"! Sooner or later, it has to
be taken into a close look at Rich's use of language and how such a tone is inferred by
many male (and female) writers. Anyway, the "fire with fire" principle was raised by the
second student, even though we hadn't yet located the cause of the fire within the Rich
essay. A woman student took the defensive, arguing that to write an essay like this, "Rich
had to be 'aggressive,' to not let up."

The discussion had become impressionistic, and we needed to get into the text itself,
to try to grapple with the "incendiary" material. John helped this happen by commenting
that the student essay was not dealing with the assignment question, or for that matter,
with "*what* Rich was saying" (as opposed to how). So we began to scout for passages in
which the student made any reference at all to any aspect of the assigned text. The first
gold we struck was not Rich's text, but the editors' text introducing the essay in the
anthology. That was good enough for the moment; I was desperate for any intertextuality
we could work with:

> It would be one thing if Ms. Rich was simply
> an advocate, but she goes a step beyond. She in-
> sists that she trash and deface accepted norms
> along her way of proving her point; for example in
> her <u>Of Woman Born: Motherhood as Experience</u> the
> editor even agrees that despite a fine job she
> still "calls for the destruction of motherhood as
> an institution."

Obviously, since the writer is drawing his material from the editors' introduction, he
is already predisposed away from dialogue with the text that ensues. Finding this gave
us the opportunity to discuss the influence of paratextual discourse (be it present or
removed) on our readings of a given text. From there, we followed John's lead by looking
for other "hookups" with the assignment or Rich texts, locating this oasis about midway
through the paper:

> She [Rich] suggests that major works of liter-
> ary art be re-examined to find sleeping messages
> that may prove new points to an "awakened" audi-
> ence. . . . Not only do major works of male au-
> thors [need to be scrutinized], but more important
> lost and "buried" works from female authors need to
> be "unearthed" in order to gain the complete pic-
> ture. <u>I disagree</u> with Ms. Rich on the point of
> "unearthing" all females' work simply because until
> the 1920s most women were not accepted. . . .

Here, this textual moment breaks down as the writer repairs to the political issues
he infers from the text (and it is exactly this process of inference that would need to be
externalized in a revision, as in "Here all we get is Z, but we, your readers, are clueless.
Please walk us through the process of getting from A to Z."). From this point, the writer

never returns to the text, as we noted in class, but rather culminates his detour with a chilling anecdote that serves as a conclusion:

> I'll never forget the homosexual killed in my town when I was in ninth grade, he was dragged behind a pickup truck on a rope for a mile at high speed by some seniors. They went to jail but did so freely, feeling that they were protecting a way of life, much as Ms. Rich feels she's protecting hers.

(I said it was an extreme example of an adversarial, pro and con approach.) It wasn't difficult (as it is in much more subtle versions of this approach) to move into a discussion of the incongruity not only of the frightening analogy drawn up by this text, but of the dialogical relationship between this text and the Rich essay. Also, in keeping with the question, "What aspect of Rich's text is this essay in dialogue with?" this final passage connected clearly in students' minds to the information proferred in the editors' introduction: that Rich was committed to gay and lesbian rights. This piece of information had furnished paratextual noise in many students' own readings of Rich, and so they quite readily pointed to it.

From this extreme (and clearly antisocial) example of the adversarial model over the dialogical one, which is always only ideal, we moved to a less vituperative student essay which does quite the opposite. It defers to and privileges the Rich text and keeps the student writer's voice at bay. Here is the writer's conclusion:

> She [Rich] began her career writing like men, for men, but changed. She was able to see changes in her writing and make other changes. After following tradition she actually went against it. Rich overcame conformity of men and found a way to write like a woman. <u>She often used renaming in her poetry to get this point across.</u>

Because the editors' assignment question had asked students to apply Rich's assertion that "writing is re-naming" to a reading of her poetry, this student is careful to include the importance of renaming in this capsule summary of the Rich text. But throughout the essay, the concept itself is never worked out through reading and writing of both the prose and poetry that form "When We Dead Awaken." There is, however, a paragraph in the center of the essay that brings the idea in proximity to a reading of Rich's poem "The Loser"; and we made this our center for critical discussion in class:

> The renaming used in this poem, as I see it, is not something in the poem being renamed but the narrator being renamed. The point of view should be of the author who is female, but because females were criticized by men, Rich wrote "The Loser" from the point of view [of] a man. . . . Tradition is not renamed but only followed in "The Loser."

This is the productive center of the student's essay, where the text is engaged in understanding a concept introduced expositorily through its assumed manifestation in the poetic artifact. My mimeographed copy of this essay has marginal notes gleaned from discussion — "go back to the place where Rich discusses renaming" — this, with an arrow indicating the first sentence of the cited passage (the place where the reader makes a decision either to go back and dialogue with Rich on this idea or to move forward, following the "evolutionary" line of Rich's sequence of poems). In other words, she prematurely gave the "floor" back to Rich (or at least, back to her generalized outline of Rich's thesis and narrative).

In picking up the superficial line of Rich's expository/narrative text, the student safeguards herself against taking a plunge into "back and forth" reading and writing — and thus running the risk of kicking up more questions than answers. Right beyond that point is the shrug of despair that I associate with relativism. Who wouldn't want to put that off, especially in her first weeks at the university, when she doesn't know what's expected of her? And so this second student, when she notices her own insight emerging, steps aside and lets stand what the author tells her "The Loser" represents in her "evolution." Only it's doubtful the author would have needed to include the poems if that's all she wanted the reader to gather.

As the student essay stands, "renaming" is present in name only, and to follow the paper's analysis of the poem, we must refer back to Rich's text, of which the student text is only an index. But it can be more, and the work of the critical reading/writing course is to locate such places not as faults but as "windows of opportunity." As a group, we located every moment in this student's essay where the word "renaming" appeared. Each of these places was seen as an opening back to the text, where "going back" is not a penalty but a real instance of "reading against the grain." At each opening this student had a chance to do more than indicate the concept. But I think the presence of poetry in the Rich essay made her cautious — and rightly so — about stopping the progress "with the grain" of the text. It doesn't help that the phrase "writing is re-naming" has a tautological aspect to it. In short, the reputedly "endless" possibilities for interpreting poetry, the spectre of relativity, were preempted by this student's referring back to the general line of Rich's essay, for which the concept of "renaming" could be seen as a transcendent rubric.

Regardless of which *Ways of Reading* essay you use to open your course, I recommend selecting two such student essays and juxtaposing them in class. In this way, you set the stage for a movement away from both the extratextual debate approach and the deferential, or indexing, approach, in both of which, the dialogue is markedly lopsided. I should point out that these essays should not be painted as failures. For instance, a student's deferring to the grain of a given text — as well as the opposite approach — is an effort to contain an abundance of ideas, reactions, and a convergence of many texts both written and unwritten. You can help to stem this overwhelm through your written comments and through in-class discussions that try to narrow the focus or find, as we did in the previously cited essay, a "productive center." For this latter student, the following Rich assignment presented a reasonable point of entry back to the poems and to the concept of "renaming": The assignment asked students to explore, again through Rich's poetry, another idea Rich offers, that "revision is an act of survival." Here, the student has two "re" words to work with. How are they related? And how might we see "The Loser" as a revision of "Aunt Jennifer's Tigers"?

Helping students to narrow the focus is one way to reduce the fear we all have (and no one more than the instructor) of opening cans of worms that can't ever be closed. It's the uneasiness we feel when a dialogue gets further and further away from the prospect of a conclusion. But this is the nature of critical reading and writing, isn't it? The first student cited, the "belligerent" one, attempted to be, in his words, "more diplomatic" with the Rich text in his revision. But the text remained for him an object to deflect in the name of larger issues external (or tangential) to it. Not one citation appeared in this second essay, although quotation marks do not necessarily guarantee dialogue, as anyone who's ever "strip-mined" a reference book for a research paper will admit. In retrospect, I think that this student might have been better served by the very model I wished he would abandon.

What might have happened had he tried (as the tradition of debate sanctions) to take on the alien perspective, that is, to debate on behalf of the Rich text? Would he, under these circumstances, have been able to keep the text at a distance, as an object? It's only recently that this "hair of the dog" intervention occurred to me. I'll take it up again shortly, in relation to John Berger's "Ways of Seeing."

By discouraging monolithic pro and con positions, I hope to discourage entrenchment and to encourage critical reading. To do this, we must question the nature of conclusions, and by implication, the construction of knowledge and discourse. A resounding, definitive conclusion may be like sealing the final car payment in an envelope, making the text one's own; but I work against this proprietary impulse and replace it with the sense that a text can never be owned outright.

By stressing that no one reader can "own" a text entirely, I find that the next wall we often encounter as a group, beyond the adversarial model, is that of relativism. Certainly, it's a wall you want to encounter. But to return to the analogy of dialogue, acknowledging the varying perspectives of the speakers is usually not an end in itself.

I would like now to work through examples of moments when students are wading in relativism, or what Jane Tompkins calls her "epistemological quandary." When a reader feels s/he can only end in relativism, I propose that, as Jane Tompkins illustrates in "'Indians': Textualism, Morality, and the Problem of History," the only way over the "wall" is a shift in the discourse, or what Tompkins calls "a change of venue." This shift can involve taking stock, backtracking, and it is usually self-reflexive and metadiscursive.

Tompkins's essay can be seen as a model of the process composition students and instructors work through in the course of a term. Like Tompkins, a group of readers and writers set out with a project. Whereas Tompkins sets out to research the relationship between Native Americans and colonists in seventeenth-century New England, the composition group has a more mixed agenda, but certainly it has something to do with getting somewhere, hitting on knowledge, and making progress.

Not long into the course, you notice the ground shifting, the compass points of progress jerking erratically in every direction. Tompkins discovers that history, even that conveyed by "primary" sources, offers varying perspectival facts about the Anglo-Native encounters in New England. This leads her back to the only "sources" left — her own subjectivity, her postmodern formation, her reading practices — all of which have contributed to her arrival at a quandary. "It may well seem to you at this point that, given the tremendous variation among the historical accounts, I had no choice but to end in relativism." (*Ways of Reading*, p. 597)

It's desirable that students, too, reach a point where they feel they have no choice but to *end* in relativism. But it's easy to mistake the beginning for the end. In Sheri's paper, a response to John Berger's "Ways of Seeing," the ending on a relativistic note becomes a way back into dialogue with the text:

> As I approach the end of my paper I ask my-
> self what I have found. I guess really all I've
> found is that <u>I'm still at the place I was before
> I began:</u> not quite sure of what mystification is,
> or why it exists. However, on the positive side,
> I realize that the way I see something stems from
> who I am, where I've been, what I've done, every-
> thing that has come from my existence. I am a
> unique individual who is entitled to have unique

```
thoughts.   What  I  see  is  what  I  know,  and  neither
can  really  be  wrong.
```

To make this assertion is important to a student; it draws a connecting line between the reader and the text, recognizing that the reader does make a mark on the text; it positions the reader as active and subjective; and it recognizes that writing needn't end in mastery to be successful.

On the other hand, I read the final assertion on two levels: first, as an application of Berger's claims — that nonexperts can "read" art and the world without intervention by powerful and interested experts; and second, as a plea to me, the instructor, for indulgence about her not nailing down the concept of "mystification." To be part of the university, to admit oneself into the confederacy of subjectivities, a student does need to disown the fear of being wrong. Yet, as the editors of *Ways of Reading* point out in the anthology's introduction: "Think of yourself . . . as a writer intent on opening a subject up rather than closing one down." Declaring all opinions, perspectives, and readings as equally viable is a generous move (and a nice break from the adversarial model), but as Tompkins notes in "'Indians,'" "The notion that all facts are only facts within a perspective has the effect of emptying statements of their content" (*Ways of Reading*, p.599). Just as the definitive conclusion closes down the dialogue between reader and text, so, too, does a disclaimer in the name of relativism. Where the former anchors down the text, the latter sends it floating like smoke with no significance apart from a reader's subjectivity.

To try to get Sheri to substantiate the text and her reading of it, I asked her to think about her own metadiscourse, the final disclaimer about everyone's being entitled to an opinion: "Why do you feel the need to assert this? Who might judge your individual way of seeing as 'wrong'?" I followed these questions up with another, having to do with the concept she was struggling with. "How might this move you make help you to understand how mystification can work against an individual's way of seeing?" Invoking relativism might be a more sophisticated way of expressing an insecurity in relation to the text or the instructor. "This is only my opinion" becomes, "Since even published writers are not totally objective, I stake out the right to go out on a limb, too." In both cases, instead of calling for these assertions to be cut, I try to use them as windows back into the reading/writing project.

If Sheri's defensiveness comes from her sense that she does not have a hold on Berger's concept of "mystification," the defensiveness itself becomes an occasion for returning to that concept. What is daunting about Berger's discussion of mystification? Which words block her (and she is not alone) from seizing what the text is trying to say? Earlier in her essay, as she tries to make meaning of the concept, she writes:

```
    Berger  focuses  mainly  on  mystification  and  its
role  in  art.    He  never  really  gives  a  straightfor-
ward  definition  of  mystification  within  his  essay,
but  he  does  say  that  "mystification  is  the  process
of  explaining  away  what  might  otherwise  be  evi-
dent."    I  took  this  to  mean  that  something  simple
and  undistorted  can  become  obscured  by  searching
for  a  hidden  meaning.    Being  of  the  analytical
type,  I  have  a  habit  of  doing  this.    [emphasis
added]
```

This is a key paragraph to return to for revision, because here the writer is hitting on the problem of mystification in her very attempt to define it. By searching for a "straightforward definition," she is missing Berger's development of concepts functioning through examples. She is searching for a concise hidden meaning as if it were a bedrock in the maze of text that is actually Berger's process of showing what mystification does rather than what it is.

In an assignment requiring students to describe a work of art on their own terms and "in the spirit" of John Berger, it is necessary to understand what that "spirit" is. His discussion of mystification is at the core of it. So students' initial impulse to break off dialogue with Berger's text and go into a monologue about their chosen work of art is a short-lived but probably necessary step. A self-reflexive assignment for revision, "Ways of Seeing Your Ways of Seeing," sets the table for a return to the text, through which a student can then look at his or her description on a metadiscursive level. Here, too, is a chance to expand on the notion of mystification, to add to Berger's delineation of its function among art historians. Is it something only art historians do, by trying to put forth single, valorized (and often esoteric) meanings for works of art? How might saying, "Everyone who looks at a painting will form his or her own meaning" also be a sort of mystification?

Here, the "hair of the dog" might be helpful. I might try, for instance, to put a spin on the *Ways of Reading* assignment for "Ways of Seeing," which asks students to evaluate a work of art of their own choosing in "the spirit of John Berger." My spin — and I can't say whether it would be successful — would be to require students to pair off, each pair choosing the same work of art, but with the stipulation that the partners could not discuss their readings until after their essays were written and turned in. In-class discussion would then juxtapose these individual readings of the same work of art (with a reproduction of it available for the group to see). I am curious whether there would be a tendency to valorize one reading over another, or if, in group discussion, students would take refuge in the clause "Everyone has his or her own opinion," which so many of the Berger-related essays I've read seem to seize upon. I would hope that the classroom jury might turn to the Berger text for help in reading and commenting on the student essays. . . . If the jury didn't do this on its own, I'd ask some questions to facilitate this return to the text.

The point is not to force students to take firm positions, but rather to be aware that these positions shift during the course of a dialogue. It is important to establish through large group work with student papers that relativism, too, is a certain position assumed and gesture made by the writer to both the reader and the text discussed. It is also to call a writer's attention to her own discursive shifts. Metadiscussion is not the sole property of advanced writers. "This is only my opinion," that seeming nervous writing tic, underlies and precedes more developed instances of self-reflexivity. But if we point it out in class as a superfluous truism or as a flag in textual confidence, we lose the chance to build around it a larger discussion and a conscious way back into the close reading project.

Returning to the essay by Jane Tompkins, I'd like to discuss how my students' readings of that text show how much of a wall the point of relativism can be. The initial assignment asked students to relate their own stories of either an academic research project or a personal discovery in which, like Tompkins, they found conflicting facts and ended up reflecting on how knowledge is constructed. As with the Berger essay, this assignment gave students the chance to read their own experience, a frame of reference that easily pulls writers toward monologue over dialogue. The writer of the following essay does not succumb to this temptation. She reads her experience through Tompkins's experience; but while Tompkins gets around the wall of her quandary by changing the venue, Rhee parts company with the "'Indians'" parallel at the point of relativism:

> In my experience of being a Korean-American, no one can truly understand what I experience unless they themselves experience it with me. I am able to tell about cultural shock, but <u>telling and</u>

<u>experiencing are different:</u>   no one can get the
full effect.   That is what Tompkins is saying; we
have to be there to fully understand because
everyone's perception of what occurred is different.   [emphasis added]

Rhee relates the dilemma of historical otherness to her own dilemma of making her experience understandable to contemporary others. Like most students I've worked with on the Tompkins text, she sustains a dialogue with the text up to the point where the quandary of perspectivism is discussed. What is more difficult for students to work with in a parallel writing assignment is Tompkins's metadiscussion on what to do about the quandary, which occupies the closing section, or "zone," of the essay. In the same paper, Rhee summarizes Tompkins's project in this way:

Basically what Tompkins said initially is that
you, the observer, had to be there to know and
understand what happened, since everyone's point of
view differs from others.   Then, she began to research the Puritans and Indians by consulting "expert" sources to see what they claimed as factual
information about what had occurred between the two
groups.   After she had completed her research she
tried to tie together what she researched, but was
unable to do so.   All the "experts" she consulted
had slight variations in their point of view.   At
the end of the essay it was as if she had given
up trying to formulate an opinion from the factual
information she researched about their [the Puritans' and the Native Americans'] relationship.

Rhee concludes her synopsis with a partial quote from Tompkins. "She finally states that, 'someone else's facts are not facts because they are only the product of a perspective.'" This partial quote is interesting primarily because it has been cut to suit the needs of the summary's line of thinking and to "end in relativism." But when the clause is put back into context, the meaning is quite different. The full sentence from which it is taken is in Tompkins's metadiscussion of her quandary and how the assumptions she held about history and perspective were getting in the way of her making a moral judgment on an historical event. In effect, this discussion helps her to work her way out of her postmodern corner:

. . . the argument that a set of facts derives from some particular world-view is no longer an argument against that set of facts. If all facts share this char-acteristic, to say that any one fact is perspectival doesn't change its factual nature in the slightest. It merely reiterates it.

This doesn't mean that you have to accept just anybody's facts. You can show that what someone else asserts to be a fact is false. But it does mean that you can't argue that someone else's facts are not facts *because they are only the product of a perspective*, since this will be true of the facts that you perceive as well (*Ways of Reading*, p. 600).

Here is the close of Rhee's essay:

Even though Tompkins was unable to state a
research-opinionated statement about the relation-

ship between the Indians and the Puritans, she made
a very important point: You have to be there or
experience the situation to understand what was or
is happening.

What interests me in this passage is the way in which Rhee is careful to distinguish between "what is" and "what was" happening, just as she made the distinction in a passage cited earlier between "telling" and "experiencing." In discussion, it was clear that her focus was, if taken to its logical conclusion, emptying history of its content, since we cannot be in history. Taking her own distinctions, together with part of the essay's title "the *problem* of history," we have something to work with beyond perspectivism. If history is history and now is now, how do we read history? How do we read "now"?

I have found it helpful to assign a second reading of " 'Indians' " that examines it in terms of "zones" and gestures. Early in the essay, Tompkins announces that the essay is an enactment of "a particular instance of the challenge poststructuralism poses to the study of history" (*Ways of Reading*, p. 585). The presence of space-breaks throughout the essay assumes more than a typographical significance, and asks students to summarize each of the five zones of text — with emphasis on the final one (which we could call the "twilight zone" because it's difficult to summarize and easily eclipsed by the preceding discussion of perspectivism). In rough terms, it breaks down in this way:

I. Anecdotal introduction — preconceived impressions about Indians from childhood. Introduction of research problem. Metadiscourse about purpose of the essay.

II. Initial source — Perry Miller's *Errand into the Wilderness* (1956). Observations about the author's subjective oversights.

III. Examination of other sources from the 1960s and 1970s. Discussion of contradictions in certain revisionist accounts.

IV. Examination of captivity narratives. Expression of frustration ("It may well seem to you at this point that I had no choice but to end in relativism.").

V. Self-reflexive discourse. Change of venue and reformulation of the question.

Calling attention to Tompkins's use of the phrase "change of venue" in this final, often overlooked, zone of the text raises the issue of other legal language employed in this section. Caught between the need to judge "the case" and a reading practice that makes her reluctant to accept the "evidence" of history, Tompkins appears to be using "change of venue" as a way of mediating between the adversarial model and the legacy of poststructuralism. "The change of venue, however, is itself an action taken" (p. 601).

Even though Rhee's final conclusions from the Tompkin's essay essentially beg the question and do not take Zone V into account, this idea of the perspectival nature of historical fact became one of her themes, even as the course moved into a reading of "Our Time," the excerpt from John Edgar Wideman's *Brothers and Keepers*. Comparing Wideman's text to Harriet Jacobs's "Incidents in the Life of a Slave Girl," Rhee stands by her conviction that Wideman is the more "authentic" of the two: "When I say that Wideman is objective, I mean that he tells what happens; he does use emotion but not . . . to show his bias." Rhee is on to something here, which has to do with the differences in the kinds of rhetorical/ historical constraints each writer was under. Rhee continues:

You have to be there to know and understand
what really happened to say it is a true
FACT. . . . Wideman does [not?] tell the facts as
to what happened to Robby, but he tells what <u>he</u>

> <u>saw</u>. Tompkins may say that what he saw is not a
> "true fact" because it was all from his point of
> view. A "true fact" to Tompkins is something like
> Garth died from a serious illness. To me, it seems
> like Wideman is telling what happened as it hap-
> pened, but Tompkins feels otherwise, because
> everyone's point of view and perspective differs
> from others. She is always skeptical of what is
> written down. In other words, take what is written
> with a very small grain of salt. What Wideman
> wrote may be nothing more than one big deception
> on his part in Tompkins's eyes. Everything depends
> on what the observer or reader perceives in their
> eyes <u>ONLY</u>.

As you can see, Rhee still takes from Tompkins only the notion of relativism, but perhaps, too, she has taken something else: an interest in reseeing what constitutes fact and objectivity. The highly antijournalist style Wideman introduces in his nonfiction account of his relationship with his brother could be expected to put a reader on guard against seeing the text as "objective," since objectivity is more often an effect of style than it is of content. Yet Rhee admits this text into the realm of the "historical." And more important, even though she doesn't get past the relativistic disclaimer, it's on her mind enough to carry over as a theme from one assignment to the next.

Nicole first wrote an essay about a personal experience that came to the conclusion that knowledge depends on perspective, stopping at just about the same point as Rhee did. In her second essay, Nicole decided to focus on a research project; this made her parallel with Tompkins's project more feasible, although it raised its own set of questions. She discussed researching Franklin Roosevelt's presidency and encountering conflicting views. Disposed as she was to favor the Democratic president, she acknowledged how her preexisting values mediated in her sorting through the opposing facts. By the end of the essay, Nicole has moved into a self-reflexive discourse, if not a total change of venue (since, unlike Tompkins, she solves her problem, instead of reformulating another):

> I can reach a happy medium on my approach to
> history and perspective/fact by drawing <u>from my own</u>
> <u>method:</u> Gather the perspectives, weigh the infor-
> mation carefully, and decide what, <u>in your mind</u>,
> should be considered a fact.

My comments on Nicole's paper took on a different focus than they had in response to Rhee's work. Rhee's relativism did not allow for any fact in history. Nicole's method links fact to perspective, à la Tompkins, but does not anticipate conflict between the two when they are brought together to solve a problem. Which will out in the tough cases? Perspective? The weighing of evidence? Here, a further stepping away from the individual method she proposes might be helpful. If everyone approaches history in this way, how do we account for differences and similarities in conclusions? What are the consequences of such an approach? What does this say about history and our relationship to it? And to knowledge?

The stepping back needn't lapse into generalization. Even if it does, it serves to place the relativistic relationships in a larger context. In Rhee's essay, the inexperienced other is prohibited from judging an alien experience. In Nicole's, the method of judgment is contained, atomized, and at once subjective and objective. Further, the stepping back is a necessary component of any self-reflexivity; we cannot examine ourselves without examining our place within a culture and cultures.

Relativism is a wall that usually has its windows right there in the student texts and in the texts they are in dialogue with. Those windows are usually questions, questions that multiply within student essays, instructor's comments, and group discussions. Getting there is an accomplishment. Getting "beyond" it may not happen for you or for all of your students in the space of one semester. But "climbing the walls" can't go on forever, and for many reasons it's a lot more constructive than being in the trenches. I know one thing. No student who's read Susan Willis's "Work(ing) Out" will ever again go to aerobics class in the same frame of mind. Nor does that essay go unmarked. Willis may never know, for instance, how a male student tuned himself into a text by appearing in class with a skirt on, catching me so off guard that all I could think to say as he handed in the paper was, "Uh, that's a nice skirt, Dave." Later, I read the essay he had written in response to "Work(ing) Out":

> If gender discrimination is entirely the fault of men, then why do some men suffer at the hands of this discrimination? How would a man be judged if he wore a skirt? Are not hulking male body builders seen as more manly and favorable than just a healthy physique?

Now say this aloud, three times: "If you can keep your head when all about you. . . ."

o—o—o—o—o—o—o—o—o—o—o—o—o—o—o

THE RETROSPECTIVE ESSAY:
"MAKING PROGRESS" IN A WRITING CLASS
by Steve Sutherland

> A Klee painting named "Angelus Novus" shows an angel looking as though he is about to move away from something he is fixedly contemplating. His eyes are staring, his mouth is open, his wings are spread. This is how one pictures the angel of history. His face is turned toward the past.
>
> – Walter Benjamin
> "Theses on the Philosophy of History, IX"

Halfway through the reading and writing course I teach at the University of Pittsburgh, and again at the end of it, I ask students to write a retrospective paper in which they look back upon the work they they've done in my class in order to "look for key moments and points of transition, for things that have changed and things that have remained the same" in their writing. These two assignments could be said to stand as markers of "progress" or "development" in the class, as moments when students are afforded the opportunity to think about how their writing has changed and about how they have changed as student readers and writers. In other words, the opportunity for an act of retrospection aims at enabling my General Writing class to "see" change by constructing narratives about what has happened in the course.

In a memo to graduate students teaching at Pitt, Jean Ferguson Carr offers the following rationale for this act of retrospection: "The final retrospective assignment should direct your students back to some significant rethinking of their practices and positions as readers and writers, as they have been influenced by this course, by your comments and classroom work, by their classmates, and by the texts they have read and the papers they have written. . . . This is a difficult assignment for your students, coming at a difficult time. It can be, however, a very important experience for them and a very telling assignment for you to evaluate." At first glance, the retrospective assignments might seem to offer tidy, historical evaluations of the course, mini-chronicles of what happened and failed to happen. Yet the histories that students write are "very telling" in other ways, since they are indeed functions of what Carr calls a "difficult time." This essay is about how teachers and students work within and against the constraints of that "difficult time." It's about the difficulty of writing in/about time.

Very often, the pedagogical gesture of asking students to write a mid-term and final retrospective essay reinforces their sense of the course as an unfolding history of progress, a story about a time of growth. For example, many of their retrospective narratives are structured by notion of causality ("This occurred, and it then caused that to happen") that allow students to see a chain of influence running through their successive papers.

The retrospective essays are almost always chronologically structured, so that successive moments of insight serve to reinforce a linear progression toward a conclusion in which the student frequently claims to have reached a kind of educational utopia. There is, I think, a sense in which the rhetorical demand of asking students to write these essays can often reinforce rather than challenge unproblematic accounts of history and of what it means to *become* educated. This is because the retrospective papers that my students write frequently participate in broader cultural narratives about change and progress.

For a moment, I'd like to problematize the popular notion of "course as narrative of progress" by entertaining a somewhat absurd notion of "course as Zeno's stadium." Zeno of Elea proposed the well-known "stadium paradox." Here is his scenario: If someone were to walk from one end of a stadium to another, it would be impossible to arrive at the other end. This is because the person would have to pass through an infinite number of points:" halfway, quarter-way, and so forth, *ad infinitum*. Since it is impossible to pass through an infinite number of points in a finite period of time, it would be impossible to reach the end of the stadium or even to get to a halfway point. So much for end of term and mid-term.

Since Zeno's account precludes any kind of change or movement, it seems necessary to refute his argument, not only because he is violating "common sense" in general but, more important, because his position calls into question some "common sense" notions about teaching. Plato finds a way out by positing two worlds: one of unchanging, ideal forms, and another of change and illusion. This is a familiar Platonic position, which insists that the world of change (of "becoming") is only a reflection of a more substantial, unchanging world of "being." The argument allows Plato to account for change while still preserving an essentialist notion of an unchanging reality. According to his model, change is merely something that appears to be the case, an illusion. This illusory world is, for Plato, precisely what education should not be asking students to look at. In the *Republic* he writes, "Education then is the art of . . . this turning around, the knowledge of how the soul can most easily and effectively be turned around" in order to apprehend permanence in the world of forms (171). When Plato's students are asked to "look back," they look away from change and toward permanence — that is, in the opposite direction to my students. In fact, the whole of the *Republic* might be understood as an attempt to "look at" a utopian model "laid up in heaven" (238). Plato's moment of turning and looking (his retrospective act) fails to see change. And, I'd like to argue, this particular way of looking has pedagogical and political consequences, since it is a predictable prerequisite for establishing the kind of republic Plato desires: one that is free of change and conflict.

Although it's clear that Plato's notion of change is substantially different from that of Zeno, both arguments manage to turn change into an illusion. This way of accounting for change is of considerable importance because it allows the narrative to construct utopian spaces (like Plato's *Republic*) that are free of contradiction. Utopian fiction, for example, frequently offers mystical or unreliable accounts of the historical changes that brought utopia into existence. A kind of forgetfulness often frames utopian narratives. Since utopias are almost always narrated retrospectively (e.g., More's *Utopia* or Bellamy's *Looking Backward*), one might say that an unwillingness to engage with history can all too easily produce utopia.

I want to argue that a similar construction of change is often at work in my reading/writing class, both in discussions and in student papers, and that this construction of change frequently allows students to imagine an educational model that is free of complication, unproblematic, and utopian. I'll focus first on class discussions and then on student essays. During the course of the semester, students (most are in their first year of study) read five selected texts from Bartholomae and Petrosky's *Ways of Reading*, an anthology of essays for student writers. Each week, they write a paper (about five pages in length) in response to an assigned question on a particular text. These weekly assignments are sequenced and interrelated, asking students to consider among other things, the ways in which they are enacting a particular "reading/rereading" of each text. Our class discussions center on sample student papers, which I select and distribute ahead of time. I do not choose the "best" or the "weakest" essays, neither models for imitation nor pitfalls to avoid. Instead, the samples are papers that I believe will lead the class into a productive discussion, perhaps papers that enact or raise issues that seem to crop up in many essays. I sometimes choose papers that might seem provocative, problematic, even absurdly Zenoesque. We then talk about these essays as a way of investigating student writing, and also as a way of thinking about how students are reading the assigned texts in the anthology. Two of these assigned pieces, Adrienne Rich's "When We Dead Awaken: Writing as Re-Vision" and Harriet Jacobs's "Incidents in the Life of a Slave Girl," regularly provoke conversations that can lead to important insight into the ways in which students discuss change.

Jacobs's text, an excerpted slave narrative written in order to further the abolitionist cause, is accompanied by an initial assignment question which asks students, "What is Jacobs doing in this text? What might her work as a writer have to do with her position (as a female slave) in relation to the world of her readers?" (p. 306). The second writing assignment asks students to "consider the ways she [Jacobs] works on her reader . . . and also the ways she works on her material," emphasizing that students "will need to reread the text as something constructed" (p. 307). In our class discussions, students usually see Jacobs's narrative not as a constructed account but rather as a kind of window into her life, one that allows her to "show" her story "just as it is." Students often use optical words (like "reveals") to describe Jacobs's work; they seldom use words like "selects," or "organizes." In this way, Jacobs's story is frequently seen as an accurate display of the truth, and as an autobiography that is *inevitable* in the sense that it is dictated solely by Jacob's real life rather than by her choices as a writer. What students frequently do not see is precisely what the question asks them to see, namely, that Jacobs is a writer at work, constructing a text, making decisions, making changes to her material. What seldom gets discussed is the fact that Jacobs's narrative is not identical to her life; neither is it propelled by her life in an automatic or deterministic manner.

Getting students to think about Jacobs's work as a writer might be done in various ways, but I think an effective method would probably entail managing a discussion about how Jacobs looks back on her life in a retrospective gesture that allows her to work with her material by selecting, emphasizing, ordering, or otherwise changing it. If we imagine Jacobs looking back, our account of her work can move beyond seeing only inevitability, and toward a recognition of how her narrative gets changed in the very act of writing it. Such a move can help students to acknowledge the critical choices that Jacobs makes. It's a move toward a nondeterministic/nonautomatic account of the text's production, toward seeing Jacobs as a writer who is both self-aware and aware of her choices. In this way, the absent moment, Jacobs's retrospective gesture in which changes are made, can be made present.

A similar discussion is often prompted by the two assignments on Adrienne Rich's essay, a piece about the changes she sees as she looks at a brief history of her poetry. This time, the first assignment asks students to choose a poem by Rich and to "conside[r] the poem as an act of 'renaming'" by asking, "What is transformed into what? and to what end? (p. 478). The second assignment (drawn from a previous edition) extends the first, asking students to "take three of the poems Rich offers as examples of change in her writing . . . and use them as a way of talking about revision." Both of these questions explicitly ask students to talk about "change" or "transformation." Nevertheless, the notion of change frequently disappears from our class discussions. Students are able to offer intelligent insight into the "meaning" of Rich's poetry, or passionate opinions on her homosexuality. However, they seldom talk about change. When they do, they describe an almost self-evident development in Rich's poetry. A common way of accounting for the changes they see is to imagine change that takes place *between* each poem, in a chronology that exists prior to Rich's actual writing of the essay. While this account is undoubtedly somewhat accurate, it fails to account for the revision that gets enacted by Rich's essay itself.

In order to problematize this particular construction of "change," I ask students to construct a narrative of what they think Rich actually does as a writer. They respond by saying that she writes a poem, notices that it is somehow insufficient, then writes another poem that tries to solve the problems of the earlier poem. Subsequently, Rich sees the second poem as insufficient, and she goes on to make up for its inadequacies in the third poem, and so forth. This narrative, although addressing the issue of change, locates change outside (prior to) Rich's act of writing her essay. It thus offers only one, chronologically based understanding of what our class might mean by "re-vision."

Adrienne Rich's piece reminds us that "re-vision" is an act of "looking back." I want to argue that this act, this retrospective moment, which so often disappears in our discussions of Jacobs, partially disappears in our discussions about Rich. Students frequently do not examine the absent moment in which Rich looks back on her work with a gaze that selects, connects, exaggerates, or otherwise changes her material in the very act of writing about change. My role in the discussions about Jacobs and Rich is to recuperate the moment of change, to try turning students' attention toward the retrospective gestures that could otherwise manage to disappear. In this way, I hope to provoke a conversation about how Rich and Jacobs *use* chronology, about how they construct histories, and to move beyond a discussion that views chronology only as a self-evident determinant of the texts we read.

The same might be said of the texts we write. Of course, many of the texts we read are essays written by students in the class. Our discussion of these essays is intended to get students to think about how their writing both enacts and produces a particular reading. To a large extent, then, our class is about how acts of reading and writing are connected.

When students sit down to write their retrospective assignments, they occupy what I have called the moment of constructing change, of looking backward, the same moment they learned to identify as readers. The two retrospectives ask students to "review the work you've done . . . and describe what you see. . . . You might look . . . at what stands as evidence of your efforts and achievements as a writer." As students respond to these questions, they confront rhetorical tasks similar to those undertaken by Rich and Jacobs. Students, too, have to look back on the past and construct a text that accounts for changes. They, too, are writing history; and they are rereading the readings they produced in their essays. This affords them the opportunity to enact some of what they have learned in our class discussions.

However, what frequently happens at these moments is that students again ignore what they did not initially see in our discussions of Rich and Jacobs, namely, that writers of history do not merely report, but also construct their narratives. When we talk about the retrospective papers, then, I try to get student writers to push against conventional accounts of change driven by narratives of inevitability. I remind them of the work we performed as readers of Jacobs and Rich. In short, I try to get my students to produce writing that enacts a critically self-conscious retrospection rather than utopian narratives that either banish change completely or effectively neutralize the possibility of writing a critical account of change.

Sometimes students write utopian accounts — papers that, in looking backward, turn away from change and toward closure, permanence, the end of history. At the end of my first semester teaching at Pitt, I received final retrospectives that constructed change in this way. The conclusion of Amy's paper is an appropriate example of what I've called utopian closure. She writes, "Now at the end of the term, I feel confident that I have completed the wishes of Bartholomae and Petrosky and have proved myself as an open-minded and honest writer. I see myself as a well-rounded reader with the intelligence of knowing that there are many other ways of reading, seeing, thinking, and writing." In Amy's account, the work of the course is completely over, the agenda fulfilled, the goals achieved. It's almost as if Amy's paper functions as a kind of testimony that bears witness; "I have proved myself."

This is how she describes her essay in her opening paragraph: "While I was gathering ideas for a retrospective paper I had a feeling that this paper could be considered as a confession. What I have done on the following pages was to confess to my professor what I feel I have accomplished in his class." The purpose of Amy's confession is, in part at least, to claim that she has "satisfied the desires of Bartholomae and Petrosky" in what she calls "an effort to achieve the praise of B[artholomae] + P[etrosky] and to have the satisfaction for myself." I want to point out that her paper is an astute reading of the pedagogical scene in which she finds herself. Having been asked to write about how her work has changed in the course, she reads the assignment as a request for testimony, a chance to prove to the teacher that she has performed all of the requirements. In this act of writing, though, the retrospective gesture glosses over contradictions and complexities. She does not, for example, "read against" what she sees as the "desires of Bartholomae and Petrosky," even though she describes herself as a student who is becoming a "strong and critical reader."

Rather than a precise demonstration of the changes she identifies, Amy's paper offers only a claim: "I have changed." Her essay draws on broader cultural narratives about education as an almost total transformation of the student. As such, it constructs a conversion narrative — not necessarily because Amy feels that she has converted to the course's agenda, but because she feels that this is what she is required to say.

Felicia and Damian also employ narratives of change that are relatively predictable and unproblematic. Their papers offer accounts of developmental progress that are as inevitable as organic growth. Felicia's retrospective is called "Stages," and it employs the following model as a way of talking about the changes she sees in her writing: "Just as humans go through these different stages, I strongly believe as a writer that I have encountered these stages but in a different manner. First, there is the baby stage. . . ." Felicia then goes on to talk about the "teenage stage" and the "young adult stage," comparing teenage rebelliousness with a kind of rebellion in her writing. She reinforces this developmental metaphor, but also adds a more sophisticated reading of it in her conclusion:

> One semester can't transform my way of think-
> ing. This can be compared to being raised; once
> your parents have told you to behave in a certain
> manner, if all of a sudden others tell you differ-
> ently, it will take you a while to adjust to what
> they tell you. I believe that I have adjusted dra-
> matically from the beginning of the semester, but I
> believe it will not stay.

While I admire both Felicia's fairly elaborate deployment of the "growing up" metaphor and her resistance to the utopian closure that operates in Amy's paper, I cannot help thinking that her account of change limits her ability to reflect critically on the work she has done in my class. Her narrative presents change as a matter of growing up, but she fails to problematize her metaphor by seeing its limitations or by acknowledging that the "stages" she relies upon are also socially constructed, culturally specific stages rather than phases that are chronologically inevitable. I think her metaphor disallows a critically useful construction of change because it locates change within the familiar, predictable, sequential framework of "growing up." For example, her metaphor prevents her from recognizing that she is at work in her retrospective, seeing developments or noting significant moments while she is engaged in the very act of looking backward.

Damian's paper also accounts for change, but he uses a similarly limiting metaphor, that of swimming. Looking back on his work, Damian writes, "I see this [his early work] as being shallow, but I had to start somewhere. After all, when one goes swimming at the beach, one starts off in the shallow water. It is not possible to start in the middle of everything." Perhaps Damian's swimming metaphor is suggested by the adjective "shallow," which he uses initially in a figurative sense and then employs literally in his description of wading into the water. I had hoped Damian's paper would enact an awareness of this particular move he makes as a writer, that it would trouble this metaphor of education as wading into water. It would be interesting, for example, to see a revision of Damian's paper in which he replaces the more progressive action of wading into the ocean with a less sequential metaphor like getting thrown in the deep end, or diving into water. It might certainly be argued that students begin their work in my class *in medias res:* the first text we read is Adrienne Rich's essay, which is not shallow by any means. How, then, might Damian account for change within less sequential narratives? This is the kind of question he does not pose.

My reading of retrospective essays like Damian's, Felicia's and Amy's led me to conclude that the work of recuperating the retrospective moment — making it more explicit — does not necessarily result in students' ability to construct powerful or critical accounts of change when they write. Strong student readers who learn to identify the kind of work undertaken by Rich and Jacobs do not automatically become more aware of the work they are performing when they write retrospectives themselves. I had hoped to see students move away from narratives of utopian closure or from unproblematic accounts of educational "progress" and change toward constructions of change as problematic, constructions that might allow them to think about their work of and their education in ways that are more critical, more self-aware.

In my second semester, I taught the same sequence of writing/reading assignments. This time I wanted to forestall utopian retrospectives by prompting my class to think about change and education from the beginning of the semester. My course description centered on a student's retrospective essay from the previous semester, which I asked the new students to read closely as a way of examining how a former student had accounted for my class and for the changes he and his work had undergone. I wanted them to see that change could be described in various ways, as something to be welcomed and also as something to be resisted.

At the end of that semester, I read the new set of retrospective essays with keen attention. All of them resisted utopian closure; all of them refused to engage in conversion narratives. Does this represent a success? I'm not sure if this change is because students now feel that they simply ought not to write such narratives, or because they are indeed able to see that such accounts do not allow for a complex assessment of what they've learned. Many of these papers still employ models of change as inevitable progress or growth. Laurie, for example, describes herself as "fifteen weeks old" at the end of a semester in my class. Her account echoes Felicia's paper; moreover, it assumes that a student entering my class is *tabula rasa*, or a newborn baby. I am troubled by this attitude, which strikes me as overly and uncritically forgetful.

As I come to the end of this my own retrospective paper, I feel perhaps the same as my students do: in need of utopian closure. How can I end with a story that might account for the ways in which my work works?

The most successful retrospective paper I received in the second semester was Steve's. What I admire most about his essay is that it troubles its own sense of accomplishment and questions the narrative of progress that it presents. It also problematizes and calls in question some of the pedagogical work I have described in this paper.

Steve begins his search for change in the following way: "I wondered how my writing might have improved . . . so a comparison between papers written before mid-term and later essays seemed to be a good way to see if anything had changed. I wasn't sure what to look for." Using the mid-term point as a marker, he constructs a careful discussion, which leads him to the conclusion that his earlier papers simply took for granted the kinds of implications that his words have. He explains: "In earlier essays I noticed using words . . . without any hint that they have many different contexts. I used them as easily as if I were talking to myself." He sees his later work as being more aware of the implications involved in using certain words. But then his retrospective takes an unusual turn, which I would like to quote at length:

> So there it is . . . I can now write about
> "writing." I once was lost but now I'm
> found . . . Halleluia, I've seen the light. All
> is fine with the world, right? Well, I'm not sure
> I'd go that far. I could just savor the important
> things I learned about writing, but I find myself
> with a sense of uncertainty about what happens
> next.
>
> I looked back at my writing, and as I said,
> my later essays said a lot more about the ways in
> which the texts were written. I felt my Wideman
> essays [the last in the sequence] were the best
> ones, but why then did I feel as I had once again
> missed something? Was I simply operating in the
> "General Writing frame of reference"?
>
> I looked again at my [John Edgar] Wideman pa-
> pers . . . the author's use of language, frame of
> reference, and other aspects that we discussed
> throughout the term are important for understanding
> him, but just how much consideration do they de-
> serve in the scope of the overall work and its
> moral implications in the "real" world? I made
> statements like "in Wideman, we have no such simple
> judgement," and "we have to face disturbing ques-
> tions." Earlier in the semester I would have made
> a judgment or dealt with those questions, not just
> pointed out that Wideman presents them to us with
> some technique. I guess that in the "General
> Writing frame" this is progress, but I'm not sure
> about the "responsibility frame." Maybe the ear-
> lier papers were the better ones. So, you see my
> dilemma? Here I am with a collection of texts [by
> Rich, Jacobs, Berger, Tompkins, and Wideman] about
> oppression, slavery, morality, and racial injustice,
> and I'm spending more time discussing the language
> of the author than I am the issues that he or she

has made it a point to write about. An increasing
amount of my time has been spent writing about
"writing." I'm just not sure this is progress. I
don't know what the proper balance between ethics
and semantics should be. Maybe that's what I
missed.

In Steve's account, a definition of "progress" is itself context-bound, not to be taken for granted. He locates his definition first in the "General Writing frame" and then in what he calls the "responsibility frame." For him, the former represents a gain, and the latter involves a very troubling loss — troubling because it questions the "proper balance between ethics and semantics." I find this formulation of change provocative and insightful, and its attendant critique of the educational process in my class presents an important challenge to much of what I have argued in this paper. Perhaps the course, in insisting on its own frame (what Steve calls "writing about writing" rather than writing about the "real" world), ends up "talking to itself"? I'm not sure. I know that I could respond to Steve's paper by asking him to challenge his division between "ethics and semantics" by examining, for example, how these two categories are intertwined. This might also produce a different reading of his distinction between the "General Writing frame" and the "responsibility frame." After all, knowing how words are put together — how they mean — is precisely what enables us to make the kind of moral judgment that Steve wishes to make.

Because retrospectives like Steve's are produced at the end of term, at that "difficult time" in which students are asked to reconstruct the fifteen-week time period of the course, they have a tendency to escape the kind of thoughtful revision that is so central to my reading/writing class. When I began my second year of teaching at Pitt, facing a new set of students, Steve, Amy, and the others were not there to respond to my comments and questions about their papers. We were unable to "go back" and rework what had been done. I think students know this, and I think their knowing it reinforces their desire to write "end of history" essays. My concern is to seek and imagine ways of turning this desire into a self-reflexive and critical account of history that brings a retrospective understanding back into the work of the course — making it present rather than invisible.

When I present my syllabus to the next reading/writing class I teach, I hope to direct the new group back to the "very telling" retrospectives of my former students. I would like these narratives to help situate our work on a continuum of constant and repeated retrospection, to build an awareness of a course history that is already well under way. What might begin to emerge is a more self-conscious understanding of the ways in which we (students and teachers) work within and against very powerful notions of what it means to make educational progress.

I may well use Steve's piece in my next course description. In this way, his project will continue, not as the utopian end of history or the fullness of time, but as an involvement in ongoing critical, educational work. As in the story of Walter Benjamin's "angel of history," there is no utopian space that is exempt from criticism and change, or from the often thwarted desire not only to look backward, but also to use retrospection in order to think critically about how "progress" gets made.

> "The angel would like to stay, awaken the dead, and make whole what has been smashed. But a storm is blowing from Paradise. . . . This storm irresistibly propels him into the future to which his back is turned, while the pile of debris before him grows skyward. This storm is what we call progress."

WORKS CITED

Bartholomae, David, and Anthony R. Petrosky. *Ways of Reading*, 3rd edition. Boston: Bedford-St. Martin's, 1993.

Benjamin, Walter. "Theses on the Philosophy of History, IX" in *Illuminations*. Ed. Hannah Arendt. Trans. Harry Zohn. New York: Shocken Books, 1969: 257–58.

Bloom, Damian. Retrospective Essay. Unpublished, University of Pittsburgh: 1990.

Carr, Jean Ferguson, Memo on Final Retrospective Assignment 11/23/1990, University of Pittsburgh.

Gray, Felicia. "Stages." Unpublished, University of Pittsburgh: 1990.

Nicotra, Amy. "Confessions." Unpublished, University of Pittsburgh: 1990.

Plato. *Republic*. Trans. G. M. A. Grube. Indianapolis: Hackett, 1974.

Rich, Adrienne. "When We Dead Awaken: Writing as Re-Vision" in *Ways of Reading*, 463–79.

Sheaffer, Steven. "Looking Backward, Seeing Ahead." Unpublished, University of Pittsburgh: 1991.

All student papers are used with permission of their authors, to whom I am grateful.

I would like to thank Jean Ferguson Carr and Barbara McCarthy, who provided the retrospective assignment that I have cited in this essay.

I am also grateful to Phil Smith, Joe Harris, Paul Kameen, Mariolina Salvatori, and Dave Bartholomae, who gave me valuable suggestions as I worked on this paper.

o—o—o—o—o—o—o—o—o—o—o—o—o—o—o

OPENING A CONVERSATION WITH THE TEXT
OR
"WHAT PART OF THE ASSIGNMENT SHOULD I WRITE ABOUT?"

by Kathleen A. Welsch

The question in my title was posed by one of my students after we had spent a class period closely reading and discussing one of the writing assignments in *Ways of Reading*. Although this student had been quite attentive and had dutifully taken notes during class, her frustration and exasperation at not having been told precisely what or how to write was reflected in her face and in the way she slammed her notebook closed at the end of class. She had come to class looking for answers and what she got instead was a discussion about rereading and working with the text in preparation for writing. This didn't correspond to her previous writing experiences. For her, reading and writing were two distinctly separate activities. She'd read the text already; she knew the story; the reading was done. What she wanted now was a precise definition of what she should write about: What were the important points in the text? What did I (the teacher) see as its value for students? What kind of essay did I expect her to produce? As students filed out of the classroom, she approached me in a final effort to ask, "What part of the assignment should I write about?" Because she had come to class expecting to hear an answer, she had neither seen how class work related to what she might do on her own nor heard that what she might write depended on how *she* read, what *she* noticed, why *she* was interested in this passage or image and not that one. Her final question asked for a connection to the ways of knowing and doing papers that she had come to rely on and that had worked for her in the past. In this case, however, these old ways blocked her from understanding class work and discussions, making use of the information she'd taken down in her notebook, and, ultimately, from engaging in the challenge of the assignment at hand.

This student's question, though simply stated, reveals a set of assumptions about reading and writing that many students and teachers bring to assignments like those in *Ways of Reading*. To begin with, my student wanted a clearly stated topic to *write* about, for that's what she had come to expect of a writing assignment. How reading fit into that she couldn't imagine. Her question asked me to clear a path through all the reading and to identify the topic so that she could get to work on writing her essay. Prior experience had led her to assume that an assignment defined her choices as a writer, that it possessed an authority to which she had to submit rather than being the starting point for her own work. Her readiness to tell back what an assignment asked for clashed with this new assignment that challenged her to write about her reading of a text. She didn't grasp how she could use the assignment for her own purposes: to return to the text, to open it, question it, respond to it, and then write about *that* interaction. It didn't occur to her that writing about her reading might entail looking at what she'd noticed and why, what she'd skimmed over because it seemed difficult, and what she had found out-right confusing or intriguing.

It didn't occur to her, because she assumed that this was the work of the assignment, not the writer. The assumptions about the roles of teachers, students, assignments, and texts embedded in her question worked to undermine her authority as a reader/writer. First, she imagined that the text presented a specific knowledge she needed to find; second, she expected the assignment to tell her what was important to find and write about; third, she assumed that I knew what it was she should focus on rather than her establishing that for herself. This last assumption frequently took the shape of the question, "What do you want?" as if I could tell a student what she would notice, connect with, find confusing, or feel compelled to write about.

Assignments in *Ways of Reading* imagine that writing is more than reporting what the text says, and that reading is more than finding a main point or getting the story. Students are challenged to write about their own acts of attention and making of meaning. This is no easy task, when one considers the level of complexity in each of the essays, or the possibility that one might notice something new or have a deeper understanding with each rereading. The complexity of the essays is reflected in the complexity of the assignments in this book, and attempting to simplify either assumes that an essay's complexities can be reduced to a single most important point or lesson — something to be "gotten" quickly. Students and teachers who assume assignments should provide a path to a pre-established meaning (or who have grown comfortable with such an arrangement) may be confused by the nature of assignments in this book. For this reason, learning to read the assignments (making meaning of them as one would make meaning of an essay) is just as important as reading the essays before one can write a response. As I've talked with students and teachers about the essays and assignments in this book, I've encouraged them to recognize and question their assumptions about what it means to read or write an essay, and to imagine alternatives to these old ways of knowing. My plan for the rest of this essay is to discuss some alternatives in relation to three assignments that challenge both students and teachers to imagine possibilities in essays rather than the right answer; to open a subject to the range of directions it might take rather than close it down with conclusions, the main point, or the lesson; to notice not only the complexity of each project but how one might read, write, and make meaning in one project in a way that leads to rereading, rewriting, and rethinking meaning in relation to another project. The assignments I've selected address the work of Harriet Jacobs and Alice Walker. They are based on Assignments for Writing and Making Connections in the book, but I have revised several questions for my course.

Assignments like the first Jacobs assignment for writing are particularly perplexing because they seem to say a lot about Jacobs's narrative and much less about what one should write. This particular Jacobs assignment opens with quotes by Jean Fagin Yellin, Susan Willis, and Houston Baker, is followed by a statement about "gendered subjects" and a brief discussion of the public discourse of slavery, moves on to distinguishing between a life and a narrative, and shifts to observing how Jacobs's text reflects the circumstances of her life. All this before any writing objective is suggested, and this, too, is complicated by parenthetical remarks. In response to this mass of information, inexperienced students (and teachers) tend to grasp the one part of the assignment they understand best as their focus and generally disregard the rest. This isn't surprising, since most students have plenty of experience establishing a clearly stated topic and presenting an organized explanation of it. What they have less experience in is pursuing the numerous possibilities a text might offer. They tend to note what they understand, organize it, and keep it under control rather than consider how the one part of the assignment they *do* understand relates to the parts they don't seem to have a handle on. They are less practiced in the art of questioning what confuses them in order to make meaning; more commonly, students assume they didn't read thoroughly enough or that the material is simply beyond their comprehension.

256

My students and I have addressed this particular Jacobs assignment by beginning at the end — identifying the type of rereading the writing project suggests — and then turning to the rest of the assignment as a way to address that rereading. The final paragraph in the assignment states:

> Write an essay in which you examine Jacobs's work as a writer. Consider the ways she works on her reader (a figure she both imagines and constructs) and also the ways she works on her material (a set of experiences, a language and the conventional ways of telling the story of one's life). Where is Jacobs in this text? What is her work? How do you know when you've found her? When you find her, have you found an "authentic voice"? A "gendered subject"?

In this assignment students are invited to write an essay in which they "examine Jacobs's work as a writer" by investigating how her text (chapters from *Incidents in the Life of a Slave Girl*) can be read "as something constructed." Since students have read Jacobs's text, they generally assume they know the material (the details of her narrative), and they generally assume that the narrative represents the "truth"; that is, that Jacobs doesn't deviate from or alter her experience as she writes it. To consider Jacobs's text as constructed, however, requires a different kind of reading, one in which the truth of a life is read through the truths of nineteenth-century social and literary conditions. An understanding of Jacobs's text and audience as constructed is crucial for a reader/writer who plans to reread Jacobs's narrative for the work she does as a writer. The reader needs to attend to *how* the story is told/constructed rather than being caught up in and carried along by the emotion and details Jacobs provides. The reader needs to ask: What does her text reveal about the decisions she makes as a writer with a purpose?

One way that my students and I begin talking about the kind of work one would have to do to reconsider Jacobs's story as something "constructed" is by re-examining the Houston Baker quote at the beginning of the reading from a variety of angles, since it provides a key to understanding Jacobs's text as something constructed. Baker writes:

> The voice of the unwritten self, once it is subjected to the linguistic codes, literary conventions, and audience expectations of a literate population, is perhaps never again the authentic voice of black American slavery. It is, rather, the voice of a self transformed by an autobiographical act into a sharer in the general public discourse about slavery.

The problem for many students lies in the fact that although they've read this quote, it remains an abstraction because they can't imagine how it might connect to Jacobs. So we discuss phrases that appear mystifying — "linguistic codes, literary conventions, and audience," "general public discourse" — and define them in terms of their own experience and understanding. We explore the meaning of the "unwritten self" by replacing the phrase with Harriet Jacobs's name and considering the differences between the unwritten and written Harriet Jacobs. When students have difficulty making this distinction, we shift to more personal terms by replacing the "unwritten self" with the word "student" so that they can consider what it means to them to be a written or unwritten self. For example, what linguistic codes, literary conventions, and audience expectations do they find themselves subjected to or restricted by when they go to write? We can take this question a step further by replacing the words "linguistic" and "literary" with academic codes and conventions and "audience" with teacher expectations. Such a discussion positions students to be more thoughtful about what it means to construct a text or about how what they write might be called a construction rather than a truth. We use the second paragraph following the opening quotes to establish an understanding of a "general public discourse" by exploring students' storehouses of general public discourse. The assignment explains that in Baker's formulation:

[Jacobs's] voice shares in the general public discourse about slavery and also in the general public discourse representing family, growing up, love, marriage, childbirth, the discourse representing "normal" life — that is, life outside of slavery. For a slave the self and its relations to others has a different public construction.

Students begin to investigate what it means to participate in a public discourse by considering how they, too, are sharers in it. What do they know about slavery, life outside slavery, literary expectations for a writer like Jacobs who wants to be published? If necessary, we shift to the more personal again as students consider the public discourse that describes the life of students in the university and the academic expectations they must meet to be successful. A discussion such as this allows them to see and understand their own participation in public discourses. It also allows them to begin imagining how Harriet Jacobs participated in the general public discourses of the nineteenth century as a writer, while at the same time being positioned outside those discourses for the person she was — an African-American, a slave, and a woman. We pursue this "inside but outside" conflict in Jacobs's narrative by mapping out on the blackboard the dichotomies identified in the third paragraph of the assignment.

The passages from Baker, Willis, and Yellin allow us to highlight the gap between a life and a narrative, between a person (Harriet Jacobs) and a person rendered on the page (Linda Brent), between the experience of slavery and the conventional ways of telling the story of a life, between experience and the ways experience is shaped by a writer, readers, and a culture.

As a group students compose four parallel lists on the board that identify the differences they see between a life and a narrative, Harriet Jacobs and Linda Brent, the experience of slavery and how one is expected to tell one's life story, a lived experience and the ways in which experience becomes shaped by forces outside one's life. By the time students have completed this work, they have created a context that they can complicate and explore further by considering how the Willis and Yellin quotes relate to what Baker writes.

Students have accomplished a great deal of work by this point, but that work has not yet included writing the assignment essay. Instead, they have focused on using the assignment to work closely with Jacobs's text, rereading and rethinking it from a number of critical perspectives. Students begin to see that her text is no longer only the story of a life; it is also the story of a writer's work. For readers to arrive at this distinction, they need to be willing to see the text as something constructed rather than only the flow of the writer's memory. And that requires working with Jacobs's text more than once. When I describe the variety of ways my students and I discuss a text like Jacobs's (as I did in the previous paragraphs), I want to make clear that we aren't just talking off the top of our heads from what we remember. Our books are open; we search the text for specific passages; we go home and read it again and come back to class the next day to continue our discussion by turning to what we notice today that we didn't notice yesterday. It is only after we have worked with the text in this way that we go back to the final paragraph of the assignment where the writing project is outlined. At this point I ask students to notice the verbs in the assignment; we talk about ways they have already begun to "examine," "consider," and "reread" Jacobs's text and her notion of audience as something constructed and how they might continue this work on their own. As students construct readings of Jacobs during class discussion, they model the type of work they'll need to do to construct individual readings as they write their essays. Through class work they also identify an array of possibilities for reading the text; this task, in turn, gives them the writer's responsibility of focusing, selecting, and developing what interests them most about Jacobs' work as a writer.

Reading Harriet Jacobs's work as a writer — exploring what it means for a writer to "construct" a text — positions students to move on to investigating the work of other writers who not only have different projects but who write in different contexts. Students are thus challenged to reconsider and complicate their understanding of a text as something constructed from still other critical directions. A sequence in which students move from Jacobs to Alice Walker invites a revision and complication of how they understand the choices a writer makes as she constructs a text. In the first writing assignment following Walker's essay "In Search of Our Mothers' Gardens (p. 616)," students are invited to write an essay in which they "discuss Walker's project as a creative endeavor, one in which she reconceives, or rewrites, texts from the past." Unlike the Jacobs assignment, there are even fewer directions here about what students should write in their essays. The question posed to them is simply: "What would you say . . . that Walker creates as she writes her essay?" Writing an essay that answers such a broad question entails some very specific reading; the second paragraph of the assignment offers a number of questions to begin investigating her project:

> How would you say that Walker puts that term, "contrary instincts," to use within her project? What does Walker's use of that term allow her to understand about the creative spirit of African-American women, including Phillis Wheatley and her own mother? And if you consider Walker's position as an African-American artist of today, what would you say the process of looking back at ancestral artists helped her to understand about herself?

Where students frequently encounter difficulties with such broadly stated assignments is when they focus on what to write rather than on constructing a reading through writing. Instead of using assignment questions to open a conversation with the text, some students shut down possibilities by writing essays that read like a checklist of the assignment's questions; that is, they devote one paragraph to answering each of the questions about Walker's project. Answering the questions, however, doesn't address the larger issue of what it is that Walker creates as she writes. Before students write about Walker's project, they first need to read her text closely (as they did with Jacobs) for what the project is, what influenced its construction, and how it works.

When we talk about Walker in class, we begin by examining her revision of Virginia Woolf's passage in which she defines her key phrase, "contrary instincts." We use a strategy from our work with Jacobs as we draw up parallel lists on the board to illustrate the dichotomy between these two constructions of contrary instincts and to highlight how it is that Walker is revising a text from the past. Students test their understanding of Walker's revision by drawing up another list (in class or for homework) of all the women Walker names in her essay in order to identify each woman's creative gift and how it was/might have been subjected to contrary instincts. These discussions do not move students through the set of questions in the assignment; they do, however, provide students with ways to begin formulating answers and discovering how the questions lead to an understanding of the project. And by examining the array of women that Walker brings together and how each contributes to her revision of contrary instincts, students begin to see a process of creation. As they construct their understanding of this process through their own close reading, students don't need to rely on the assignment's questions to structure their essays. Instead, they can turn to their own authority as readers as they write about how they understand Walker's creation of a project.

Both the Jacobs and the Walker assignments challenge students to develop as strong readers — readers who notice what they pay attention to as they read — who respond to and interact with a text rather than repeating it. As they read and reread these texts, students develop a method of analysis and a set of key terms for looking at and talking about a writer's project — whether it's the work of Jacobs, Walker, or the student herself. Another type of writing assignment in *Ways of Reading* invites students to participate in

259

a writer's project by extending it, either by connecting it to personal experience or by rereading one text through the frame of another. The first Making Connections assignment after the Jacobs piece calls for students to reread Jacobs through Walker's frame of contrary instincts and the creative spirit of African-American women. To do this work, students need to extend what they already understand about these two texts. Instead of seeing them as separate projects, students need to reimagine each of them as contributing to a larger project: in general, how writers construct a text and, more specifically, how these two African-American women construct texts within and against established discourses and traditions.

This assignment suggests that students "extend Walker's project by considering where and how Jacobs's work as a writer and artist would complement Walker's argument for the 'creative spirit' of African-American women in the face of oppressive conditions." To do this, students will need to return to Jacobs's text for another rereading, this time in light of Walker's frame. And likewise, they'll need to return to Walker's text, rereading for places where Jacobs's work as a writer and artist would complement Walker's argument. The work students have done with these two pieces in prior assignments provides them with a level of familiarity with content; it can also be used as a starting point for reentering the texts, for beginning a new conversation with them.

This last point is important. It would be very easy to reenter the texts and repeat what one has already seen and said about them before. For example, the second paragraph of the assignment suggests that students note the choices Jacobs makes as a writer. They are to attend to

> her use of language, her selection of incidents and details, her method of addressing an audience, the ways in which she negotiates a white literary tradition. Where for instance do you see her writing purposely negotiating a literary tradition that isn't hers? Who does she imagine as her audience? How does she use language differently for different purposes? Why?

Students have answered questions similar to these in their first essay on Jacobs. This set of questions, however, does not serve to reacquaint students with Jacobs's work but proposes that similar questions can be answered differently in relation to Walker's argument. In their first essay on Jacobs, students focused on her work on her terms; they read her text for how she constructs herself and her story in relation to traditions and public discourses that excluded her. The third paragraph in this new assignment asks them to extend this original reading by considering a new set of questions that incorporate Walker's terms:

> How would you say that the writerly choices Jacobs makes and enacts allow her to express a creativity that otherwise would have been stifled? What type of legacy does she create in her narrative to pass on to her descendants? And, as Walker writes in honor of her mother and Wheatley, what might Walker or you write in honor of Jacobs?

Answering these questions entails still more reading. This time, however, students reread Jacobs with an eye toward noticing what makes a particular writerly choice creative and how that creativity creates a legacy that Jacobs passes on to future generations. As they reread Walker, they need to attend to those places where her argument about creativity in the face of oppressive conditions relates to Jacobs's experience as a writer. The challenge of this assignment, then, lies in reseeing and rethinking both Jacobs's and Walker's work from new perspectives and in writing an essay that presents this revision.

One way that my students and I address this challenge is by identifying what we understand as the key terms or phrases in Walker's argument, for example, "contrary instincts," "creative spirit," "artist," "legacy," and "notion of song." We talk about why we chose them and how they help us understand Walker's project. We also use these terms to reread the quotes included in the first paragraph of the assignment.

> Of her mother, Walker writes: "Her face, as she prepares the Art that is her gift, is a legacy of respect she leaves to me, for all that illuminates and cherishes life. She has handed down respect for the possibilities — and the will to grasp them." And to the poet Phillis Wheatley she writes: "It is not so much what you sang, as that you kept alive, in so many of our ancestors, the *notion of song*."

Students consider how they understand the legacies created by Wheatley and Walker's mother — two women separated by time, living conditions, and legal status. From here students are prepared to shift to a discussion of how Jacobs, too, shares in and helps create this legacy out of a context and experience quite different from that of Wheatley and Walker's mother. It is when students have looked at all three of those women as possessing "creative spirits" and "contrary instincts," and as artists who have kept alive the "notion of song" and created a "legacy" that I invite students to consider what type of statement they would write in honor of Jacobs, as Walker has written in honor of Wheatley and her mother. I want students to try on Walker's way of thinking and working, to test her language in relation to Jacobs's creativity, to know where it works (or doesn't) and why, to consider how they would revise her project and why. In the end, I want my students to be responsible for constructing a reading in the essays they write rather than reporting what an author says.

My students and I devote a good deal of time to developing reading strategies for writing essays that present their understanding of a text. We read assignments closely for ways to enter the texts from different directions, work through confusions, understand complicated ideas, discover what they know, and make personal connections. One can't expect to just *do* these assignments — to go off and write a paper. It's important for both students and teachers to realize that one first needs to learn to read the assignments; they provide a guide or model of how one might go about rereading, interacting with, and responding to the essays in this book. They offer keys to opening conversations with texts, and it is these conversations that the reader writes about in response to the assignments.

Part V: Responding to Student Writing

o—o—o—o—o—o—o—o—o—o—o—o—o—o—o

WRITING ABOUT STUDENTS WRITING ABOUT MICHEL FOUCAULT'S "THE BODY OF THE CONDEMNED," AN ESSAY IN HONOR OF GOOD INTENTIONS, IMITATION, AND MALLEABILITY

by Anthony Petrosky

I

In the fall of 1991, my twenty-one Freshman Composition students began their semester by reading and writing about the first chapter, "The Body of the Condemned," from Michel Foucault's book, *Discipline and Punish*. Foucault's text was the first in a sequence of readings and writings designed to engage them in a semester long project on various notions of how the body, power, and knowledge might be thought of as related. Although my students began working with Foucault's text first, they returned to it many times — to reread and to write from it — in conjunction with other texts during the semester. "The Body of the Condemned" served as a frame, then, for all of the semester's work, and students continued to struggle with it even though they came to understand it better and differently as they read and wrote through it into other texts. After working with Foucault's first chapter, my class also read another chapter, "Panopticism," from *Discipline and Punish*. After that, we read "Workers' Revolt: The Great Cat Massacre of the Rue Saint-Severin" from Robert Darnton's book, *The Great Cat Massacre*, and from there we moved on to a chapter, "Male Bodies and the 'White Terror,' " from Klaus Theweleit's *Male Fantasies*. We ended the semester with Susan Willis's "Work(ing) Out" from her book, *A Primer for Daily Life*. My students wrote a total of fourteen essays over the course of the semester; roughly one-half of those were versions of assignments involving Foucault's first chapter.

In order to give you a sense of what my students' writing looked liked as they began their work with Foucault's text, I would like to present a range of first papers from that class. What follows are four first draft papers written in response to an Assignment for Writing for the Foucault text (a version of which appears on p. 202) asking students to write an essay in which they took this text as a problem to solve. What is it about? they were asked. What are its key or significant arguments? it's key tems? it's conclusions?

After my brief discussion of these four first draft papers, I'll present the first and second drafts in part II of this essay, of a paper written by Kate Cantrill, a student from the same class, and excerpts from a third paper that she wrote later in the semester when she was still using the Foucault text to interpret another text. I'll also present two drafts of another paper, in part III that Cantrill wrote late in the semester for you to think about and comment on so that you might try your hand at a discussion of her later work, given the agenda that I had set for the class. All of the papers except Cantrill's last two have my original marginal notes to the students on them. After you read these papers, you'll have a sense of what the beginning work from this class looked like, and you'll have a sense of the

262

difficulties students faced as they began to work with Foucault's text. Cantrill's revision should give you a feel for how she resaw the work of her first draft after two class discussions of four complete papers from other students in the class. I will comment more extensively on Cantrill's drafts and revisions in my remarks following her papers, but I'll only comment briefly on the other students' papers — they're here for you to get a feel for the way my students began to write about Foucault's text and to let you see the kinds of marginal comments I wrote to them. You should read Foucault's chapter (p. 178), of course, before reading the student papers that follow, or my comments on them won't make much sense.

As you read these papers, you should know, too, that my agenda for this class involved helping students work on beginnings and endings of their essays and their uses of sources, of other writers' language, in their papers. As you'll see, my marginal comments on their papers almost always refer to the ways they begin and end their papers. And, of course, my comments refer to the substance of their essays; in this case you'll see me critiquing their readings of passages from Foucault. In addition to my comments on the substance of their essays, you'll see that my comments begin to draw their attention to how they are using Foucault's language and to why they are using it as they are. My comments in many cases also touch on the students' need to proofread, although at the beginning of the semester I am more concerned with the intellectual "moves" that they make (that is, their identification and explanation of key arguments in Foucault's text, the way they understand and use his terms, and the way they connect Foucault's examples to what they make of his discussion at the end of the chapter on the relation of the body to power and knowledge).

Although at first glance it may seem that my agenda for these students was far-reaching and all over the place, I don't think that it was. I purposely chose to work with students' beginnings and endings and with how they used Foucault's language in their essays, because it seemed to me from my past experiences teaching freshman composition that students can use help with these three writerly moves. I thought, too, that by drawing students' attention to these three intellectual moves, I could also, in a reciprocal way, help them with the substance of their essays, particularly with how they identified, explained, and used Foucault's arguments on body, power, and knowledge relations. Getting students to proofread their writing is always a part of my agenda with these classes, and I'm not at all surprised when the first papers for the course are overrun with errors. But I've also learned from experience that for these students almost all such errors are accidental and the result of nonexistent or poor or sloppy proofreading. So, it seems to me that my agenda for this class was limited and focused. It is important, I think, to set an agenda so that students understand what they'll be working on and so that you can focus your comments on their writing.

As you read these papers, especially as you read Cantrill's various drafts of her essays and try to puzzle out how or why she made the changes that she did, it will help you to know that generally my classes proceed as discussions of students' work. At times I'll duplicate passages from their papers and at other times I'll use whole papers. Our discussions almost always begin with questions that I pose about the writing before us. For the discussions that come between the first drafts and the revisions of the papers here, I focus the class talk on the three intellectual "moves" that I mentioned earlier (i.e., their identification and explanation of key arguments in Foucault's text, the way they understand and use his terms, and the way they connect Foucault's examples to what they make of his discussion at the end of the chapter on the relation of the body to power and knowledge).

In the following papers, you'll notice that my students entered Foucault's text from a number of perspectives. Many of the students in my class saw Foucault's discussion of the changes in punishment in their own terms rather than in his, in the common, received terms, that is, of linear progress — things got better and more humane because the judicial system got better as people got smarter and more humane. A few students, like Cantrill, began to imagine Foucault's notion of change as a shift in the relations between the body, power, and knowledge; but their initial papers, including hers, as you'll see, are tangled and confusing. This doesn't mean that their work or the work required by texts such as Foucault's that present new ways of seeing old notions isn't worthwhile. It does mean, though, that students will likely try to work with such unusual texts and ideas from perspectives they already hold rather than from the new or unusual perspectives offered by the text. Foucault's chapter is a difficult text, and the two-way split in the way students approached their papers — that is, between those who saw Foucault's discussion in their own terms and those who struggled to make sense of his discussion in his terms — in my experience, typifies what happens when students work with texts that challenge the ways they are accustomed to seeing a subject. This outcome is especially likely when the subjects that they are reading and writing about are abstract ones like change, power, and knowledge. Most students, particularly after a quick rather than a careful, close reading, will see the new work in the common terms of their received language and ideas. Others will struggle to imagine the new work, but few will be able to shape coherent explanations of it on their first attempt. It's important for instructors and students to understand this to forestall conclusions about the students', the text's, or the assignment's failures. As you'll see, Cantrill's first paper is a good example of a student struggling with the new work of Foucault's chapter; but it takes two drafts, multiple rereadings of the text, and a number of class discussions for her even to begin to shape her understanding.

It's also important to realize that students will choose different points of departure into a text. In the paper (#1) that follows by Kelly Klutcher, for example, the writer stays close to Foucault's opening examples and misreads him from her third paragraph on, where she attempts to formulate the changes in judging and punishment that he discusses. She sees Foucault's notions in the common terms of a progressive, linear evolution of judging that has changed gradually over the centuries from harsh to humane. That is she sees Foucault's discussion of the change from torture in her own terms rather than in Foucault's. Now, she argues, in the twentieth century judges are more humane and punishment, likewise more mental than physical, is therefore more humane. Judith Freidl's paper (#2), on the other hand, begins with the rules that Foucault presents to describe the way his study proceeds and from there moves to an effective discussion of how he uses the term "soul." As good as that final discussion is, she doesn't try to connect Foucault's notions of the soul to the power that is in punishment and the knowledge that is, therefore, also created by punishment. Freidl finds an entry into Foucault's text that mostly manages to sidestep his notions of the interconnectedness of the body, power, and knowledge, but she does find a way in. Here are Klutcher's and Freidl's papers. Notice how differently they enter into Foucault's text and how differently they represent those of his arguments that they chose to write about.

#1

[handwritten margin note: This is a very general statement about torture. Why aren't you beginning right off with reference to Foucault's chapter?]

Kelly Klutcher

[handwritten note: This is a very big generalization. How do you know it is so? Where did time begin?]

Since the beginning of time man has been under a system of rules or guidelines. If these rules were broken some sort of discipline was given to maintain order. This punishment had to be severe enough so other members of society wouldn't want to commit any forbidden act. Cruel as it might have been, people abided by the rules and "hurt" those who disobeyed them. Soon these punishments developed into long, detailed processes with which the

264

"involved"? You mean evolved, but that's not right either. They are examples of torture.

accused was maimed or killed. For example, in some
societies, if a man stole a piece of bread his
hand was cut off or if he raped a women his genitals were mutilated. These brutal methods <u>eventu-
ally involved</u> into what Foucault calls "torture."

This is a well-written synopsis of penal workings in the 18th century a la Foucault.

At first, torture was used as public spectacle. But as time went on punishment occurred behind the walls of prisons. During the 1700s public
punishment was used to warn people that if they
committed such crimes this could happen to them.
The "visible intensity" itself would make anyone
think twice before breaking the law. Seeing a man
being pulled into different directions by horses
would not only discourage the crime itself but make
the witnesses fear the people in charge of the
justice system. <u>The judge and executioner were
thought of as some kind of gods, damning those who
defy them.</u>

your essay begins here. What comes before is like a Walt Disney time-trip. Too generalized.

However, as time passed and the legal system
changed, the role of judge and executioner also
changed. Deciding whether or not a man should be
put to death was now only one aspect of the law.
Judges had to decide if the accused should be put
into a mental hospital or rehabilitated or even set
free. I think modern judges have come down from
the "heavens" and their roles have changed into
problem solvers. <u>Now they try to help the person
rather than hurt him.</u> The court's law used to be
"guilty until proven innocent" and now it is "innocent until proven guilty."

This is your belief. The assignment asked you to only to address Foucault's ideas.

This isn't Foucault's reasoning. He says that it appears this way but it isn't so. Can you get closer to Foucault's analysis instead of your generalization here?

For the executioner, a tremendous burden was
lifted. In the past he was considered to be committing a crime that was equally as bad or close
to it. For example, he wore a black hood while
killing a man. He did this so the people could not
see his face. As Foucault says, it showed the
spectators "the frequency of crime, to make the
executioner resemble a criminal, the judges murder." Now, in most U.S. states there are more than
one executioner who kills a man. The shame and
guilt of killing a man is minimized because no one
knows which one executioner pulled the switch or
gave the lethal injection. Executions are less
painful and are private compared to the ones that
took place in the 1700s. The whole city doesn't
watch and only the warden, a priest, and doctor
are present besides the executioners.

How does shame fit into Foucault's argument for penal changes?

Therefore I feel that the word "torture" has
two meanings. One ~~with~~ which can be defined physically and the other mentally. In the early part of
history punishment was mainly physical. In more
modern times "torture" has become more mental than
physical, because in the past punishment was death
or near death. The main objects were the body and
pain. The only way to "pay" for your crime was
through severe bodily pain which most of the time
resulted in death. The longer the "physical confrontation" the better justice was served. The
whole town watched while lead was poured into a
criminal's open wounds. "Punishment had no doubt
been centered on 'torture' as a technique of pain."

In this time period, "torture" has a physical
and mental meaning. Not everyone is sentenced to
death. Some criminals have to stay in prison for
life, others have life at hard labor, and even
others are sentenced to solitary confinement. Out
of all of them, this is the worst because most
people go crazy before their time is up. Not being
able to communicate with other humans for months
affects the mind drastically. "The condemned man"
was no longer to be seen." In some parts of the
country a person who is caught watching an execution was also punished in some way. "The great
spectacle of physical punishment disappeared; the
tortured body was avoided and the theatrical representation of pain excluded from punishment." There
is almost no physical confrontation between the
accused and the executioner. Death by law is now
"less cruel, less painful, more kind and represents
more humanity." Punishment is now aimed at the
soul. The criminal had to struggle within himself
to find justice after the judge's ruling. Can he
live with himself after the act he committed? Many
people can't overcome their wrongdoings and commit
suicide or have mental breakdowns. Just because
they "repent" doesn't always mean they will survive
what lies behind the walls of the prison and their
minds.

[Handwritten margin annotations:]

Why "therefore"? This signals a conclusion logically related to what comes before.

Reread this sentence. Do you define torture physically? Both definitions are forms of the same way but refers to physical pain.

Go back to Foucault's text. He says it appears this way. But what does he say is, in the case about change?

Watch verb tenses.

This needs an anchor in time. When were these changes in effect?

This quotation hangs here. Can you connect it to what comes before and after it?

was

was

was

yes, but according to Foucault is it less cruel and so on?

How does Foucault term this mean? To mean. What does he "soul" here do with this change?

[Handwritten note at bottom:]

You do a pretty decent job of recounting the literal ways Foucault says punishment changed but you don't mess with the last two-thirds of the essay where he discusses why — in terms of power and knowledge — he hypothesizes the changes happened. That remains for you to do.

#2

Judith Freidl

In Chapter One of his book <u>Discipline and Pun-</u>
<u>ish</u>, Michel Foucault states that he intends to
write a history of the present scientific and legal
theory of the modern judicial system in the Western
countries (Europe and the U.S.). He sets himself
four general rules to follow in his study, para-
phrased below.

1. To regard punishment as a complex function
of society with good and bad aspects.

2. To see punishment as a "political tactic"
and its methods as "ways of exercising power."

3. To attempt to find a common derivation from
what Foucault calls the "technology of power" in
the evolution of the social sciences and modern
penal practice.

4. To find out if the joining of social science and legal practice is an effect of a metamor-
phosis in the way power and its methods relate to
"the body," i.e., the physical presence of the individual human.

Foucault begins with a graphic description of
the torture and execution of a man named Damiens
in 1757. He has committed a major crime and his
punishment is terrible. One theme that surfaces
over and over in the various accounts of the execution is the man's desire to be forgiven his sin
by God and by the priests attending him. He seems
to be resigned to his fate and even to see it as
the penance that will earn him the ultimate for-
giveness for his crime.

Contrast Damiens's hope with the stultifying
sameness of the daily round in the "House for
young prisoners," eighty years later. The young-
sters are being used as cheap labor, every moment
of their day regulated, warehoused without hope of
a break in the ongoing tedium. Damiens's bloody,
cruel death at least gave him a sense of hope for
his soul while killing his body, while the "Young
Prisoners'" bodies are being fed, clothed, and
housed while their souls are dying. To quote Foucault and Mably,

> The expiation that once rained down upon
> the body must be replaced by a punishment

from this point back to the beginning of your paper, you are retelling the general movement of the chap. Quite a lot of retelling and well done, but why is it here?

that acts in depth on the heart, the
thoughts, the will, the inclinations. Mably
formulated the principle once and for all.
"Punishment, if I may so put it, should
strike the soul rather than the body."
(Mably, 326)

your list of purposes takes care of what Foucault up to.

This great change in the focus of punishment
is the core of Foucault's chapter. The switch from
punishing the body to punishing the "soul" is the
cornerstone of the great complex of modern criminal
justice. Crimes are not seen as law given and law
broken, but as law given and law broken "because"
--with a whole new system of experts and circumstances and past deprivations to excuse the act.

I take it that this is, for you, significant in the chap.: but, why? How would you explain this use of "soul" as it is to this chap.

Foucault's use of the word "soul" is different
from the religious use of the word. Here, Foucault
is defining the "soul" as "the present correlative
of a certain technology of power over the body."
He says that this soul "is born . . . out of
methods of punishment, supervision and constraint."

you work your interpretation into Foucault's use of "soul" and you do well.

This soul, through the effects of knowledge and
power, is the ground for psychological concepts and
social and scientific theories, such as consciousness, subjectivity, personality, and humanism. It
is the result of power's mastery over the body and
is the "prison of the body." I interpret this to
mean that the power of society is the great mass
of convention and life experience and shared belief
that made up the concept that an individual has of
his social environment: his political system, his
upbringing, his view of himself as a member of the
society, his world view. The "soul" is indeed the
prison of the body in this interpretation, because
it decrees all of the body in this interpretation,
because it decrees all of the body's deeds. The
new punishment of the "soul," therefore, seems to
me to punish a person's attitudes and self-view as
much as his actions; the new power to punish the
"soul" is fused with the knowledge of modern humanity put together by the social sciences.

*You write well. You know how to use punctuation con-
ventions, and you paraphrase and retell well. Your interpretation
of Foucault's use of "soul," compared to a more conventional
use of the notion, is also well said. But, why are you doing
all of the retelling? Think of the whole of your essay and
its purposes: to say what you see Foucault is up to and to
identify key moments in the essay. You identify one key
moment but, even then, you haven't gone on to explain why
it's key. When you draft your essay, think about the weight
of what you're doing.*

Mark Blumer, whose paper you are about to read (#3), dances around the idea that punishment has changed over the past two hundred years in the first two paragraphs of his paper and then, in his third paragraph, makes the case that one of the reasons punishment has changed has to do with the observation that torture breeds torture. Blumer identifies a number of key passages from Foucault that he represents with quotations, but essentially he misreads Foucault, at least from the fourth paragraph of his paper on, when he claims that punishment has become more humane because, rather than torturing prisoners, it now takes away their freedoms. Foucault points to this surface change and argues that it's an illusion, that the body is still the focus of the power of the penal system, and that within the obvious surface changes there remain traces of torture. About one-half of my class didn't go beyond Foucault's discussion of these apparent but illusory changes in punishment in their first drafts for this assignment. Indeed, Foucault's position is easy to misread, especially if the readers work quickly rather than carefully and closely, expecting that the text will fall into place with what they already know or think they know about changes in punishment, and not rereading difficult, puzzling passages. Blumer closes his paper, then, by arguing for torture and the death penalty. Geoff Marton's paper (#4), which follows Blumer's, begins with a mini-lecture to his readers on the need to fully understand Foucault's essay and to see beyond his surface arguments into his deeper, more abstract thoughts. He moves quickly from this to his argument that Foucault is really commenting on human nature; and he uses his second and third paragraphs to develop an argument on the rehabilitation of prisoners. Although Marton refers to Foucault's text a number of times, he stays close to Foucault's observation that in fact there appear to have been dramatic changes in punishment over the last two hundred years; but he doesn't push beyond his grasp of Foucault's observations to comment on Foucault's use of them for his argument about the relation of the body, power, and knowledge. He ends with claims for unchanging human nature and a kind of aside to his readers to demonstrate that he knows authors like Foucault like to get us to think about these abstract things. Here, then, are Blumer's and Marton's papers.

#3

Mark Blumer

Much of what I, or any of us, know about torture and punishment is from television. We see Rambo getting cut with a hot knife so he will tell his captors what they want to hear. That is basically what most of us believe torture really is. That is until you read Foucault. He shows that torture was once the only way of dealing with crime and that if the crime was harsh, the punishment was even worse.

[handwritten left margin: Help. what does your second ¶ have to do with Foucault and your first ¶?]

[handwritten: I have a mixed reaction to your opening but mostly it compels me to read on.]

The United States is one of the few industrial nations that still has a death penalty for some of its convicted criminals. This is a far cry from the eighteenth century, as Foucault points out in the first chapter of <u>Discipline and Punish</u>, when almost every country had some sort of death penalty, usually by way of torture first. Today such public displays of torture that Foucault describes would be protested and definitely not allowed. [He asks the question of why could punishment go from one extreme to the other in less than two hundred years.]

[handwritten right margin: O.K. you discussed the text, but your first sent. once threw me off.]

[handwritten: Yes. This is the big Question he asks.]

I believe that one of the main reasons that punishment changed so much was that, as Foucault pointed out, "the public execution is now seen as a hearth in which violence bursts again into flame." When people saw that torture was a responsible way of dealing with things, the public then began to also use this violence to deal with problems. Punishment then became "the most hidden part of the penal process."

[handwritten left margin: what does Foucault argue for, to explain this question?]

[handwritten right margin: you lose me here with the last sentence. How can you explain why punishment—what kind?—because hidden?]

The new punishment for the convicted, instead of bodily harm, was a "system of constraints and privations, obligations and prohibitions." Now instead of pain and torture for the convicted, he now had to live in a cell 8' x 12' and have all of his rights to freedom taken away. Even the death penalty was changed. The worst punishment known to man also became humane, by letting the accused die but not feel any pain. Today executions still follow this process, "the disappearance of the spectacle and the elimination of pain."

Another point Foucault emphasizes is how the penal system has altered in the last two hundred years. The way crimes are judged has changed. Some

[handwritten bottom: what conclusions about change and change of power does Foucault draw from his assertion that punishment became hidden?]

270

what does Foucault say these changes mean in terms of changing power relations?

crimes have ceased to exist and others have lost some of their harshness. Also things that have been used to judge crimes have changed. Now it seems as though crimes are judged more from what was in one's mind more than what he actually did. Foucault points this out by saying how it is common for a judge to hear a psychiatrist's view of the criminal and what should be done with him. There is a bigger emphasis on how the criminal's mind works. And it seems as though the judge is there to decide if his mind needs time to heal or if it can be healed at all. *Up to here you recount the literal changes in the penal system, mostly through paraphrase handled well.*

you are repeating what you said earlier

The penal system has changed drastically over the last two hundred years. It was once that people would be tortured and killed every day. Now we have the death penalty but it is very rarely that we use it. Criminals were once judged on physicality of the crime but now are often let off because of their mental status. Foucault's point in the first chapter is how the punishment of crimes has gone from physical to mental. Punishment was once physical, as Foucault points out with the seventeenth-century torture at the beginning of the chapter, then the punishment became a suspension of rights and activities to try and change the criminal's mind. [I would like to see a reversal of this trend. I believe that if people could see what could happen to them if they are caught then maybe we could curb some of the crime in this country. My point is that we have the death penalty, so use it.]

This is a personal reaction—not called for by this assignment.

O.K., but what does this change say, according to Foucault, about changes in the power relations involving the state, the body, and knowledge?

you recount the literal changes in the penal system, as I said, mostly through well-handled paraphrase. you still have to address the difficult part of Foucault's essay where he explains the reasons for these changes, as he sees it, as the result of power and knowledge.
What, too, does the "soul," as Foucault defines the term, have to do with changes in the penal system?

you're setting yourself up for a fall.
You can identify key moments #4
while working to understand it.

Geoff Marton   This way, you can work on & with
the chap. to condense it.

why are y
lecturing n
on how to
read this
text?

If we are to decide what is important in
Foucault's essay, the first thing we must do is
fully understand it; not just read it, but fully
understand its meaning, on both the surface and
secondary levels. On the surface, Foucault simply
writes about punishment and how it has evolved; he
does this from many standpoints--that of the punished, that of the judge(s), and even that of him
who carries out the punishment. But surface meaning
is not our concern. I think Foucault has more than
just that in mind. He is trying to subtly comment
on human nature. Speaking of the changing of punishments, he suggests that this change could be
"the incidental effect of deeper changes. . ."[1]
By saying "deeper changes," he brings up the question of whether human nature itself is changing.

who is
"our"?

what leads
you to
believe he
is talking
about
human
nature &
not power or
society?

Great.
yes, cite
reference

Help! I'm
lost.

Foucault first focuses on the nature of the
punisher. By punisher I mean not only those who
carry out the punishment, but the judge as well.
Judges, he suggests, have become more personal in
their judgments, while those carrying out the punishment have become far more anonymous. At the same
time, those being punished also became more anonymous. In France, for example, executions by guillotine began being carried out quickly, quietly, and
unannounced, and eventually were not done in public. He suggests a reason for this anonymity: "It
is ugly to be punishable, but there is no glory in
punishing."[2] By saying this he makes the suggestion
that humans now tend toward hiding the imperfec-
tions of their kind rather than making a spectacle
of punishing those who are imperfect. By human nature, no one likes to admit faults, and even
though there was a change, any way punishment was
carried out, this tendency to eliminate flaws is
supported, whether that elimination is by denial or
by complete destruction of the problem; in this
case, by execution. Judges became less personal
first, with uniform sentences. These sentences were
more fair, however, and also much less gruesome;
the French, for example, instituted use of the
guillotine in order that all executions would be
quick and painless. This tendency away from personal judgments and subsequent punishments was on
the way to having almost totally personalized punishments. This was helped by an article (Foucault

what,
according to
the text, are
the results
of changes
in judging?
Foucault
doesn't
argue that
punishments
became
more
human.
What does
he argue?

He focuses
first on
punishment
I don't
recall
persona
judges
the begin

you kee
using
this ter
as if Fouc
does?, & a
these
were some
universal
sense of
agreement
or their isn't
Find anoth
term or qu
one.

Help! I'm
lost
again.
what
sentences?

where are you reading this
I can't find it anywhere.

Those
cited in the opening are uniformly gruesome.
fairness seems a complicated issue in
relation to those.

272

you're confusing terms here — "personal judgements" and "personalized punishments."

refers to it as article 64) which assumed mad
people were innocent, which I believe led to the
assumption that by human nature, all people are
good, and therefore can be treated rather than punished.

Punishment has always supported the human tendency to survive as a race. (Early on,) when punishment was gruesome and not hidden, it was thought
that this would make a would-be criminal think
again before committing a crime, and this was supposed to save the lives of would-be victims.
Today's punishments are less public, and tend toward rehabilitation rather than elimination. It is
thought that people are generally good, and that
this good can be brought back in most criminals.
Capital punishment still does exist, one might argue, but in today's society, it is, for the most
part, limited to those who are believed to be in-
curable. *→ All of what? the previous ¶?*

(All of this) leads us to the question of
whether or not human nature is actually changing,
but more importantly for this essay, whether Foucault believes human nature is changing. I firmly
believe that human nature is the same as it always
has been, and never will change; this is the whole
basis of the words "human nature." Foucault likes
to make his readers think about abstractions like
this, as do many other essayists. He makes us
think on a much deeper level than, say, a textbook
does, by raising questions about very deep topics
such as human nature. Foucault seems to agree with
my view about unchanging human nature, as the arguments in this essay suggest.

You sweep through hundreds of years here. For what purpose? How does this address the assignment?

what do you accomplish, in terms of the assignment, with these sentences.

Footnotes

1. <u>Discipline and Punish</u>, by Michel Foucault,
p. 8.

2. <u>Discipline and Punish</u>, by Michel Foucault,
p. 10.

You cite references and use quotations properly. You also begin to develop a thesis on change and human nature but in doing so you lose sight of the assignment — to identify and explain key moments in the essay. I've raised a number of questions about your overly generalized sweep through Foucault and your use of terms like "human nature." When you revise, focus on Foucault's discussion of how the penal system appears to have changed and how he thinks it actually changed. What are the changes in the power relations as punishment becomes hidden? And what does the "soul," as Foucault uses the term, have to do with the changes in punishment?

You can see from these first drafts that although students were working from a common assignment, they wrote in various directions, given the points of entry they defined for themselves with Foucault's text. Freidl, for example, touches on Foucault's guidelines for his project and his use of the term "soul," while Blumer and Marton replicate Foucault's observations on the apparent changes in punishment over two hundred years. None of them writes about Foucault's argument for the relation of the body, power, and knowledge. Their various points of entry into the assignment and the reading are not a sign of their failures or the assignment's, even though three of them misread the passage where Foucault claims that change in punishment was not a linear progression resulting from growth in intelligence and humane sensibilities even though it is commonly thought of as such. Like any other piece of writing students read, they respond to assignments differently, no matter how much trouble one goes through to limit their responses. And, I would argue, good assignments open up rather than shut down ways into texts for students, so that tightly locked assignments that insist on only one way of approaching a text usually put students and instructors into the not so useful position of arguing over whether students actually did the assignment — which is not to say that students should't be held accountable for doing the assignment. It is to say, though, that students will approach assignments from different directions that define, for them, ways into it. The first Assignment for Writing in *Ways of Reading* (p. 202) for the Foucault selection, for example, poses a number of questions that offer students ways into the reading. When students engage Foucault's text to make something of his ideas and his terms, then they are doing the assignment, and most likely they are not following the sentences and questions in the actual assignment to the letter. You can see that here in these examples of students' writing from my class. And I would say, too, that an assignment bears the responsibility to present students with a project, one defined well enough for them to understand what they are supposed to do and why they are being asked to do it. Assignments should also present students with some help; therefore, I usually ask two or three questions carefully focused on the project rather than, say, asking a shotgun array of questions that try to cover too much ground at once.

Besides getting a sense of the various ways students entered this assignment from these papers, you can also see my obsession in my comments with drawing students' attention to multiple levels of work in their writing. My students can handle various kinds of comments and, then, various kinds of work on their writing. For this particular class, as I've said, you can see my concerns over the beginnings and endings that they write, the substance of their essays, and their proofreading.

II

Now that you have had an opportunity to look at some typical first papers from my class, along with my comments on those papers, I'd like to present the following first draft of Kate Cantrill's paper. You'll see the same concerns being played out in my marginal comments. And you'll see Cantrill struggling to shape Foucault's thinking with her language. Her particular perspective on it, her particular way into his text, has to do with his notion that the concealment of punishment is power, and that punishment inflicts shame on both punished and punishers. Although she doesn't pull these and other thoughts together in this first paper, you can see the beginnings of the threads that she'll work into a more coherent statement for her second draft on Foucault's notion of the concealment of punishment and the relation of that concealment to the power and knowledge of the state.

[handwritten: quotation marks around → chapter, essay, story titles!] #1

"The Body of the Condemned"

Katherine Cantrill

[handwritten margin notes: your opening is an account of your day. Can your imagination in opening lines appropriate for an essay, a text that would engage your readers' attention regarding ideas?]

After a long day of little food, diet soda, and neverending classes, "The Body of the Condemned," by Michel Foucault, was not the easiest thing to stomach. His extremely graphic descriptions of tortures inflicted upon criminals in the eighteenth century left me feeling nauseous, yet strangely interested in what was about to follow. I have to admit that what followed bothered me just as much, but not in the same way. Instead of my stomach feeling abused, my mind felt it. Foucault seems to go off on tangents that are very hard to follow, as most tangents are, so keeping my mind focused on what he was saying became increasingly difficult. There were a few times when my interests were peaked, however, usually by a new idea or declarative statement.

[handwritten margin notes: your discussion of the punishers to dangle out of context of the whole chap. How could you in your writing so context it to the larger discussion project.]

"Punishment, then, will tend to become the most hidden part of the penal system." This statement seemed to begin an idea that would flow and develop throughout the course of this chapter. Foucault says that by the turn of the century being in the position to punish was no longer a glory. Those who punished, judges and executioners, were becoming more and more affected by the "shame inflicted on the victim. . . ." This infliction caused the people to "pity" the offenders, and turn the "legal violence of the executioner into shame." The justice tried to keep its distance from the execution itself because of this change in the attitudes of the people. As Foucault puts it plainly, "It is ugly to be punishable, but there is no glory in punishing." [handwritten: → This implies steps here, as if what you said in the ¶ before was the 1st step & this]

[handwritten right margin: How are 2nd & 3rd its connected?]

[handwritten: Foucault 2nd, not so, so transition doesn't work.]

[handwritten margin note: What does this mean to be an act against an instrument when I'm lost.]

The next important step [circled] according to Foucault in the handling of convicts was the punishment-body relation. He says that the body became an "instrument of intermediary" between the law and the convicted. Any action made toward the body, such as forced labor or imprisonment, is questioned to be an act against this instrument. This begins the discussion of where the body ends and the [sp] soul begins, in respect to the punishment it recieves. The question is then raised about whether or not it is ethical to not consider imprisonment, forced labor, and even deportation as corporal punishments.

[handwritten: How does Foucault mean "soul"? What's its connection to the body? to power?]

276

your opening sentence's "this" leads me to think that you're discussing imprisonment as corporal punishment,

(This) type of consideration for the convicted,

but you're whether or ~~not~~ it be for the sake of justice to

not at all stay clear of (shame) leads up to the more recent

lose you views on punishment. We now ask ourselves questions

completely about the responsibility the convicts hold for

when you their accused crimes. Was the crime a product of

subject of insanity, "instincts, unconscious, environment, he-

this it reditary?" Is the convicted person, "curable, or

becomes readjustable?" The questions pose new variations on

"shame." the punishment itself. Should mandatory institution-

alization be the sentence? Should a jail sentence

be given? Should there be any punishment at all?

Because the entire judicial system has become more

complex throughout the years, more and more people,

in varying positions and ranks, are responsible for

the lives and deaths of convicted criminals.

what specifically? Pages 5 to top of 7 retell in sweeping

(These) are some of the vital points made by *sentences*

what does this Foucault in his thought-provoking, and at times *the general*

kind of haphazard, piece of work. If broken down idea *movement of*

writing idea, this chapter would contain an amazing *Foucault's chap.*

address in of valuable points for such a condensed piece of

the work. If a thousand people summarized "The Body of

assignment the Condemned," I think there would be the same

number of different papers, each stressing varied,

but equally important points.

This is very much an exploratory first draft. You identify a key moment - in the 2nd ¶ - then you go on to retell some general moves of the essay, but you lose sight of the assignment completely. How can you get yourself to focus on the assignment? How can you discuss Foucault's claims for the relations among the body, power, and knowledge? You begin this in ¶3. How can you use that to begin again?

As you can see, my marginal comments to Cantrill raise questions about the beginning and ending of her essay. They call into question the purpose of her writing her introduction as a personal account of her reading, and they question the purpose of an ending that says, in effect, "there are a lot of valuable points in this essay, and even though all of us reading it undoubtedly found different ones, they're all good." As her paper demonstrates, beginnings and endings pose numerous problems for students. They are easily seduced by beginnings ranging from anecdotal accounts of how it felt to read a particular selection and to lockstep formulas that repeat sentences from the assignment. From early on in the semester my comments both raise questions about what students write for beginnings and endings and, of course, begin to reveal the kinds of beginnings and endings I value. After three or four assignments with my comments on them, it becomes pretty obvious to students that I value beginnings that start right off into the essay with no posturing or rhetoric and endings that leave me (and readers) with ideas to think about further instead of, for instance, restatements of already written sentences into a tidy, sum-it-up conclusion.

Before going on to say more about my responses to Cantrill's draft, I would like to digress for a few pages to discuss my expectations for my students' writing and the notion, which I share, that students learn a great deal about what to write and how essays should work from imitation. When my classes first meet, I hand out the syllabus and we spend two class sessions discussing writing. I bring in examples of past work by my former students, and we spend considerable time finding ways to say what we admire and don't admire about the examples before us. Lately, my initial focus in these discussions has been on the work that beginnings and endings of essays might accomplish; my repertoire of examples of students' work is fairly large and meant to demonstrate the plasticity and malleability of writing. It's also fair to say, however, that my students certainly see the possibilities and limits of what I value through these examples. I see these early class discussions as the beginnings of a semester-long conversation between me and my students, a conversation that will touch on numerous aspects of writing, not just beginnings and endings, and one that will require us to reveal what we value or think we should value in writing. My expectations certainly come into play during all of our discussions of writing, no matter how much work I do to turn the conversation over to my students, to get them to say what they value and why they value it. They always want to know what I think, and my job, as I see it, is to tell them, albeit in ways that honor variability and what I have referred to above as the plasticity and malleability of writing. So I speak always from examples that we can discuss in common. It's taken me years to learn a manner or style for doing this, and I'm pedantic when I wish I weren't. Still, the upper hand is always mine because I give the grade, and my students know that. So my expectations matter to them, and I think it's my responsibility both to reveal them in our discussions and to reflect on or explain them as best I can without being pedantic. Sure, my students will do what I tell them to, but they learn when they solve their own writing problems, not when I solve their problems for them.

Imitation is, I think, the most powerful way I learned to write. It's not that I spent time trying to write sentences or essays like George Orwell or Virginia Woolf, but I did spend considerable time reading and rereading writing I came to admire. And that writing made its way into my writing. It's certainly more an indirect, oblique process than it is a direct one, although the results or effects of it can be startling and immediate. I always catch myself, no matter what I'm writing — an essay, a poem, a letter — imitating and resaying others' words and sentences. After I read an essay, for example, that my friend and colleague David Bartholomae is working on, I write and speak in long sentences with multiple embeddings and qualification much as he does, especially if I admire and "get into" the work. After I read poems by Yehuda Amichai, I work to form sentences in poems with light and joy in them. And when I change the kind of writing I'm doing — say, going from writing an essay to writing poetry — I always read the kind of writing that I'm about to begin before I write, so that I can get back into that language. My reading of the kinds of text that I'll be writing is also a form of imitation.

I like to explain these things about imitation to my students during those early class meetings; and I think it's critically important that I let them see what I do about writing, especially if it strikes me as possibly valuable to them as writers. After all, most of them come to my classes with at least six years of poor, weak examples of writing to imitate — essays of almost all the same kind put before them year after year to imitate — and they're at a loss for alternatives. They usually aren't even aware of the imitation they have been doing. Cantrill, for instance, learned in high school to begin her essays "personally," as she called it, with comments on how she read the selection and how it affected her; and she began her first paper for my class exactly that way. She could have used any number of formulas, as Blumer and Marton do, for example, in their beginning paragraphs when they write the overgeneralized rhetoric of "us" and "we" that is commonly taught and put before students as an example of how to begin an essay. It's not so much that these are wrong or useless — although I would argue that they are "bad" writing — it's more that for students they're limiting when they're all that the students know; they don't give credence to the plasticity, the variability, and malleability of writing. They also allow students to believe that writing is simply posturing and repeating received voices and formulas. And if students don't read widely, it's likely that these voices and formulas are all they'll ever know. The formulas, one might argue, can be useful in situations where they're called for, like standardized essay examinations, but they mislead students as to both the purposes and range of writing.

I ask students to imitate the readings from the semester that they admire and to imitate as well the writings they admire from other students. (Later in this paper, you'll read an excerpt from Cantrill's paper on the Darnton essay, which she begins with an epigraph — imitating, I think, the way I wrote the assignments for the class.) At times, I create assignments that ask students to work in the spirit and with the methods of particular authors. And I am also aware that my students learn to imitate the kinds of questions I ask them and the kinds of comments that I make to them on their papers. My talk in class about their work and the texts we're reading serves just as well as examples that both reveal my expectations and offer them ways of talking and thinking to imitate. As their teacher, I enact particular, limited habits of writing and thinking. And my students, like my children, pick up the habits that they see enacted before them, especially when they see that I value those habits. This is a part of what it means to me to be a teacher (and, of course, a parent).

Now that I have digressed to the point where Cantrill's essay on the Foucault text seems like a moment in the distant past, let me once again shift subjects and draw you back to her first draft (which at this point you should probably reread) by saying that the substance of that paper — her attempts to discuss Foucault's notions of the relations among the body, power, and knowledge — begins, for me, with the second paragraph and moves through her next two paragraphs. She's working quickly, though, almost as if she's getting a feel for the language, using it to think rather than to present her thinking. She identifies the quotation on punishment being the hidden part of the penal system as a key moment, but she hasn't made the connection from hidden punishment to concealment to power. She quotes a number of Foucault's terms — the "instrument of intermediary" and the notions of "soul" and "shame," particularly as the punishers are shamed as well as those punished — and her remarks seem to be drawing her to make connections between the invisibility of punishment, the body as an instrument of intermediary, and the soul (although she doesn't explain Foucault's use of the term) and reasons for punishment. But her work on this first reading of Foucault's text is, nevertheless, terribly disjointed and almost incoherent, particularly as a statement of what Foucault's text is about. But this is where she began, and she's struggling.

So, finally, here's Cantrill's revision of that first draft. You should notice that even though her paper has problems of many sorts, she has done quite a good job, particularly in the first, second, and third paragraphs (even though this last one trails off into a tangle) of reformulating her original sentences on Foucault's notions of the power in the concealment of punishment in the penal system; and she's made dramatic changes to her beginning and ending. What has happened with Cantrill's second draft is typical, in my experience, of the way students gradually move into the ideas and space of a complex text like Foucault's through their writing and rereadings. In a sense, it's like watching a shape — here the shape of Cantrill's understanding — begin to form on a surface that is already marked by other learned and received shapes.

279

#2

"The Body of the Condemned"
Katherine Cantrill

[handwritten: Not the most exciting of beginnings.]

[handwritten: no. no. no. How do you signal and punctuate book titles?]

[handwritten: All the centuries? What centuries?]

Foulcault uses examples of governmental discipline through the centuries to illustrate his ideas on the relationships between the Body-the State-Power-Knowledge, in a chapter from his book, "Discipline and Punish." When comparing present times to the eighteenth century tortures, Foucault states that, "Punishment . . . will tend to become the most hidden part of the penal system" (9).

[handwritten: this leads to expect essay on the hidden aspect of the penal system before.]

[handwritten: who was distant? People watched, executioners, participated, judges, watched]

[handwritten: you build a visible and effective argument for power through concealing good. Church writing.]

Public tortures of the eighteenth century seemed to portray an incredible distance between the punishers, the State, and the people, the Body. It seems only natural the the State must have had an incredible amount of Power over the Body to be able to enforce their rules with such a gruesome spectical as public torture. But as Foucault shows in his piece, "The Body of the Condemned," the State of today might possess more Power over the Body, although public tortures would never be tolerated. For instance, despite the oppressive nature of the tortures, the State nevertheless was directly involving itself with the welfare and punishment of the Body. As judicial time continues, the State seems to be distancing itself from the act of punishment more and more. This separation between the Body and the State shows an increase of power from the one to the other, in that order.

[handwritten: when you convey a word to special mea like when you mean body be the bad society? A the word in quotation]

[handwritten: Help me see what you mean by the interesting from one to u one in u order]

[handwritten: Do you mean "Body in to be the bad politic? Are you playing with the book w/ the physical the body politic is the word?]

Because the Body does not witness punishments as it has in the past, it is left uninformed, and therefore powerless. This helplessness of the Body only increases the power that is enforced po it by the State. The State has used the opinions and reactions of the Body to make them look better. An example of this is the very fact that tortures do not occur today. To maintain and even gain power over the Body, the State must reform their tactics to the approval of the Body. "It is ugly to be punishable, but there is no glory in punishing" (10). The State has realized this fact, and has hidden punishment as much as it can in order to lose respect for the Body. Actions such as this prove the fact that even in the most oppressive of nations, the State needs the Body to possess any Power.

[handwritten: writing is getting cl here afte the argu is alrea establi]

[handwritten: not?]

[handwritten: you're beginning to define the relation of "hidden" punishment to the state's power. Good.]

[handwritten: This quotation doesn't connect very well to the sentence before it. It seems disjointed.]

Is this the power Foucault discusses?

...s seems to be it
n opinion as it
...esn't
...ne from
...rcault

   Power is relative. If you are armed with fifteen lethal weapons, and there is no one around to threaten them with, then you are powerless. Therefore, essentially, the State was originally placed in Power by the Body, and has used this opportunity to possess Knowledge over the Body. "We should admit . . . that power produces knowledge (and not simply by encouraging it because it serves power, or by applying it because it is useful)" (26). For example, the Body now has no say in what is considered knowledgeable. The State has achieved Power over the Body and now what is knowledgeable to the State is knowledgeable to the Body, which only enforces the hold that the State has over the Body.
   Foucault brings up these points to prove his argument on the ethical and effective components of disciplines that are used today. A shared paper in class by an anonymous author seems to have stated Foucault's ideas clearly. "It is not the severity or the brutality of the punishment which is to be feared, it is the inevitability of the punishment." This shows that the electric chair, solitude, deprivation of pleasure through jailing, and other modern methods of punishment, are just as oppressive as the tortures of three centuries ago. Foucault states that recent prison revolts are extremely representative of the tortures still inflicted upon the condemned. Foucault states that the issue of the revolts is not, "whether the prison environment was too harsh or too aseptic, too primitive or too efficient, but its very materiality as an instrument and vector of power" (30). He goes on to say that the very idea of anyone having power, or control, over one's soul causes anguish enough to provoke revolts and other forms of rebellion. "They were revolts against an entire state of physical misery that is over a century old" (30).

p! But
at is
knowledge
about?

When? (over "now")

What points? you need to say what or else em lost.

you
an to say
ese
deas
um-up
caults
deas?
what?

his is a
ood ques-
use here
ut it does
ers. you
eed to
make the
use for
what it
might
help you
or readers
understand

I don't see the "share-fire" relationship here.

you are building a logical claim - the state has power over "the body" & therefore controls what "the body knows," but it's so abstract without a discussion of what you mean by Knowledge.

Do you need to say these ideas sum-up Foucault's ideas? Or what?

Foucault's term "soul" is not the usual, common sense of it. How can you signal this use of the term as different from the common use of it?

This is your best essay yet this semester. Your writing is focused & your major arguments are visible. You need to work on using quotation &, in particular, how to introduce them & connect them to sentences before them. You must proofread more closely, too. You have too many spelling errors, too many accidental, sloppy errors. Did your essay line up to the expectations that it set in your 2nd sentence of your 1st ¶?

I chose Cantrill's two drafts for my discussion because I admire the way she demonstrates her evolving understanding of a number of Foucault's interrelated ideas. She has found a way into understanding Foucault's text that has to do with a quotation ("Punishment, then, will tend to become the most hidden part of the penal system") that she identifies as key in her first draft. Her second draft takes the notion of concealment in punishment and develops it for the better part of her first three paragraphs. She concludes that "Because the Body does not witness punishments as it has in the past, it is left uninformed, and therefore powerless." She connects power to knowledge in these first three paragraphs by focusing on the shift in the visibility of punishment. The body — the body politic, that is — no longer sees the punishment; consequently, it's not knowledgeable and is, therefore, powerless. The power, then, has been concentrated in the state, which administers and, therefore, knows punishment. Cantrill, I think, has unraveled a difficult and subtle piece of Foucault's writing — a quite sophisticated notion of how the concealment of knowledge affects the relation between power and the body — and rewoven it in her own language. She doesn't, either, try to resay or restate Foucault's sentences or paragraphs. She's visibly working his notions into her language with attention to his terms.

At the end of the second paragraph and throughout the third paragraph of this second draft, she's struggling again. I see her at the end of her second paragraph trying to connect another quotation ("It is ugly to be punishable, but there is no glory in punishing") to her sentences on power through concealment. It seems that she's working toward saying that the state has had to hide punishments from the body politic because the state needs the respect of the body politic to maintain power and the ugliness of punishment was causing the state to lose that respect, and, therefore, its power. This reading is, as I see it, true to Foucault's text, but it's important to realize that it's not a complete reading, and it would have been unreasonable for me (or Cantrill) to expect a complete or summary reading, even if such things are possible. Cantrill misses a lot in the text, but with her second draft she does now have a way to begin to discuss a number of the text's related issues. Her revision is admirable, I think, because she used her first draft, my comments, and our class discussions to continue her writing to make sense of Foucault's line of thought on the power and knowledge that comes with the concealment of punishment. She carved out a piece of Foucault's project for her work, and her shaping of that work is quite visible from her first to second draft.

Cantrill's third paragraph begins to tangle again, especially about midway through, and her analogy of power as a person armed with lethal weapons isn't explained well enough for me to see if it works to represent the social power she just wrote about. Problems of ambiguity make it difficult to see how she's using the quotation in the second-last sentence of that paragraph with the example that follows it and ends the paragraph. Her last paragraph is interesting, though, for the tensions it carries. At first, with the example of the sentence from a classmate's paper, she tries to wrap up Foucault's argument, and she says that this anonymous author from the class "seems to have stated Foucault's ideas clearly." My marginal comment at this point was meant to draw her attention to what she's doing, because I didn't know why all of a sudden she felt compelled to sum up Foucault's ideas. I wanted her at least to see that she was doing this. Perhaps she does it because she's learned that this is how essays should end, by wrapping up and shutting down the discussion, or perhaps she makes this move because she's so wrapped up in her line of thought into Foucault's text that she's left thinking it is *the* line of thought. It's difficult to say, and maybe it's both of these tensions working together, but she doesn't stay with the wrapup very long. Her sentences, from the moment when she writes, "This shows that the electric chair . . ." down through the end of the paper, go back to her original discussion in the beginning of the paper and echo pieces of paragraphs from her first draft.

Punishment, she says, has concealed itself, but it's just as oppressive as torture. This misery, she concludes (from Foucault's sentences on revolt and rebellion in prisons) has to do with "the very idea of anyone having power, or control, over one's soul." My comments in the margin at this point raised the question of what she meant by "soul," because Foucault uses the term to represent that which is produced in the body by punishment, supervision, training, and correction. He doesn't use the term in the usual Christian sense as that which is created by God. Since Cantrill doesn't explain her use of the term in her sentence, and since it's a pivotal term in Foucault's text (and in her closing remarks), I drew her attention to her use of it.

To give you a sense of how Cantrill continued to work with Foucault's text as she read other texts during the semester, I'd like to present now the first two paragraphs of her first draft of her fourth paper. She wrote this essay in response to an assignment that asked her to read Robert Darnton's essay on "The Great Cat Massacre of the Rue Saint-Severin" as Foucault might, as an example of how the body, power, and knowledge might be related. (In the essay workers massacred the owners' cats, Darnton argues, in a symbolic rebellion that took advantge of cultural fears and beliefs about cats and what they represented.) As you read these paragraphs, you should notice how she's transformed Foucault's discussion of the body, power, and knowledge into an equation. She picked this up from one of the students in class who began to think of Foucault's argument as an equation. She also picked up the habit of beginning her papers with an epigraph, and she used this approach for the next three papers she wrote for the class. It happened that one day a student commented on my assignments beginning with epigraphs, and when I turned the comment back to the class as a question (Why would I begin with an epigraph?), we had a good discussion of what this device allows one to do. Cantrill, as she commented in class, was taken with the notion that an epigraph can place an essay in a tradition, in a space occupied by other texts by implication. As you can see from my marginal comments, I thought she did a very good job of representing the cat massacre as another instance of Foucault's equation, but I didn't comment on the usefulness of reducing Foucault to an equation, although I had many reservations about this reductive move when it happened in the class discussion and then began to appear in students' papers. Now, with hindsight, I think that we should have discussed the implications of reducing complex ideas to simple equations.

Here, then, are the first two paragraphs of Cantrill's first draft of the fourth assignment, which asked her to read "Workers' Revolt: The Great Cat Massacre of the Rue Saint-Severin" by Robert Darnton as a case for trying out and testing Foucault's argument concerning how the body, power, and knowledge might be related.

> In a declining state of society--increasing misery of the work; in an advancing state--misery with complications; and in a fully developed state-- static misery.
>
> > -Karl Marx,
> > *Economic and Philosophical Ms. of 1844*, p. 68

> According to Marx, the worker suffers regardless of the conditions of the state. The state oppresses the worker whether its economy is declining, rising, or maintining its stature. Such oppression can often cause rebellions and uprisings by the workers, for they feel resentment toward their dominating bourgeois, and in the instance

discussed in the "Workers' Revolt: The Great Cat Massacre of the Rue Saint-Severin," by Robert Darnton, they "resolve that they will not be the only ones to suffer" (Darnton, 102). This resolution seems to be the provoking factor in the massacre of cats in Paris in the eighteenth century.

When related to Michel Foucault's equation of the Body-State-Power-Knowledge, The body can represent all who are oppressed: the workers by the bourgeois, and the cats by the workers. The state can be those oppressors: the bourgeois and the workers. There are exchanges of power in this equation that can be attributed to the dependency that the cats have on the bourgeois, that the workers have on the bourgeois, and finally the dependency that the bourgeois have on the labor of the workers. The knowledge is the awareness of this dependency, which allows for oppressions to occur. For instance, the bourgeois are very aware of the dependency that the workers have on them; therefore they are free to cut their wages, increase their hours, and treat them in a condescending manner, without fear of severe rebellion. In the instance of the dependency of the bourgeois upon the worker, there is not a great deal of knowledge of this dependency, therefore there is not a great deal of oppression from the direction of the worker. There is just enough knowledge of this dependency for the workers to "stage strikes, and sometimes force up wages," yet they still remained "subordinate to the bourgeois" (101).

Even with the problems posed by her attempts to reduce Foucault's ideas to an equation, I admire the way Cantrill has come to understand Foucault's use of knowledge in the relationship of power and the body, and the way she uses her understanding to represent the relations between the employers and workers. She presents knowledge and power as being intertwined — the knowledge that the workers are dependent gives the bourgeois power over the workers, but the workers' knowledge of that dependency also allows the workers a certain power — the power to strike, to resist. Her writing in these paragraphs is more focused than it is in the first two drafts of the papers on Foucault's text. I think this focus speaks to her changing sense of herself as a reader who is capable of writing about difficult texts. From her earlier work with the Foucault text, she now has a point of departure derived from Foucault's text that she can use to read the Darnton essay.

III

The next examples of Cantrill's work for the semester are the first and second drafts of her eighth paper written for an assignment on Klaus Theweleit's "Male Bodies and the 'White Terror.' " The first draft of this assignment asked students to identify two key moments in the essay that they could use to represent Theweleit's claim that the German military machine transformed the sexual desires of young boy recruits into killing desires.

Once students did this, they were asked, in the assignment for the second draft, to place their work with the Theweleit selection into a larger context by drawing on the other readings from the semester. I wanted them to try their hands at theorizing, to see what kinds of patterns or threads they might find across these various texts, given their past work with the notions of how power, knowledge, and the body might be related. The second assignment also asked students to write for people who had read the Theweleit selection (p. 525), so you'll want to do that in order to understand what Cantrill is working with.

I'm not going to comment on these final examples from Cantrill's work, nor am I going to provide the marginal comments that I made on her paragraphs. So, in a sense, she gets the final word. But let me suggest that you use these final examples of Cantrill's work as points of departure, as further examples of her writing that you can discuss and comment on, given the agenda that I enacted for her and her class. You might see these papers, then, as an occasion to play, in a Derridian sense, with my agenda, her writing, and your own critical reading of both the agenda and her work. If you think of these two papers of hers as an extension of the project that I began with this essay, then this is an invitation to continue that project. First, more directly, it's an invitation to continue the discussion of Cantrill's work as represented by these two papers. But it's also an invitation to critique my work, that is, to critique my agenda for her and for others from this class and my comments to her and the others.

If you began with the first part of this project, how would you describe changes in her writing from all of the drafts that you've read to these two papers of hers? How would you characterize the beginning of these essays in comparison to the beginnings of her other essays? the endings? How would you describe, in contrast to her other papers, the ways she uses and explains key passages from the texts she's working with in both these drafts? What do you notice about her use of others' language? What, too, would you say are her continuing problems? her new ones? And, finally, what comments would you write or give to Cantrill on both of these essays?

Now, in the spirit of the second part of this project, how, from my comments to these students, would you describe my notions of "good" writing? the writerly moves that I value? What does my agenda, including my comments, allow me to do with students' writing? What does it prevent me from doing? How would you revise my agenda? What, specifically, would you choose to draw students attention to? How, and for what reasons? What, then, does your agenda reveal about your notions of "good" writing? the writerly moves that you value?

#1

"The Nazi Time Bomb"

Katherine Cantrill

The Pygmalion-like story of the making of the Nazi soldier, which is discussed in Klaus Theweleit's "Male Bodies and the 'White Terror,'" illustrates the sculpting of the young German boy into the ultimate soldier to suit the needs of his superiors. The tension created through this transformation of boys into soldiers was manipulated until it made the German army, and every soldier in it, an extremely dangerous time bomb.

First, the young men were stripped and carved into the most basic form of life--flesh and bones-- and then reconstructed, by way of demented discipline, into a mechanical killing machine, seemingly void of human emotions, feelings, and desires. The only sense of self that these soldiers possessed was their personal barriers, limits, or frontiers-- which Theweleit describes as their armor--and using the analysis of ego by Freud, this armor had become their ego. Through torturous physical training, these men learned of their limits and forever strove to defeat them. This striving to break through this armor caused a great deal of tension in the individual German soldier. These limits are very significant, according to Theweleit, but first it is important to show how these new soldiers were "capable of seamless fusion into larger formations with armorlike peripheries" (p. 164).

This "seamless fusion" into a greater mechanical body is where the power of the German army comes from. These men came together--in their absolute strictest mode--to create the ultimate battle machine. They marched as one, with each limb moving in sync--with each thundering step, the soldiers became more a part of their fellow marchers than they were of themselves. For instance, the stiff legs, when extended, became more closely associated with the legs stepping with them than with their own attached torso. These soldiers are no longer individuals when they march like this, they are now each a vital part of a machine so powerful that it creates its boundaries on three sides, while its only restriction is Germany--the fourth boundary-- which is attached to an "umbilical cord that feeds it with bread, spare parts, and munitions" (p. 155).

Theweleit presents the many phallic symbols incorporated into this machine: stiff limbs, pulsing pressure and tension, and the forward, penetrating movements of the machine. These protruding symbols seem to be a result of the smothering of human feelings during this suppressing fusion process. Sexual desire, a very basic human instinct, and an unaccepted one in the Nazi army, is expressed in these stiff, forceful, actions and movements, and creates an almost unbearable amount of pulsing tension within each individual soldier, and therefore within the entire machine. This machine, as with each soldier, is now a highly dangerous and determined bomb, whose only outlet for a much-needed discharge can be found in the instance of war. Only then can both the boundaries of the machine in totality, and of each individual soldier, be broken.

This brings us back to the issue of the boundaries created by the individual soldier. During training, according to Theweleit, there is really only one instance where the soldier can partially break through this boundary and experience a partial release. This is during a fainting spell--a blackout. In a system where weakness is never tolerated, oddly enough, blackouts are not only accepted, but praised. To the commander it means that the soldier, although probably very aware of his physical limitations, pushed himself beyond to the point of collapse. Theweleit compares blackouts to orgasm. In both, the man reaches a climax of tension, pushes past it, releasing the tension, then collapses in fatigue. For the soldier this is a period of rest, and it also unites him with "the person for whose sake he makes the physical effort" (p. 167). Namely, his commander, who, according to Theweleit, is penetrating in his stare and unceasing commands.

This fainting action seems to be one of the only human reactions permitted in the training period when, strangely enough, once in battle we see how the training is all in preparation for the absolute confrontation with life. The soldiers fight, and describe the fight in a process of conceiving, birthing, and dying. For instance, the heaving of the slowly submitting earth--the way it "swelled and breathed" (p. 176) toward the ever determined soldier can be seen as intercourse (appropriately enough--"Mother Earth," "The Source,") while the rush of blood, tears, screams, and other forms of release, can be seen as the ejaculation that leads to the birth of life--"Explosion is likened to birth" (p. 176). This extremely powerful and violent instance seems to make the entire battlefield "come to life" (p. 178). Then the soldier meets his enemy, sees that he is a human, something tangible that can feel the pain of the soldier's pent-up fury. The soldier can now make the greatest attempt ever to free himself of the crippling tension that has been building up since training--

blood must flow. In a Fascist society such as the Nazi one, blood is "the only thing permitted to flow from within him" (the soldier) (p. 185), it is the pulsating factor within him--what drives him to kill is his need to release his tension by the flow of blood, no other accepted form of release is as effective.

Tension seems to be the guiding factor in the Nazi army--gearing it up for a battle where the army as a whole, and the individual soldier, may finally experience the most extreme release possible. So much has been stifled in the once young German boy, that I find it hard to believe that a total release is ever possible, save for the death of the soldier himself. Although Theweleit discusses in detail the sexual innuendos of the Nazi soldier, I feel that they are not the most vital factors in the army, but instead the results of the stifled human in each of the soldiers. I think he says it best when he states that "erection itself may simply be an unsuccessful attempt by the genitals laden with unpleasurable qualities to separate themselves from the rest of the bod" (p. 196). In this sense we can attribute the entire Nazi army to a huge erection, waiting to explode.

#2

"The Nazi Time Bomb" Revised

Kate Cantrill

Instead of pinpointing the two main ideas in Klaus Theweleit's "Male Bodies and the "White Terror," I'd rather use the idea he presents that the German soldier--and therefore the German army--was fueled by tension caused by repressed human emotion, and I'd like to focus on this use of repression to create tension in our culture and others because, as Theweleit would attribute this to an erection that when manipulated would lead to orgasm, many areas of our existence are run on this need to explode.

> I stand, in the dark, start to unbutton. Then I hear something, inside my body. I've broken, something has cracked, that must be it. Noise is coming up, coming out, of the broken place in my face. Without warning: I wasn't thinking about here or there or anything. If I let the

noise get out into the air it will be
laughter too loud, too much of it, someone
is bound to hear, and then there will be
hurrying footsteps and commands and who
knows? . . . It could be fatal.

from The Handmaid's Tale,

Margaret Atwood, p. 189

The idea of repressing or creating tension can
also be used to hold someone captive as illustrated
in the above quotation. Offred, a woman no longer
needed or wanted for anything but her viable ova-
ries, must repress all feelings not directly associated with giving birth. Her forced repressions
are not directly manipulated as the German
soldier's were to create fear in others, but indirectly manipulated to create fear, and therefore
obedience in her. This same idea can be attributed
to present-day penal systems--not only is the body
imprisoned, but also the soul--and also in a capi-
talistic system where the worker is not only alienated from his product, but also the emotions involved in the making of the product. The tensions
could be the cause of worker revolts (such as
those in "The Great Cat Massacre"), worker disobe-
dience (the worker attempting to but being too in-
timidated to explode), and finally the worker who
sometimes feels so much pressure to explode, he or
she turns to drugs and alcohol on the streets.

In these latter examples, the power built up
inside of the person can be extremely detrimental
to him/her if it is exploded, whereas the Nazi
soldier was applauded for his release or explosion
as long as it took place during wartime. First,
the army releases tension by dispersing the different parts onto the battle field so that they become individual soldiers again, who then in turn
exploded with the display of human feelings so that
the soldiers became individual men again.

The aspect of individuality is important in
the repression process also. If someone is being
forced to repress certain aspects of themselves
then they are not being permitted to be individuals, and therfore are not free (according to some
people--J. S. Mill, for example). To release tension, therefore, is a way to become free. Freedom
is an important aspect of being whole, but in a
society that uses the technique of repression--

which seems to be every organized society--this
aspect of becoming free is not always easy. Henri
Charrière, author of "Papillon," says this about
becoming free after years of oppressive captivity.
"It's not all that easy to step out of chains
you've been dragging around for fourteen years.
They tell you you're free, then turn their backs
on you, you're no longer being watched. It's that
simple. Yet you still wonder . . ." (457). A.
Anatoli Kuznetsov, the author who recounted the
Holocaust in "Babi Yar," says this about the importance of freedom: "I wonder if we'll ever understand that the most precious thing in this world
is a man's life and his freedo" (404). Kusnetsov
was stating this in response to the freedoms of
the victims of the Holocaust that were taken away,
but as shown by the Theweleit piece, the soldiers
themselves were forced to give up their freedoms
and become part of a killing machine that had no
human traces. "When machines start delivering themselves . . . I guess that's when people better
start really worrying" (Vonnegut, 15). Worrying is
an understatement, because the violent power that
humans are capable of when they are no longer really human is astounding and terrifying. Even
scarier than this, is the fact that people such as
Hitler were aware of this, and through intimidation
have learned to manipulate human feelings and use
them for their own self advancement--no matter how
warped that advancement may be.

o—o—o—o—o—o—o—o—o—o—o—o—o—o—o

Annotated Bibliography

Note: This is a selective, not a comprehensive, bibliography. It is, in fact, a list of the books, chapters, and articles we use in seminars and give to colleagues when they are planning to read or write about reading or writing.

Atwell, Nancie. "Writing and Reading from the Inside Out." In *Breaking Ground: Teachers Relate Reading and Writing in the Elementary School*. Edited by Jane Hansen, Tom Newkirk, and Donald Graves. New York: Heinemann, 1985.

While the essay speaks directly to middle school teachers, Atwell has much to say to all teachers about the institutionalization of reading.

Bartholomae, David. "Inventing the University." In *When a Writer Can't Write*. Edited by Mike Rose. New York and London: Guilford Press, 1985.

Argues, through examples, that students have to write their way into the ways of thinking and speaking that seem "natural" to university life.

Bartholomae, David, and Anthony Petrosky. *Facts, Artifacts, and Counterfacts: Reading and Writing in Theory and Practice*. Upper Montclair, N.J.: Boynton/Cook, 1986.

An account of a curriculum designed for students who have trouble imagining the ways of thinking and speaking that seem natural to university life — includes essays looking at revision and class discussion in a reading and writing class.

Bizzell, Patricia. "Cognition, Convention, and Certainty: What We Need to Know About Writing." *PRE/TEXT* 3 (Fall 1982): 213–43.

Makes a crucial distinction between theoretical models that locate reading and writing inside the mind and those that locate it in a social context.

Coles, William E., Jr. *The Plural I: The Teaching of Writing*. New York: Holt, Rinehart and Winston, 1978.

An account of a class where students learn to pay attention to written texts, both their own and others'.

Annotated Bibliography

Culler, Jonathan. "Readers and Reading." In *On Deconstruction.* Ithaca, N.Y.: Cornell University Press, 1982.

A powerful demonstration of how to imagine and discuss reading as an act of composition: "To read is to play the role of a reader and to interpret is to posit an experience of reading. This is something that beginning literature students know quite well but have forgotten by the time they get to graduate school and begin teaching literature."

de Castell, Suzanne, and Allan Luke. "Defining 'Literacy' in North American Schools; Social and Historical Conditions and Consequences." In *Perspectives on Literacy,* eds. Eugene R. Kintgen, Barry M. Kroll, and Mike Rose. Carbondale: Southern Illinois University Press, 1988: 159–74.

This brief history argues that literacy education always takes place within the context of values, and aims at creating a certain kind of individual within a certain kind of culture.

Fish, Stanley. "Interpretive Authority in the Classroom and in Literary Criticism." In *Is There a Text in This Class? The Authority of Interpretive Communities.* Cambridge, Mass.: Harvard University Press, 1980.

The standard reference for discussions of the classroom as an "interpretive community" where students learn to operate within a set of peculiar rules and conventions.

Graff, Gerald and Reginald Gibbons, eds. "The University and the Prevention of Culture." In *Criticism in the University.* Evanston, Ill.: Northwestern University Press, 1985.

A response to Fish. Graff argues that the problem with students who can master the classroom routines is that they have not learned how or why to ask "Why am I doing such a thing?"

Harris, Joseph. "The Idea of Community in the Study of Writing." *College Composition and Communication* 40 (1989): 11–22.

It might be more powerful to think of teaching composition as a way of complicating students' language use, rather than a process of moving them into an academic "community."

Koch, Kenneth. "Preface." In *Rose, Where Did You Get That Red?* New York: Random House, 1973.

A powerful demonstration of how imitation can become a way of understanding complex texts.

McQuade, Donald, ed. *The Territory of Language: Linguistics, Stylistics, and the Teaching of Composition.* Carbondale, Ill.: Southern Illinois University Press, 1986.

A remarkably rich and provocative anthology. It is a fine introduction to the methods and concerns of those who write about composition and teaching.

Miller, Susan. "What Does It Mean to Be Able to Write? The Question of Writing in the Discourses of Literature and Composition." *College English,* 45 (March 1983): 219–35.

Charts the complicated social and historical context represented by any moment of writing and argues that such an awareness is essential for both research and teaching.

Newkirk, Thomas, ed. *Only Connect: Uniting Reading and Writing.* Montclair, N.J.: Boynton/ Cook, 1986.

A collection of essays from a conference devoted to the issue of how reading and writing connect in introductory classes.

Petrosky, Anthony R. "From Story to Essay: Reading and Writing." *CCC,* 33 (February 1982): 19–36.

Defines a method for moving a student from immediate reactions to a text, to those more structured responses that characterize formal ways of understanding and representing experience.

Petrosky, Anthony. "Imagining the Past and Teaching Essay and Poetry Writing." In *Encountering Student Texts: Interpretive Issues in Reading Student Writing,* eds. Bruce Lawson, Susan Sterr Ryan, and W. Ross Winterowd. Urbana: NCTE, 1990: 199–219.

An account of a reading/writing class in which productive questions and responses enable close attention to be paid to student essays and poems.

Petrosky, Anthony, and David Bartholomae, eds. *The Teaching of Writing.* Chicago: NSSE and the University of Chicago Press, 1986.

A collection of essays surveying key issues and methods in composition teaching and research.

Pratt, Mary Louise. *The Imperial "I."* New York: Routledge, 1992.

Although her specific focus is the discourse of European capitalism in travel narratives, Pratt's book is broadly about how structures of writing are implicated in issues of culture and ideology.

Rich, Adrienne. "Resisting Amnesia: History and Personal Life" in *Blood, Bread, and Poetry, Selected Prose 1979–1985.* New York: Norton, 1986: 136–55.

This moving essay focuses on the need for students and writers to acknowledge questions of historical responsibility in their work.

Rosenblatt, Louise M. *Literature as Exploration.* New York: MLA, 1968.

One of the first studies to ever consider reading as a transaction between a reader and a text, a transaction mediated by the language of instruction.

Salvatori, Mariolina. "Reading and Writing a Text." *College English*, 45 (1983): 657–67.

An examination, through examples of student work, of how reading might be imagined as writing and writing as reading.

Sale, Roger. *On Writing*. New York: Random House, 1970.

A useful and influential series of lectures on student writing and schooling.

Scholes, Robert. *Textual Power: Literary Theory and the Teaching of English*. New Haven: Yale University Press, 1985.

Winner of the 1986 Shaughnessy Award from MLA. The opening chapters present a powerful set of terms ("reading," "interpretation," and "criticism") for imagining reading and the teaching of reading; the opening chapters also provide a demonstration of those terms at work.

Spellmeyer, Kurt. "Foucault and the Freshman Writer: Considering the Self in Discourse." *College English* 51 (1989): 715–29.

An interesting account of how Foucault's work on discourse and authorship might inform a teacher's reading of student papers.

WRITING WORTH READING
A Practical Guide
Paperback Second Edition

Nancy Huddleston Packer, *Stanford University*
John Timpane, *Lafayette College*

■ paperback edition reprints the highly-praised rhetorical chapters of *Writing Worth Reading*, Second Edition, without the handbook section ■ emphasis on critical thinking and reading ■ in-depth treatment of specific writing assignments across the curriculum ■ extensive coverage of the research process and documenting sources for various disciplines ■ thorough Instructor's Manual

1993/paper/
471 pages/
Instructor's Manual
$9.50 net

A POCKET STYLE MANUAL
Diana Hacker, *Prince George's Community College*

■ brief, pocket-sized handbook without exercises ■ concise — but never skimpy — coverage of topics students most frequently consult a handbook for ■ less than half the price of larger handbooks ■ incorporates proven reference features from Diana Hacker's other handbooks: clear writing style, hand-edited examples, and two-color design that highlights crucial material ■ fuller coverage of using sources and MLA and APA documentation than other very brief handbooks ■ based on *The Bedford Handbook for Writers*, Third Edition, and *A Writer's Reference*, Second Edition

1993/paper/
140 pages
$7 net

CRITICAL THINKING, READING, AND WRITING
A Brief Guide to Argument
Sylvan Barnet and **Hugo Bedau,** both of *Tufts University*

■ brief and inexpensive guide to critical thinking and writing—comprising the text and appendices of *Current Issues and Enduring Questions* ■ an ideal text for bringing critical thinking into a writing course ■ 21 model arguments for critical analysis ■ thorough coverage of research and documentation including MLA and APA style ■ 4 unique appendices on different argumentative perspectives, including Toulmin and Rogerian models

1993/paper/
256 pages/
Instructor's Edition
$8 net

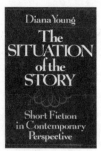